FOUNDATIONS *of*
HIGHER EDUCATION
LAW *&* POLICY

NASPA
Student Affairs Administrators
in Higher Education

PETER F. LAKE

FOUNDATIONS *of* HIGHER EDUCATION
LAW & POLICY

Basic Legal Rules, Concepts,
and Principles for Student Affairs

NASPA
Student Affairs Administrators
in Higher Education

Foundations of Higher Education Law & Policy: Basic Legal Rules, Concepts, and Principles for Student Affairs

Published by
NASPA–Student Affairs Administrators in Higher Education
111 K Street, NE
10th Floor
Washington, DC 20002
www.naspa.org

Additional copies may be purchased by contacting the NASPA publications department at 301-638-1749 or visiting http://bookstore.naspa.org.

NASPA does not discriminate on the basis of race, color, national origin, religion, sex, age, gender identity, gender expression, affectional or sexual orientation, or disability in any of its policies, programs, and services.

Library of Congress Control Number: 2010939480
ISBN 978-0-931654-42-8
Printed and bound in the United States of America
FIRST EDITION

CONTENTS

Preface vii

Introduction xi

CHAPTER 1 1
Law in the Life of the Student Affairs Administrator

CHAPTER 2 47
A Brief Student-Affairs-Centered History
of Higher Education Law

CHAPTER 3 91
Managing the Institution of Higher Education Environment
Part I: Safety, Risk Management, Wellness, and Security

CHAPTER 4 179
Managing the Institution of Higher Education Environment
Part II: Promoting and Protecting the Core Academic Mission

CHAPTER 5 197
Student Empowerment, Civil Rights, Inclusion, and Diversity

CHAPTER 6 251
A Brief Overview of Powers and Governance

Conclusion 261

Bibliography 265

Appendix 303

Table of Cases 307

Table of Laws 317

Subject Index 321

For Coyote, who made his indelible mark on my life,

and for Jennifer who brought the light back into my life.

PREFACE

Aslan, the lion hero of the *Chronicles of Narnia*, said you can never have the same experience twice, even if you return to a familiar place.

Every book is different, too. If you happened to read the preface to my last book, *Beyond Discipline*, you know that the process of writing that book was . . . *trying*. Writing this book was an entirely different matter and a much more positive experience. I am an Irish writer at heart, so it is not in me to claim that the process of writing any book is rainbows and leprechauns. For a few weeks I never left the house in the stunning Florida summer and missed out on life.

Writing this book made me realize that my greatest professional blessing has been to have the opportunity to be *your* voice of the law of higher education in student affairs. NASPA has generously entrusted me with this role. As you read the chapters that follow, I hope you realize that I carefully crafted discussions of legal doctrine, cases, and so on with deep respect for your work in student affairs. I have sought to demystify the law, help you understand what I believe is most important, and most of all empower you in your relationship with law. I want you to see all the ways the law defers to you and your good work, and how the law counts on your best efforts to make higher education and the law of higher education work. I had fun with this, always trying to speak with you, not to you, and connect the law to the culture that surrounds student affairs practice. It is a great honor to have had such an opportunity: If I stumble, please tell Aslan it was I who failed and not the cohort who supported this work.

ACKNOWLEDGMENTS

I wish to thank all of my friends at NASPA for their patience and confidence in me. Executive Director Gwendolyn Dungy and I first spoke of this project many years ago—Gwen, you really are the best, thank you! Melissa Dahne went far and beyond in seeing this manuscript from proposal to final form—always supportive, even when I missed deadlines. I also wish to acknowledge Stephanie Gordon, Kevin Kruger, and Joseph DeSanto; although not directly involved in the production of this book, we all work together on a variety of related projects.

I also wish to thank Stetson University College of Law for its generous research grants and leave time in support of this work. Mark St. Louis, coordinator of the Center for Excellence in Higher Education Law and Policy, is my right-hand man and nothing good in my work happens without his help. Mark, thank you 1,000 times for all you do to help me and the Center and for your invaluable assistance on this book. You are one of the finest men I have ever known. Thank you to Terra, too; I knew she would say "Yes!"

Stetson is blessed with the best faculty support services imaginable. Very special thanks to Dianne Oeste, who worked on the entire manuscript. I am not a good typist, so I dictated the book to cassette tapes. Day after day—for weeks—Dianne would transcribe the tapes; she must have been sick to death of listening to my voice, but you would never know it. One day, before school started, she "asked" me if it was okay to take a half-day off—she didn't want to let me down. Can you believe that kind of dedication? Dianne, you rock.

This book also came to fruition because of the efforts of my research assistants. Dara Cooley slaved away day after day for weeks on end, researching absurdly complex issues of higher education law and finding quotes from obscure cases, esoteric music, and movies that only I had seen. I am not sure Tristan Overcashier should be called a research assistant. He volunteered to help me after graduating, and immediately dug in after taking the Florida Bar Exam. Tristan was so dedicated to helping me finish my adventure that he literally moved in with my family for several days so we could work around the clock.

As deadlines loomed and passed, I called in more help. Stacey Rowan helped immensely in the final push. Her finely honed law review skills were exactly what the team needed to close out the manuscript. Very special thanks also go to Brooke Kernan and Chelsea Harrison, who gave much-needed valuable assistance in bringing the manuscript toward final form. Aaron Swift came on late in the fourth quarter to give us fresh legs when we were all getting a little fatigued. As soon as I saw his ink—"This too shall pass"—I knew he was the man of the hour.

Brooke Bowman. What can I say? Another book, and another herculean effort to move a manuscript of mine to final form. I have run out of ways to thank you and praise your work in this lifetime. I never knew law professors like you in law school; you have reinvented the way I think of colleagues and law teachers. You make everything you work on better and everyone who works with you better off. Smart, diligent, selfless, and kind is the way to go through life and you can tell Dean Wormer I said so!

My wife, Jennifer, again helped in every conceivable way to get the manuscript to final form. I have been blessed to have a true partner like her. Lilo and Stitch did their part, too—rarely barking at random events and patiently waiting for me to emerge from "the hole" where I did most of my writing.

In every adventure, as new companions emerge, some dear friends cannot complete the voyage. In the past I always wrote with my cat Coyote nearby, manuscripts covered in fur. Coyote passed away peacefully on August 22, 2009, at home in my arms. I finished writing the first draft of the manuscript exactly one year later to the day.

To all of you, especially Jennifer, thank you. You have literally lifted me up; and without you there would be no book.

Peter Lake
Bradenton, Florida
August 2011

INTRODUCTION

This book is designed to provide current and future student affairs administrators with a concise, readable, and accessible discussion of the foundations of higher education law for student affairs practice.

Sooner or later, in various ways, higher education law affects student affairs administration practice. However, in my experience, attempting to master advanced levels of competency in higher education law without firm foundations leads to frustration and error. I have found that even among student affairs administrators and lawyers who reach advanced competency levels, a return to the study of fundamentals is helpful. I recall speaking at a National Association of College and University Attorneys (NACUA) event with Robert Bickel, the co-author of my first book, *The Rights and Responsibilities of the Modern University: Who Assumes the Risks of College Life?* (Carolina Academic Press 1999). In a room full of attorneys, one lawyer had the temerity to ask, with regard to negligence law, "Could you two go over that duty/breach/causation/damage thing again?" We smiled, because that subject is covered in the first six weeks of law school; but, as in football and fashion, it's all about fundamentals and foundations.

We start with fundamentals, and we continually return to them, regardless of our skill level or experience. My hope is that this book ends up on your desk for years to come—dog-eared, marked up, and eventually falling apart, like *ropa vieja*.

Any time you try to select foundational information and sort it out from the whole of the law of higher education you will encounter challenges of breadth and depth of coverage. For instance, employment law affects student affairs practice, but only highly experienced student affairs administrators will routinely encounter advanced questions, such as disparate impact claims under

Title IX. Such complex issues are for senior student affairs administrators and must be dealt with in conjunction with human resources staff and legal counsel. In fact, much of higher education employment law is the black diamond slope. I occasionally see a legal skier who can start on a black diamond slope; most of us mere mortals, however, will end up breaking our necks if we go too fast too soon.

I have tried to select the essential topics to promote firm foundations for further coverage at an advanced level. If you find yourself craving more, you might become a law junkie and end up like one of us, a—*gasp!*— *lawyer!* A few of you will become so enamored of law that you will leave student affairs practice to sojourn in the law world. At the same time, the legally trained are entering the student affairs field as well. If you are among the latter, you can hide this book in your desk and tell people "I already knew that." There is a dirty little secret in law school—that the most essential foundational material is taught early and quickly to students who are not really equipped to master it. Law school does not test for essential competencies, and the bar exam is at best a crude tool for this. In short, even lawyers discover gaps in their foundational knowledge base.

This book will be enormously helpful to current and former student affairs administrators who seek to achieve competencies in law, policy, and governance in the NASPA LPG competency area, which "includes the knowledge, skills, and attitudes relating to policy development processes used in various contexts, the application of legal constructs, and the understanding of governance structures and their effect on one's professional practice."[1] The book will greatly assist the reader in achieving basic level LPG competency and is very useful for intermediate level LPG competency as well. Of course, competency is not just the mastery of information but involves skill development as well—something a book cannot provide on its own.

However, if this book is used in conjunction with courses on law and higher education in master's level programs or with a variety of other NASPA-sponsored presentations and conferences, or supplemented by participation in NASPA-sponsored, -branded, or -endorsed law and policy events (e.g., the annual NASPA Law and Policy Conference, the Certificate program, the Gehring Institute,

---

[1] ACPA and NASPA, *Professional Competency Areas for Student Affairs Practitioners* (July 24, 2010), *available at* http://www.naspa.org/programs/prodev/Professional_Competencies.pdf.

or the Stevens Institute), it can help a student affairs administrator master LPG competencies at all levels, from basic to advanced. Think of the book as a Rosetta Stone that will give student affairs administrators the foundational information they need to access more advanced levels of LPG competency.

The book is organized primarily around four areas of interest or spheres of activity that connect law to student affairs practice, from entry-level residence staff all the way to vice presidential levels of operation.

The first area, treated in Chapter 2, is history and context. Student affairs administration practice and the law relating to it are organic and constantly evolving. Starting to work without a sense of context and history will leave a student affairs administrator bewildered, confused, and misdirected. For example, without context, it is virtually impossible to fully understand the new Family Educational Rights and Privacy Act (FERPA) regulations (January 2009).[2]

Second, to function in the modern higher education environment, student affairs administrators must be proficient in a daunting, multifaceted set of interrelated tasks. For convenience, this sphere is divided into two parts: Chapter 3 treats law and policy issues related to student safety, wellness, security, and risk management; Chapter 4 deals with related issues in the educational environment that focus on the context of managing student populations via discipline codes and the like. This is the sphere that most directly affects core mission delivery, and many administrators subspecialize in practice areas—such as discipline and enrollment management—that have overt connections to core mission delivery.

Chapter 5 addresses major issues of student empowerment and development related to inclusion, diversity, civil rights, and social justice. This chapter refers to key Supreme Court cases in discussing basic student constitutional rights and federal statutory and regulatory approaches to promoting civil rights. Chapter 5 also covers the rights and responsibilities of registered student organizations and other groups and speakers on campus.

Chapter 6 provides an overview of basic principles of governance and the powers of student affairs administrators. This chapter is very pragmatic—it will help student affairs administrators understand their somewhat unique employment posture in the current higher education environment and how the field of

---

[2] *See infra* at Chapter 5.

student affairs administration will evolve in the future.

These four spheres of activity are the distillation of more than 20 years of experience in the field—as an administrator, teacher, lawyer, facilitator, workshop leader, presenter, and consultant. The questions student affairs administrators find most pressing almost always relate back to one or more of these four spheres of activity or areas of interest. Sometimes student affairs administrators think they need highly specific legal resolutions to questions or situations. However, in many instances, clarification of certain foundational information is all they need to get them off and running, empowered to make decisions for themselves.

This book offers more than just basic legal information. How the law functions in the daily life of a student affairs administrator is the primary topic of Chapter 1, and this theme—how to mold student affairs administration practice to law and vice versa—permeates the book. Understanding the foundations of higher education law as it applies to student affairs administration is more than memorizing legal principles and rules; a foundational level of understanding includes how student affairs administrators can and should act with regard to the law.

Student affairs administrators work in a fluid field, one that is heavily influenced by law and in which accountability under legal principles seems to be expanding faster than the known universe. It is easy to become frightened by the law—to feel disempowered, to become bewildered by legal jargon, or to become technical-compliance oriented and lose the spirit of the law and the power of student affairs administration. This book offers a sense of perspective and empowerment. Believe it or not, the law has a great deal of respect for student affairs administration practice, and it protects the space that student affairs administrators need to accomplish their critical mission. In turn, the law counts on student affairs administrators to step up and assert their rights and powers, and to exercise their academic freedom.

We are only the second generation of student affairs administrators who have made law a major feature of the higher education experience. Higher education law generally—and, as it relates to student affairs practice, particularly—is still in its relative infancy. Try not to expect too much from the law; it was only a constitutional yesterday that students were expelled from college for exercising their First Amendment rights, and some were even shot dead by National Guard troops while demonstrating. Soon the first generation of student affairs administrators who brought law to campus will fade away, and it will be up to us to carry the juridical torch forward. It is a heavy responsibility that can elude us in the din of "compliance."

A generation ago, our profession and students fought the law and won, but that form of civil disobedience and that relationship to the law are not ours. We must constantly redefine our relationship with the law and be careful not to lose our power in a sea of regulations and legal cases, threats of lawsuits, and oppositional legal discourse. We have a sacred obligation to continue to make the law work for us and for our students—we must realize that it plays out a little differently for each generation.

A good foundation is the beginning—the platform from which you can challenge and change the law, understand your relationship to the law, revise perceived wisdom, and find creative new solutions to the challenges of being a college student in a world that all too often seeks to eat its own young. *Harry Potter's* Hogwarts is fantasy; but Voldemorts exist in the real world, and the law is a powerful form of magic to meet and defeat them. Now, let's pick out a wand.

CHAPTER 1

LAW IN THE LIFE OF THE
STUDENT AFFAIRS ADMINISTRATOR

At no point in human history has law exerted a larger influence over higher education and student affairs administration. Indeed, the very fabric of higher education has become highly legalistic, even where the law itself does not extend its reach. We are not just governed by law; in many situations we have embraced the law and legalistic concepts for our own use. To paraphrase Madonna, we live in a juridical world and we are juridical girls.

This is a time of protective accountability, even as legal protections for institutions of higher education are slowly diminishing and accountability is on the rise. The law often strives to protect our core mission, but we find ourselves increasingly subject to questions such as "Why did you do this?"

The law of higher education is not static, and it is important to step out of the tangle of legal minutia to see the larger forces—legal vectors—at work. Some of these vectors march on over centuries; some change quickly with political winds and other social forces. The law of higher education is dynamic; lawyers speak of law as a practice, in which perfection is sought but rarely achieved.

Although one can speak of higher education law, in fact, most law applicable to higher education is not specific to the field. Rather, higher education is governed, regulated, and facilitated by laws that apply to many other entities and activities. We are rarely singled out for special rules applicable only to us, although the way certain rules operate in our world often differs significantly from the way they operate in other spheres. The law of higher education is influenced heavily by legal trends and developments that may have little to do with higher education specifically.

THE LANGUAGE OF LAW AND LAWYERS

The law in the United States is written largely in English. However, this is not conversational English; it is more like a dialect that we could call "law-English."

Law-English is more challenging to learn than many foreign languages, because it often pretends to be nothing more than common English. The language of lawyers can lure the legally untrained into thinking that commonly used words are being used commonly in a legal context. Beware! In law, every word has a special meaning that may or may not match its common meaning.[1] It takes lawyers years of training (and being berated by judges and professors) to unlearn common English.

Law-English is often the language of mistrust, in which people posture in lieu of communicating. Thus, it is exactly the opposite of most discourse in higher education among administrators and students. Educational discourse depends on trust, candor, and openness to succeed. In this sense, law is a very foreign language to most higher education administrators. It is not the language of s'mores and team building.

The language of law has a tendency to project fear, mistrust, or stultifying boredom to those who are not legally trained. Legal discourse is often impregnated with the mistrust/disdain that crafted it—with a frightful Nancy Grace-like "I win, you lose" feeling. People talk and listen differently when they are afraid, especially when they are posturing so as not to appear to be afraid. Fear is the antithesis of learning, which requires openness and receptivity.

Much of the language of law is crafted in conflict, sometimes extreme conflict. It is also a language that has to speak across time—even ages—and be used by people to communicate with others about whom they know very little. As a

---

[1] Consider the following. A person coming to another's property may occupy the status at law of a "business invitee" without ever being invited. Some individuals called "licensees" never have a license. And many relationships that the law considers to be "special" would not be on any list of relationships most people would consider "special."

result, law-English has a tendency to be very reductionist and objective—very left-brain in orientation. This is foreign to many people in higher education, who are more likely to use English to communicate in prosaic or emotive ways and may use language in a very generation-specific way (OMG!).

Law-English is also very directive, even when it appears not to be. It is a language of doers and orders, although it often tones down a command or demand. Perhaps most perplexing for nonlawyers is the fact that legal terms are often simply signifiers in a complex conceptual system. Nonlawyers typically seek *definitions* but instead find *concepts* and become frustrated in the process. Conceptualization in law requires lawyers to work fluidly in a topic area, balancing many considerations; conceptualization is something lawyers learn to do. Lawyers can conceptualize an area of the law but lack a sense of cognitive resolution—to nonlawyers it seems that something doesn't quite fit or make sense, or that there is more to learn. On the one hand, it is tempting to be cynical about legal concepts that may appear ambiguous. On the other hand, it is easy to become glibly enamored of legal concepts such as due process and civil rights. Lawyers seek to reduce concepts to rules, but some concepts defy description in a complete set of rules. For example, try to describe all the rules of love.

This book is a Rosetta Stone for student affairs administrators who want to understand the law better in their daily work. As you proceed through the chapters, imagine yourself in a conversation with someone who speaks only law-English. What types of things might you say that would be valid and understandable to both of you? This is an important heuristic for student affairs administrators. There will be many times in your career when no translator will be available to help you when law-English is being spoken. You may find yourself trying to speak to lawyers as efficiently as possible and realize that you need to bridge the communication gap.

For a student affairs administrator, the key to understanding law is communication. How can an administrator hear the language of law and lawyers and incorporate it into good student affairs practice? All too often, student affairs administrators are baited into trying to play the role of the lawyer, cast against type and job description. This is not why interdisciplinary work among lawyers and administrators has evolved in higher education. The true goal of interdisciplinary training is not to make mini-me lawyers but to enhance student affairs practice with an understanding of law. The language of law is not the language of higher education; in learning about a new dialect, student affairs administrators should be careful not to lose their own language.

THE ROLE OF HIGHER EDUCATION LAWYERS

Some institutions of higher education are fortunate enough to have in-house counsel, which usually means that one or several lawyers are on staff full time. Many institutions—including a host of small private colleges—are not so fortunate and must employ outside counsel to deal with legal issues. Even institutions that have in-house counsel must employ outside counsel as well. There is simply too much work to be done.

The heavy workload is a key feature of legal counsel's role on campus. Higher education is an under-lawyered business, with high client-to-attorney ratios. Key campus decision makers typically have limited access to direct legal guidance. Lawyers are often hard at work on employment disputes, transactions, athletics, and so on. Day-to-day legal questions from student affairs administrators typically are referred to secondary or even tertiary sources. It is not uncommon for administrators to receive "legal" information from persons who have no formal legal training.

In many ways, higher education is a legal self-help culture. Lawyers are directly involved only in the most pressing matters; thus, perceptions of law are often as crucial as the reality. Higher education is a business that functions under both law and mythologies of law. The latter can be very hard to correct and very dangerous. Consider, for example, the common misunderstandings about the Family Education Rights and Privacy Act (FERPA) (see note 10 below) that emerged in reports following the shootings at Virginia Tech in April 2007.[2]

---

[2] "Much of the frustration about privacy laws stems from lack of understanding. When seen clearly, the privacy laws contain many provisions that allow for information sharing where necessary." Virginia Tech Review Panel, *Mass Shootings at Virginia Tech, April 16, 2007—Report of the Review Panel Presented to Governor Kaine, Commonwealth of Virginia* 63 (2007), available at http://www.vtreviewpanel.org/report/index.html. "Information from educational records cannot be shared unless authorized by law or with consent of a parent, or if the student is enrolled in college or is 18 or older, with that student's consent." *Id.* at 66. "FERPA provides the basic requirements for disclosure of health records at campus health clinics, and state law cannot require disclosure that is not authorized by FERPA." *Id.* "FERPA also has a different scope than HIPAA. . . . FERPA applies

For higher education administrators, branding is a major issue in receiving legal information. The highest brand quality obviously comes from lawyers working directly for the institution. After that, brand identification and quality assessment are more challenging.

Another interesting feature of the role of higher education lawyer is that the line between system administrator and lawyer can become blurred. Lawyers at institutions of higher education work closely with presidents and governing boards or bodies. Membership and leadership on the boards may change, but the lawyer may continue to serve the institution for many years and may become a key source of institutional memory. Strong ties with governing boards and the institution's president can place the attorney in a unique position vis-à-vis student affairs administrators. Technically, the role of the institution of higher education lawyer is to advise and give counsel; however, in many cases, the lawyer directs student affairs administrators to do or not do certain things. From the point of view of student affairs administrators, the lawyer may assume the role of a super-administrator.

When lawyers at institutions of higher education give direction instead of advice, they may seem to be overstepping their roles and not fully respecting their client's autonomy. Often, however, the attorney is merely reflecting the goals and directives of administrators, including the board or president. In this situation, it is critical that the lawyer clarify his or her role of messenger. Sometimes it is expedient for a senior administrator to have a lawyer tell a subordinate administrator that the law forbids a path of action. In the end, however,

---

only to information in student records. Personal observations and conversations with a student fall outside FERPA." *Id.* (emphasis in original). "Many records kept by university law enforcement agencies fall outside of FERPA." *Id.*

    FERPA authorizes release of information to parents of students in several situations. First, it authorizes disclosure of any record to parents who claim adult students as dependents for tax purposes. FERPA also authorizes release to parents when the student has violated alcohol or drug laws and is under 21.

    FERPA generally authorizes the release of information to school officials who have been determined to have a legitimate education interest in receiving the information, . . . [and] unlimited disclosure of the final result of a disciplinary proceeding that concludes a student violated university rules for an incident involving a crime of violence (as defined under federal law) or a sex offense. *Id.* at 67 (citations omitted).

"FERPA also contains an emergency exception. Disclosure of information in educational records is authorized to any appropriate person in connection with an emergency 'if the knowledge of such information is necessary to protect the health or safety of the student or other persons.'" *Id.* (quoting 20 U.S.C. § 1232g(b)(1)(I)(2006)).

the lawyer does not typically represent the board or president but the institution itself. It is natural for a lawyer to personify the institutional client and the individuals who occupy senior leadership roles. But lawyers must be careful not to become enmeshed in conflicts of interest or complicate governance issues.

Student affairs administrators should remember that while a lawyer may work collaboratively with them in transactions or contested matters, the lawyer may not technically represent them. In some cases, dual representation is possible, but only if the lawyer can ensure fidelity to the institution of higher education as the primary client. If a conflict of interest exists, the student affairs administrator may need to secure his or her own counsel. Thankfully, this is a rare occurrence.

Most often, the goal of a student affairs administrator is to work collaboratively and efficiently with institution of higher education lawyers. Lawyers are highly trained to be time and efficiency oriented. Lawyers account for their time in increments of minutes throughout the day, a form of time management that is foreign to most student affairs practitioners. Student affairs administrators can maximize the time they spend with lawyers if they are well prepared, prompt, candid, and to the point. The field of law has certain similarities with the field of medicine; one is that educated clients are usually easier to work with. Thus, pursuing interdisciplinary law studies can be valuable for student affairs administrators and their host institutions.

A student affairs administrator will want to determine which of the following three situations he or she is in when dealing with lawyers: (1) making decisions with little or no direct legal input; (2) making decisions with direct or directive input from lawyers; or (3) making decisions in a collaborative manner with lawyers. In other words, a student affairs administrator will usually work in a self-directed, lawyer-directed, or collaborative way with respect to issues that have legal dimensions.

In the first mode, the student affairs administrator has the opportunity to make the most of his or her professional higher education judgment. The risk is that decisions will be made without due regard for or understanding of legal consequences. In the second mode, the decisions are likely to be both legally and administratively sound; however, the risk is abdication of student affairs responsibility and the lawyer's assumption of the role of super-administrator. In the third mode, the opportunity exists to create positive solutions by combining the best instincts of lawyers and student affairs administrators. However, the correlative weakness is inefficiency—collaborative lawyering is time-intensive and costly. Thus, collaborative student affairs practice is a luxury for many institutions of higher education.

It is a common belief that a student affairs administrator should consult the law and then make sound student affairs decisions—this is the two-step model. In reality, there is no two-step process in most situations. Administrators do not routinely treat the law as a minimum or floor; instead, the law informs choices and becomes part of the complex calculus of decision making. The principles and policies that underlie rules and regulations are often as important as the rules themselves.[3] Sometimes legal principles and policies are also those of good student affairs practice; law and sound student affairs practice often converge. However, in a lawyer-directed engagement mode, student affairs administrators may feel like captives of a two-step process: "Do this; don't do that."

Too often, however, a lawyer's use of directive language means a disempowered client. (Sometimes 'direction' comes via formulating questions.) Lawyers are trained in posing and formulating questions, and then answering them. While the Socratic method is no longer the primary mode of teaching in law schools,[4] the process of legal education is still highly didactic. Often a lawyer who frames the best question first wins—almost like the TV game show "Jeopardy."[5] Clients do not usually have the kind of training or orientation to formulate questions the way lawyers do, or to reframe the question when they get "No" for an answer. Student affairs administrators should be prepared to hear "No" to their first question and even to their second and third questions. Student affairs administrators should keep asking questions until they find a path to accomplish their goals. It is always appropriate to say to a lawyer, "Am I

---

[3] Consider the following recent example. Hastings Law School had a complex anti-discrimination rule and endeavored to interpret and understand the spirit of that rule in its educational context relative to registered student organizations—which led to the adoption of an "all comers" policy that itself became the subject of major litigation. *See generally Christian Legal Society at Hastings College of the Law v. Martinez*, 130 S. Ct. 2971 (2010).

[4] "Nurturing is the trend in law school today." Scott H. Greenfield, *In Defense of the Socratic Method (Update)*, Simple Justice: A New York Criminal Defense Blog, (May 11, 2009, 6:29 AM), http://blog.simplejustice.us/2009/05/11/in-defense-of-the-socratic-method.aspx. Although still adversarial, law school is much kinder and gentler than 30 years ago.

[5] Sony Pictures International, *JEOPARDY!*, http://www.jeopardy.com/ (last visited Jan. 31, 2011).

asking the right question?" or "That doesn't seem like the right question to me."

By training, lawyers are risk-averse, or at least very calculating. If clients never took action, lawyers could reduce their litigation risk to near zero. But higher education is a business that creates risk, which in turn creates legal risk. Clients in higher education have a tendency to ask permission of their lawyers to do their jobs. Student affairs administrators who ask permission might assume that they will be directed one way or another. Rather than seeking permission from a lawyer, they should ask about legal options and the costs and consequences of a choice, and explore other choices. Remember, the lawyer for an institution of higher education is not just experienced in lawsuits and contracts; these lawyers know a great deal about higher education as a business and are often fabulous institutional resources.

You may wonder how higher education attorneys perceive student affairs administrators. Usually, lawyers are among the best educated individuals in a higher education setting. However, few lawyers have terminal degrees or master's degrees in student affairs administration. Some lawyers believe that the education of a student affairs administrator (and other members of the academic community) is more intellectually rigorous than their own legal education. In particular, lawyers may have "PhD envy," because a Juris Doctor degree is not usually considered the equivalent of a terminal degree in academic departments.

Moreover, higher education attorneys regularly deal with clients and others who are not as "compelling" as higher education clients. If you spend a few days in a courtroom, you'll see a mix of seasoned criminals being prosecuted, a bitter divorce, large economic interests slugging it out for financial advantage, a case involving a car crash caused by someone speeding and not paying attention, and so on. On any given day, courtrooms are filled with deadbeats, the greedy, and the downtrodden. In comparison, higher education administrators are great clients. With few exceptions, student affairs administrators are highly educated, responsible people who are genuinely dedicated to the best interests of students and others. Student affairs administrators solve problems on their own; they do not routinely displace their conflicts onto others. Student affairs administration draws people for noneconomic rewards—no one goes into higher education administration to get rich. Honest, good-hearted clients are hard to find. Although higher education administration is not an angelic calling, it is far from diabolical. In short, higher education attorneys respect their clients.

It does not hurt that higher education administration is also a "lifestyle job" like the law. Working long hours under stress and with constant criticism is typical of both law practice and student affairs administration. Higher education administrators are simpatico with their lawyers; their work ethics are similar.

LEGAL COMPLIANCE AND DEFENSIVE STUDENT AFFAIRS PRACTICE: THE SPIRIT OF THE LAW

It is very easy to imagine that a student affairs administrator should first seek to find the correct legal compliance solution, do that, and then move on to perform student affairs services. And it is tempting to view the law from a defensive standpoint: Do what is legally required to stave off the law wolves or at least minimize their impact. Indeed, there are times when a student affairs administrator must perform clear legal compliance steps and times when student affairs administrators must load their guns with silver bullets. However, this idealized relationship is generally too primitive for the modern institution of higher education environment and disserves the profession of student affairs administration as well as the law.

The hobgoblin of legal compliance is reductionism; that is, trying to reduce the law to a finite set of compliance solutions or one simple solution. In reality, legal compliance often requires the exercise of *judgment*—especially in higher education—and there is a range of possible legal compliance solutions. Often, there are no clear right or wrong answers at all—simply various choices with relative pros and cons. Indeed, it is the *process* of reaching decisions that is most important. Legal compliance may require weighing and balancing and generating decision trees. One judge I worked for told me that the right solutions are usually the ones that you feel a little uncomfortable about, and I think this is what he meant.

Moreover, since the student affairs administrator is not the lawyer for the institution of higher education, the administrator's job is not to generate legal arguments in court but to work with law as an element in the overall sound decision-making process for the institutional environment. Too often, student affairs administrators feel the need to reach decisions as if they were lawyers, or they allow legal advice to supplant their own sound judgment in a student affairs dimension. Bright-line yes or no answers are not ubiquitous in the student affairs world.

A related phenomenon is turning easy issues of student affairs administration into hard questions of law (or vice versa). I worked with a young lawyer who, like other Wall Street lawyers, had impeccable educational credentials. We called him the "human hornbook" (a hornbook is a legal book that contains a compendium of precise statements of law), because he had tremendous knowledge of the law at the tip of his fingers at all times. One day, shortly after his wife had a baby, he was unexpectedly transferred to one of our offices in another city. He had recently signed a long-term lease on his house. He walked into my office with a long "demand letter" for his landlord. The letter was full of threatening legal language and essentially said, "Dear Landlord, I am leaving my lease and if you don't let me out of the lease I will crucify you legally." The letter had taken quite some time to write, and he had used all his skills to compose a message that was sure to get the landlord's attention. He asked me, "What do you think?" I said, "Have you called the landlord?" Startled, he replied, "Well, no, not yet." I said, "Try calling your landlord; tell him you had a baby and you've been transferred." He said, "Do you think that will work?" I said, "Try it." He came back a little later, beaming: "I asked the landlord if we could break our lease and he said, "Of course—you just had a baby! I'll help you move." The lesson is this: A situation with an easy resolution could have become a nasty legal issue.

The concept of "defending" higher education from the law—ingrained in the formative moments of higher education law and those of its college attorney group, the National Association of College and University Attorneys (NACUA)[6]—misses the mark in today's complex law and higher education environment. Often the law exists to protect or facilitate and is not an opponent. In Chapter 5, the discussion of disability law in the context of student affairs illustrates that disability law is very much on the same page with the core values of higher education: attending to individual students, facilitating, developing and working with special aptitudes and weaknesses, mentoring, and so on. The spirit of disability law overlaps the spirit of higher education. There is nothing to defend against.

In the search for compliance—and in playing legal defense—we should be careful not to lose sight of the fact that compliance with the spirit of the law is our real goal. In many areas, the law needs us to embrace and internalize

---

[6] NACUA, founded in 1960–1961, is the primary higher education attorney group in the United States. Its purpose is to educate institutions of higher education, and their administrators and attorneys, regarding legal issues relating to campuses. *See* NACUA, *History and General Information*, http://www.nacua.org/aboutnacua/index.asp (last visited Nov. 6, 2010).

that spirit in our practice. If we do not, the law has no chance to succeed on its own. It may not occur to student affairs administrators that the law needs *us* to perform good and conscientious student affairs practice. The founding fathers, for instance, recognized that if citizens lose the spirit of the First Amendment, there is no chance that protection of speech or religion under law will work.[7]

Often, it is our task to pass this spirit on to students. Millennial students in particular are known for their adroit avoidance skills: We make a rule and they quickly find a way to circumvent it. Teaching the value of internalizing the purposes of rules may be especially imperative for this generation.

Sometimes student affairs administrators—and students—are commanded by the law to do or not do a particular thing. Sometimes it is not obvious what purposes the law hopes to achieve, or those purposes seem inconsistent or incoherent. However, that kind of relationship with the law is not the most common. Instead, higher education law usually seeks to integrate with and respect the professional practice of student affairs administration.[8]

LIMITS OF THE LAW AND THE DANGER OF LEGALISMS

The law is an important tool in student affairs practice. The law can help create fairness, combat discrimination, facilitate good student affairs practice, and protect institutions of higher education from forces that would thwart their objectives. Law is a very powerful force in our environment; however, there are limits to what the law can accomplish, especially

---

[7] A complete index of the *Federalist Papers* is provided on the Library of Congress web page *at* http://thomas.loc.gov/home/histdox/fedpapers.html (last visited Jan. 31, 2011).

[8] As the court stated in *Christian Legal Society at Hastings College of the Law*:

> The campus is, in fact, a world apart from the public square in numerous respects, and religious organizations, as well as all other organizations, must abide by certain norms of conduct when they enter an academic community. . . . The RSO [Registered Student Organization] forum is no different. It is not an open commons that Hastings happens to maintain. It is a mechanism through which Hastings confers certain benefits and pursues certain aspects of its educational mission. Having exercised its discretion to establish an RSO program, a university must treat all participants even-handedly. But the university need not remain neutral—indeed, it could not remain neutral—in determining which goals the program will serve and which rules are best suited to facilitate those goals. These are not legal questions but policy questions; they are not for the Court but for the university to make.

130 S. Ct. at 2997–98 (Stevens, J. concurring).

on its own, and there are risks associated with being too legalistic in higher education.

Many times in legal history, the law has been asked to fix a social ill, right a wrong, or promote a social good. As with any human enterprise, there are shining examples of success and spectacular Hindenburg-like failures as well. The key lesson for student affairs administrators is that we should not expect the law to fail or always make things better. We need to set reasonable expectations for our relationship with the law.

As discussed in more detail in Chapter 2, American higher education has embraced a culture of legalisms in managing student affairs. But it is dangerous to expect too much from the tools of a lawyer: Rules and procedures can complement student affairs practice, but they cannot supplant it. Sears sells some truly great power tools, but most would work poorly if the task involved cooking fine French cuisine.

Student affairs administrators should be conscious of when student affairs practice is imitative of law; for example, when it uses legal language and policies or asserts that the law requires or forbids something. Playing the law card can completely change student affairs administration discourse and how administrators react to an issue or manage it—and even how they think about issues.[9] As an example, consider how beliefs about FERPA led student affairs administrators to mismanage dangerous students before the events at Virginia Tech in April 2007.[10]

---

[9] An excellent book that will help student affairs administrators better understand the psychology, culture, and language of law is Benjamin Sells' *The Soul of the Law* (Element Books 1994). You might find yourself feeling sorry for lawyers after reading this book.

[10] In a report to President George W. Bush after the 2007 Virginia Tech tragedy, Department of Health and Human Services officials found "[a] consistent theme . . . that this confusion and differing interpretations about state and federal privacy laws and regulations impede appropriate information sharing." Michael O. Leavitt, Margaret Spellings, & Alberto R. Gonzales, *Report to the President on Issues Raised by the Virginia Tech Tragedy* (June 13, 2007), http://www.hhs.gov/vtreport.html#key. Teachers, administrators, and institutions were "concern[ed] and confus[ed] about the potential liability . . . that could arise from sharing information, or from not sharing information, under privacy laws, as well as laws designed to protect individuals from discrimination on the basis of mental illness." *Id.* "[F]ears and misunderstandings likely limit the transfer of information in more significant ways than is required by law." *Id.* While canvassing the nation, officials found institutions to be aware of FERPA and HIPAA but also found "significant misunderstanding about the scope and application of these laws and their interrelation with state laws." *Id.* An American Psychiatric Association document stated, "The perceived impediments to disclosures by college

The message is simple: Use law and legalisms to manage higher education environments, but be careful not to allow law and legalisms to supplant good student affairs practice.

LIABILITY INSURANCE, INDEMNIFICATION, AND PAYING FOR LAWYERS

Student affairs administrators often find themselves in situations that trigger questions about liability insurance and indemnification. Indemnification is simply a complex way of talking about picking up the tab for someone else. If you allow your son or daughter to use your credit card, essentially you are indemnifying them for the charges they make. Insurance is a complex indemnification agreement based on the occurrence of certain events—such as accidents that create legal liability.[11] Insurance agreements or contracts (policies) also provide valuable rights to legal representation at little or no cost to the insured. Many times, the cost of lawyers significantly exceeds the potential indemnification cost. Translated into English: It may cost more to defend a case than is at stake in the case. Insurers must also defend against claims even if they might be "groundless, false, or fraudulent."[12] Moreover, insurance policies require insurance companies

officials in situations in which the health or safety of students may be endangered seem often the result of a misunderstanding of FERPA and other relevant laws and regulations." American Psychiatric Association, *College Mental Health and Confidentiality* (June 2009), http://www.psych.org/Departments/EDU/Library/APAOfficialDocumentsandRelated/ResourceDocuments/200905.aspx. After the tragedy, NACUA published information on FERPA to correct misunderstandings and allay "[c]oncerns about the ability to communicate critical information in an emergency." Nancy E. Tribbensee & Steven J. McDonald, *FERPA and Campus Safety*, 5 NACUA Notes 4 (Aug. 6, 2007), *available at* http://www.nacua.org/documents/ferpa1.pdf.

[11] "The basic insuring agreement of the CGL (Commercial General Liability Policy) provides: The company will pay on behalf of the insured all sums which the insured shall become legally obligated to pay as damages because of A. bodily injury, or B. property damage to which this insurance applies caused by an occurrence during the policy period." Robert H. Jerry, II, *Understanding Insurance Law* § 65[a], 440–43 (2d ed., Matthew Bender 1996).

[12] In *Boccone v. Eichen Levinson LLP*, the insurance policy stated in relevant part, "'[t]he company shall defend any [c]laim to which this insurance applies, even if any of the allegations of the claim are groundless, false, or fraudulent.'" 301 Fed. Appx. 162, 166 n. 4 (3d Cir. 2008) (quoting the policy). The court stated that "[i]n determining whether an insurer has a duty to defend, New Jersey law instructs us to 'compar[e]' the allegations in the complaint with the language of the policy. When the two correspond, the duty to defend arises, irrespective of the claim's actual merit." *Id.* at 168 (quoting *Voorhees v. Preferred Mutual Insurance Co.*, 607 A. 2d 1255, 1259 (N.J. 1992)). The court agreed with the district court's finding that "the underlying claim fell 'within the scope of coverage afforded

to continue defending their insureds until a case is dismissed or settled, or goes to judgment. Insurance policies, therefore, provide two key and distinct rights for insureds: indemnification in the event of legal liability and legal defense costs.

The institution of higher education is typically the insured for indemnification purposes, and policies usually cover the acts of many employees, such as student affairs administrators. However, in the event of a successful lawsuit, insurance usually only indemnifies the institution of higher education itself; it does not cover personal liability of a student affairs administrator. Through application of rules of law or agreement to indemnify employees such as student affairs administrators, an institution may bear responsibility for the errors of student affairs administrators; however, administrators can be sued personally for their errors, and a winning litigant could theoretically attempt to collect from the administrator personally instead of the institution. The institution's insurance policy would not typically cover the student affairs administrator in this situation. Moreover, the lawyer paid for by the institution's insurer represents the institution, not its employees, unless the insurer, the institution, and the employees agree to joint representation and there is no manifest conflict of interest in representing all parties simultaneously. In practice, this means that if a student affairs administrator and an institution of higher education do not have common interests, the administrator will have to find his or her own legal representation. However, the student affairs administrator may find that no insurance company will offer such defense costs, unless that administrator has purchased an insurance policy covering professional liability in his or her capacity as a student affairs administrator.

There are several ways a student affairs administrator can draw some comfort in situations such as these. First, most plaintiffs name student affairs administrators in lawsuits for tactical or procedural reasons; the true aim of the litigation is to seek redress from the institution of higher education, with its typically much larger resources, including insurance policies. If an institution is to be held vicariously liable[13] for any negligence of its student affairs administrators, plaintiffs often must first show that the administrator was negligent and sue him or her personally. Rules of law can make the institution of higher

---

by the policy," and that American Safety breached the policy by denying coverage." *Id.* (quoting *Voorhees*, 607 A. 2d at 1259); *See also Peterson v. Ohio Cas. Group*, 724 N.W.2d 765, 773 (Neb. 2006); *Vulcan Engineering Co. v. XL Ins. America, Inc.*, 201 Fed. Appx. 678, 680 (11th Cir. 2006).
[13] *See infra* Chapter 2.

education directly responsible for any judgment rendered against its employees acting in the scope of employment (although technically the plaintiff could seek direct recourse against the student affairs administrator). In short, the student affairs administrator is rarely the true target in litigation.

Also, many institutions can, and do, indemnify their key employees for negligent errors and omissions committed in the course of their duties. It is advisable to work out what, if any, indemnification arrangements are available and appropriate for student affairs administrators at your institution. A few words of caution: Some institutions cannot or will not indemnify employees. Moreover, acts outside the course of official duties and certain wrongs, such as intentional wrongs and many crimes, are not subject to indemnification—or to insurance coverage, for that matter. Also, indemnification and insurance apply in civil actions only. If a student affairs administrator lands in criminal court (which is highly unusual), that person is on his or her own to hire and pay for counsel in all but the rarest situations.

Finally, a student affairs administrator may attempt to purchase special insurance products for student affairs administrators.[14] This is not a common practice in student affairs, and usually only the most senior or litigation-averse student affairs administrators consider this option. In fact, one school of thought holds that having insurance actually makes student affairs administrators a bigger target for litigation, because they are seen as having "deep pockets." Plaintiffs' lawyers rarely seek money damages from student affairs administrators personally, because student affairs practice is not likely to be a source of wealth. It is quite expensive and time-consuming to collect money damage awards from ordinary people unless they have insurance—and then even if they do. In addition, successful litigation against student affairs administrators in institutions of higher education arising out of student affairs practice is still highly unusual, and little evidence exists to suggest that lawyers target student affairs administrators in the hopes of gaining judgments from them as individuals. (See Chapter 3 for more reasons not to purchase personal insurance.)

But here is another thought to consider: If an institution of higher education pays money damages to a plaintiff under a doctrine of vicarious liability,

---

[14] For example, United Educators offers insurance for student affairs administrators. United Educators—Education's Own Insurance Company, http://www.ue.org/home.aspx (last visited Nov. 5, 2010). (Obviously, the Author cannot endorse any one company's products or services.)

see below, arising from the negligence of a student affairs administrator in the scope or duties of employment, that institution technically has the right to seek repayment of those sums directly from the administrator. Yikes! Employers in general, and institutions of higher education in particular, almost never act on such rights, and I would venture to guess that many institutions do not even realize these rights exist. However, should the employment culture in higher education change, institutions could choose to exercise these rights; in that case, student affairs administration insurance would be advisable, even essential.

STUDENT AFFAIRS PROFESSIONALISM AND THE LAW

It is common to speak of the "profession" of student affairs administration. Student affairs is highly worthy of the status of profession, but the law usually reserves a special meaning for the word. The traditional learned professions—such as law, medicine, architecture, engineering, and accountancy—are primary examples of spheres of activity that the law brands professions.[15] A few states, like Florida, expand the definition somewhat.[16] Typically, a learned or recognized profession requires special training and a license to practice, and features some form of self-regulation, including a disciplinary function for members who transgress stated norms.[17] If a field achieves such status, the law typically grants special privileges; for example, the profession essentially sets its own standard of care, and questions of negligence are transformed into questions of whether the professional has acted in accordance with good and customary practices in the profession, accounting, of course,

---

[15] Generally, in negligence cases, liability is determined by the defendant's "failure to act as a reasonably prudent person." John L. Diamond, Lawrence C. Levine & M. Stuart Madden, *Understanding Torts,* § 7.01, 91–92 (3d ed., Lexis 2007). However, "professional negligence" is determined using a different standard of care. *Id.* "Because of the specialized skill and training needed to be a doctor, lawyer, accountant, architect, or engineer, courts defer to the expertise of the profession to determine the appropriate standard of care.... [C]ustom plays a determinative role." *Id.*

[16] Florida law imposes a professional standard of care upon a wider class of allegedly negligent professionals; that is, "a duty to perform the requested services in accordance with the standard of care used by similar professionals in the community under similar circumstance." *Moransais v. Heathman,* 744 So. 2d 973, 975–76 (Fla. 1999) (finding a cause of action to exist against the professionals, individually, for negligent acts committed while in providing professional services (i.e., professional negligence)). *Id.*

[17] "The professional standard of care applies only where there is specialized skill and training, and often, post-graduate education." Diamond, *Understanding Torts,* at 91 note 2.

for variations in professional judgment.[18] Customs and practices of the profession typically become the controlling standard against which a professional's actions or inactions are judged.

Student affairs administration does not have full professional status but is perhaps semi-pro. Student affairs administrators are required to conform to good and customary practice when it exists,[19] and there is some literature in the field on some topics that purports to provide good or best practices. However, the law may or may not recognize such practices, or "best practices," for its own purposes unless they meet minimum legal thresholds. Student affairs administrators should be particularly wary of purchasing snake oil. First, something branded a "best practice" (implying some level of legal protection) may or may not work effectively in litigation management. Second, even if it is a true customary practice under the law, the law might still inquire whether compliance with that practice is sufficient.[20] The litigation process may ask student affairs administrators to do more than, or something other than, what is considered customary practice in the industry.[21]

The practice of student affairs has been moving steadily forward since the 1960s and may someday achieve the status equal of a so-called learned profession. The legal system has shown substantial deference to student affairs administrators.[22] This deference arises in part from historical patterns of legal deference to higher education and in part from an overlay of academic freedom as it relates to the practice of student affairs administration. Yet a movement currently exists to make student affairs practice more professional.

---

[18] "There may be some elitism at work in the determination of which 'professions' are afforded the professional standard of care, and which are not." *Id.*

[19] Usually, for a practice to rise to the level of good and customary, it must be widely accepted and followed in an industry as a protective or safety practice. Dan Dobbs, *The Law of Torts*, §§ 163–64, at 393–99 (West 2000).

[20] *The T. J. Hooper v. Northern Barge Corp.*, 60 F.2d 737, 740 (2d Cir. 1932).

[21] A good example comes from the Massachusetts Supreme Court in *Mullins v. Pine Manor*, the first case in higher education law that imposed responsibility on institutions of higher education to deploy campus security to protect students from violent assault on campus. 449 N.E.2d 331, 335–36 (Mass. 1983). Before *Mullins,* campus security or police saw their primary mission as protecting buildings and grounds. This custom and practice had to yield to transitions on the modern campus and in the law.

[22] "As a general matter, courts should respect universities' judgments and let them manage their own affairs." *Christian Legal Society*, 130 S. Ct. at 2998. (Stevens, J. concurring).

Consider, for example, recent efforts by the American College Personnel Association and the National Association of Student Personnel Administrators to develop more competencies for student affairs administrators.[23] The devel-

---

[23] The competency areas include: Advising and Helping; Assessment, Evaluation, and Research; Equity, Diversity, and Inclusion; Ethical Professional Practice; History, Philosophy, and Values; Human and Organizational Resources; Law, Policy, and Governance; Leadership; Personal Foundations; and Student Learning and Development. ACPA and NASPA, *Professional Competency Areas for Student Affairs Practitioners* (July 24, 2010), *available at* http://www.naspa.org/ programs/prodev/Professional_Competencies.pdf. The competency areas are defined as follows:

The Advising and Helping competency area addresses the knowledge, skills, and attitudes related to providing counseling and advising support, direction, feedback, critique, referral, and guidance to individuals and groups. *Id.* at 6. The Assessment, Evaluation, and Research competency area (AER) focuses on the ability to use, design, conduct, and critique qualitative and quantitative AER analyses; to manage organization using AER processes and the results obtained from them; and to shape the political and ethical climate surrounding AER processes and uses on campus. *Id.* at 8. The Equity, Diversity, and Inclusion (EDI) competency area includes the knowledge, skills, and attitudes needed to create learning environments that are enriched with diverse views and people. It is also designed to create an institutional ethos that accepts and celebrates differences among people, helping to free them of any misconceptions and prejudices. *Id.* at 10. The Ethical Professional Practice competency area pertains to the knowledge, skills, and attitudes needed to understand and apply ethical standards to one's work. *Id.* at 12. The History, Philosophy, and Values competency area involves knowledge, skills, and attitudes that connect the history, philosophy, and values of the profession to one's current professional practice. *Id.* at 14. The Human and Organization Resources competency area includes knowledge, skills, and attitudes used in the selection, supervision, motivation, and formal evaluation of staff; conflict resolution; management of the politics of organizational discourse; and the effective application of strategies and techniques associated with financial resources, facilities management, fundraising, technology use, crisis management, risk management and sustainable resources. *Id.* at 16. The Law, Policy, and Governance competency area includes the knowledge, skills, and attitudes relating to policy development processes used in various contexts, the application of legal constructs, and the understanding of governance structures and their effect on one's professional practice. *Id.* at 20. The Leadership competency area addresses the knowledge, skills, and attitudes required of a leader, whether it be a positional leader or member of the staff, in both an individual capacity and within a process of how individuals work together effectively to envision, plan, effect change in organization, and respond to internal and external constituencies and issues. *Id.* at 22. The Personal Foundations competency area involves the knowledge, skills, and attitudes to maintain emotional, physical, social, environmental, relational, spiritual, and intellectual wellness; be self-directed and self-reflective; maintain excellence and integrity in work; be comfortable with ambiguity; be aware of one's own areas of strength and growth; have a passion for work; and remain curious. *Id.* at 24. The Student Learning and Development competency area addresses the concepts and principles of student development and learning theory. This includes the ability to apply theory to improve and inform student affairs practice, as well as understanding teaching and training theory and practice. *Id.* at 26.

opment of core competencies for a profession is an exercise that could mature into setting disciplinary and professional standards. Student affairs administration is in the process of becoming a legally recognized profession; however, it does not yet require a license or continuing education, or support self-regulating disciplinary bodies. Thus, it retains its semi-pro status for now.

THE LITIGATION PROCESS

The civil litigation process is unnerving to many student affairs administrators. It is like being in a dance contest where you only know some of the steps. Litigation and education are very dissimilar in their goals and structure, and are often populated by very different professional personalities. As I told one law student, "There are no hugs in law."

Civil litigation can be a very costly, time-consuming enterprise, and as the litigation proceeds farther and farther down its path, litigants tend to lose more and more control over their futures and fates. Moreover, the civil litigation system runs essentially parallel to other legal systems (e.g., the criminal system), many of which are far more urgent and demanding. The American legal system is hardly waiting to put everything on hold for parties who wish to argue over civil matters. The justice system is very busy, and higher education's biggest controversies are rarely the biggest in the overall system.

The most common legal processes that student affairs administrators become embroiled in are civil litigation involving claims of breach of contract, depravation of civil rights, or negligence. Higher education attorneys will experience the full range of legal processes—including bankruptcy proceedings, regulatory matters, and city council meetings—but the first three areas dominate the student affairs administrator's experience in the civil justice system.

This chapter explores the litigation process through the lens of a typical contested civil matter. Litigation does not always follow the same path, but we can describe the critical steps in the process. The following litigation schematic may help.

LITIGATION SCHEMATIC

1. Preventative steps to manage risks, events, or occurrences that might trigger potential liability
2. Triggering event
3. Formal or informal demand from plaintiff following incident or event
4. Complaint or other initiating legal document
5. Discovery, including court-ordered mediation
6. Summary judgment
7. Trial, including post- and pretrial motions
8. Appeals
9. Post-litigation management
10. Alternative Dispute Resolution (ADR)

Litigation has a life cycle: Highly contested matters are born and eventually die, while some matters never come to term and still others are "false positives"—they appear pregnant with litigation potential but never materialize. The litigation schematic displays a typical life cycle, although no two are ever exactly the same. Many litigations skip steps or follow a different sequence. Indeed, no one schematic could ever truly capture the world of complexity in civil litigation.

Step 1. Preventative Steps

The best way to avoid litigation is to avoid events or occurrences that could trigger litigation in the first place. Student affairs administrators often do not realize that their day-to-day best efforts prevent litigation, particularly when they are engaging in proactive risk management efforts and overt litigation avoidance steps. Step 1 is the contraceptive part of litigation. From a litigation risk standpoint, student affairs administration often works best when nothing happens. This makes it difficult for student affairs administrators and their managers to understand and quantify their achievements, but it is crucial to realize that an ounce of student affairs administration prevention can stave off a pound of lawyers.

Step 2. Triggering Event

Every civil litigation has at least one triggering event—in insurance law, we often speak of an accident or occurrence.[24] These are the events that have the potential to mature into full-blown litigation.

A good example would be a set of injury-producing events—loosely speaking, an accident or breach of contract. Usually, for an event to trigger talk of liability, the consequences must be severe and not easily mitigated by corrective or reparative actions. The cost of civil litigation—and of the duties after loss or injury to take proactive steps to reduce or eliminate damage—are so high that only very significant matters percolate up from the triggering event stage. After you have read Chapter 2, it will be clearer that the framework for safety law in the United States is a filtering framework that tends to eliminate small or manageable matters. Often, small issues are resolved only heuristically, as if they were subject to legal scrutiny or with an eye toward Step 1—preventing similar incidents that might be serious enough to trigger legal action.

Student affairs administrators have a great deal of power at Step 2 to manage the risk of litigation. Effective communication with legal counsel and others can forestall litigation or eliminate litigation risk. Not surprisingly, many people who proceed to lawsuit against a college do so because they feel mistreated or ignored, or because of poor communication with the institution after an incident. A bunker mentality on the part of the institution sometimes can be its own worst enemy. Counsel may tell clients to be silent and take no further action, but this advice may relate to past events only and not to action after an incident.

The immediate aftermath of an event or occurrence is the critical time during which litigation risk is most likely to increase or decrease. Keep in mind, however, that if injuries are extremely severe—such as major head or spinal cord injuries or significant contested constitutional rights—litigation may be inevi-

---

[24] See *Understanding Insurance Law, supra* note 11, at 440–47.

table or even desirable. Sometimes going to court is the best alternative and the right choice to manage conflict.

This is also the time for student affairs administrators and others to determine whether relevant insurance policies have been triggered and insurance companies should be notified. Many insurance policies have broad language that requires the insured to provide timely notice of claims, events, and lawsuits—typically before a complaint is filed.[25] Some insurers also help institutions of higher education develop preventive practices.[26]

Step 3. Formal or Informal Demand

An aggrieved party may elect—or be required—to initiate the litigation process via a formal demand for relief, such as a written demand letter, notice of claim, or intent to sue letter.[27] Formal demand letters and notices of intent to sue are not themselves complaints; rather, they precede litigation or may be a necessary precondition to proceed to litigation via complaint.[28] Nonetheless, a demand letter is a strong indicator that a complaint and litigation may be coming.

Demand letters can be very formal and hard for the layperson to comprehend. They are often oppositional, positional, and even accusatory in tone. Also, they typically insist on unrealistic or unreasonable actions or forbearances, even if they do include reasonable demands. The language and tone can be off-putting to a student affairs administrator, but these documents are part of the litigation process and do not necessarily reflect how a dispute will ultimately be resolved. Student affairs administrators should not assume that it is their job to respond to such a letter; rather, they should immediately forward it to counsel for review. For the student affairs administrator, the demand letter should signal the beginning of an oppositional legal process and the need to prepare for what may lie ahead.

---

[25] *Id.*

[26] *See* United Educators—Education's Own Insurance Company, http://www.ue.org/home.aspx (last visited Nov. 5, 2010).

[27] Stefan H. Krieger & Richard K Neumann, Jr., *Essential Lawyering Skills* 355–70 (3d ed., Aspen 2007).

[28] For instance, consider the following: "As a condition precedent to filing any action for benefits under this section [§ 627.736], the insurer must be provided with written notice of an intent to initiate litigation." Fla. Stat. § 627.736(10)(a) (2010). Constitutional or other legal issues sometimes affect statutory requirements for demand letters. See, for example, *Turner v. Staggs,* 510 P.2d 879, 882–83 (Nev. 1973), in which the court held that the statute requiring a person to give six months notice before suing a government entity for tort claims is void.

A demand letter or notice of intent to sue also can signal the start of a negotiation or alternative dispute resolution process. Parties engaged in a dispute are free to negotiate an agreement or settlement. Sometimes demand letters precede a very quick settlement, and no complaint is ever filed. For example, a demand letter might call for the retraction of and apology for a defamatory statement; the person who made the statement might quickly agree to retract and apologize in lieu of litigation.

However, potential adversaries do not always send a letter or notice to signal that they may institute legal proceedings. Some litigants proceed directly to Step 3, and it is not uncommon for an institution of higher education to receive its first written notice of a claim right at the statutory time limit for taking action.[29]

Some people who are aggrieved with an institution of higher education will make their concerns known less formally. Informal demands for relief are not uncommon. For example, an attorney representing a client with a grievance may request to meet or to discuss the matter. Often the purpose of the discussion is to convey a demand or a potential position in litigation, or to invite negotiation. Sometimes potential complainants are litigation-averse. They may not want to air grievances publicly, or they simply lack the time or resources to engage in the litigation process. The presuit process can be a little bit like playing poker—brinksmanship and bluffing are part of the game.

Step 4. The Complaint

The most common way to initiate a civil action in a court of law is to file a complaint.[30] A complaint seeks to invoke the jurisdiction of the court.[31] It is a highly

---

[29] A statute of limitations is like the shot clock in basketball—it sets the time allowed to file a lawsuit for a given cause of action, and if the lawsuit is not filed within that time frame, the buzzer goes off and the suit is no longer allowed to be litigated. Federal and state statutes of limitations set maximum time frames to bring a legal proceeding for a particular event.

[30] *See* Fed. R. Civ. P. 3. "A civil action is commenced by filing a complaint with the court." *Id.* A complaint is considered a pleading. Fed. R. Civ. P. 7(a)(1). "A pleading that states a claim for relief [a complaint] must contain: (1) a short and plain statement of the grounds for the court's jurisdiction, unless the court already has jurisdiction and the claim needs no new jurisdictional support; (2) a short and plain statement of the claim showing that the pleader is entitled to relief; and (3) a demand for the relief sought, which may include relief in the alternative or different types of relief." Fed. R. Civ. P. 8(a)(1)–(3).

[31] *Id.* at R. 8. There are two branches of jurisdiction: personal jurisdiction and subject-matter jurisdiction. Personal jurisdiction is the court's ability to exercise power over the particular defen-

stylized document that typically features recitations and "counts"—each of which typically attempts to set forth "facts," legal theories for relief, and usually a demand for relief from the court (often money damages, sometimes in enormous sums).

Here are a few things to keep in mind about complaints:

1. The facts—and even the persons—described in the complaint may be completely incorrect. Although attorneys are not allowed to make up facts or knowingly plead false facts, they are granted wide latitude in presuit investigation processes. A generous way to look at this is to say that the law understands that a plaintiff (the one bringing the complaint) may not know exactly what happened, or which laws apply, or who did what to whom.

   If a student affairs administrator has been involved in an incident that matures into a complaint, he or she might be perplexed that persons who had little or nothing to do with the incident are named as defendants, or that the complaint includes obvious factual errors. This is common and is an important part of the discovery process. Student affairs administrators can be excellent assets to litigation teams preparing a defense for an institution of higher education.

2. The relief sought by the plaintiffs might be an extraordinary sum of money. For a variety of reasons, it is common to set forth unrealistic amounts in so-called "ad damnum" clauses.[32] The actual monetary award rarely comes close to the figure in the complaint. Think of these numbers as aspirational.

3. A complaint will likely be amended several times in the course of litigation.

4. An institution of higher education will have the chance to answer the complaint and offer affirmative defenses.[33] In addition, a defendant

---

dant or item of property. Subject-matter jurisdiction is the court's ability to exercise power over the type of case.

[32] *Id.* at R. 8(a)(3).

[33] "In responding to a pleading, a party must: (A) state in short and plain terms its defenses to each claim asserted against it; and (B) admit or deny the allegations asserted against it by an opposing

can proffer counterclaims against the plaintiff; in essence, playing offense from the defensive side of the field.

5. A complaint does not have inherent survivability. A plaintiff must allege sufficient facts that, if proven, would support a viable cause of action.[34] A complaint typically has to survive a motion to dismiss, which tests the basic legal sufficiency of that complaint.[35] Many lawyers refer to this as a "12(b)(6) motion," after the applicable federal rule of civil procedure.[36] Not long ago, many complaints lodged against institutions of higher education failed at exactly this point. Lawyers like to win cases at this point—it typically means little or no discovery (see below Step 5), and the matter is concluded favorably. Thus, lawyers naturally gravitate toward arguments that might win cases in this way. "No-duty" arguments (discussed in Chapter 2) are a prime example of arguments at the motion to dismiss level.

However, it has become increasingly less common for institutions of higher education to win cases in this way. Subtle changes in the procedural rules—a shift away from resolving cases at the level of a complaint—have fueled a litigation-reality shift. This situation substantially elongates the litigation process, makes settlement more likely, increases litigation costs, and ramps up the level of scrutiny of student affairs administrator decision making.

The shift away from quick and decisive win options for institutions of higher education has promoted an increased sense of accountability among student affairs administrators. Once litigation proceeds past the complaint stage, the discovery process (see Step 5) tends to scrutinize student affairs administrator decision making from the vantage

---

party." Fed. R. Civ. P. 8(b)(1). Further, "[i]n responding to a pleading, a party must affirmatively state any avoidance or affirmative defense." *Id*. at 8(c)(1).

[34] "Every defense to a claim for relief in any pleading must be asserted in the responsive pleading if one is required. But a party may assert the following defenses by motion. . . . (6) failure to state a claim upon which relief can be granted." Fed. R. Civ. P. 12(b)(6).

[35] *Id*.

[36] *Id*.

point of 20/20 hindsight. As litigants proceed through discovery, they are posturing and often accusatory. Moreover, despite some legal tools to control the flow of information in discovery, some information may make its way to the press and the larger community.

But student affairs administrators should not think that this accusatory/adversarial process sets the standard for administrator professionalism or even the ultimate standards of evaluation in the legal system. The legal system will judge student affairs administrator behavior in real time, not from the point of view of a Monday morning quarterback. In fact, it is actually very difficult to successfully prosecute an action to conclusion; often, a plaintiff's best hope is to posture for a better settlement offer.

Step 5. Discovery

After the complaint is filed, the process of discovery can begin. Discovery is the period (often lengthy) during which litigants develop facts and legal theories before trial and posture to make a critical series of pretrial motions (discussed below).

Discovery is more of a structured event than a free-for-all process. Most litigants are subject to case management orders (CMOs) that set deadlines for discovery. Moreover, litigants can seek protective orders to stem inquiries in which the flow of information goes beyond the litigation. The discovery process is a preparatory phase before a trial, but it is also preparation for pretrial motions, especially in the critical summary judgment phase. Institution of higher education lawyers use summary judgment as a critical tool to terminate litigation, and discovery is often oriented toward this goal.

Several key aspects of the discovery phase apply to student affairs administrators:

1. *Depositions*

Depositions are a key component of discovery. A deposition is an information-gathering event at which a witness testifies under oath. Parties appear with counsel, but no judge or neutral referee is present. Depositions typically involve both an audio and video recording, and are usually transcribed. The deposition can last for as little as a half hour or can go on for days. It is acceptable to ask questions that would not be asked at trial and to ask them in a form that might not be acceptable in court. Lawyers may use deposition transcripts later at trial, and often do. The witness may be asked to bring key documents (*duces tecum*[37]), which will be marked as "exhibits at the deposition."

The pace and tone of a deposition depend on the styles of the lawyers involved, so they can vary widely. Some depositions are so short and serene that a witness might almost doze off; however, many depositions involve heated arguments and some even lead to physical fights. Few student affairs administrators have experience being deposed, and their personal experiences in depositions will vary considerably. Recent professional and judicial efforts have attempted to reduce the likelihood of extreme behavior,[38] but given the adversarial nature of the process and the fact that judges are rarely present, some conflict is inevitable.

---

[37] *Duces tecum* is a Latin term that means "bring with you." *Black's Law Dictionary* 227 (8th ed., West Group 2004).

[38] The American Bar Association created Model Rules of Professional Conduct to maintain the integrity of the legal system and preserve the administration of justice. Regarding interactions between opposing counsel, the ABA Model Rules set forth Rule 3.4: Fairness to Opposing Party and Counsel, which states in part:

> A lawyer shall not: (a) unlawfully obstruct another party's access to evidence or unlawfully alter, destroy or conceal a document or other material having potential evidentiary value. A lawyer shall not counsel or assist another person to do any such act; (b) falsify evidence, counsel or assist a witness to testify falsely, or offer an inducement to a witness that is prohibited by law; ... (d) in pretrial procedure, make a frivolous discovery request or fail to make reasonably diligent effort to comply with a legally proper discovery request by an opposing party.

Model R. Prof. Conduct 3.4(a, b, d) (ABA 2008). The purpose behind this rule is to ensure that evidence is in front of the trier of fact so the law unfolds fairly, based on truth, and thus maintains the integrity of the judicial system. Additionally, this rule ensures that while both sides are encouraged to use the system to win, counsel are fair, respectful, professional, and put their faith in the judicial system.

Documents and other items of evidence are often essential to establish a claim or defense. Subject to evidentiary privileges, the right of an opposing party, including the government, to obtain evidence through discovery or subpoena is an important procedural right. The exercise of that right can be frustrated if relevant material is altered, concealed or destroyed. Applicable law in many jurisdictions makes it an offense to destroy material for purpose of impairing its availability in a pending proceeding or one whose commence can be foreseen. *Id.* at 3.4 cmt. 2.

2. *Interrogatories and requests for admission*

Litigants often put forth formal written questions or request to "admit on the other side." Student affairs administrators may be involved in the process of responding to such discovery, especially regarding requests for documents. Administrators must always have a clear picture of what is being requested and why. Discovery is the fishing expedition phase of litigation—plaintiffs often cast a wide net in their search for information that can help their cases survive to go to trial or increase the value of their case for settlement.

3. *Experts*

During discovery, institutions of higher education often identify experts who may assist in litigation. Student affairs administrators may help counsel identify relevant experts and then work closely with them. The use of experts is a relatively new phenomenon in higher education litigation, which has evolved to the point at which it is similar to commercial litigation.

4. *Case preparation with counsel*

Student affairs administrators typically work hand-in-hand with counsel during the discovery process; for example, preparing for a deposition, gathering documents, or helping counsel understand how a particular situation was handled. Counsel will also set boundaries in discovery matters with others, including the media. For instance, counsel may seek and receive 'protective orders' that limit access to and dissemination of materials; or may instruct clients not to speak to the media. Student affairs administrators often work with counsel to develop post-event practices; for example, helping a severely injured student return to class or counseling roommates who have experienced a traumatic incident. Student affairs administrators must realize that civil litigation can often continue for years; the discovery process alone can last for a very long period.

Step 6. Summary Judgment

Modern higher education litigation is focused on the summary judgment phase. To some extent, this focus mirrors trends in civil litigation in general, but it also reflects the rising culture of accountability in higher education. Courts are less inclined to dismiss cases at the complaint/motion to dismiss stage; on the other hand, higher education cases rarely go to trial. Litigation surrounding summary judgment can end a matter, frame it for settlement, or set it up for appeal. Summary judgment is often the last step in a long litigation process. Ironically, the civil justice system conceives summary judgment as a pretrial preparatory stage; in reality, it is a filtering process that weeds out most cases before a trial begins.

For seasoned litigators, the concept of summary judgment is so familiar that it feels instinctive. For a student affairs administrator with no formal legal training, the concept can seem a bit strange.

The typical standard for summary judgment is something like this: A party (either side or both sides can make motions for summary judgment) is entitled to summary judgment if the material facts are not disputed and the law compels a result on these undisputed facts.[39]

Functional standards for summary judgment are subtly different in the federal and state systems, from state to state, and even from court to court. A non-lawyer is in a poor position to assess the subtleties of summary judgment without assistance from counsel; however, there are some fairly consistent themes.

First, parties will invariably debate many facts and, especially, the coloration of those facts. Yet, there may be no *material* factual dispute. In other words, the key facts necessary to reach a clear legal result may not be in dispute. Some disputed facts are irrelevant in making decisions based on clear legal standards.

Second, summary judgment can be reached on some issues but not all issues. A court may grant a partial summary judgment and set other disputed matters for trial. The purpose of a trial is to determine facts and apply them to the law. Judges are always looking for ways to avoid unnecessary trials and reduce trial time—hence, summary judgment. Summary judgment can set the predicate for settlement, especially if a court is willing to show the parties how it might or might not rule if certain facts are proven or demonstrated. Thus, par-

---

[39] *See* Fed. R. Civ. P. 56; *see also* N.Y. C.P.L.R. 1411.

tial summary judgment frames what could happen if a trial were to take place.

Third, a court can deny summary judgment for one or both parties. Some judges would rather let evidence come in at trial and make legal rulings after the close of the plaintiff's case or when all evidence has been presented. There is talk in decisional law that parties are *entitled* to summary judgment,[40] but in reality the decision to grant or deny summary judgment is at the discretion of the trial judge. This decision is subject to appellate review, but appellate courts routinely defer to trial judges with respect to their discretion to grant or deny summary judgment.[41]

Fourth, different versions of what took place during an event may vary wildly, but summary judgment is still available in some instances. Consider the board game Clue.[42] If we all agree that the butler did it in the pantry, we might be able to award summary judgment. Even if we do not know whether he used the knife or the candlestick, we agree that it was murder.

Fifth, sometimes summary judgment on a linchpin issue will end a case even if other issues are hotly debated. One classic situation is causation. In many causes of action, evidence of a causal relationship between a wrong and an injury is necessary for the plaintiff to succeed. No causation, no cause of action—even if there was wrongdoing. Lawyers try to identify the linchpin issues and attempt to win cases by winning on those issues. In modern higher education safety litigation, for example, lawyers often argue that the institution owes no duty to a student because the existence of a duty is essential to a plaintiff's case. In higher education litigation, duty is frequently a linchpin issue.

Sixth, summary judgment separates issues of fact from questions of law (although a question can be a mixed question of law and fact).[43] When judges have difficulty sorting through contested sets of facts, or applicable legal rules are extremely complex, they tend to set matters for trial, perhaps hoping that the parties will settle or the issues will become clearer during the trial.

Seventh, generally (although not always), when institutions of higher edu-

---

[40] *Marcus v. St. Paul Fire and Marine Ins. Co.*, 651 F.2d 379, 382 (5th Cir. 1981); *Vangsguard v. Progressive Northern Ins. Co.*, 525 N.W.2d 146, 147 (Wis. App. 1994).

[41] Appellate courts do sometimes disagree with a trial judge's decision on summary judgment. *See Allen v. Cox,* 942 A.2d 296, 299–301 (Conn. 2008); *Englert, Inc. v. LeafGuard USA, Inc.,* 659 S.E.2d 496, 498–99 (S.C. 2008); *Harris v. Showcase Chevrolet*, 231 S.W.3d 559, 561–62 (Tex. App. Dallas 2007).

[42] Wikipedia, Cluedo, http://en.wikipedia.org/wiki/Cluedo (last visited Aug. 9, 2010).

[43] *See Nelson v. Piggly Wiggly Central, Inc.*, 390 S.C. 382 (S.C. App. 2010).

cation are the defendants in litigation they seek summary judgment, while plaintiffs prefer to go to trial. This is an issue of legal culture and law. Plaintiffs' lawyers may hope to put sympathetic facts in front of juries in the hope of winning favorable (and large) verdicts. A large verdict that survives trial motions (discussed below) provides an extremely powerful weapon in settlement. On the other hand, the defense counsel for an institution of higher education wants to win the case before a trial begins. Summary judgment can be used to play offense effectively, but most litigators realize that it is primarily a defensive tool. A victory on summary judgment is far better for the institution than winning in trial, while losing summary judgment may mean that the settlement value of a case has grown significantly and the plaintiff has won the right to go to trial. A trial is extremely expensive and time-consuming, and delays the ultimate resolution of the matter.

Step 7. Trial

It is very rare for civil cases to go to trial—most cases settle or otherwise resolve. Very few student affairs administrators will ever go to trial in their careers.

Although litigants typically have the right to a trial by jury, a trial can also be in front of a judge only—this is known as a "bench trial."[44] Actions against the government (i.e., public universities) are not likely to include the right to trial by jury. In some cases, parties willingly waive their right to trial by jury.[45] At trial, a judge may determine that the case lacks merit, either at the close of the plaintiff's case or after all the evidence has come in from both sides. A judge can also rule after a jury renders a verdict.[46] The plaintiff has a number of hurdles

---

[44] "Bench trial" is defined as "[a] trial before a judge without a jury" where "[t]he judge decides questions of fact as well as questions of law." *Black's Law Dictionary* at 733.

[45] "The right to trial by jury as declared by the Seventh Amendment to the Constitution—or as provided by a federal statute—is preserved to the parties inviolate. . . . A party waives a jury trial unless its demand is properly served and filed. A proper demand may be withdrawn only if the parties consent." Fed. R. Civ. P. 38(a)(d).

[46] "A motion for judgment as a matter of law may be made at any time before the case is submitted to the jury." Fed. R. Civ. P. 50(a)(2). "If a party has been fully heard on an issue during a jury trial and the court finds that a reasonable jury would not have a legally sufficient evidentiary basis to find for the party on that issue, the court may: (A) resolve the issue against the party; and (B) grant a motion for judgment as a matter of law against the party on a claim or defense that, under the controlling law, can be maintained or defeated only with a favorable finding on that issue. *Id.* at 50(a)(1)(A–B). After the trial is over, the movant who filed a motion for judgments as a matter of law may renew this motion and "the court may: (1) allow judgment on the verdict, if the jury returned a verdict;

to cross to win a case, even if the verdict is favorable: Judges must respect jury verdicts; however, in certain cases, if the judge believes that the verdict is not warranted, he or she may enter judgment notwithstanding the verdict.[47] It is not uncommon for a judge to order a new trial or substantially reduce the amount of damages awarded to the plaintiff.[48]

Thus, a trial is not over simply because the jury has rendered a verdict. It is up to the judge to enforce the jury verdict and make it a judgment.[49] Moreover, even after a judge enters judgment—either after a jury verdict or following a bench trial—the plaintiff still faces two hurdles: First, is the judgment enforceable and recoverable? Second, will there be a successful appeal?

In modern litigation, the burden is on the plaintiff to "recover" after judgment, which may require additional legal proceedings. A judgment can be like confederate money—worth little except for its historical value. Many judgments are unrecoverable; others may cost a great deal to recover. Often a verdict and judgment create a settlement value that is less than the actual judgment.

The winning plaintiff must also calculate the likelihood of appeal and success of appeal. Defense lawyers create records at trial to preserve issues for appeal. This tends to reduce the present value of any verdict and judgment. Parties may choose to settle after trial—again, usually for quite a bit less than the jury verdict.

---

(2) order a new trial; or (3) direct the entry of judgment as a matter of law." *Id.* at (b)(1–3).

[47] The standard of review for a JNOV (judgment *non obstante veredicto*) "tests the legal sufficiency of the evidence supporting the verdict, not the weight of the evidence." *Martin v. Bd. of Instn. of Higher Learning*, 993 So. 2d 833, 835 (Miss. App. 2008) (quoting *Corley v. Evans*, 835 So. 2d 30, 36 (Miss. 2003)).

When confronted with a motion for a JNOV, the trial judge must: 'consider the evidence in the light most favorable to the non-moving party, giving that party the benefit of all favorable inferences that reasonably may be drawn therefrom. The trial court should consider the evidence offered by the non-moving party and any uncontradicted evidence offered by the moving party. If the evidence thus considered is sufficient to support a verdict in favor of the non-moving party, the motion for JNOV must be denied.' *Id.* at 835–36 (emphasis omitted) (quoting *Corley*, 835 So. 2d at 835). '[I]f there is substantial evidence in support of the verdict, that is, evidence of such quality and weight that reasonable and fair-minded jurors in the exercise of impartial judgment might have reached different conclusions, affirmance is required.' *Id.* at 836 (quoting *Corley*, 835 So. 2d at 837).

[48] Fed. R. Civ. P. 59; *Moody v. Pepsi-Cola Metropolitan Bottling Co., Inc.*, 915 F.2d 201, 211–12 (6th Cir. 1990).

[49] Fed. R. Civ. P. 58.

Step 8. Appeals

Losing parties often have the opportunity to appeal to an appellate court and ask that court to grant them relief; for example, a new trial or a reversal of the judgment. Successful appeals are not common, however. First, appellate jurisdiction is often discretionary in some way. In other words, the appellate court can choose which cases to take and which to reject. Second, litigants may choose not to appeal for a variety of reasons, including the lack of any realistic chance of success on appeal or settlement before appeal. Third, some determinations by trial courts and juries are not reviewable or, if they are reviewable, the standard for appellate review is so narrow and deferential as to preclude any realistic hope of relief.[50]

Appellate litigation is statistically uncommon, and it is even rarer for appellate litigation to result in a published opinion or result in several rounds of appellate litigation. The U.S. Supreme Court, for example, hears and decides only a small number of cases each term. Thus, it is unlikely that student affairs administrators will find themselves directly involved in a matter in appellate litigation. However, if such litigation does result in a reported decision, the student affairs administrator may be connected to a fixed point in decisional law. Reported appellate decisions on matters involving student affairs administration will not always comport with a student affairs administrator's experience of the facts or the experience of litigation. In other words, the case takes on a life of its own.

In higher education law, appellate litigation is a preferred tactic primarily of defense lawyers rather than plaintiffs' lawyers. Plaintiffs will sometimes appeal when they lose at trial, but many plaintiffs cannot afford to appeal. Plaintiffs must finance lawsuits out of their own pocket, or their lawyers must stakehold the case for them. After a defeat at trial, a plaintiff may lose the will or means to continue fighting. Moreover, the culture of plaintiff litigation is largely trial-oriented— many plaintiffs' lawyers are not anxious to move cases to appellate litigation.

Even when plaintiffs win, it is the institution lawyers who decide whether litigation will continue to an appellate level. Injured parties can face years of waiting if they choose to fight to preserve a verdict or judgment on appeal. An

---

[50] "'[A] ruling by the trial court in an area where it has discretionary power will not be disturbed on review, unless it [is] clearly shown that there was an abuse of such discretionary power.'" *Colorado Nat. Bank of Denver v. Friedman*, 846 P.2d 159, 166–67 (Colo. 1993) (quoting *Moseley v. Lamirato*, 370 P.2d 450, 456 (Colo. 1962)).

injured person may need compensation now and may be unwilling or unable to engage in protracted dispute. Reasonable offers to settle on the verdict or judgment are difficult to turn down—defense lawyers know this and proceed accordingly. If a higher education lawyer thinks a published appellate decision will favor the institution, he or she will not be willing to settle a judgment or verdict against the institution on favorable terms to the plaintiff. If, on the other hand, the institution lawyers are concerned about "making bad law," they will settle, thereby cutting off the opportunity to create a record of published opinions that will come back to hurt their clients in other litigation.

The American justice system puts a great deal of control over which cases become candidates for appellate review in the hands of the parties themselves. Plaintiffs are rarely martyrs to a cause, but institution lawyers must consider that today's case is precedent for tomorrow's. Lawyers for institutions of higher education can skew the appellate record by selecting cases for appeal that are more likely to be favorable. They have a tremendous amount of power to create a record of appellate case law that is likely to protect their clients' interests in the long run. In short, plaintiffs act locally, while defense lawyers think globally.

Step 9. Post-litigation Management

Litigation never dies, it just fades away. Even after settlement or final appeal, work remains to be done. This is the post-litigation phase. First comes the logistics period, during which clients and lawyers debrief and decide what to do with litigation files and other documents. Then they take action to carry out the terms of the settlement or requirements of a court order. After compliance activities are completed, the institution of higher education and its student affairs administrators must determine what comes next. How should the institution manage perceptions of the completed litigation? This is an important moment for student affairs administrators, who must interpret the signs and signals of the litigation system and translate them into the educational context and environment.[51]

---

[51] As a case study, student affairs administrators should study the Kent State tragedy and its legal aftermath. *See, e.g.*, Judith Areen, *Higher Education and the Law: Cases and Materials* 108–19 (Foundation Press 2009).

Step 10. Alternative Dispute Resolution

The litigation process includes opportunities—even requirements—for alternative dispute resolution (ADR), which takes three major forms: negotiation, mediation, and arbitration.

Litigants are free to negotiate with one another and reach settlements. In fact, the litigation process may set the stage for settlement. Negotiation often occurs in tandem with every other major step in the litigation process, and may determine when, if, and how parties proceed. Judges are often aware of ongoing negotiations and may make decisions in light of that knowledge. The civil litigation system is a settlement system, after all!

Some litigants seek the help of trained mediators to facilitate the negotiation and settlement process.[52] The mediator is a neutral, disinterested person who facilitates decision making but does not make the decisions. Mediators are often very helpful in getting parties to see the nonlegal options and the consequences of continuing their dispute. First, the parties agree on the mediator they will use, or at least on the process to select a mediator.[53] Mediators are often selected for their experience in a particular field and their overall success rate. They have no power to command the parties to do anything, but they are frequently instrumental in helping parties devise carefully crafted agreements—they know how to use specific language and how to structure settlement documents. Increasingly, courts are ordering litigants into mediation as part of the pretrial process; however, it is most successful when all parties genuinely want to agree on a settlement, or at least narrow the range of their disputes.[54]

Institutions of higher education are not very likely to find themselves in arbitration over student affairs issues. This may change, as arbitration is on the rise in other fields. In fact, in many circumstances outside higher education, insurance policies or contracts require arbitration for resolution of disputes. However, contracts with students rarely include arbitration clauses (although they could); and insurers do not yet offer arbitration clauses in insurance policies that relate to student affairs issues. Student affairs administrators are unlikely to

---

[52] Robert B. Moberly, *Ethical Standards for Court-Appointed Mediators and Florida's Mandatory Mediation Experiment*, 21 Fla. St. U. L. Rev. 701, 709 (1994).
[53] American Arbitration Association, *Commercial Arbitration Rules and Mediation* (2009) at M-4, http://www.adr.org/sp.asp?id=22440; Moberly, *supra* note 52, at 705–6.
[54] Fla. R. Civ. P. 1.710.

see much arbitration in their work, at least for the time being.

When arbitration does occur, the most common forms are binding and nonbinding. In the former, the arbitrator issues an award "that is not binding but advisory."[55] This may be helpful to parties that are trying to reach a settlement and need to get a better sense of what reasonable solutions to their dispute might look like. On the other hand, in binding arbitration, the award has a binding effect; that is, it can be enforced in much the same way as a court judgment.[56]

The panel of arbitrators (usually one to three persons) is often chosen through a prearranged process. Like mediators, arbitrators are neutral and may be sought out for their expertise in a particular field of arbitration. Arbitration is less formal than trial. However, in some cases, the litigants make arguments and provide evidence as they would in a court of law. Arbitral awards are not typically published, nor are they precedent for cases in courts of law. Arbitration is far less expensive than some litigation and is typically much faster than the civil litigation system. Having their disputes heard by experts in their field is another advantage to both parties. In uncommon instances, arbitral awards are subject to limited review in the courts, as if by appeal; however, most arbitral awards are final.[57]

COURTS AND JURISDICTION

The United States has the world's most complex court/jurisdiction system for two main reasons: (1) our unique love/hate relationship with law and lawyers, and (2) federalism—50 states, some territories, tribal courts, and a federal government. A person could spend a lifetime studying how our court system operates; I will present a basic snapshot of the system.

Jurisdiction and Justiciability in a Juridical World

Student affairs administrators live in a world in which it seems that someone has jurisdiction over everything and everything is justiciable. We live in a juridical age in which we turn to courts for answers to almost everything, in which human endeavors and conflicts are routinely translated into "court-

---

[55] 9 U.S.C.A. § 9 (2010).

[56] *Id.*; Colo. Rev. Stat. §§ 13-22-201 to 13-22-207 (2010); Fla. Arbitration Code §§ 682.01–.22 (2003); Mass. Gen. Laws. ch. 251, §§ 1–19 (2010).

[57] *See Wieder v. Schwartz,* 829 N.Y.S.2d 125 (N.Y. App. Div. 2006).

speak." It was not always so; in earlier times, the concepts of jurisdiction and justiciability were much easier to understand.

What is jurisdiction? Jurisdiction is the legal power to interpret and apply the law, resolve disputes, and issue legal remedies. We most often refer to the jurisdiction of courts, but jurisdiction can relate to other legal entities as well, as in the jurisdiction of the federal government over a territory. In the United States, jurisdiction must be granted by the constitution or a legislature. In unusual instances, once a court has some jurisdiction, it may acquire other forms of jurisdiction, but this is an esoteric issue that need not concern student affairs administrators.[58] Suffice it to say that a court with jurisdiction can be like bamboo planted in a suburban yard: Once it's there, it's hard to root out and tends to take over, slowly but surely.

Grants of jurisdiction are usually limited, although for just about every matter or controversy, some court has jurisdiction. A virtually seamless web of jurisdiction exists in the United States.

Consider the jurisdiction of federal courts, which extends to "federal question" jurisdiction and "diversity" jurisdiction.[59] Federal courts have the power to interpret federal law under federal question jurisdiction, although state courts may have power in some cases.[60] And when citizens of different states have disputes, they may qualify for diversity jurisdiction.[61] These litigants may bring their dispute to federal court even though the matter might be heard in a state court as well. When courts compete for jurisdiction, incredibly complex rules govern where a case is heard.[62]

Because colleges often host students from other states, issues of accident liability and contract interpretation can land in federal court under diversity jurisdiction. In these matters, a federal court exercises jurisdiction but applies the substantive law of the state in which the contract was formed or the ac-

---

[58] Perhaps the classic example is the famous case of *Marbury v. Madison*, 5 U.S. 137 (1803), in which the U.S. Supreme Court essentially gave itself final jurisdiction over the interpretation of the U.S. Constitution. It was not clear at all that the founders intended such a thing, but acquiescence from other branches of government essentially ratified this assumption of jurisdiction, and we take it for granted today.

[59] 28 U.S.C. § 1331 (2006) (Federal Question); 28 U.S.C. § 1332 (2006) (Diversity Jurisdiction).

[60] 28 U.S.C. § 1367 (2006).

[61] 28 U.S.C. § 1332 (2006).

[62] *See* 28 U.S.C. §§ 1441, 1446 (2006*); Younger v. Harris*, 401 U.S. 36 (1971).

cident occurred, usually the institution of higher education's home state.[63] In this situation, the federal court makes a so-called "*Erie* guess" as to how the state court would rule were it hearing the case.[64] However, federal courts do not always guess correctly, and state courts do not review the decisions. Thus, higher education law includes notable federal court decisions regarding state law that are incorrect *Erie* guesses but are frequently cited by other courts because they have not been "overruled." These *Erie* ghosts haunt the legal system even after the death of the legal principles contained in them.

The potential for different results in the state and federal systems motivates litigants to engage in forum shopping—fighting over which court will hear the case. Federal courts try to discourage this phenomenon. One reason for forum shopping is political: Federal district court judges tend to be more conservative, because conservatives controlled the federal judicial nominating process for so long. Many business litigants prefer federal court because they believe that conservative judges are more likely to favor their cases. However, litigation is complex, and it is not always easy to guess which system will be more favorable to a particular dispute. In fact, some attorneys ask a federal judge to "remove a case to state court"[65] so that a party does not have its preferred venue of choice.

Courts are not the only entities with jurisdiction. For example, the Office for Civil Rights (OCR), an office of the federal Department of Education (DOE), has the power to enforce civil rights laws.[66] A letter from OCR can be a powerful motivator to change institution of higher education behavior even if, in the end, a federal court has the final say on whether a violation of civil rights laws occurred.[67] Similarly, state attorneys general often issue opinions that state their view of the law and their intention to enforce certain aspects of the law.[68] And some agencies have the jurisdiction to regulate an area via the promulga-

---

[63] The leading case requiring federal courts to apply state law in diversity cases is *Erie Railroad Co. v. Tompkins,* 304 U.S. 64, 71–73 (1938). See also *Hanna v. Plumer,* 380 U.S. 460, 473–74 (1965).
[64] *Erie Railroad Co.,* 304 U.S. at 64.
[65] 28 U.S.C. § 1441.
[66] U.S. Department of Education, *Office for Civil Rights,* http://www2.ed.gov/about/offices/list/ocr/index.html (last visited Jan. 22, 2011).
[67] *Parker v. Bd. of Sup'rs Univ. of Louisiana-Lafayette,* 296 Fed. Appx. 414, 418 (5th Cir. 2008).
[68] Michael O. Leavitt, Margaret Spellings, & Alberto R. Gonzales, *Report to the President on Issues Raised by the Virginia Tech Tragedy* (June 13, 2007), http://www.hhs.gov/vtreport.html#key.

tion of regulations and to adjudicate certain issues related to legal compliance.[69]

Student affairs administrators often speak of jurisdiction metaphorically—as in the "jurisdiction" of their codes of conduct—but in reality the vast majority of such codes are contractual and do not derive their power over students from any authority or grant of legal power other than actual or implied consent. This is no more real jurisdiction than if a person were to assert jurisdiction over a lost dog in a park. "Common law" in an institution of higher education is also a metaphor.[70] Common practices may have legal implications because they set expectations or induce reliance, but this is not law or jurisdiction.[71] A deputized police force can exercise jurisdiction, but note the difference: A duly constituted body of law creates such power and makes it a legal power, not just a power with legal implications.

It is also important to understand the difference between jurisdiction and justiciability. A court may have jurisdiction but a given dispute may not be justiciable. Various situations raise issues of justiciability. A matter must usually be in controversy, and it must be ripe for adjudication and not moot. Courts usually consider matters only when there is a controversy; they are not routinely proactive the way good student affairs administrators are. Most judges are not willing—or jurisdictionally empowered—to hear hypothetical disputes or provide advice. If a court does so, it is usually in the context of a case or controversy; that is, the case provides the predicate for offering a vision beyond the controversy. This method of intervening is foreign to student affairs practitioners. Can you imagine managing student populations by always waiting for a state of conflict before intervening? Parties in an oppositional state think and act differently—they posture and argue, and do not usually engage in positive educational discourse.

While some courts do issue advisory opinions from time to time, most do not; thus, student affairs administrators often must wait for the law to form.[72] Some in-

---

[69] *See* Administrative Procedure Act (APA), 5 U.S.C. §§ 551 et seq. (2006).

[70] There is something called "common law" that arises from the courts; but this is not the same thing as common practices of an institution. *See* William A. Kaplin & Barbara A. Lee, *The Law of Higher Education*, 26 (4th ed., Student ed., Jossey-Bass 2007). "Common law, in short, is judge-made law rather than law that originates from constitutions or from legislatures or administrative agencies." *Id.*

[71] *See* John Austin, *The Province of Jurisprudence Determined* (Wilfred E. Rumble ed., Cambridge Univ. Press 1995).

[72] *See generally* Peter F. Lake, *Still Waiting: The Slow Evolution of the Law in Light of the Ongoing Student Suicide Crisis*, 34 J.C. & U.L 253 (2008).

dustries—such as banking and public utilities—have co-opted and collaborated with regulatory systems to build the rules they need on a day-to-day basis. In this sense, higher education is a primitive industry under law—reacting to the legal system.

The reality of judiciability means that student affairs administrators often experience law as an intrusive, haphazard, and crisis-driven system. They can feel a sense of powerlessness and victimization by law—a feeling made even worse by the fact that lawyer-to-client ratios are poor in our industry, and much legal training occurs vicariously through persons who have little direct legal training.

In addition, a matter must be ripe but not moot to be justiciable, so some controversies have not yet ripened to the point at which legal issues are raised. Think of that bad driver as an accident waiting to happen; a lawsuit in negligence is not ripe for adjudication until someone gets hurt. On the other hand, some disputes become moot. A court may hear a matter after the parties have acted in such a way as to make controversy disappear; for instance, in contract disputes, payment in full of disputed sums often moots a case.[73]

One crucial feature of justiciability is nearly lost in our modern world, in which we often equate the reach of jurisdiction with justiciability. Some controversies simply do not belong in court, even though a court could theoretically exercise jurisdiction. Judges know that the greatest power of a lawmaker is knowing when not to make law. The parallel in student affairs can be seen in moments when administrators choose not to intervene in a situation for developmental reasons. We want our students to learn from their mistakes so they will grow. Judges know that many disputes will never end if people can run to court to sublimate and transform every conflict into a legal battle. In a world in which people believe there should be a law to govern every dispute, judges find themselves in a "justiciability squeeze." People in conflict have a tendency to complain that others are not exercising their responsibility to resolve disputes—without recognizing the irony.

The limits of justiciability are often apparent in subtle ways. Later in Chapter 4, when I consider due process, you will see how the U.S. Supreme Court has sent the message that courts should perhaps not set legal rules for resolving controversial educational evaluations.[74] This viewpoint is also apparent in state

---

[73] E. Allan Farnsworth, *Contracts* (4th ed., Aspen 2004).
[74] *See Board of Curators of the Univ. of Missouri v. Horowitz*, 435 U.S. 78, 84 (1978); *Regents of the Univ. of Michigan v. Ewing*, 474 U.S. 214, 222–23 (1985).

law cases involving educational malpractice[75] and in the recent U.S. Supreme Court ruling in *Christian Legal Society* regarding "all-comers" policies for registered student organizations.[76] Showing deference to higher education is a way of limiting the justiciability of disputes.

Overview of the Court System

There are a bewildering number of courts in the United States. This situation is a direct result of the American love affair with adjudication to resolve disputes, federalism, the need for specialization, and even residual colonialism. However, student affairs administrators are fortunate, because only a rudimentary knowledge of the court system is required for most situations they will encounter.

At the most basic level, the federal government and state governments operate systems of trial and appellate courts—the latter usually in two layers: an intermediate appellate court system and a court of last resort.

In the federal system, U.S. district courts, which sit in every state, are the principal trial courts for cases that fall under federal jurisdiction. Federal magistrates typically help federal district court judges manage the vast work of the federal trial court system. Magistrates are a special kind of judge; they are not appointed for life as are federal district court judges.[77] The federal system also has several specialized courts—such as bankruptcy court—that operate in tandem with federal district courts and have limited jurisdiction in special areas.[78] These courts have judges with particular areas of expertise, and they divert cases away from the overworked U.S. District Court System.[79]

---

[75] Peter F. Lake, *Will Your College Be Sued for Educational Malpractice?*, Chronicle of Higher Education (Aug. 11, 2009), *available at* http://chronicle.com/article/Education-Malpractice-Ma/47980/. *See, e.g., Ross v. Creighton Univ.*, 957 F.2d 410, 414–15 (1992).

[76] 130 S. Ct. at 2995.

[77] Federal Judicial Center, *How the Federal Courts Are Organized: Federal Judges and How They Get Appointed,* http://www.fjc.gove/federal/courts.nsf/autofram!openform&nav=menu1&page=/federal/courts.nsf/page/183 (last visited Aug. 10, 2010). Federal magistrates usually have eight year terms and can be reappointed.

[78] U.S. Courts, *Bankruptcy Courts,* http://www.uscourts.gov/FederalCourts/UnderstandingtheFederalCourts/BankruptcyCourts.aspx (last visited Aug. 10, 2010); U.S. Courts, *Jurisdiction of the Federal Courts,* http://www.uscourts.gov/FederalCourts/UnderstandingtheFederalCourts/Jurisdiction.aspx (last visited Aug. 10, 2010).

[79] Julia Preston, *Lawyers Back Creating New Immigration Courts*, N.Y. Times (Feb. 8, 2010), *available at* http://www.nytimes.com/2010/02/09/us/09immig.html. "[R]egardless of what you think,

Litigants who have rights to appeal decisions of the federal district court (not everything is appealable) bring their cases to a U.S. Court of Appeals (USCA). USCAs are largely geographical and are designated in circuits that include several states and may cover vast areas. Among the 13 USCAs are the Second Circuit, which includes New York and other states; the Ninth Circuit, which includes California and several other states; and the Fifth Circuit, which includes Texas and other states. Each USCA has multiple judges, who usually work in panels. (District court judges are usually lone wolves.)

In the federal system, student affairs administrators are most likely to encounter district court judges. These judges are some of the most powerful individuals in the judiciary, as they can, more or less single-handedly, alter the course of history. For example, individual district court judges have broken up the telephone system (Judge Harold Green) and resolved Agent Orange claims (Judge Jack Weinstein). Lawyers joke that a federal district court judge is more powerful than the captain of a nuclear-force submarine, because all the captain can do is destroy the world. District court judges—indeed, all federal judges—undergo an extensive screening process that requires an extremely high level of credentials.[80]

The final step in the federal system is the U.S. Supreme Court. Among other cases, the Supreme Court hears appeals from the various circuits. The Court has other jurisdiction as well, including the power to adjudicate some matters coming out of the state system. However, it is not the final court of review for matters of state law. Under our system of federalism, that kind of review is entrusted to the states themselves, which means that litigants can expect diverse answers to many legal questions, depending upon the state in which the controversy arises. The Supreme Court reviews only a small number of cases each year; one way it selects cases is via a writ of certiorari, court-speak for "We will review your case."[81]

The state systems are similar to the federal system. States have trial courts with jurisdiction over a wide variety of matters, and litigants have the right to appeal to an intermediate court of appeal. States also have Supreme Courts,

---

federal district judges are some of the most overworked individuals in our society." Mark Kernes, *Stagliano Obscenity Trial: The Post-Game Wrap-up* (Aug. 5, 2010), *available at* http://news.avn.com/articles/Stagliano-Obscenity-Trial-The-Post-Game-Wrap-Up-406388.html.

[80] ABA Coalition for Justice, *Judicial Selection: The Process of Choosing Judges* (June 2008), http://www.abanet.org/justice/pdf/judicial_selection_roadmap.pdf.

[81] S. Ct. R. 10–16, *available at* http://www.law.cornell.edu/rules/supct/index.html.

sometimes called Courts of Appeals.[82] As in the federal system, special jurisdiction courts exist at the state level.[83]

State courts primarily determine issues under state law, although they sometimes have jurisdiction over issues that arise under federal law. State court decisions are not binding on federal courts or on other states. Oddly, under our system of federalism, federal courts sometimes find themselves deciding questions of state law, and states find themselves dealing with federal law, or the law of other states. There are complex rules for making determinations under another jurisdiction's law and complex rules about who gets first and final opportunity to review a matter. Student affairs administrators will need to consult lawyers to understand what goes to federal court and what goes to state court, and who goes first.[84] Most cases are not hard on grounds of federalism, but the hard ones are really hard to figure out.

The Role of Precedent

Each year, many decisions by a variety of courts are published, although some are not.[85] Published opinions of courts are often referred to as "precedent."

Precedent comes in two forms: controlling and persuasive. Opinions of a court of superior jurisdiction in a system (such as the State Supreme Court)

---

[82] The Court of Appeals is the highest court in New York State; in other states, the State Supreme Court is the highest court. New York State Unified Court System, *Court Structure: Civil Court Structure* (last updated Aug. 9, 2004), http://www.courts.state.ny.us/courts/structure.shtml.

[83] Michigan has courts with limited jurisdiction, such as its municipal court that handles mostly minor cases and marriages. Michigan Judicial Institute, *Your Guide to the Michigan Courts: A Quick Reference Guide to the Court System*, http://courts.michigan.gov/plc/AccessMichCourts.pdf (last visited Aug. 10, 2010). Washington has municipal courts, established by city ordinance, that have exclusive jurisdiction over certain legal infractions. Washington Courts, *Municipal Courts*, http://www.courts.wa.gov/appellate_trial_courts/?fa=atc.crtPage&crtType=Muni (last visited Aug. 10, 2010).

[84] A series of cases relating to the 1999 bonfire collapse at Texas A&M University are helpful to understand the interplay between state and federal courts. *See*, e.g., *Davis v. Southerland*, 2004 WL 1230278 (S.D. Tex. 2004); *Bowen v. Comstock*, 2008 WL 2209722 (Tex. App. Waco Dist. 2008); *Texas A&M Univ. v. Bading*, 236 S.W.3d 801 (Tex. App. Waco Dist. 2007).

[85] "An 'unpublished case' is a term of art that means that the case was not selected by the court for official publication. The general rule is that unpublished cases cannot serve as binding precedent; indeed, many courts prohibit attorneys from citing unpublished cases." ALWD & Darby Dickerson, *ALWD Citation Manual* 96 (3d ed., Aspen Publishers 2006). An example of court rules relating to unpublished opinions is taken from the United States Court of Appeals for the First Circuit: "Unpublished opinions may be cited only in related cases. Only published opinions may be cited otherwise." 1st Cir. R. 36(b)(2).

bind the lower courts in that state. However, opinions from another state may only be persuasive, not controlling. A court is free to accept, reject, or even ignore such published opinions. Similarly, opinions from the various U.S. Courts of Appeals do not bind other circuits, although federal district courts in that circuit are bound by the decisions of the USCA in their jurisdiction. Obviously, a federal district court opinion cannot bind a USCA; however, USCAs are often persuaded by opinions from federal district courts and even state courts.

The simplest way to explain the role of precedent in our judicial system is to say that, all things being equal, litigants may have some rights to have like cases treated alike, although this is often not the case.[86] Precedents set expectations and become *stare decisis*.[87] A court might have good reasons for changing course and ignoring precedent, but courts usually do so reluctantly and rarely. Previous decisions of a court are *stare decisis* but not written in stone, although, like childproof bottle caps, they may take some effort to uncork. Courts sometimes engage in complex mental gymnastics to give the appearance of following a previous decision while actually significantly rewriting it. Courts sometimes behave just like parents.

Student affairs administrators are most likely to see the use of precedent in negotiations, during which a lawyer can help administrators understand the relative weight and power of published opinions. Precedent can be a powerful tool in establishing objective standards to use in negotiation. For example, if a parent threatens to sue a student affairs administrator under FERPA, the administrator can point out that in *Gonzaga v. Doe*,[88] the U.S. Supreme Court disallowed the possibility of any private lawsuits to enforce FERPA.[89] Or (a personal favorite) you can remind students at a private college that they have no federal right to due process.

The most important feature of precedent is that it has motion and vector, and is rarely an entirely fixed point. The cases are always heading somewhere: trending. Detecting vector and motion takes a great deal of experience and

---

[86] *See generally* Ronald Dworkin, *Taking Rights Seriously* (Harvard Univ. Press 1978).

[87] *Stare decisis* is a Latin term that means "to stand by things decided." *Black's Law Dictionary* at 672. *Stare decisis* is "[t]he doctrine of precedent, under which a court must follow earlier judicial decisions when the same points arise again in litigation." *Id.*

[88] 536 U.S. 273 (2002).

[89] *Id.* at 280.

training, which is why student affairs administrators often seek guidance from lawyers and legalists. Law has its prophets and prognosticators—no two cases are ever entirely alike, and the future is always in motion. Neither the law nor student affairs is static.

CHAPTER 2

A BRIEF STUDENT-AFFAIRS-
CENTERED HISTORY OF HIGHER
EDUCATION LAW

Before World War II, very little law related specifically to higher education. In many ways, higher education law is a baby boom topic—much of the law of higher education in America has been written since baby boomers and their children (and now, in some instances, their grandchildren) arrived at college.[1] The history of higher education law in the United States is a study of the generations of Americans who have brought a quest for fairness and a legalistic culture to higher education.

The arrival of law on campus has been at times a cause for celebration and at other times disconcerting. What follows is a brief history of higher education law from the viewpoint of a modern student affairs administrator.

---

[1] Baby boomers essentially invented the concept of college-aged adolescence and mythologized the college experience. They brought a penchant for safety, recreational sex, alcohol, and other drug issues. And they fueled real estate run-ups and busts—the financial fuel to pay for college—and showed a love of college sports and competition in general. In addition, post-World War II populations have been much more concerned with rights discourse, law, legalisms, justice, and fairness in higher education.

THE FOUR ERAS

The Era of Legal Insularity

The period before World War II has been described as the era of legal insularity[2]—an era of protecting the power and prerogative of institutions of higher education.[3] The law rarely considered matters relating specifically to higher education; when it did, it created doctrines that protected the power of the institutions and their prerogative to self-govern. Higher education did its work in a prelegal world; it was not subject to any truly significant external judicial restraints. American higher education operated much like Hogwarts in Harry Potter's world—with wizards free from the laws of the Muggles.[4]

A certain amount of mythology surrounds higher education before the arrival of law on campus. Some of this mythology is built on the so-called doctrine of *in loco parentis*,[5] which is usually overemphasized and badly misunderstood. *In loco parentis* was not what most commentators and courts have believed it to be,[6] and it was not a critical feature of higher education law until it became a strawman concept in later periods. The *in loco parentis* myth is one of the great misunderstandings in higher education law, and it

---

[2] Robert D. Bickel & Peter F. Lake, *Rights and Responsibilities of the Modern University: Who Assumes the Risks of College Life?* 17–33 (Carolina Academic Press 1999).

[3] *See* Peter F. Lake, *Beyond Discipline–Managing the Modern Higher Education Environment* 27–32 (Hierophant Enterprises, Inc. 2009).

[4] Muggles are non-magical folk. *See generally, e.g.*, J. K. Rowling, *Harry Potter and the Sorcerer's Stone* (Scholastic 2001).

[5] *See* Bickel & Lake, *supra* note 2, at 17. "*[I]n loco parentis* performed an important if counter-intuitive function: in this era, university student relations were far less "legal" than today because that doctrine, along with others of the period, made law less important in college/student relations. . . . In its heyday, *in loco parentis* located power in the university—not in courts of law, or in students. *In loco parentis* promoted the image of the parental university and insured that most problems were handled within the university, by the university, and often quietly." *Id.*

[6] *See, e.g.*, *Bradshaw v Rawlings,* 612 F.2d 135, 140 (3d Cir. 1979) (explaining that "[a]t one time, exercising their rights and duties *in loco parentis*, colleges were able to impose strict regulations"); Bickel & Lake, *supra* note 2, at 29. "Given the broad statements of some of the earliest cases and developments of *in loco parentis* as applied to school age children (in K–12 education today, *in loco parentis* is the basis for imposing duties of care), it was easy for commentators and courts to fall into a subtle but important trap regarding notions of *in loco parentis*. *As a technical legal doctrine,* in loco parentis *was not—ever—a liability/responsibility/duty-creating norm in higher education law.*" *Id.* (emphasis added).

has carried forward into modern student affairs administration practice.[7]

In loco parentis was simply one doctrine that a few courts referenced in affirming the plenary power of institutions of higher education vis-à-vis students and others. However, the era of insularity, power, and prerogative was built on a complex interlocking set of legal principles and rules that protected higher education.

Before the 1960s, colleges typically enjoyed the following legal protections:

1. Colleges had government (if public) or charitable (if private) immunity.[8] These immunities were unqualified and complete.[9]

2. They enjoyed *in loco parentis*—parental immunity—status, which was also unqualified.[10]

3. College was considered a constitutional privilege; therefore, students had no constitutional rights.[11]

4. Colleges enjoyed favorable contract law interpretation. The private college student contractual relationship was completely one-sided in favor of colleges well into the 20th century.

5. No viable causes of action existed for educational malpractice, negligent admission, or negligent retention. A college was typically free

---

[7] The principal error is that the doctrine of *in loco parentis* did not impose any form of responsibility on institutions of higher education. The belief that *in loco parentis* created some form of safety responsibility in higher education arose from a false comparison with K–12 law. K–12 law features its own form of *in loco parentis* doctrine that does impose safety duties on schools to use due care for pupil safety. However, that rule was never the law in higher education at any time. See Bickel & Lake, *supra* note 2, at 29.

[8] Bickel & Lake, *supra* note 2, at 29. "The tools used to immunize the university in those circumstances were governmental or charitable tort immunities." *Id.*

[9] *See id.* at 29–30.

[10] *See id.* at 29 ("*In loco parentis* was the specific tool used to protect, to *immunize*, university conduct from legal review when *deliberate* or *intentional* actions were taken to *discipline* and *regulate* students.").

[11] *See* William A. Kaplin & Barbara A. Lee, *The Law of Higher Education* 10 (4th ed., Jossey-Bass 2007). "[I]n cases such as *Hamilton v. Regents of the University of California*, 293 U.S. 245 (1934), which upheld an order that student conscientious objectors must take military training as a condition of attending the institution, courts accepted the proposition that attendance at a public post-secondary institution was a privilege and not a right."

to fail in its core mission and to admit and retain students with legal impunity.

6. Higher education was not subject to any meaningful, broad-based state or federal regulation.

7. Accreditation processes and self-studies were not aimed at systematic regulation of core mission delivery, especially within the field of student affairs. The power of accrediting bodies grew exponentially after World War II as colleges became increasingly dependent on student tuition dollars underwritten by state and federal largess.[12]

8. Legal redress in the tort system was primarily for innocent victims only. Before World War II, victims of torts (primarily negligence) had viable claims against others only if they did not assume a risk and did not engage in any contributory negligence.[13] It is difficult to find a situation in which a college student is injured and that student did not willingly and knowingly participate in a risk or have some fault or blame for the injury. Largely as a result of the enormous volume of automobile accidents and injuries after World War II, the law of negligence ultimately softened its hard line against faulty plaintiffs. However, most of the reform did not occur until the 1970s and 1980s.

9. The law regarded the voluntary drinker as the "sole proximate cause of harm."[14] A very large percentage of college injuries are and have always been alcohol-related. Higher education institutions and the law traditionally took the position that the drinking victim or the drinker who caused harm was the sole responsible party for any harm

---

[12] *See, e.g.*, Judith Areen, *Higher Education and the Law: Cases and Materials* 85–86 (Foundation Press 2009).

[13] *See* Dan B. Dobbs, *The Law of Torts* 535 (West Group 2000). "Courts traditionally held that a plaintiff who assumed the risk of the defendant's negligence could not recover." *Id.* at 495. "The traditional rule, subject to some exceptions . . . held that contributory negligence of a plaintiff . . . was a complete bar to the claim." *Id.*

[14] *See id.* at 472. "This attitude explains why courts at one time held that negligent sellers of alcohol to intoxicated drivers were never responsible; in spite of the fact the there can be many proximate causes, they said it was the drinker, not the seller, who was 'the' proximate cause." *Id.*

or injury resulting from alcohol use. The "proximate cause" rule was simply a complex legal way of expressing this position. Dram shop and alcohol responsibility law evolved slowly from the 1950s through the millennium.[15]

10. Premises safety responsibility was a public, not a private, responsibility. Before the crime waves of the 1960s, courts rarely entertained the idea that private landowners were responsible for protecting people from foreseeable criminal attack or danger on their property. The original mission of campus security was to protect buildings and grounds, not people.[16]

11. The concept of mental health therapeutic liability on campus did not exist, nor did the duty to prevent self-harm, suicide, or danger to others arising from mental health issues.

12. Before the 1960s, campuses were largely free to discriminate on the basis of race, gender, disability, and so on. This changed with the enactment of sweeping civil rights laws in the 1960s and thereafter.[17]

Higher education in the era of power and prerogative enjoyed the privileges of the cornerstone institutions of industrial society: family, charity, and government. The current focus on child safety was unknown. Until the automobile forced changes in liability law, American negligence law did not evolve to imagine shared responsibility for injuries arising in complex ways. In responding to the unprecedented slaughter on the highways, the law changed many rules relating to accidental loss.[18] Before the legal revolution brought about by automobile risk, essentially only faultless plaintiffs had legal recourse. It is tempting to proj-

---

[15] "Dram shop" is a legal term referring to a bar, tavern, or the like where alcoholic beverages are sold. "Dram shop liability" refers to the body of law governing the liability of taverns, liquor stores, and other commercial establishments that sell alcoholic beverages. Dobbs, *supra* note 13, at 839 ("These statutes, enacted in a small number of states, did not merely regulate the sale of alcohol. Instead, they provided expressly for civil liability of alcohol providers."). Even today, social host liability is not widely accepted. *See infra* at 11–12.

[16] *See* Lake, *supra* note 3, at 92–93. This changed in the 1980s with the landmark ruling in *Mullins v. Pine Manor College*, 449 N.E.2d 331, 337 (Mass. 1983), discussed *infra*.

[17] *See infra* Chapter 4.

[18] *See infra* Chapter 3.

ect the concept of individual accountability backward, but the law in that era simply did not imagine a large role for itself in the management of society, and usually intervened only to protect entities with power and prerogative. But the emergence of alcohol responsibility law did not foster any sense of college responsibility for alcohol-related risk; on the contrary, the unique timing of law's arrival on campus cemented laissez-faire attitudes toward alcohol risk.

In this era, the law was not in evidence on campus. The movie "Animal House" was set in the early 1960s, and was released in 1978. Notice that no lawyers appear and litigation is never mentioned. Imagine the legal storm today in the wake of similar events!

The Civil Rights Era

The era of legal insularity ended when the law began intervening in higher education to protect basic public law rights for students and faculty.

From the early 1960s on, the law steadily chipped away at the notion of higher education as a privilege.[19] Systematically, the U.S. Supreme Court held that college students have First Amendment rights of association,[20] press,[21] speech,[22] and free exercise of religion.[23] Congress passed sweeping civil rights legislation that told institutions of higher education they could not discriminate on the basis of race, gender, or disability.[24] Congress also passed the Family Education Rights and Privacy Act of 1974 (FERPA) to protect students from blacklisting and give them access to their educational records, along with rights to correct errors in those records.[25] The landmark 1954 Supreme Court ruling in *Brown v. Board of Education*[26] launched a desegregation movement that first primarily hit K–12 and later more heavily influenced higher education.[27]

---

[19] *See, e.g., Dixon v. Alabama State Board of Education*, 294 F.2d 150, 156–57 (1961).
[20] *See Healy v. James*, 408 U.S. 169, 183 (1972) (upholding the student right to freedom of association).
[21] *See Rosenberger v. Rector and Visitors of the University of Virginia*, 515 U.S. 819, 836 (1995).
[22] *See Tinker v. Des Moines Independent Community School District*, 393 U.S. 503, 511 (1969).
[23] *See Widmar v. Vincent*, 454 U.S. 263, 269 (1981); *Rosenberger*, 515 U.S. at 831.
[24] *See Lake, supra* note 3, at 68–69 (detailed in footnote 15).
[25] Family Educational Rights and Privacy Act (FERPA), 20 U.S.C. § 1232(g) (2006). FERPA also essentially created an era of professional registrars. Before FERPA, many schools used nonprofessionally trained staff to manage educational records.
[26] 347 U.S. 483, 495 (1954).
[27] *See U.S. v. Fordice*, 505 U.S. 717, 729 (1992). It was several decades before *Brown's* sweeping language had a wide impact on higher education.

Interestingly, the U.S. Supreme Court provided clear due process mandates for K–12 students and higher education faculty, but hesitated to apply similar principles to college students.[28] Some lower federal courts did impose due process requirements on colleges, but many did not.[29] The Supreme Court has never squarely held that college students had sufficient liberty or property interests (prerequisites for due process) to justify imposition of due process requirements on colleges.[30]

For complex reasons, most colleges voluntarily embraced concepts of due process after making due process-like requirements part of their contracts with students.[31] Colleges have often operated as if due process were required, and courts are increasingly willing to enforce this presupposition.[32] However, the Supreme Court has hesitated to take this path out of concern about interfering with the academic process and academic freedom. A showdown over due process looms in the future, and it seems almost inevitable that the Supreme Court will impose *some* form of due process requirements on higher education.

Revolution in the application of public law to colleges was only partially mirrored in the application of private law. The civil rights era was focused on the application of political and civil liberties rather than economic equality or status, safety rights, or rights to equality and valuable education. The civil rights era was an incomplete revolution for students. It moved them closer to being the central focus of higher education, but they did not suddenly become the sole or primary focus of higher education.

The law was moving steadily toward recognizing the contractual status of students,[33] and this shift in status would bring students some rights they never

---

[28] *See, e.g., Goss v. Lopez*, 419 U.S. 565 (1975); *Perry v. Sinderman*, 408 U.S. 593 (1972); *Roth v. U.S.*, 354 U.S. 476 (1957); *Board of Curators of the University of Missouri v. Horowitz*, 435 U.S. 78 (1978); *Ewing v. California*, 538 U.S. 11 (2003).

[29] *See, e.g., Dixon*, 294 F.2d at 156.

[30] *See Board of Curators of Univ. of Missouri*, 435 U.S. at 84 (1978); *Regents of Univ. of Michigan v. Ewing*, 474 U.S. 214, 223 (1985).

[31] Lake, *supra* note 3, at 137–38.

[32] *See, e.g., Flaim v. Medical College of Ohio*, 418 F.3d 629, 633 (6th Cir. 2005); *Gorman v. Univ. of Rhode Island*, 837 F.2d 7, 12 (1st Cir. 1988).

[33] *See Atria v. Vanderbilt Univ.*, 142 Fed. Appx. 246, 255 (2005) (unpublished); *see also* Areen, *supra* note 12, at 700 ("*Atria* demonstrates that students at private universities may successfully challenge arbitrary actions as violations of tort or contract law." (citations omitted)). *See also*

had before.[34] However, in comparison with other major consumer transactions, the college contract and the law of college contracts has lagged behind. Consumers of pharmaceuticals, health care, food, automobiles, insurance, and housing have far greater legal protections in contract law than students have in higher education. Higher education is the last major transaction area to undergo a widespread consumer revolution. The application of public law principles helped delay the onset of a transactional consumer consciousness; however, recent changes in federal lending (including new rules of federal direct lending and the regulation of for-profit institutions of higher education) are moving higher education closer to being regulated as other industries are. Student affairs administrators can expect additional—perhaps even rapid—evolution of the regulation of core mission delivery.

The civil rights era is associated with two other notable developments in higher education law and policy: the rise of the academic/conduct distinction and a rise in a legalistic culture in student affairs.

Modern institutions of higher education have embraced academic/conduct distinctions as if they were ineluctable. The academic side of the house is managed with a separate set of administrators. Institutions have honor *and* conduct codes. Faculty and student affairs administrators often have different training and career paths.

Academic/conduct distinctions are mostly creatures of the period since the civil rights era, and this bifurcation of higher education has not always served core mission delivery successfully. The events at Virginia Tech in April 2007, and subsequent state and federal reports on those events, show how dangerous "silos" and compartmentalization can be.[35] Student affairs administrators in the postmillennial period will increasingly be charged with responsibilities to reconnect the educational mission into whole cloth. However, academic/conduct distinctions are five decades in the making and it will take time—perhaps even

---

Russel v. Salve Regina College, 890 F.2d 484, 488 (1st Cir. 1989)." *Id.*

[34] *Atria*, 142 Fed. Appx. at 255.

[35] Virginia Tech Review Panel, *Mass Shootings at Virginia Tech, April 16, 2007—Report of the Review Panel Presented to Governor Kaine, Commonwealth of Virginia* 40–53 (2007), *available at* http://www.vtreviewpanel.org/report/index.html (detailing the totality of Seung Hui Cho's behavior and concluding that there was a failure to share, collate, and synthesize the information that would have brought Cho's behavior to the administration's attention).

one or two generations of student affairs administrators—to reconnect all the features of a student's higher education experience into a seamless whole.

How did academic/conduct distinctions take hold in higher education? There are several causes.

First, the rapid rise in largely residential student populations after World War II forced institutions of higher education to staff up to meet student needs such as safety, housing, food service, and activities. The ranks of administrators experienced a sudden swelling.

Second, institutions of higher education chose to expand the administrative ranks largely with cost-effective, nontenured, nonteaching staff. It would have been virtually impossible to fill all the necessary jobs in higher education with PhDs—there just were not enough candidates. Institutions of higher education could not ask faculty to shoulder the responsibility of managing the new student populations—classrooms were beginning to grow, and the focus of teachers was increasingly being drawn away from teaching.

Third, institutions of higher education largely chose to assign faculty to teaching, classroom, and scholarship activities; while "service" was often reframed in ways that did not involve direct service to student populations in capacities outside the classroom. Faculty were not completely divorced from tasks performed by student affairs administrators, but a clear pragmatic delineation of job descriptions emerged overall.

Fourth, courts—including the U.S. Supreme Court[36]—articulated academic/conduct distinctions in the context of analyzing student due process issues and thus may have unintentionally fueled the bifurcation process.

And fifth, later courts seized upon academic/conduct analysis in due process case law and used that analysis in safety cases to deny student claims for safety rights.[37] Some courts of the bystander era (discussed below) held that student life tasks are different in kind from academic tasks and that academic tasks have primacy. These courts fueled the darkest aspect of the academic/conduct distinction—the belief that the classroom mission is more important than other tasks in higher education and that pure academics are a higher caste than other

---

[36] *See, e.g.,* Dixon, 294 F.2d at 158; *Board of Curators at Univ. of Missouri,* 435 U.S. at 85; *Regents of Univ. of Michigan,* 474 U.S. at 225.
[37] *See, e.g., Beach v. Univ. of Utah,* 726 P.2d 413, 419 (Utah 1986).

employees at an institution of higher education. This damaging perception of a hierarchy of personnel and tasks persists to this day.

Sixth, as the law entered the life of the academy, it directly affected the job descriptions of student affairs administrators. Student affairs administrators were charged with dealing with issues such as free speech, free association, and freedom of the press. The new tasks of legal compliance fell disproportionately to nonclassroom employees; that is, student affairs administrators.

Seventh, higher education lacked (and still lacks) significant business organizational theory, a situation that encouraged intuitive, incremental development of the business model. No serious opposition arose to the bifurcation of higher education; boards of trustees, for instance, either embraced bifurcation or acquiesced.

Eighth, higher education lacked (and still lacks) a broad base of scientifically valid learning theory. In the post-World War II period, education research money went largely to K–12 learning theory, so little or no learning theory was developed to validate or invalidate major shifts in core mission delivery. Higher education was free enough from science to walk on its own moon.

The civil rights era also set in motion a legalistic culture in higher education. Institutions of higher education believed that new due process "requirements" demanded legal compliance that had to be heavily legalistic.[38] At least in student discipline, institutions of higher education came to favor systems of student discipline that are highly imitative of the legal system itself. An entirely new caste of student affairs administrators emerged: professional disciplinarians.[39]

The Bystander Era

The civil rights era gave students new public law rights. Higher education was no longer a privilege, and students gained constitutional status with basic public law rights. This trend would, in turn, facilitate the development of private

---

[38] Lake, *infra* note 3, at 14.

[39] *See id.* at 194. "Today, the association named the Association of Student Conduct Administrators (ASCA), formerly the Association of Student Judicial Affairs (ASJA), has become the primary and leading association for individuals charged with administering discipline in higher education. According to legend, the idea for the association began in conversations between Donald Gehring and Robert Bickel in the hallway of the annual Stetson Law Higher Education Conference in Florida sometime before the association formed. The rapid evolution and success of ASCA followed." *Id.* It's not a legend.

contract law rights. Private law lagged behind in many areas, especially safety rights and rights related to core mission delivery. There was no federal mandate (like the Supreme Court decisions creating rights of speech and association) on the law of student safety or core mission delivery. It was left to the various states to determine what, if any, rights students had in these areas. Conceiving these matters largely as matters of state law ensured that student empowerment outside the realm of public law would take a long time to develop.

In a series of oft-cited cases from the 1970s and 1980s, courts applying state law held that institutions of higher education had no legal duty to protect college students who voluntarily became intoxicated or engaged willingly in high-risk behaviors.[40] The language of some of these cases was very strong and became emblematic of the judicial attitude of a generation ago.

Two particularly famous cases, *Beach* and *Bradshaw*,[41] made the following assertions about college students and college life in the 1970s and 1980s:

1. College students are adults and are principally responsible for their own welfare.

2. College alcohol use—even by minors—is uncontrollable.

3. College is the place where young adults learn to use alcohol, hopefully responsibly.

4. Colleges are not the "insurers" of student safety.[42]

Although *Beach* and *Bradshaw* are frequently cited even today,[43] neither case presents an entirely accurate statement of current law in its state jurisdiction.[44] Even more striking is the fact that all four key assumptions made by these courts are now known to be false.

---

[40] *See, e.g., Beach,* 726 P.2d at 419; *Bradshaw v. Rawlings,* 612 F.2d 135, 141 (3rd Cir. 1979); *Baldwin v. Zoradi,* 123 Cal. App. 3d, 275, 288 (Cal. Ct. App. 1981).

[41] *See Beach,* 726 P.2d at 418; *Bradshaw,* 612 F.2d at 139.

[42] *Beach,* 726 P.2d at 419; *Bradshaw,* 612 F.2d at 138.

[43] *See* Areen, *supra* note 12, at 811–17.

[44] The Utah Supreme Court essentially eviscerated *Beach* in *Webb v. Univ. of Utah,* 125 P.3d 906 (2005), and rewrote the law of student safety in Utah. The current law regarding alcohol responsibility in Pennsylvania would dictate a different result if the same incident occurred today; indeed, criminal charges might be brought.

First, studies of human brain development show that the human brain continues to mature well into one's 20s—past the age of traditional college students.[45] Moreover, the part of the brain that is still forming controls judgment, among other things, and high-risk alcohol use can delay maturation.[46] Biologically, traditional-age college students are not fully formed adults, and they are susceptible to safety and developmental risk from high-risk alcohol use. Moreover, millennial students tend to have very strong bonds with family members, particularly their parents, well past traditional college age, making them much less independent than previous generations at the same age.[47]

Second, alcohol and other drug prevention science has shown promise for reducing high-risk alcohol and drug use.[48] Modern risk management approaches can also reduce the frequency and severity of harm to students.[49] Institutions of higher education have the power to influence and reduce, if not eradicate, college alcohol use and the negative consequences associated with it.

Third, studies show that most college students who drink started well before college—in some cases, in middle school or earlier.[50] College is no longer the point of socialization into drinking for most college drinkers.[51]

Fourth, the law of negligence differs significantly from the law of insurance. Insurance involves a contract in which one party receives certain sums on the occurrence of a contingency (a loss occurrence or the like) for which there exists an insurable interest.[52] Negligence liability for physical injury does not usually arise from a contract (at least not in the college context), and the contingency on which liability is predicated is fault—usually the lack of due care (see below). Insurance, on the other hand, is rarely concerned with fault; it operates more like strict liability, in which ordinary proof of fault is not necessary for re-

---

[45] Darby Dickerson, *The Millennial Brain and Risk,* Campus Activities Programming 10 (November 12, 2008), *available at* SSRN: http://ssrn.com/abstract=1300625.
[46] Darby Dickerson & Peter F. Lake, *Alcohol and Campus Risk Management,* 18 Campus Activities Programming (October 2006), *available at* SSRN: http://ssrn.com/abstract=1097120.
[47] The "millennial generation" roughly encompasses students who were born between 1982 and the present. Neil Howe & William Strauss, *Millennials Go to College: Strategies for a New Generation on Campus* 19 (Am. Assn. Collegiate Registrars & Admissions Officers 2003).
[48] Dickerson & Lake, *supra* note 46.
[49] *Id.*
[50] *Id.*
[51] *Id.*
[52] Robert H. Jerry, II, *Understanding Insurance Law* 237 (2d ed., Matthew Bender 1996).

covery. The language regarding 'insurance' in cases such as *Beach* and *Bradshaw* is legal hyperbole. If a college were to be liable, it would not be an "insurer"; rather, it would be asked to perform reasonable care or due diligence. No one has ever seriously argued that colleges should be strictly liable for student injuries. Perhaps the courts in *Beach* and *Bradshaw* were tempted to exaggeration because they believed (incorrectly) that no care by an institution of higher education could ever prevent college student injuries when students are intoxicated or voluntarily engage in high-risk tomfoolery.

In the bystander era, the following were widely accepted:

1. The primary issue in a negligence case against a college was the existence of legal duty (see below).

2. Colleges should be wary of assuming duties (see below). Starting in the 1970s, many institutions of higher education pursued policies of active disengagement from certain aspects of student life and were very cautious in what they chose to regulate. Even today, many campuses debate whether to extend "jurisdiction" of their conduct codes off campus—a vestige of the bystander era.

3. Some courts cast the potential liability of institutions of higher education for student injury in terms of rescue law (see below) and essentially analogized institutions of higher education to "bystanders" of dangerous student behavior. Institutions of higher education legally became much like someone driving past an accident on the highway.

4. Institutions of higher education had a strong legal posture in cases involving student injury. They could argue that no duty was owed; this argument could end litigation very fast and avoid significant litigation costs. Even today, higher education attorneys prefer to meet cases at the courthouse door with various "no duty" arguments. This has been a bread-and-butter maneuver in college litigation for at least two decades.

5. The practice of student affairs steadily grew apart from the rhetoric higher education lawyers used in court. College recruiting and

marketing became a crucial feature of the higher education business plan, and retention became a major focus for most institutions. The discourse used to recruit students and retain them was very different from the discourse used after a student became injured.

It is important to put the bystander era law in perspective. To some extent, cases such as *Beach* and *Bradshaw* represented a judicial backlash against the students of the 1960s and 1970s.

First, some courts seemed to believe that the price of newfound public law rights was a student's responsibility to manage his or her own affairs—hence the dicta in cases like *Beach* and *Bradshaw* regarding the fall of *in loco parentis* (which had never imposed safety duties on institutions of higher education in the first place).

Second, higher education was in the nascent stages of a business boom from World War II to the great recession of the 2000s—over a half century of a mostly up business cycle. It is not unusual for the law to be protective of industries in a growth phase—consider how wildly unregulated the Internet was at the beginning. The development of higher education law was heavily influenced by larger legal and social forces. Institutions of higher education were slowly but surely being put on the same footing with other businesses under private law.

Just as higher education entered the juridical world in the civil rights era, the law relating to the regulation of alcohol had reached its most laissez-faire extreme. Before World War II, America had Prohibition—a social experiment that failed.[53] After World War II, the dominant legal norm regarding alcohol risk was "personal accountability" of the drinker. A voluntary drinker was considered the sole proximate cause of harm and was therefore the responsible party for harm.[54] The server or vendor of alcohol was not liable for over-service. Modern "dram shop laws" would come later for most states (1980s for many).[55] "Social hosts"— nonvendors who served for casual or social purposes—were also not considered responsible for their intoxicated guests' mistakes,[56] an attitude that persists today in many states.[57] Driving under the influence (DUI) and open container law en-

---

[53] U.S. Const. amend. XXI.
[54] Dobbs, *supra* note 13, at 535.
[55] Dobbs, *supra* note 13, at 899.
[56] Dobbs, *supra* note 13, at 901–2.
[57] *See id.* "But liability of social hosts has proved to be unpopular with many courts and legis-

forcement was lax, as was enforcement of underage drinking laws.[58] Laws against being drunk in public were falling into disfavor.[59] The American legal system had not yet made the connection between vehicular accidents and intoxication: The notion that drunk driving is a public health crisis would come later, in the 1980s and 1990s.[60] In short, the law of the 1960s and 1970s was very favorable to businesses and social hosts, and enforcement of alcohol laws was lax.

This was the context of the bystander era. American courts were simply applying the drinker-is-responsible rule to American colleges, refusing to impose liability for alcohol risk on colleges that other actors in society did not also shoulder.

Three points are noteworthy. First, in cases *not* involving alcohol use by the victim or the victimizer, courts applied different rules even in the bystander era. Beginning in 1983 with *Mullins v. Pine Manor*, institutions of higher education were charged with the responsibility to use reasonable care to protect students in the campus environment.[61] This ruling mirrored the development of law outside colleges.[62] The bystander era initiated a form of parallelism in business law for colleges and other businesses. However, because alcohol risk is the signature risk of the modern institution of higher education, it was easy to overgeneralize alcohol cases such as *Beach* and *Bradshaw* and miss the larger trend of the application of business law principles to higher education.

Second, institutions of higher education sometimes argued that they should not have a duty to use reasonable care to reduce risk to students in context outside alcohol risk—with embarrassing consequences on occasion.[63] By-

---

latures. Social host liability today remains the exception rather than the rule." *Id.*

[58] Wikipedia, *Drunk Driving in the United States: History of Drunk Driving Laws,* http://en.wikipedia.org/wiki/Drunk_driving_in_the_United_States#History_of_drunk_driving_laws (last visited Aug. 5, 2010).

[59] *Id.*

[60] *See* Mothers Against Drunk Driving, http://www.madd.org/Drunk-Driving/Drunk-Driving/Laws.aspx (last visited Aug. 5, 2010) (under "Laws," the relevant DUI laws are provided in a clickable state-by-state menu).

[61] *Mullins v. Pine Manor College,* 449 N.E.2d 331, 335 (Mass. 1983).

[62] *See, e.g., Nixon v. Mr. Property Management Co., Inc.,* 690 S.W.2d. 546, 550 (Tex. 1985).

[63] In several cases, universities asserted indefensible positions and were rebuked. *See, e.g., Nero v. Kansas State Univ.* 861 P.2d 768 (Kan. 1993) (university places sexual predator in dormitory, asserts "no duty," and loses); *Gross v. Family Services Agency and Nova Southeastern University, Inc.,* 716 So. 2d 337 (Fla. App. 1998) (university sends student to dangerous off-site externship, asserts "no duty" and loses); *Tarasoff v. Regents of the University of California,* 551 P.2d 334 (Cal. 1976) (a psychotherapeutic patient with dangerous intentions attacks victim, uni-

stander era rationales were connected to a general philosophy of disengagement or minimal engagement from a variety of facets of student life. This reluctance to assume duties (discussed below) persists and often influences student affairs administration policymaking.

Third, the law relating to alcohol responsibility changed slowly and steadily from the Rat Pack era in the 1950s to the 1970s. Almost all states eventually passed dram shop laws[64] and rapidly increased their enforcement of DUI and underage drinking laws.[65] Crucially, the law relaxed the traditional "drinker is sole proximate cause" rule and accepted the possibility that vendors, servers, and other facilitators of alcohol risk could bear some share of blame.[66] By the 1990s, the great booze-soaked office party culture visible in "Mad Men"[67] was over, largely because of changes in the law that chilled such business-facilitated risk.[68] Nonetheless, the social host has not typically been found to be responsible for alcohol risk, although there are notable and a steadily growing number of exceptions to that rule.[69] Shifts in alcohol law have affected college campuses in complex ways. This topic is discussed in Chapter 3; for now, suffice it to say that colleges win some cases and lose some, and the divided authority represents the complexity of current negligence and alcohol responsibility law, not a policy of protection for colleges per se or a general belief that the student drinker is always the sole responsible party if someone is injured.

The Facilitator Era

The next era was one of broad application of principles of business law and accountability to higher education. In the civil rights era, institutions of higher education had experienced the broad application of many public law principles but fewer private law principles. Meanwhile, from the 1960s on, higher educa-

---

versity asserts "no duty," and loses).

[64] Dobbs, *supra* note 13, at 899.

[65] *See* Mothers Against Drunk Driving, *supra* note 60.

[66] *See* Dobbs, *supra* note 13, at 900. "Dram Shop statutes aside, the courts began reversing themselves about 1960. Most courts without a Dram Shop statute now recognize a common law duty of reasonable care and impose liability when the licensed seller of alcohol negligently sells to a minor or intoxicated person who, as a result, causes injury to the plaintiff." *Id.*

[67] *Mad Men* (AMC 2007).

[68] *See Balk v. Austin Ford Logan, Inc.*, 221 A.D.2d 795, 796 (N.Y. App. Div. 1995).

[69] *See* Mothers Against Drunk Driving, *supra* note 60.

tion became a big industry with expanding commercial activities: large endowments, huge capital projects, and student services that mimicked services provided in the commercial sector. Higher education became more visibly similar to business, and the law increasingly, if cautiously, applied business law principles to institutions of higher education (sometimes with special adaptations for the college environment).

The period from the 1960s to the 1980s saw a meteoric rise in the application of negligence law to businesses generally. Private law itself was changing, and higher education would not be immune to these changes. Indeed, the application of private law to individuals and businesses expanded so rapidly that American tort law faced a backlash in the form of tort reform (beginning in the 1980s and peaking in the late 1990s and early 2000s). Tort reform did not wipe out all the changes in negligence law that had occurred in the 1950s through the 1970s. Much of the focus of tort reform was on strict product liability, particularly liability for design defects in commercial products. Noticeable variations in safety law from state to state emerged, and the law in many states became unfavorable to injured plaintiffs. In the past, it mattered very little from a safety law standpoint whether a student went to college in Texas or Massachusetts; at the millennium, as a result of tort expansion and tort reform, it started to matter a great deal which state's safety law applied, even if the differences were only visible to lawyers. At the same time, large social forces and changing attitudes were reforming approaches to alcohol risk and child and adolescent safety.

A tectonic shift in the law of contracts as applied to higher education was creating the framework for expanded promise-based responsibility for institutions of higher education.[70] The increase in contractual freedom for students has been a notable development in the law. In the era of power, prerogative, and insularity, courts had acknowledged that the higher education relationship was contractual, but they usually thought of the contract as one with parents, not students. In addition, the courts interpreted the contract in a narrow and one-sided way, heavily in favor of institutions of higher education.[71]

Thus, just as higher education was maturing into a business in the eyes

---

[70] Sara Lipka, *Ties Between Colleges and Students Increasingly Look Like Contracts*, Chronicle of Higher Education (June 29, 2010), *available at* http://chronicle.com/article/Ties-Between-Colleges-and/66088/.

[71] *See Anthony v. Syracuse*, 224 A.D. 487, 491 (N.Y. App. Div. 1928).

of private law, business law was changing, as were social attitudes toward the allocation of risk and responsibility, particularly with regard to alcohol risk and youth.

On the public law side, institutions of higher education saw nothing like the meteoric increase in accountability that occurred in the civil rights era; however, in the decades following that era, public law steadily extended its reach into the affairs of higher education. On one hand, Congress added specific regulatory requirements for higher education, including the ever revolving and expanding campus crime reporting act known as the Clery Act.[72] Meanwhile, the courts, including the U.S. Supreme Court, consolidated and expanded public law application to higher education.[73] In the facilitator era, the Supreme Court struck down gender-biased admission systems at public colleges and held that college students are entitled to some constitutional protections when mandatory student fees are used to fund speakers and ideas that students do not approve of.[74] The law moved to consolidate the gains of the civil rights era and to create a more seamless web of the application of public law to higher education. The current Supreme Court, led by Chief Justice John Roberts, seems particularly interested in expanding First Amendment freedoms and appears willing to hear more cases involving higher education. Litigants have postured in court with the implicit assumption that they are entitled to key answers relating to the application of public law principles to higher education, and courts have frequently obliged.[75]

PUBLIC/PRIVATE DISTINCTIONS

In many ways, public/private distinctions are for lawyers to argue in court, not for student affairs administrators in everyday practice. This is so for several reasons. First, public law reaches broadly into the lives of student affairs admin-

---

[72] The Clery Act, 20 U.S.C. § 1092(f) (2006).
[73] *See, e.g., Rosenberger,* 515 U.S. 819; *Board of Regents of Univ. of Wisconsin v. Southworth* 529 U.S. 217 (2000); *Christian Legal Society at Hastings College of the Law v. Martinez,* 130 S. Ct. 2971 (2010).
[74] *See, e.g., Rosenberger* 515 U.S. at 840–41; *Southworth* 529 U.S. 217, 221.
[75] For example, several lower federal courts became frustrated that the U.S. Supreme Court refused to clearly answer questions of whether or not college students are entitled to due process and simply answered those questions themselves. (See Chapter 4 *infra*).

istrators whether they are in public or private institutions. Second, a noticeable parallelism exists in the application of public law principles and private law principles. Pragmatically, the work of student affairs administrators at public and private institutions differs primarily because of employment issues, funding and accountability issues, and scale (many public colleges enroll tens of thousands of students, while few private colleges have those enrollment numbers).

In dealing with students and student issues, what differs most between the two realms is usually language systems. Higher education is more seamless than it may appear on the surface—or than lawyers allow it to appear. Only in the past half century have public/private distinctions mattered in any significant way. The era of power and prerogative was equally generous to both public and private institutions. And public versus private is a modern concept: Most of American higher education started as theocratic state-sponsored religious training.[76] As you take this brief tour of public/private distinctions in higher education law, remember the overall similarity of all higher education institutions.

State Action

"State action" doctrines are often considered to be the quintessential distinction between public and private: Federal constitutional principles and many other federal laws[77] do not apply unless there is state action . . . except when they do.[78] (State constitutional requirements are a whole other ball of wax and are beyond the scope of this book.[79]) A private actor not engaged in state action is not subject to federal constitutional principles.

What is state action? There are two answers: the pragmatic answer and the lawyer's answer. Let's start with the pragmatic answer. If you work at a public college, most everything that happens in the course of the day is state action. If you work at a private college, most of what you do is not state action. For

---

[76] *See* Lake, *supra* note 3, at 10–61.

[77] Sherman Antitrust Act, 15 U.S.C. § 1 (2006); *see, e.g., Rendell-Baker v. Kohn*, 457 U.S. 830 (1982); *Hack v. President and Fellows of Yale College*, 237 F.3d 81 (2d Cir. 2000), *cert.denied*, 534 U.S. 888 (2001); *Commodari v. Long Island Univ.*, 62 Fed. Appx. 28 (2d Cir. 2003) (unpublished).

[78] *See, e.g., Pruneyard Shopping Center v. Robins*, 447 U.S. 74, 80 (1980). "State action" is not the only way in which public law may apply. For instance, state constitutional law may project public law onto otherwise "private" actors.

[79] *See Princeton Univ. v. Schmid*, 455 U.S. 100, 102 (1982).

Christmas one year, my father gave me a horsehair barometer. He said, "Son, if it's wet, it's raining; and if it's dry, it's not."

Lawyers will be quick to point out that in *Powe v. Miles*,[80] the Second Circuit held that at a university event, some students were entitled to constitutional free speech protection while others at the same event were not. In *Powe*, the university was both public and private at the same time.[81] *Powe* illustrates that an institution can include both public and private enclaves. Pragmatically, however, this situation is unusual. *Powe* is not legal sophistry, but it would be easy to place too much emphasis on it. Lawyers will also point to a variety of U.S. Supreme Court cases that deal with the issue of state action.

We'll begin with what is *not* state action. First, most American colleges are heavily dependent on tuition, and most tuition comes from federally subsidized lending programs. In 2010, the federal government entered the business of direct lending.[82] However, the fact that an institution of higher education depends heavily on federal or state subsidies for tuition does not in itself create state action.[83] Similarly, receiving grant money or other assistance from the government does not create state action per se.[84] These days, just about everyone in higher education is on the government payroll in one way or another. The fact that an institution of higher education is subject to regulation by federal or state govern-

---

[80] *Powe v. Miles*, 407 F.2d 73 (2d Cir. 1962).

[81] The case was very fact-specific. One program, the ceramics college, was a state-operated and state-sponsored creation, which transformed the relationship with students into a state action. The liberal arts college was not state sponsored. In essence, Alfred College was two colleges with one event.

[82] Health Care and Education Reconciliation Act of 2010, Pub. L. 111–152, §§ 2201–13, 124 Stat. 1029 (2010).

[83] "The Supreme Court, however, has consistently held that financial aid to an institution, without more, is not sufficient to elevate a private entity's conduct to the level of state action." *Carson v. Springfield College*, 2006 WL 2242732, at *2 (Del. Super. 2006) (finding the college student unsuccessful in seeking to establish the private college as a state actor, despite the private school's acceptance of financial aid from the federal government) (citing *Rendell-Baker v. Kohn*, 457 U.S. 830, 842 (1982)).

[84] Private action may be deemed state action "when the private actor is a willful participant in joint activity with the State or its agents." *U.S. v. Price*, 383 U.S. 787, 794 (1966). However, "mere allegations of State financial or other support, without more, are insufficient to convert an otherwise independent entity into a joint venture with the state." *Commodari v. Long Island Univ.*, 89 F. Supp. 2d 353, 373 (E.D.N.Y. 2000) (quoting *Madon v. Long Island Univ.*, 518 F. Supp. 246, 249 (E.D.N.Y. 1981)).

ment does not create state action either.[85] Everything seems to be regulated to-day, but mere regulation is not determinative of state action.[86] And the granting of a charter to an institution of higher education does not create state action.[87]

The U.S. Supreme Court has devised various tests for state action. There is no one simple rule to determine state action for all purposes. State action in higher education can arise in a variety of ways; two are common. First, the government can act through an entity as its agent; for example, when the state government sets up a state school or contracts with a company or college to provide specific government services.[88]

Second, the U.S. Supreme Court has acknowledged that sometimes the government entangles itself with a private entity in a way that can transform the action of that entity to state action.[89] This is a classic question of degree and does not admit a bright-line analysis. For example, the Supreme Court has said that there must be a sufficient "nexus" between state and private actors or the state must be in a joint "venture" or have a "symbiotic relationship" with a private actor.[90] These tests are very fact-specific, and lawyers and nonlawyers alike will be hard-pressed to accurately guess how courts will rule in all situations. Student affairs administrators should think of state action in terms of "The Matrix,"[91] when an Agent assumes the body and takes over the will of another. Few cases find state action when the "relationship" is very hard to call.[92] State action is like love: If you have doubts that you are in it, you probably are not.

---

[85] *Powe*, 407 F.2d at 81.

[86] *Hu v. American Bar Assn.*, 568 F. Supp. 2d 959, 964 (N.D. Ill. 2008) (finding that "neither general government involvement nor detailed and extensive regulation or public funding is sufficient to find state action").

[87] *See Greenya v. GWU*, 512 F.2d 556, 560 (D.C. Cir. 1975).

[88] *Id.*; *see also Powe*, 407 F.2d 73.

[89] *Burton v. Wilmington Parking Authority*, 365 U.S. 715, 722 (1961) (determining a private entity's entanglement with the government, and thus becoming a state actor, based upon the facts and circumstances of the case). "Only by sifting facts and weighing circumstances can the nonobvious involvement of the State in private conduct be attributed its true significance." *Id.*

[90] *Id.*; *see Commodari*, 89 F. Supp. 2d at 373; *Jackson v. Metropolitan Edison Co.*, 419 U.S. 345, 351 (1974).

[91] *The Matrix*, (Warner Bros. 1999) (motion picture).

[92] *See, e.g., Benner v. Oswald*, 592 F.2d 174, 179 (3d Cir. 1979). A notable exception may be found in certain discrimination cases; however, public/private distinctions operate differently in the discrimination context. *See infra* Chapter 5.

Commerce Clause in the Fourteenth Amendment

For student affairs administrators, Congress's plenary power[93] to pass regulatory legislation under the commerce clause is significant in their experience of the public/private distinction. Congress also has a broad grant of enforcement power under the Fourteenth Amendment.[94]

Under these two grants of authority, Congress has been able to extend public law principles to the actions of many public *and* private actors. The reach of federal power to regulate commerce and to pass laws in the name of equal protection is not limitless or entirely uncontroversial,[95] but for student affairs administrators the extension of public law principles to day-to-day operation blurs the line between public and private. The reach of federal power is not itself a state action doctrine; that is, private institutions are not transformed into state actors because of such regulation. However, from the perspective of the student affairs administrator, it often feels as though the reach of regulatory enforcement power is so great that the public/private distinction is unclear.

Public/Private Under State Law

The higher education industry is largely regulated by state law. For example, the law of contracts and torts is highly state-specific. However, states also extend the reach of public law into the affairs of higher education, sometimes with laws that are more aggressive than their federal counterparts.

The U.S. Supreme Court and a few state courts have blurred the lines between public and private even further (for example, in the famous Supreme Court case *Pruneyard*).[96] Some states broadly apply the principles of their constitutions to campuses in that state;[97] thus, while many private colleges do not

---

[93] "The Congress shall have power to lay and collect taxes, duties, imposts and excises, to pay the debts and provide for the common defense and general welfare of the United States; but all duties, imposts and excises shall be uniform throughout the United States." U.S. Const. art. I, § 8; *see Frye v. United States*, 421 U.S. 542, 552 (1978).

[94] "The Congress shall have power to enforce, by appropriate legislation, the provisions of this article." U.S. Const. amend. XIV, § 5; *see Katzenbach v. Morgan*, 384 U.S. 641, 648–49 (1966).

[95] *See, e.g., Oregon v. Mitchell*, 400 U.S. 112, 286–87 (1970).

[96] *Pruneyard*, 447 U.S. at 80–89 (holding that states have the power to determine that some private spaces are so imbued with public space qualities as to be subject to state constitutional public law principles).

[97] *See State v. Schmid*, 423 A.2d 615, 619 (N.J. 1980).

have state constitutional obligations to provide free speech and expression, colleges in some states do have such obligations under some circumstances.

Some Public/Private Chimeras

State government/state officers immunity.

Mel Brooks once said, "It's good to be the king."[98] But it's not nearly as good as it used to be—sovereign immunity includes many complexities. The feature of sovereign immunity most likely to affect student affairs administrators is that state government entities and actors have vestigial legal protection from many lawsuits; that protection varies considerably from state to state.[99]

Government immunity originally arose from 'received' English legal doctrine protecting the Crown from lawsuits. The English doctrine evolved in the United States to completely block tort lawsuits against federal and state governments and their employees.[100] This doctrinal protection extended to the government entity itself and to most of its operatives. Cities and towns represented special challenges for doctrines of sovereign immunity; they were not always immune.[101] Colleges, however, invariably were protected under the privilege doctrine, which made it magically irrelevant whether they were more like a city or the state.[102]

---

[98] *History of the World: Part I* (Brooksfilms 1981) (motion picture).
[99] The Eleventh Amendment preserves some state immunity in federal court. A college or university can qualify for this immunity if it is an "arm of the state" and not of a political subdivision. *Joseph v. Board of Regents of Univ. of Wisconsin System*, 432 F.3d 746, 748 (7th Cir. 2005). Many colleges and universities qualify as an arm of the state. *See, e.g., Hall v. Medical College of Ohio*, 742 F.2d 299, 301 (6th Cir. 1984) (listing cases finding public colleges or universities as "arms of the state" under the Eleventh Amendment). That being said, no one really understands the Eleventh Amendment, so student affairs administrators should not be expected to have special powers to interpret it. *See, e.g., Ho v. Univ. of Texas at Arlington*, 984 S.W.2d 672 (Tex. App. Amarillo 1998); *Daniel v. American Bd. of Emergency Medicine*, 988 F. Supp. 127 (W.D.N.Y. 1997); *Hall v. Hawaii*, 791 F.2d 759 (9th Cir. 1986).
[100] *See* Edwin M. Borchard, *Governmental Liability and Tort*, 34 Yale L. J. 1 (1924); *see also Molitor v. Kaneland Community Unit Dist.*, 163 N.E.2d 89, 94 (Ill. 1959) ("[I]n preserving the sovereign immunity theory, courts have overlooked the fact that the Revolutionary War was fought to abolish the 'divine right of kings' on which the theory is based").
[101] *Monell v. N.Y.C. Dept. of Social Services*, 436 U.S. 658, 701 (1978) (holding that "municipal bodies sued under § 1983 cannot be entitled to an absolute immunity" and declining to explain the scope of any municipal immunity).
[102] *Prairie View A&M Univ. of Texas v. Mitchell*, 27 S.W.3d 323, 325–26. (Tex. App. 1st Dist. 2000) (demonstrating that public universities and colleges can use sovereign immunity as a

State government immunity typically arises from state statutes that "partially waive" sovereign immunity. Many of these 'partial waiver' statutes were passed in the 20th century. State government immunity systems often exclude entire categories of torts, such as intentional torts, from potential lawsuits,[103] and many provide caps on liability and special provisions for suit against the state.[104] Even when the government entity (e.g., the institution of higher education) can be sued (usually for negligence),[105] state law often provides that "discretionary functions" remain immune, while "ministerial acts" are not.[106] (Lawyers learn that discretionary functions are policy-making decisions, while ministerial acts are merely actions taken to carry out the policy decisions.[107]) The decision to place a red light at a dangerous intersection is immune, but once the red light is approved and in place, the state must maintain it using reasonable care.[108] Routine maintenance is usually considered ministerial.[109] The determination that something is or is not immune as a discretionary function is not always as clear as the simple illustration suggests. Courts have devised very complex tests to determine how a close case will tip.[110]

Public officials enjoy varying degrees of government immunity. Sometimes the government entity (the college) is immune but the individual student

---

defense); *Hamilton v. Regents of Univ. of Cal.*, 293 U.S. 245, 257–58 (1934).

[103] *See* Haw. Rev. Stat. § 662-15 (2010); Idaho Code Ann. § 6-904 (2010); Mass. Gen. Law Ann. ch. 258, § 10 (2010).

[104] Minn. Code Ann. § 3.736 (West 2010); Tex. Civ. Prac. & Rem. Code Ann. § 102.003 (2010); Va. Code Ann. § 8.01-195.3 (West 2010).

[105] Occasionally, litigants can sue for injuries sustained by "encounters" with state defendants acting more than merely negligently.

[106] *Heigl v. Bd. of Educ.*, 587 A.2d 423, 427 (Conn. 1991) (determining that the board of education's action in establishing an open campus policy is a discretionary act and the board is protected from tort liability by the doctrine of governmental immunity).

[107] "Generally, liability may attach for a negligently performed ministerial act, but not for a negligently performed governmental or discretionary act." *Kolaniak v. Bd. of Educ.*, 610 A.2d 193, 195 (Conn. App. 1993).

[108] *Elgin v. Dist. of Columbia*, 337 F.2d 152, 156–57 (D.C. App. 1964) (holding the District of Columbia liable for injuries to a school child from a defective guardrail, as the function of repairing the guardrails was ministerial rather than discretionary).

[109] *See Kimps v. Hill*, 546 N.W.2d 151, 157–59 (1996).

[110] "The public/private duty distinction and the ministerial/discretionary test may appear to overlap and this has resulted in a lack of consistent analysis by this state's courts." *Gordon v. Bridgeport Housing Authority*, 208 Conn. at 168. "The finding of a public duty is often, but not always, dispositive of whether the act is a discretionary one." *Id.* at 169.

affairs administrator is not, or vice versa.[111] When student affairs administrators are entitled to government immunity, it is typically "qualified immunity."[112] In most cases, if a government official's actions are not purely ministerial (for which there often is no immunity), the question of qualified immunity turns on whether the official acted in good faith or without malice or other similar factors.[113] The determination of the level of immunity is complex because of the following factors:

1. State public official immunity law varies from state to state, and for various classes of officers.

2. State officials who allegedly deny individuals' civil rights while acting under the color of state law may be subject to federal civil rights law under section 1983,[114] and the U.S. Supreme Court has crafted official immunity law just for section 1983.[115] Section 1983 immunity is similar but not identical to the immunity state officials enjoy under state law.

---

[111] The litigation involving Texas A&M University and the 1999 bonfire collapse best illustrates, in a series of cases, the dichotomy of student affairs administrators in their official versus individual capacities and the resulting liability. The university was shielded from liability, while the individual school administrators were not. *Davis v. Southerland*, 2004 WL 1230278 (S.D. Tex. 2004) (finding the defendants, high-level employees or university officials of Texas A&M University, were entitled to qualified immunity from § 1983 claims); *Bowen v. Comstock,* 2008 WL 2209722 (Tex. App. Waco Dist. 2008) (finding university administrators barred possibly liable for acts done in the course and scope of their employment as it relates to the 1999 bonfire collapse at the university); *Texas A&M Univ. v. Bading*, 236 S.W.3d 801, 808 (Tex. App. Waco Dist. 2007) (holding that sovereign immunity barred claims against the university by a construction company arising from the collapse of the 1999 bonfire).

[112] State university officials are entitled to qualified immunity when performing discretionary functions, and the civil damage suit arises from the performance of their official duty. *Purisch v. Tenn. Tech. Univ.*, 76 F.3d 1414, 1423 (6th Cir. 1996); *Yohn v. Coleman*, 639 F. Supp. 2d 776, 788–89 (E.D. Mich. 2009) (finding university officials protected by qualified immunity against a professor's § 1983 action alleging First Amendment and due process violations).

[113] *Watts v. Wayne Co. Bd. of Educ.*, 412 S.E.2d 541, 543 (Ga. App. 1991) (holding that a school principal could invoke the defense of official immunity for his discretionary decision when no showing of willfulness, malice, or corruption existed).

[114] *Goldbarth v. Kansas State Bd. of Regents*, 9 P.3d 1251, 1260 (Kan. 2000) (finding administrators, in their individual capacity, entitled to qualified immunity in a § 1983 claim).

[115] *See, e.g.*, *Wood v. Strickland*, 420 U.S. 308, 318 (1975); *see also Harlow v. Fitzgerald*, 457 U.S. 800, 818 (1982).

3. The scope of qualified immunity is often highly debatable and may take significant litigation to clarify. For student affairs administrators who are not legally trained, litigation over immunity issues and actual liability issues may seem almost indistinguishable at times. Moreover, as a practical matter, qualified immunity operates to deter some cases from being brought in the first place. In some situations, student affairs administrators will not find out whether they have qualified immunity until well into litigation. This is like putting sunscreen on your face the first day of vacation and not finding out if it works until you get back home—not very satisfying or comforting.

As we review the protections afforded institutions of higher education and their staffs, it is tempting to conclude that things are very different in the public and private sectors. But do not be misled. Although differences exist in the language used and the precise processes of litigation, student affairs administrators at public and private schools experience roughly the same overall litigation outcomes. Private sector administrators do not enjoy overt forms of legal immunity; however, the law is very protective of higher education, and private colleges and their staffs are more likely to face accountability rather than liability—just like their public counterparts.

In some litigation against private institutions of higher education, it is appropriate and even necessary to sue both the institution and the individual student affairs administrator.[116] In some instances (like some cases in the public sector), lawsuits involving private higher education proceed only against individual student affairs administrators and not the institutions themselves.[117]

In short, student affairs administrators of public and private institutions of higher education can expect high levels of accountability but low risk of liability. Many student affairs administrators find themselves sued individually and sometimes solely. Legal language and procedural systems differ (and the

---

[116] See the discussion of *respondeat superior, infra,* Chapter 3.

[117] *See Shin v. Mass. Inst of Tech.*, 19 Mass. L. Rep. 570 (Mass. Super. 2005) (denying the motion for summary judgment asserted independently by MIT's medical professional, Girard, due to an issue of material fact as to whether Girard was part of the "treatment team," which establishes a physician-patient relationship at the time of the student's suicide).

points of distinction can be fine), but student affairs administrators at public and private institutions generally experience very similar litigation risk.

Student lending and the federal government.

Until very recently, the federal government was heavily involved in *indirect* lending.[118] Virtually every institution of higher education in the United States is highly dependent on tuition. Without federally subsidized loans, the higher education system as we know it would not have evolved. Indirect lending was a cornerstone of federal government support of American higher education after World War II. Until 2010, the government favored an indirect lending approach: It subsidized private lenders, who were the direct lenders to students, and entrusted accrediting bodies with the power to determine which institutions would qualify for indirect loans.[119] To qualify for a loan, students had to attend colleges with accreditation or the equivalent.[120] This put billions of dollars in the hands of banks and bank-like entities and great power in the hands of accreditation groups. If an institution of higher education failed to achieve or maintain accreditation, that institution was mortally wounded.[121]

This longstanding system gave public regulation of higher education a very private feel. The federal government was not setting standards directly for institutions of higher education the way a state might set specific standards for K–12

---

[118] Health Care and Education Reconciliation Act of 2010, Pub. L. 111–152, 124 Stat. 1029 (2010).

[119] Sam Dillon, *Drilling Down on the Budget, Student Loans,* N.Y. Times (Feb. 26, 2009), *available at* http://www.nytimes.com/2009/02/27/Washington/27web-edu.html.

[120] Jonnelle Marte, *New Rules for Loans,* Wall Street Journal (July 18, 2010), *available at* http://online.wsj.com/article/SB127940788035718231.html.

[121] "Students who attend unaccredited colleges are not allowed to receive federal financial aid. As a result, many colleges find it impossible to survive without accreditation." Beth McMurtrie, *Southern Accrediting Group Penalizes 21 Colleges,* Chronicle of Higher Education (Jan. 11, 2002), *available at* http://chronicle.com/article/Souther-Accrediting-Group-/12176. When Morris Brown College lost accreditation, it suffered "a crippling blow" because of the inability to award federal financial aid. Audrey Williams June, *Southern Association Strips 2 Black Colleges of Accreditation,* Chronicle of Higher Education (Jan. 3, 2003), *available at* http://chronicle.com/article/Souther-Association-Strips/23712. Not only do universities risk low student enrollment when accreditation is suspended or stripped, they become incapable of attracting new faculty members. "Colleges must be accredited by an organization that is recognized by the U.S. Department of Education for its students to be eligible to receive federal financial aid." Eric Kelderman, *Universities Sue Accreditor for Putting Their Pharmacy Programs on Probation,* Chronicle of Higher Education (Mar. 27, 2009), *available at* http://chronicle.com/article/Universitities-Sue-Accreditor/47138.

education. Even states that provided substantial support for higher education often deferred substantially to accrediting bodies.[122]

This system has changed. The federal government now favors *direct* lending, and it remains to be seen how the government will exercise power over core mission delivery and how students will qualify for financial aid.[123] Very recently, the government promulgated controversial new rules relating to lending at for-profit colleges.[124] As this situation develops, institutions of higher education may perceive a much greater public law regulation of higher education, in which it will matter very little whether institutions of higher education are public or private. It may matter more whether an institution is set up as an entity of state government, a nonprofit organization, or a for-profit organization.[125]

Contract law: public or private.

Contract law was once quintessentially private law; however, courts have made it crystal clear that the relationship with students is primarily contractual

---

[122] U.S. Dept. of Educ., *Database of Accredited Postsecondary Institutions and Programs*, http://www.ope.ed.gov/accreditation (last visited Aug. 8, 2010).

[123] Health Care and Education Reconciliation Act of 2010, Pub. L. 111-152, 124 Stat. 1029 (2010).

[124] "The Obama Administration released [July 23, 2010] its proposed regulations requiring for-profit career colleges to better prepare students for 'gainful employment' or risk losing access to federal student aid. The proposed rules seek to protect students from taking on unsustainable debt they cannot repay and to protect taxpayers from high loan default rates." Justin Hamilton, *Proposed Rule Links Federal Student Aid to Loan Repayment Rates and Debt-to-Earnings Levels for Career College Graduates* (July 23, 2010), http://www.ed.gov/news/press-releases/proposed-rule-links-federal-student-aid-loan-repayment-rates-and-debt-earnings. "Congress plans to put for-profit colleges under the microscope on Thursday,[June 24, 2010] asking whether a higher-education model that consumes more than double its proportionate share of federal student aid is an innovation worthy of duplication or a recipe for long-term economic disaster." Paul Basken, *New Grilling of For-Profits Could Turn Up the Heat for All of Higher Education,* Chronicle of Higher Education (June 22, 2010), *available at* http://chronicle.com/article/New-Grilling-of-For-Profits/66020. Further, the U.S. Department of Education examines the definition of "credit hour" in order "to ensure that students and taxpayers, through federal financial aid, are not footing the bill for courses that are not worth the amount of credit being awarded. If it's a for-profit institution that is getting more money for a course than it's really worth . . . the awarding of credit hours could become a part of a company's business plan to bolster profits." Eric Kelderman, *Credit Hours Should Be Worth the Cost, House Panel Members Say,* Chronicle of Higher Education (June 17, 2010), *available at* http://chronicle.com/article/Credit-Hours-Should-Be-Wort/65986. This may be a harbinger of things to come for higher education.

[125] *Id.*

at both public and private colleges.[126] This blurs the line between public and private for student affairs practice.

Consider the following: First, even at a public college, constitutional law provides only *some* parameters. Most of the legal obligations at a public college arise from contract law. A public college governed solely by public law would be a weird Dali-like[127] space, where things would seem out of order, or pieces would be incongruously linked. Student affairs administrators at public colleges would scarcely recognize their campuses if private law were to disappear.

Second, even where public law principles—constitution, statute, and regulation—are in play, the interpretation of these principles often turns heavily on promises made, actions causing reasonable reliance, and expectations. In other words, contract and contract-like norms (private-law-like stuff) influence the interpretation of public law principles at colleges. This lack of clarity is especially obvious in due process law (discussed *infra* in Chapter 4). Many lower federal courts, confused by the mandates of the U.S. Supreme Court, have created a form of quasi-contractual, quasi-constitutional due process law.[128] The promises that public colleges make to students in student handbooks and the like inform reasonable expectations to the extent that some lower federal courts are willing to enforce them under the public law heading of due process.[129]

Third, private colleges have a tendency to promise to deliver services to students (such as discipline systems) on terms that mimic public law requirements.[130] Contract law at private colleges resembles public law at public colleg-

---

[126] *Zumbrun v. Univ. of Southern California*, 25 Cal. App. 3d 1, 10 (Cal. 1972) (holding that the nature of the relationship between a private university and a student is contractual); *Kashmiri v. Regents of Univ. of California.*, 156 Cal. App. 4th 809, 825 (Cal. App. 1st Dist. 2007) (explaining that other courts recognize the nature of the relationship between public/state universities and students as contractual).

[127] Salvador Dali Museum, Inc., *Collection Highlights*, http://thedali.org/collection/collection_highlights.html (last visited Jan. 31, 2011).

[128] *See, e.g., Gorman*, 837 F.2d 7; *Flaim*, 418 F.3d 629.

[129] *See Than v. Univ. of Tex. Med. Sch.*, 188 F.3d 633, 634-35 (5th Cir. 1999); *Williams v. Wendler*, 530 F.3d 584, 586-89 (7th Cir. 2008).

[130] See, for example, *Schaer v. Brandeis Univ.*, 735 N.E.2d 373, 384 (Mass. 2000), which held that while the university handbook governing discipline proceedings discussed topics including information gathering and disciplinary determinations based upon evidence, the handbook did not require the exact procedure the university must employ when gathering information, nor did the handbook provision prohibit the board from using "their own common

es and vice versa, because public colleges often use contractual language similar to that used by their private counterparts. Lawyers must try to distinguish contract law from constitutional law; but for a student affairs administrator, more or less the same principles apply in public and private. Where differences do appear, they are usually differences in the interpretation of promises made by individual institutions of higher education and reasonable expectations arising from such promises.

Concluding Thoughts on the Public/Private Distinction

At least two generations of student affairs administrators have been taught the importance of public/private distinctions. Actually, public/private is a complex and related *set* of distinctions and, in many ways, they are lawyers' distinctions, not student affairs administrators' distinctions. Post-millennial student affairs administrators will continue to experience higher education in nonseamless ways, and public/private distinctions, like academic/conduct distinctions, will persist. However, these distinctions can distract us from the reality that higher education is a unitary experience that manifests for students in diverse ways. Public law and private law are complexly intertwined in both public and private institutions. The use of public/private distinctions and academic/conduct distinctions is lawyers' work—it is how lawyers conceptualize the application of general principles of law to higher education.

ACADEMIC FREEDOM

"Academic freedom" is a somewhat overused term in higher education law;[131] however, it is sadly *under*used in student affairs practice, where administrators tend to assume that academic freedom is for academics and institutions (and perhaps students) but has little application to their work.

---

sense and expertise" in place of evidence. *Id.* at 379. "A university is not required to adhere to the standards of due process guaranteed to criminal defendants or to abide by rules of evidence adopted by courts. A college must have broad discretion in determining appropriate sanctions for violations of its policies." *Id.* at 381.

[131] Robert M. O'Neil, *Colleges Face Ominous New Pressures on Academic Freedom,* The Chronicle of Higher Education (Feb. 8, 2008), *available at* http://chronicle.com/article/Colleges-Face-Ominous-New-P/14752/#top.

But it does, and the easiest way to lose academic freedom is to give it away.

In the 20th century, the American Association of University Professors (AAUP) became a leader in articulating concepts of academic freedom for professors in institutions of higher education. AAUP was founded in 1915 at a time when national unionization of higher education teachers was a real possibility. Unionization became the norm for K–12 but did not take hold in higher education nationwide. AAUP and most university professors preferred to articulate a vision of academic freedom in lieu of broad national unionization (although some professors are unionized in some places.)[132] Over the years, these principles have worked their way into many institutions of higher education through contracts and accreditation standards.[133]

AAUP guidelines—heavily oriented to classroom, research, and scholarship academics—provide for the following:

1. Teachers are entitled to full freedom in research and in the publication of the results, subject to the adequate performance of their other academic duties, but research for pecuniary return should be based on an understanding with the authorities of the institution.

2. Teachers are entitled to freedom in the classroom in discussing their subject, but they should be careful not to introduce controversial matters that have no relation to the subject. Limitations on academic freedom based on religious or other aims of the institution should be clearly stated in writing at the time of the appointment.

3. College and university teachers are citizens, members of a learned profession, and officers of an educational institution. When they speak or write as citizens, they should be free from institutional censorship or discipline, but their special position in the community imposes special obligations. As scholars and educational officers, they should remember that the public may judge their profession and their institution by their utterances. Thus, they should try to be accurate, ex-

---

[132] *See* American Federation of Teachers, *University Professionals of Illinois, Local 4100: About the AFT,* http://il.aft.org/041000/index.cfm?action=article&articleID=e46ec50c-0565-4539-a6d5-eed4de797d4d (last visited Jan. 31, 2011).

[133] *See* Areen, *supra* note 12, at 306-9.

ercise appropriate restraint, show respect for the opinions of others, and make every effort to indicate that they are not speaking for the institution.[134]

The U.S. Supreme Court has determined that academic freedom is guaranteed by the First Amendment.[135] The amendment does not explicitly refer to academic freedom, but the Court has had little difficulty expanding the reach of First Amendment protections for free speech and association to higher education.[136] The Court became very interested in government attempts to suppress the freedom of professors, especially during the attacks on left-leaning academics during the McCarthy era of the 1950s.[137] Thus, when the Court entered the fray, it picked First Amendment cases and issues primarily focused on the rights of professors vis-à-vis the state. This may have fueled the belief that academic freedom is for "pure academics" and not for others who work in the academy.

The Supreme Court chose to write in broad strokes about academic freedom. In *Sweezy*, the Court acknowledged four foundational academic freedoms:

> It is the business of a university to provide that atmosphere which is most conducive to speculation, experiment and creation. It is an atmosphere in which there prevail "the four essential freedoms" of a university—to determine for itself on academic grounds who may

---

[134] American Association of Univ. Professors, *1940 Statement of Principles on Academic Freedom and Tenure* (2006), *available at* http://www.aaup.org/AAUP/pubsres/policydocs/contents/1940statement.htm.

[135] *See, e.g., Sweezy v. New Hampshire*, 354 U.S. 234, 250-51 (1957); *Keyishian v. Bd. of Regents of Univ. of N.Y.*, 385 U.S. 589, 603 (1967).

[136] "The essentiality of freedom in the community of American universities is almost self-evident. No one should underestimate the vital role in a democracy that is played by those who guide and train our youth. To impose any straight jacket upon the intellectual leaders in our colleges and universities would imperil the future of our Nation." *Sweezy*, 354 U.S. at 250. "Our Nation is deeply committed to safeguarding academic freedom, which is of transcendent value to all of us and not merely to the teachers concerned. That freedom is therefore a special concern of the First Amendment, which does not tolerate laws that cast a pall of orthodoxy over the classroom." *Keyishian*, 385 U.S. at 603.

[137] *See, e.g., Sweezy* 354 U.S. at 236. Some college teachers were attacked for their political views during the era before the 1960s. Academic freedom became a defensive doctrine. "Subordination was everywhere in the pre-1960s American college. Professors taught recognized doctrine—when they strayed they were sometimes persecuted and dismissed." Lake, *supra* note 3, at 78.

teach, what may be taught, how it shall be taught, and who may be admitted to study.[138]

The four academic freedoms of whom to teach, how to teach, who may teach, and what may be taught would seem to apply to institutions as well, and lower federal courts have acknowledged this.[139] Very recently the Supreme Court, in *Christian Legal Society*, acknowledged the importance of higher education institutional autonomy, free from government interference.[140]

Addressing the academic freedom of students is a relatively new phenomenon at the Supreme Court, which in the past has preferred to address student rights directly as rights of speech, assembly, press, and so on, not through derivative concepts such as academic freedom.[141] Students' constitutional freedoms clearly play against academic freedom in a variety of contexts, such as admissions (see *Grutter* and *Gratz* on race-conscious admissions).[142] A recent effort to craft a concept of student academic freedom has been written into legislative proposals that some states have adopted[143] and some have rejected.[144] The con-

---

[138] *Sweezy* 354 U.S. at 263 (Frankfurter J., concurring).

[139] *See, e.g., Feldman v. Ho*, 171 F.3d 494 (7th Cir. 1999); *Webb v. Bd. of Trustees of Ball State Univ.*, 167 F.3d 1146 (7th Cir. 1999); *De Stefano v. Wilson*, 233 A.2d 682 (N.J. Super. L. Div. 1967).

[140] *Christian Legal Society at Hastings College of the Law v. Martinez*, 130 S. Ct. 2971 (2010).

[141] *See Rosenberger*, 515 U.S. 819; *Southworth*, 529 U.S. 217; *see infra* Chapter 5.

[142] *Grutter v. Bollinger*, 539 U.S. 306, 343 (2003); *Gratz v. Bollinger*, 539 U.S. 244, 275 (2003). For risk management, see *Southworth*, 529 U.S. at 233. For registered student organization management, see *Healy*, 408 U.S. at 180; *Christian Legal Society, supra* note 73.

[143] David Horowitz wrote an academic bill of rights and began a national campaign in September 2003 to convince colleges and universities to adopt this bill, which promoted and extended academic freedom to students (and to some extent, professors). The first university to adopt the academic bill of rights was Temple University. David Horowitz, *After the Academic Bill of Rights,* Chronicle of Higher Education (Nov. 10, 2006), *available at* http://chronicle. com/article/After-the-Academic-Bill-of-/2767. Horowitz continues his campaign through the David Horowitz Freedom Center, see http://www.horowitzfreedomcenter.org (last visited Jan. 31, 2011). He has gained the support of a student advocacy group, Students for Academic Freedom, which distributes *The Academic Bill of Rights,* which can be found at http://www. studentsforacademicfreedom.org (last visited Jan. 31, 2011). The State of Georgia passed a resolution (Ga. S. Res. 661(2003)) adopting the academic bill of rights (*see* Appendix on page 303 for the Georgia Resolution).

[144] For an in-depth discussion of the Academic Bill of Rights, see Cheryl A. Cameron, Laura E. Meyers & Steven G. Olswang, *Academic Bills of Rights: Conflict in the Classroom,* 31 J.C. & U.L. 243 (2005). Further, the AAUP details the state legislative progress, or lack thereof, of the Academic Bill of Rights. *See Academic Bill of Rights 2006* (last updated April 2007), http://

cept of student academic freedom is controversial and may even be unconstitutional as framed in some of the proposed legislation. So far, few legal tests of the constitutionality of the statutes have materialized in reported opinions.[145] Much of the legislation is aimed at rights relating to instruction and classroom management, but some may affect student affairs practice as well. Some of the rights are new, however, many of the noninstructional and classroom rights are already protected by policies at most institutions of higher education.

As the law, the practice of student affairs, and the management of institutions of higher education evolve to reconnect academic and student affairs activities into a seamless whole, academic freedom will become more important for student affairs administrators. Student affairs administrators play an important role in the broadly conceived teaching mission and should have academic freedom commensurate with the responsibilities of managing a modern higher education institution and its environment.[146]

WHAT IS A COLLEGE, ANYWAY?

The history of American higher education has led us to an intriguing place: The very concept of "college" is evolving, even dissolving, in front of our eyes. For hundreds and hundreds of years in western higher education, distinguishing an institution of higher learning from other social institutions was so easy—even obvious—as to obviate the need for elaborate definitions or classifications.[147]

---

www.aaup.org/AAUP/GR/Archive/camp/ABOR/aborstateleg.htm.

[145] Some critics view the Academic Bill of Rights as "an attack on academic freedom" and claim that the founder of the bill, David Horowitz, is a "conservative activist" who "wants to force colleges to hire more conservatives." Scott Jaschik, *More Criticism of Academic Bill of Rights* (Jan. 9, 2006), http://www.insidehighered.com/news/2006/01/09/resolutions. Another critic found the bill to be "a very dangerous incursion on academic freedom" and opined that nobody "should ever be forced to conform to the kind of simplistic, two-sided worldview that Horowitz is, in effect, trying to pass into law." Graham Larkin, *What's Not to Like About the Academic Bill of Rights?* (Sept. 22, 2004), http://www.aaup-ca.org/Larkin_abor.html.

[146] "Public universities serve a distinctive role in a modern democratic society. Like all specialized government entities, they must make countless decisions about how to allocate resources in pursuit of their role. Some of those decisions will be controversial; many will have differential effects across populations; virtually all will entail value judgments of some kinds. As a general matter, courts should respect universities' judgments and let them manage their own affairs." *Christian Legal Society*, 130 S. Ct. at 2997-98 (Stevens, J. concurring).

[147] *See Hacker v. Hacker*, 522 N.Y.S.2d 768, 769-70 (1987); *Philip Crosby Assn., Inc. v. St. Bd. of Indep. Colleges*, 506 So.2d 490, 492 (Fla. App. 5th Dist. 1987). "In brief, it does not appear

The rise of proprietary colleges has captured a great deal of attention,[148] but other major changes are also afoot in American higher education. The rapid growth of virtual and distance learning, developments in modern library science, the sheer pervasiveness of technology and digital learning, the expansion of higher education learning theory, the change in the demographics of learners, the constitutional and contractual law overlay in higher education, the evolving value of higher education to individuals in society, and the new discourse over what a degree is and what it means to achieve in higher education—all these and other factors constitute a revolutionary moment in what it means to be a college.

The law provides some intriguing answers to issues of what an institution of higher learning is. Expect more to come.

On one hand, freedom of speech and association issues are clearly implicated when the state attempts to regulate the use of the word "college." Courts are sensitive to issues of censorship, prior restraint, and the potential chilling effect of a law when they consider whether someone or something can use the word to identify its activities.[149] There may or may not be a per se First Amendment right to call an entity a college,[150] but there are constitutionally protected rights associated with assembly and speech (core activities of a college).[151] It is probably a little overbroad—but not far off—to assume that you may call yourself a college.[152]

---

that the common definition of the term 'college' has changed much since Judge Lehman spoke for the Court of Appeals in 1941." *Hacker*, 522 N.Y.S.2d at 770.

[148] "The Department is proposing to require proprietary institutions of higher education and postsecondary vocational institutions to provide prospective students with their programs' graduation and job placement rates, and that colleges provide the Department with information that will allow it to determine student debt levels and incomes after program completion." Justin Hamilton, *Obama Administration Proposes Student Aid Rules to Protect Borrowers and Taxpayers; Key Elements of Gainful Employment on a Separate Track* (June 16, 2010), http://www.ed.gov/news/student-aid-rules-protect-borrowers-and-taxpayers. *See, e.g., Proposed Rule Links Federal Student Aid to Loan Repayment Rates and Debt-to-Earnings Levels for Career College Graduates, supra* note 124. As of August 8, 2010, the proposed rule, based on congressional hearings, was still up for notice and comment at 34 C.F.R. 668 (July 26, 2010).

[149] *See, e.g., Crosby v. Florida State Board*, 506 So. 2d 490, 492 (1987).

[150] *See Plano v. Fountain Gate Ministries*, 654 S.W.2d 841, 843 (1983).

[151] "Congress shall make no law respecting an establishment of religion, or prohibiting the free exercise thereof; or abridging the freedom of speech, or of the press; or the right of the people peaceably to assemble, and to petition the Government for a redress of grievances." U.S. Const. amend. I.

[152] It seems plausible that you might be able to call yourself "Mr. College" or "Ms. College" under some circumstances.

Moreover, the use of the term "college" to describe oneself may not have the desired effect in some contexts. As institutions of higher education in Florida have learned, colleges will be treated like other businesses under Florida tort law.[153] Sometimes higher education achieves special concessions; other times, it does not.[154] It is conceivable that calling oneself or one's organization a college could be a deceptive or fraudulent trade practice, but a legal plebiscite hardly exists against that sort of thing.[155] On the other hand, in a legal system so permissive of what a college can be, it is interesting that there are few South Harmon Institutes of Technology.[156]

The freedom to be any college you want to be is somewhat illusory in a world that requires accreditation or the equivalent in order for students to qualify for financial aid. Over the years, accreditation became a much more powerful tool than the court system for determining what defines a college. Theoretically, a college could be "radical" and accredited or could survive without accreditation, but neither scenario is common. With regard to the former, courts have applied Catch 22-like logic when alternative colleges have attempted to achieve accreditation or its equivalent.[157] For the most part, colleges themselves control the accreditation process and, therefore, have played a strong role in limiting innovation—at least until the rise of for-profit institutions. There are some notable examples of colleges surviving and thriving without accreditation, but to do so an institution of higher education needs massive donations or must offer education in an extremely cost-effective way with a clear path to developing job skills or opportunities.[158]

---

[153] *See Nova Southeastern Univ. v. Gross*, 758 So. 2d 86, 90 (Fla. 2000) (holding the university liable in tort when a student was injured while participating in an internship off campus and the university knew the site was unreasonably dangerous but gave no warning to the student).

[154] *See, e.g., Plano*, 654 S.W.2d 841; *Janzen v. Atiyeh*, 743 P.2d 765, 768-69 (Or. App. 1987).

[155] *See In re Name Change of Handley*, 736 N.E.2d 125, 126 (Ohio Prob. 2000) (finding the request of a man to change his name to Santa Claus to be against public policy, as allowing him to represent himself as Santa Claus would mislead children in the community and lead to a potential for fraud and misrepresentations to society; thus, the name change was not reasonable or proper).

[156] In the motion picture *Accepted*, the main character decides to create his own unique college after being rejected from several traditional colleges. Students attending this fictional college create their own majors and classes. (Universal 2006).

[157] *See Beth Rochel Seminary v. Bennett*, 825 F.2d 478, 481-82 (D.C. Cir. 1987). In *Beth Rochel*, a rabbinical program for females was forced to seek accreditation (or the equivalent) from the very all male programs which had not historically accepted such an alternative program.

[158] *See supra* note 121.

Traditionally, accreditation processes were not considered central to student affairs practice. However, as accreditation standards become more directly linked to outcomes and assessment of outcomes (such as time to graduation, demonstrated competencies, and debt-to-outcome ratios),[159] student affairs administration will become more integral to self-study processes and accreditation processes.

THE RISE OF CONTRACTUAL RELATIONSHIPS WITH STUDENTS

Considerable authority exists for the proposition that the relationship between students and institutions of higher education is contractual at both public and private institutions. Certainly, there is quite a bit more to the relationship than a contract—institutions and students are complexly related through public law and other private law norms and concepts.[160] Nonetheless, private contract law plays a crucial role in higher education practice. The law prefers to style student private law rights under the rubric of contract law rather than accepting the idea that the college/student relationship is inherently special vis-à-vis tort law. The law's preference for the private law–contract paradigm has important implications for safety law on campus, because courts rarely imagine safety obligations arising from contracts in the higher education context. (See *infra* Chapter 3.)

Saying that the institution/student relationship is contractual is a complex assertion for several reasons. First, we have to develop a sense of what a contract is. Second, the law of contracts is complex and has been evolving rapidly in the same period that higher education has been adopting contract paradigms. Third, it is not entirely clear that contract law adapts easily to the institution/student relationship. It may be that contract law is not the appropriate private law paradigm at all for higher education—just the best legal category of thought that can be tailored for use in this area.

---

[159] *See supra* note 124.
[160] See discussion *infra* "What Is a Contract?"

What Is a Contract?

Contract law is the law enforcing promises; tort law deals with accidents. People make many promises—some they do not intend to keep. Not all promises are legally binding; the law of contracts identifies the ones that are enforceable.

A great deal of the law of contracts is devoted to the role of the Sorting Hat in *Harry Potter*.[161] In classical contract law, the creation of a valid contract required a certain amount of magic and many formalities:

1. An offer had to be made and accepted on mirrored terms. Even a slight variation of terms between "I accept" and "I offer" would trigger, at best, a counteroffer. Modification was rejection of the original offer.[162]

2. Offers had to be accepted only in the way they were transmitted.[163]

3. "Consideration" or its equivalent was considered essential to the formation of a contract. The law required that parties show they were serious about their promises. This meant that you had to show that you were giving up something of value (usually) or conveying some benefit to another to get them to deal.[164] Alternatively, some contracts could be executed under seal.[165] The law evolved to recognize that one might also make some promises that would cause others to behave to their detriment, and this would work as a substitute for consideration.[166]

4. An enforceable contract had to specify key items such as price, terms, duration, quantity, and timing.

It is easy to see why classical contract law became burdensome in a modern industrial society. Think of the myriad transactions you were involved in just this week: "Would you like fries and a hamburger and a medium drink?" "Why, yes,

---

[161] J. K. Rowling, *Harry Potter and the Sorcerer's Stone* (Scholastic 1998). The Sorting Hat sorts incoming students into various houses at wizard school.
[162] E. Allan Farnsworth, *Contracts* (4th ed. 2004).
[163] *Id.*
[164] *Id.*
[165] *Id.*
[166] E. Allan Farnsworth, *Contracts* § 2.19 (2nd ed. 1990).

I would like fries and a hamburger." "Are you counter offering?" No one bargains like this, especially with respect to common goods. Most contracts today are a lot of "okays" and nods and grudging acquiescence, and then they forget your apple pie.

In the 20th century, the law of contracts evolved to accommodate the rapid increase in consumer transactions and standardized take-it-or-leave-it deals. The law of contracts (and the law of torts) also had to deal increasingly with abuses in the transactional world. Some abuses arose because of vast differences in bargaining power between parties.

Contract law now features special rules for transactions involving goods,[167] which relaxes many historical formalities and permits transacting parties to work within the framework of their ordinary course of dealing. An entire theory of contract law is dedicated to contracts of adhesion (take-it-or-leave-it deals) and unconscionable and inappropriate contractual terms and behavior.[168] A growing body of relational contract theory recognizes that many areas of transactional activity are more relational than oriented toward discrete one-time transactions. Contract law is increasingly more concerned with expectations and mutual understanding at the center of such relations.[169]

The law of contracts is not fully formed in higher education law; other areas of transactional behavior are more clearly regulated, and very little contract law theory is directed at higher education law. Hazel Beh, the leading theorist in this area, has stated that "traditional judicial deference toward institutions of higher education makes courts reluctant to apply general contract principles liberally. . . ."[170]

In most states, the debate continues regarding what exactly creates and forms the college contract. Many, but not all, states hold that the student handbook and other publications are part of the contract with students.[171] Some courts have held that the college contract can cover many things, includ-

---

[167] U.C.C. §§ 2-102-725 (2002).
[168] E. Allan Farnsworth, *Contracts* § 4.26 (2nd ed. 1990).
[169] Ian Roderick Macneil, *The Many Futures of Contract*, 47 S. Cal. L. Rev. 691, 694 (1974).
[170] Hazel Beh, *Student Versus University: The University's Implied Obligations of Good Faith and Fair Dealing*, 59 Md. L.R. 183, 197, n. 67 (2000).
[171] *See Atria v. Vanderbilt Univ.*, 142 Fed. Appx. 246, 255 (6th Cir. 2005); *Havlik v. Johnson & Wales Univ.*, 509 F.3d 25 (1st Cir. 2007); *Johnson v. Lincoln Christian College*, 501 N.E.2d 1380 (Ill. App. 4th Dist. 1987).

ing, for example, course of dealing.[172] Unlike other transactions of similar size, duration, length, and importance (e.g., purchase of a car, a house, a boat, or life insurance), the college contract is not a clear preprinted transaction with detailed elaboration of mutual rights and responsibilities. Instead, it often resembles Calvinball,[173] that old game between Calvin and Hobbes in which they made up the rules as they went along. The law has evolved away from a period when double secret probation was acceptable,[174] but not as far from caveat emptor[175] as other similarly important transactions have. The college contract begins and ends somewhat indefinitely, has many indefinite terms, is not entirely devoid of form but is not entirely formed, and remains one of contract law's odd ducks.

Student affairs administrators can draw several practical conclusions from this discussion:

1. Contractual relations with students are strongly one-sided. For example, you may alter your student handbook—even the student rules—with little more than reasonable notice, and not always even that.

2. Courts will likely require substantial performance, which means that an institution of higher education can fail to perform some of its contractual obligations and still not be in breach of contract.[176]

3. Specific contracts for specific auxiliary services (such as a housing contract) will be interpreted much like analogous contracts of that type in the business world.

4. Courts have shown more interest in offering students meaningful contractual rights in specific types of cases (most notably situations involving promises relating to graduation or certificate requirements) and student discipline systems. Breach of contract arguments are

---

[172] *See* note 171, *supra.*
[173] *See* Wikipedia, *Calvin and Hobbes: Calvinball,* http://en.wikipedia.org/wiki/Calvin_and_Hobbes#cite_ref-45 (last visited Aug. 8, 2010).
[174] *See Anthony v. Syracuse Univ.* 224 A.D. 487, 489-91 (N.Y. App. Div. 4th Dept. 1928).
[175] Caveat emptor is Latin for "let the buyer beware"; it is a legal doctrine that holds that "purchasers buy at their own risk." *Black's Law Dictionary* (8th ed., Thompson/West 2004).
[176] *See Schaer, supra* note 130, 735 N.E.2d at 381.

increasingly common in the latter area, perhaps because public law has been reluctant to provide clear guidelines for student discipline-process rights. As discussed later in Chapter 4, institutions of higher education once routinely won discipline cases; now they win in non-routine ways, if at all.[177]

5.   Student affairs administrators must be aware of contract law's close cousin, the law of agency, which deals with who has authority to bind in contract and when. Usually a job description and the ordinary course of operations informs the student affairs administrator when he or she does or does not have such authority. However, one of the great challenges in student affairs administration is dealing with employees acting *ultra vires*—beyond the scope of their authority. This topic is discussed in Chapter 6.

Can Contract Law Adequately Express the Institution/Student Relationship?

Several courts that have used the contract law paradigm to analyze student/institution of higher education relationship issues have noted that this contract is unique and not like an ordinary commercial transaction.[178] Can contract law capture and describe the relationship between colleges and students?

For some time, a significant amount of attention has been devoted to the increase in consumer relationships between students and colleges.[179] Congress also has increasingly taken up consumer rights regulation, including textbook cost issues.[180] Perhaps the greatest change in American higher education law has been the drift away from religious instruction—with strong charitable and familial overtones—to a transactional focus.[181]

---

[177] *See Than*, 188 F. 3d at 635; Lake, *supra* note 3, at 208-15.

[178] While courts have recognized that the relationship between both public and private universities and students is contractual, "they have recognized that contract law should not be strictly applied." *Kashmiri*, 156 Cal. App. 4th at 824.

[179] Peter F. Lake, *Will Your College Be Sued for Educational Malpractice?*, Chronicle of Higher Education (Aug. 11, 2009), *available at* http://chronicle.com/article/Education-Malpractice-Ma/47980/.

[180] Hazel Beh, *supra* note 170; Don Troop, *Will a New Federal Rule Do the Trick?*, Chronicle of Higher Education (June 6, 2010), *available at* http://chronicle.com/article/New-Rule-to-Curb-Textbook-C/65788/.

[181] *See Williams*, 530 F.3d at 586-89.

The courts are hesitant to go too far too quickly with this. The concerns in this area include fear of flooding the courts with new cases; worries that a heavy transactional focus will make education more oppositional, ruining the very thing the law is trying to protect; and concerns over academic freedom (e.g., cases arguing for educational malpractice).[182]

Is higher education truly a contract/bargain at all? My colleague, the eminent uniform commercial code scholar Bradford Stone, once told me that education is the only deal in which the consumer wants to be cheated.[183] Higher education is highly connected to the effort students put into it. Moreover, we want professors and students to take risks, grow, fail, and succeed—a striving that defies the usual sense of promising and contracting. Perhaps the most we can promise is to be facilitative and to do whatever we can to create conditions under which students have a reasonable chance to grow and learn. Is this the sort of promise we can breach and for which we can sue in contract law? Should it be?

Postmillennial student affairs administrators live and work at a time when images of commodification, consumerism, transactionalism, and commercialization are at an all-time high in western education. This situation is partially due to the fact that the cost of higher education has been shifted to learners and has increased dramatically in a short period. The law is acutely aware of this shift, which accounts for the rise in accountability even as the law hesitates to impose liability on institutions of higher education.

Conclusion

The history of higher education law is dominated by the rapid rise in the application of legal categories originally developed for other social institutions. Very little modern higher education law was developed specifically to fit higher education.

In many ways, the law slapped together a framework for conceptualizing higher education law without creating a truly independent (or, in some cases, truly appropriate) body of law. The leading treatise in the field—a monumental work—is *The Law of Higher Education*,[184] but the title is slightly misleading.

---

[182] *See, e.g., Ross v. Creighton Univ.*, 957 F.2d 410, 414-15 (7th Cir. 1992).

[183] If you want to understand the basics of commercial law relating to the sale of goods, see Bradford Stone and Kristin David Adams, *The Uniform Commercial Code in a Nutshell* (7th ed., West 2008).

[184] William A. Kaplin & Barbara A. Lee, *The Law of Higher Education* (4th ed., Jossey-Bass 2007).

Most law applicable to higher education was adapted from elsewhere; and the framework for higher education law is a construct of various doctrines, principles, statutes, and so on. Higher education law is not a coherently designed system like, for example, banking or bankruptcy law. Our identity crisis under law is compounded by the fact that institutions of higher education have often resisted being conceptualized under law,[185] the way that wizards resist Muggle rule in the Harry Potter books.[186] We remember our prejuridical world and often long for that time—sometimes to the point of rewriting history.[187]

Higher education has evolved incrementally as opposed to holistically and in response to crisis as opposed to proactively. Unlike the computer HAL in "2001 Space Odyssey," we have not yet fully achieved consciousness in the law, which affects our identity, our integrity, and our accountability.

Higher education is still in its infancy with the law. Consider the fact that higher education has spent just 50 years or so experiencing law in a meaningful way. Other social institutions have been working for centuries, or even longer, under law. The current generation of student affairs administrators is among the first to experience student affairs practice in a world permeated with law and legal accountability. If you are just entering the practice of student affairs administration, congratulations and welcome to one of the best careers on the planet! You might work in higher education at a time in the future when the law of higher education has matured to a new level. If so, you will have watched higher education being born into an age of law and legal accountability, making your generation one of the most significant in the history of student affairs practice.

---

[185] *See* Bickel & Lake, *supra* note 2.

[186] J. K. Rowling, *Harry Potter and the Sorcerer's Stone* (Scholastic 1998), J. K. Rowling, *Harry Potter and the Chamber of Secrets* (Scholastic 1999), J. K. Rowling, *Harry Potter and the Prisoner of Azkaban* (Scholastic 1999), J. K. Rowling, *Harry Potter and the Goblet of Fire* (Scholastic 2000), J. K. Rowling, *Harry Potter and the Order of the Phoenix* (Scholastic 2003), J. K. Rowling, *Harry Potter and the Half-Blood Prince* (Scholastic 2005), J. K. Rowling, *Harry Potter and the Deathly Hallows* (Scholastic 2007).

[187] "Modern commentators make far too much out of *in loco parentis*, and the idea of a legal return to *in loco parentis* is illogical and fanciful, and demonstrates a lack of understanding of tort and higher education law." Lake, *supra* note 3, at 32.

CHAPTER 3

MANAGING THE INSTITUTION
OF HIGHER EDUCATION
ENVIRONMENT

PART I: SAFETY, RISK MANAGEMENT,
WELLNESS, AND SECURITY

The task of managing a modern higher education environment is daunting. Institutions of higher education often subdivide the task into student life and academic components—an artificial, collapsing, but historical divide that is reflected in the division in this book between Chapters 3 and 4. This chapter focuses primarily on the law related to physical danger, wellness, premises security, and so on. Chapter 4 focuses primarily on issues associated with the integrity of the learning process, accountability for core academic mission delivery, and discipline. The modern institution of higher education realizes that these are not distinct or independent tasks. Success or failure in one of these tasks correlates with success or failure on others. Institutions of higher education approach the task of managing an education environment holistically and environmentally, and the law has been progressing in this direction as well.

The principal physical and wellness risks that students encounter involve vehicular transportation, particularly automobiles; violence; self-inflicted injury; alcohol- and drug-related risk; and risks associated with participating in sports and activities. Alcohol risk connects to most of the other risks students face—it is associated strongly with every major negative outcome on campus. For the modern institution of higher education, all risk roads lead to alcohol, although it is possible to identify other risk factors in student affairs practice. A campus that successfully combats high-risk alcohol use will likely be safer, more academically sound, and less litigious.

The law of safety in any environment tends to evolve in response to core risks associated with that environment. American safety law in general in the post-World War II period has evolved primarily in response to physical risk associated with automobiles, medical practice, and pharmaceutical products. Similarities exist between institution of higher education risk and background social risk, and the evolution of law relating to safety in both spheres has been similar. For example, our core risk—alcohol risk—is one of the risks that the law has struggled most with in society at large. However, the law as applied to institutions of higher education has been influenced heavily by our particular educational environments. For example, laws imposing responsibility potentially compromise academic freedom.

In addition, the law of safety responsibility in the United States has been evolving rapidly along a dialectical continuum from enterprise responsibility (in which a business or actor bears the costs of its risks) to personal accountability (in which individuals are responsible for their own choices in behavior). This has been the theoretical essence of so-called "tort reform."[1] The path of the law has influenced higher education in interesting ways. Many courts simply equate institutions of higher education with businesses;[2] however, unlike other busi-

---

[1] *See generally* Kenneth S. Abraham, *What Is a Tort Claim? An Interpretation of Contemporary Tort Reform*, 51 Md. L. Rev. 172 (1992); Joseph Sanders & Craig Joyce, *Off to the Races: The 1980s Tort Crisis and the Law Reform Process*, 27 Hous. L. Rev. 201 (1990); Michael J. Saks, *Do We Really Know Anything about the Behavior of the Tort Litigation System—And Why Not?* 140 U. Pa. L. Rev. 1147 (1992).

[2] *See Nova Southeastern Univ. v. Gross*, 758 So. 2d 86 (Fla. 2000) (higher education is a business and will be treated as such). The relationship between a student and university "is essentially the relationship between an adult who pays a fee for services, the student, and the provider of those services, the private university. The service rendered is the provision of an educational experience

nesses, a major purpose of higher education is to teach individual student responsibility and foster student growth. Still, much of the experience of a college student is facilitated and crafted by the institution. So, for example, personal accountability must at least nod to the reality that living in doubles or triples is a fact of college life and not fully a student "choice." The law of higher education is constantly torn between holding students responsible for their decisions and creating space for them to grow, and applying ordinary principles of business accountability.

Student affairs administrators should also realize that the law is not a monolith. The law, particularly safety law, evolves in response to risks presented and greater social forces.[3] For instance, institutions of higher education should keep close watch in the coming decades for potential overhauls in American safety law in response to recently adopted medical health care legislation: America's safety law is very active in part because victims of accidents historically have been forced to sue in tort to fully recover their medical bills. National health care may change that to some extent: Large social reform may precipitate significant changes in safety law.

OVERVIEW OF AMERICAN SAFETY LAW

Lawyers have a peculiar way of discussing and conceptualizing safety and accidents. The language system lawyers use to discourse about and conceptualize safety law is quite well settled, even if it is not always precise. There is a certain agreed-upon level of precision *and* ambiguity in legal safety language. Like any language system, the law-language for safety, risk, and accidents has idioms and terms of art that do not translate well into other languages.

When the law discusses safety issues, the primary dialect is the law of torts. Tort is a made-up word derived from the Latin word "tortus," describing twisting or breaking something.[4] (In civil law systems, which govern most of Europe, the law uses the word *delict* to describe much of what we call "torts."[5] The word

---

designed to lead to a college degree." *Id.* at 87.

[3] *See* Keeton, Page, R. Keeton, L. Sargentich & Henry J. Steiner, *Tort and Accident Law* (2d ed., West 1989).

[4] Answers Corp., *Answers.com: Tort* (2010), http://www.answers.com/topic/tort (last visited Jan. 31, 2011).

[5] "Delict" is defined as "[a] violation of the law; tort." *Black's Law Dictionary* (8th ed., Thomp-

derives from Roman law principles.[6]) The law of torts is broad and includes rules for intentional acts causing harm, product liability, certain forms of so-called strict liability, and—most important for student affairs administrators—rules for negligence, which refers to causing harm from the failure to use reasonable care.[7] The law of negligence is the workhorse of the tort system generally and dominates the higher education safety law landscape.

Negligence law in its current form is about 100 years old; it has formed and reformed in the decades since World War II. Many unresolved issues exist in negligence law (some of which are discussed in this chapter), and jurisdictions disagree about some rules and how to resolve some issues. Lawyers often speak of "majority" or "minority" rules or "emerging trends" to describe these differences. However, agreement is widespread on many core concepts, so do not let border skirmishes mislead you into thinking a civil war exists. The classic negligence formula is as follows:

---

son/West 2004).

[6] Encyclopedia Britannica, *available at* http://www.britannica.com/EBchecked/topic/156569/delict (last visited Aug. 11, 2010).

[7] This chapter focuses primarily on the law of negligence, although student affairs administrators may encounter other forms of tort liability including vicarious liability, defamation, invasion of privacy, and intentional infliction of emotional distress, some of which are discussed *infra*.

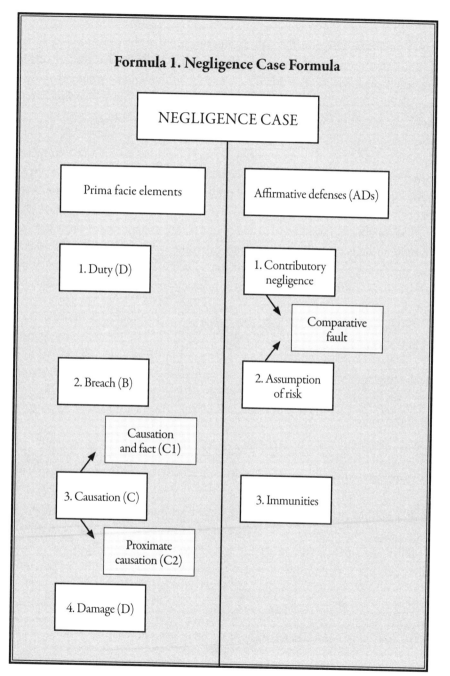

Formula 1. Negligence Case Formula

To win a negligence case, a plaintiff must successfully prove each element of a prima facie case, usually with a preponderance of the evidence. Thus, the plaintiff must establish that the defendant owed a legal duty that the defendant breached, and that the defendant's negligence in fact and proximately caused the plaintiff harm—a type of harm, called *damage*, that the law compensates. Evidence need not be beyond a reasonable doubt—it must only tip in favor of the plaintiff.

But that is not all. The plaintiff must survive a legal counterattack from the defendant, who can defeat or diminish liability (or erect other barriers, such as additional procedural requirements) by successfully asserting, with a preponderance of the evidence, affirmative defenses such as contributory fault on the part of the plaintiff, the fact that the plaintiff assumed a risk, or some form of immunity, such as government immunity or immunities arising from workers' compensation statutes.[8] A defendant can also attack a plaintiff's prima facie case, which is a form of defense, but not necessarily the same as asserting affirmative defenses.

Thus, liability (L) in negligence can be expressed roughly by the following simple formula:

Formula 2. Formula for Determining Liability

$$D+B+C(C1+C2)+D-ADs=L$$

Formula 2 contains an important lesson: It is hard for a plaintiff to win a negligence case outright—several moving parts must work together to establish liability. Despite what you may glean from media stories, in negligence law some accidents just happen, and no one is legally liable.[9] Often, plaintiffs are just aim-

---

[8] *See* discussion of affirmative defenses, *infra*.
[9] See, for example, *Jordan v. Jordan*, 257 S.E.2d 761 (Va. 1979), in which Mrs. Jordan ran over Mr. Jordan when she backed up the family vehicle. For unknown reasons, Mr. Jordan was crouching behind the car. Mrs. Jordan did not check her rearview mirror. A reasonable person would normally look in a rearview mirror to ensure that no object or person was immediately behind the

ing to win technical victories on one or another element or on an affirmative defense in hopes of prolonging the case or moving it forward procedurally. If they are successful, the case may have a higher settlement value, all things being equal.

At this point, substantive law and procedural law intersect: Defendants often want to win cases at the level of a motion to dismiss or summary judgment, while plaintiffs hope for trials and favorable verdicts. Both sides face the possibility of appeals, usually from final determinations that seal a case.[10] The potential for appeal often helps determine the settlement value of a case as well.

Winning and losing outright are not usually on the table in civil litigation, although institutions of higher education used to win many cases decisively. Negligence litigation usually aims to move one party or another into a better settlement position. When you realize that the negligence system is actually a settlement formulation system, your perspective on the liability formula may shift. The liability formula has a settlement formula equivalent as follows:

Formula 3. Settlement Formula

Where $S(X)$=strength of argument:

$$S(D)+S(B)+S(C)+S(D)-S(ADs)=SV$$

Settlement value (SV) is a complex calculus of many factors, some of which (such as public perception) have little to do with potential liability. By focusing on the strengths and weaknesses of liability arguments, this formula captures the way lawyers reason and make arguments about the relative settlement value of their cases.[11]

---

vehicle, and clearly the operation of a motor vehicle is misfeasance. However, the court in *Jordan* pointed out that even if Mrs. Jordan had looked in the rearview mirror, she would not have seen Mr. Jordan crouching behind the vehicle. Motorists are not required to patrol the perimeter of their vehicles before backing up. Therefore, Mrs. Jordan's conduct scientifically caused Mr. Jordan's injury but was not, legally speaking, a cause and fact of his injury.

[10] Fed. R. App. Prac. 4(a).

[11] After you have read this chapter, try this tabletop exercise: Plug facts into "elements" and discuss how the new facts have just affected the settlement value in the scenario. You can do the same by

The mathematical heuristic—like any—makes certain assumptions but works roughly most of the time. If you are trying to shoot a BB gun at a tree, these three formulas work very well; however, if you want to launch a spacecraft to the moon, the formulae get a little more complicated.

Imagining negligence law formulaically is not the only way to understand it and may be off-putting to those who are not mathematically inclined. Some additional information can help legally untrained student affairs administrators move a step closer to understanding the law. First, it will be helpful to consider the elements of negligence in a little more depth to gain greater understanding of how lawyers conceptualize and discourse about safety, risk, and responsibility. Second, keep in mind that "lawyer's language" is designed to work with accidents and the unpredictable. The law of torts is an attempt to create a precise language describing exactly that which is imprecise and unpredictable. At times, negligence law and its elements sound deceptively simple, but they are deviously complex in application. What else could we expect from the "law of accidents," which is just a little oxymoronic, no?

Duty

Let's start with the element of duty. In negligence law, if no legal duty is owed, there is no liability. No-duty arguments are decisive if they are successful. However, they have fallen out of favor in the modern negligence system, which prefers positioning parties for settlement over all-or-nothing litigation victories in court (much to the dismay of institutions of higher education, which were spoiled in earlier legal periods when no-duty arguments were common and likely to succeed).

Duty in negligence law is very simple to grasp on one level and maddeningly complex on another. Think of duty like a dive in the Caribbean. At 15 to 20 feet, the crystal-clear water warmly embraces you as beautiful tropical fish swim by, but at 1,000 feet, you experience nitro-

---

imagining a legal change (such as a new ruling on legal "duty") in your jurisdiction. Or you can imagine cases from other jurisdictions that are relevant to the facts of your case and discuss how these cases affect the settlement value in your jurisdiction. Keep in mind that settlement value is also determined by factors other than liability. Formula 3 is only part of the calculus of determining settlement value, although in most cases it is a dominant part.

gen narcosis and think and you are at Thanksgiving dinner in a swimming pool.

Let's start with the shallow dive. (If you find yourself getting in too deep at any point in negligence law, swim back to shallow waters.)

"Duty" is essentially a legal construct of the 20th century; it has been used by judges to keep cases from going to a jury, largely out of concern that juries might disrupt businesses with unwieldy verdicts or that the courts might be flooded with huge numbers of cases. Thus, we say that the existence of duty is a question of law for the court (the judge), not a jury, to decide.[12] Duty is a legal gatekeeper—a way to weed certain cases out early on. Some cases do not belong in court or in front of a jury. The role of juries is to determine facts, but not every case needs to be resolved at the level of factual findings.

Duty has also served in most jurisdictions, to varying degrees, as an analytical vehicle to balance and weigh a variety of policy factors that influence whether a matter should be in court or in front of a jury.[13] Foremost among these factors is foreseeability—whether the type of accident that occurred was reasonably foreseeable in the context of the risks associated with the defendant's conduct or activity that caused the injury.[14]

Many courts have also considered a wide variety of factors first articulated by the California Supreme Court in a series of key post-World War II deci-

---

[12] *See Palsgraf v. Long Island R. Co.*, 162 N.E. 99, 101 (N.Y. 1928); *see also McCain v. Fl. Power Corp.*, 593 So. 2d 500 (Fla. 1992).

[13] *See* Peter F. Lake, *Common Law Duty in Negligence Law: The Recent Consolidation of a Consensus on the Expansion of Analysis of Duty and the New Conservative Liability Limiting Use of Policy Considerations*, 34 S.D. L. Rev. 1503 (1997).

[14] *See Pitre v. Employers Liability Assurance Corp.*, 234 So. 2d 847 (La. App. 1st Cir. 1970); *see also McCain*, 593 So. 2d at 502–4. "The duty element of negligence focuses on whether the defendant's conduct foreseeably created a broader 'zone of risk' that poses a general threat of harm to others. . . . Where a defendant's conduct creates a *foreseeable zone of risk,* the law generally will recognize a duty placed upon defendant either to lessen the risk or see that sufficient precautions are taken to protect others from the harm that the risk poses." *Id.*

sions.[15] Recently, the view of duty as a "sum total of policy considerations"[16] has evolved even farther into the controversial position taken by the *Restatement (Third) of Torts* that duty usually should be presumed and that it is the defen-

---

[15] *See* Lake, *supra* note 13, at 1516–19:

> The effects of the decisions of the California Supreme Court during the period of the 1960's–1970's cannot be (and have not been) underestimated. Cases like *Dillon v. Legg, Rowland v. Christian, Greenman v. Yuba Power Products, Inc., Biakanja v. Irving,* and *Tarasoff v. Board of Regents,* have altered the landscape of American tort law by either becoming the majority rule, the basis of the majority rule, the modern trend, or the baseline from which we judge the development of the law, including tort reform. These cases did a great deal to expand the reach of tort law, particularly negligence law and its paradigm of reasonableness, and may have created their own backlash in the more conservative and tort-reform oriented moments of the 1980's and 1990's. These cases have an unmistakable liability-expanding potential and are often evaluated from that frame of reference. . . .
>
> . . . *Dillon, Rowland, Biakanja,* and particularly *Tarasoff* have become famous and widely cited for several foundational points with respect to duty. The analysis of questions of duty generally espoused by these cases has become, in one form or another, the single most dominant approach in American decisional law and is an analysis that drew heavily from [Judge] Cardozo and [Professor] Prosser ([and Professor] Green).
>
> *Dillon, Rowland, Biakanja,* and *Tarasoff* are now commonly relied upon in support of one or some combination of the following propositions:
>
> 1. Analysis of negligence liability begins with the question of duty.
> 2. Duty is not sacrosanct; it is a changeable concept.
> 3. A statement that a duty is owed is a conclusion that given these circumstances and conditions liability should (or should not) attach.
> 4. The determination of duty is based upon consideration of a number of factors (often, but not necessarily, called policy factors).
> 5. Such "major considerations" include:
>   1. foreseeability;
>   2. degree of certainty that plaintiff's injury occurred;
>   3. closeness of conduct and injury;
>   4. moral blame;
>   5. the policy of preventing future harm;
>   6. burden and consequences of imposing a duty on the defendant and the community; and
>   7. insurance cost, availability, and prevalence.
>
> Propositions 1 through 4 are predominantly propositions that were asserted by Prosser (Green) and hence reflect what I refer to as the Prosser (Green) approach to questions of duty. These propositions in whole or in part form the basis of an overwhelming consensus on the analysis of duty which has congealed in American courts in the last few decades. Although the prominence of the questions of duty itself and the foreseeability factor can also be traced also to Cardozo, Prosser was critical of Cardozo's typical unwillingness to explicitly analyze the factors underlying his duty determinations (footnotes omitted).

[16] *See Rowland v. Christian,* 443 P.2d 561 (Cal. 1968).

dant's burden to show that no duty is owed.[17] This is a somewhat radical idea that few courts have accepted to date, but it is plausible largely because, in many instances, a legal duty is indeed owed by someone to an injured plaintiff. However, most courts have been reluctant to give up the power to weed out cases in traditional ways, especially in a new and more conservative era in tort law.[18]

One area of duty law is of limited significance in the negligence system generally but has gained great significance in higher education law. (Here's where it gets hard.)

From a larger legal perspective, the evolution of the law of duty in higher education law is strange, particularly because of the unusual emphasis on "rescue rules." In negligence law generally, pockets of no-duty law have been shrinking. Courts have shifted to analyzing the *fault* of parties instead of using social policy arguments to protect the status of various entities or individuals via no-duty rules. No-duty law was once a very convenient way to protect certain groups or individuals from widespread liability; today, individual assessment—as opposed to status-based assessment—is more the norm in the law of torts. (However, see the discussion of immunities below). But one rarely used pocket of no-duty law has been shrink-resistant and has shown remarkable staying power—this is the law relating to the duty to rescue. American law traditionally has provided that there is no duty to rescue others, except under special circumstances. The law of rescue is a very small subset of the greater negligence system and is rarely invoked outside higher education law; however, in higher education law, it has become supremely important. Very strange, indeed.

Generations of law students have struggled with various murky distinctions in the law of rescue. In higher education law, weird compounds with weirder. (But trust me—we will sort this out.) Students learning American

---

[17] *Restatement (Third) of Torts* § 7 (2010). Section 7 states, "(a) An actor ordinarily has a duty to exercise reasonable care when the actor's conduct creates a risk of physical harm. (b) In exceptional cases, when an articulated countervailing principle or policy warrants denying or limiting liability in a particular class of cases, a court may decide that the defendant has no duty or that the ordinary duty of reasonable care requires modification." *Id.*

[18] *See* Lake, *supra* note 13, at 1527. "The relatively recent consolidation of consensus on Prosser (Green) notions of duty (many cases coming in the 80's and 90's) has, however, featured an intriguing turn. Prosser (Green) notions, and even California-influenced variants, have been used to limit liability and/or curtail the growth of liability law. Duty has thus been used in conservative ways." *Id.*

rescue law must distinguish "negative duty" from "affirmative duty," and "misfeasance" from "nonfeasance." Consider the "explanation" of these ideas in a treatise by a famous commentator:

> The starting point for a duty analysis in some areas of negligence law is the well established distinction between misfeasance, for which a duty is typically found, and nonfeasance, for which it usually is not. Professor Francis H. Bohlen explained . . . the difference well:

> "There is no distinction more deeply rooted in the common law and more fundamental than that between misfeasance and nonfeasance, between active misconduct working positive injury to others and passive in action, a failure to take positive steps to benefit others, or to protect them from harm not created by any wrongful act of the defendant. . . . [I]n the case of active misfeasance the victim is positively worse off as a result of the wrongful act. In cases of passive inaction plaintiff is in reality no worse off at all. His situation is unchanged; he is merely deprived of a protection which, had it been afforded him, would have benefitted him."

It is not always easy to distinguish between misfeasance and nonfeasance. Consider the case where the defendant told the decedent to jump into deep water, refusing to rescue him after realizing that he was about to drown. Although the court characterized this as a case of nonfeasance on the part of the defendant, it could also be seen as involving affirmative conduct by the defendant leading to the harm. Similarly, many other contexts such as the failure to make promised repairs, to arrest a drunken driver, or to inspect equipment can be portrayed as either inaction or an affirmative act that creates an unreasonable risk of harm to others. This distinction can be critical because the plaintiff's ability to recover damages often turns on whether the court characterizes the defendant's conduct as misfeasance or nonfeasance. To reiterate, in general, an actor is liable for affirmative acts that cause an unreasonable risk of harm, but not for nonfeasance.

The analysis is further complicated by the concept of *negligent omissions*, which are just a species of misfeasance. Misfeasance often consists of affirmative acts of misconduct—doing something the reasonable person would not do—such as firing a gun in the center of town. Misfeasance can also be shown by negligent omission— failing to do something that a reasonable person would do while engaged in other activity—such as not paying attention while driving. Either risk creating affirmative acts or risks creating omissions generally give rise to duty.[19]

Huh? To make this pretzel logic even more complicated, courts recognize exceptions to the nonfeasance rule that do create duty (discussed below). Welcome to the Galapagos Islands of tort law, which are *your* islands.

In modern American tort law, complex discussions about misfeasance or nonfeasance are almost entirely confined to discussions of the law of rescue. Rescue law is a very tiny subset of a much larger negligence system, but this type of "logic" is often used to justify broad legal propositions that are sometimes inaccurate or misleading, such as "[T]here is generally no duty to rescue a stranger in American law."[20] Courts have also used this rescue law logic to make statements to the effect that nonfeasance may raise questions of moral responsibility even if there are no legal duties.[21] Commentators have attributed the cold-bloodedness in American law (which is very unusual in the rest of the world[22]) to its prefer-

---

[19] John L. Diamond, Lawrence Levine & M. Stuart Madden, *Understanding Torts* 107–108 (3rd ed., Lexis Pub. 2007) (quoting Francis H. Bohlen, *The Moral Duty to Aid Others As a Basis of Tort Liability*, 56 U. Pa. L. Rev. 217, 219–20 (1908) and *Yania v. Bigan*, 155 A.2d 343 (Pa. 1959) (citations omitted)).

[20] *Union Pacific Railroad Co. v. Cappier*, 72 P. 281, 282 (Kan. 1903).

[21] *See* Diamond, *supra* note 19, at 115. "The clear general rule remains that a person does not have a duty to aid another. Courts have consistently refused to require a stranger to render assistance, even when faced with seemingly egregious examples of nonfeasance, and even when the person could have rendered aid with little risk or effort. Because this result appears to many as outrageous and immoral, few topics have generated more scholarship . . . to date as . . . commentators wrestle with why the Olympic swimmer can ignore a drowning child or a passerby can disregard a baby in front of an oncoming train." (citations omitted).

[22] John M. Adler, *Relying Upon the Reasonableness of Strangers: Some Observations about the Current State of Common Law Affirmative Duties to Aid or Protect Others*, 1991 Wis. L. Rev. 867; Richard A. Epstein, *A Theory of Strict Liability*, 2 J. Leg. Stud. 151 (1973); James A. Henderson, Jr., *Process Constraints in Tort*, 67 Cornell L. Rev. 901 (1982); William M. Landes & Richard A. Posner, *Salvors, Finders, Good Samaritans and Other Rescuers: An Economic Study of Law and*

ence for Anglo-Saxon individualism[23] and concerns over expanding liability too far and intruding on the rights of bystanders to go about their business.[24]

Most likely, however, this quirk in American law is a historical and jurisdictional anomaly. Before the American Revolution, English courts ran a system of justice for the king or queen in parallel with ecclesiastical courts, which enforced canonical law. Ecclesiastical courts did not keep records like other courts, which created gaps in the historical records. Recent evidence strongly suggests that English legal courts deferred jurisdiction over issues of Good Samaritan behavior to ecclesiastical courts; thus, there was essentially no evolution of a secular duty to rescue in English legal history. When the United States 'received' the law of England, it did not receive canonical or ecclesiastical principles, so enforcement of such duties fell into desuetude. Rescue law is the direct result of the unique history of the English legal system and its reformation into American law. The failure to properly think this through may be one of the great legal missteps in the transition from English colonies to an independent nation. The anomaly persists in large measure because very few real-world illustrations of duty to rescue principles exist.

However, duty to rescue factors heavily into higher education law. The unique business of higher education triggers a need to study the evolutionary path of creatures on the Galapagos Islands.[25]

Higher education safety law has been heavily influenced by the law of rescue for several reasons. First, the enterprise of higher education is not typically considered a physical-risk-generating enterprise, at least in its core mission. Delivering higher education is not like selling cars, food, or pharmaceuticals, or delivering medical services. Courts rarely see physical injury to students arising from *misfeasance* by institution of higher education administrators, although when

---

Altruism, 7 J. Leg. Stud. 83 (1978).

[23] *See Diamond, supra* note 19, at 108.

[24] *See* Bohlen*, supra* note 19, at 220.

[25] For those of you who are interested (and I am not sure why you would be), it was this esoteric area of the law that first drew me to higher education law. Before my involvement in higher education law, my scholarly research focused on affirmative duty law, joining the chorus of legal scholars who have argued for various forms of reformation of affirmative duty law in America. *See* Diamond, *supra* note 19, at 108 n. 7. I have always credited my colleague Robert D. Bickel, who recognized my interest in affirmative duty law, made the connection to higher education law, and encouraged me to move my work more overtly into the higher education field.

they do—as when a classroom exercise or program creates a physical hazard—courts have little trouble determining that a duty is owed (liability, of course, is another matter). Second, courts typically view physical injury to students as arising commonly from the misfeasance of *others* (including the student him- or herself) and/or otherwise arising only from the *non*feasance of an institution of higher education or administrator. College safety law is analytically skewed to affirmative duty analysis, which sets higher education apart from most other industries (in K–12 education, a student safety duty is widely accepted).

Analysis of affirmative duty is often excruciatingly complex. Distinctions such as that between misfeasance and nonfeasance may seem clear to scholars such as Francis Bohlen, but they are not terribly clear to anyone else. Student affairs administrators will rarely be in a position to know to a particular certainty whether a situation that risks or causes physical injury will result in the existence of legal duty. There are many examples of courts determining that institutions of higher education or administrators owe no legal duty when students are injured,[26] and lawyers may have some level of confidence that such determinations will naturally result. Student affairs administrators may also have some confidence that they or their institutions will not be held liable or face very large settlement values. But even here such knowledge is easier in hindsight, as there are also many examples of courts determining that a duty *is* owed.[27]

---

[26] *See Bash v. Clark Univ.*, 22 Mass. L. Rptr. 84 (Mass. Super. 2006).

[27] *See, e.g., Knoll v. Bd. of Regents of Univ. of Nebraska*, 601 N.W.2d 757 (Neb. 1999). The Supreme Court of Nebraska expanded the foreseeability analysis to a question of fact for the jury versus a question of law for the judge. *A.W. v. Lancaster Cty. Sch. Dist. 0001*, 2010 WL 2789339 (Neb. July 16, 2010) The Nebraska Supreme Court stated that "[t]he extent of foreseeable risk depends on the specific facts of the case and cannot be usefully assessed for a category of cases; small changes in the facts may make a dramatic change in how much risk is foreseeable. Thus, courts should leave such determinations to the trier of fact unless no reasonable person could differ on the matter." *Id.* In the *Knoll* case, a student was severely injured in a fraternity hazing incident. 601 N.W.2d at 759–65. The fall precipitating injuries to the student occurred off campus, and initially it may have appeared that the University of Nebraska would owe no duty to the student. *Id.* The Nebraska Supreme Court held that duty was owed; however, the University of Nebraska system settled the case for a mere $25,000—a fairly small settlement value in the torts system. *Id.* at 761–65.

Consider also the summation of recent case law and commentary preferred by the *Third Restatement of Torts*:

> (a) An actor in a special relationship with another owes the other a duty of reasonable care with regard to risks that arise within the scope of the relationship. (b) Special relationships giving rise to the duty provided in Subsection (a) include: . . .

Student affairs administrators must operate as if a duty were owed, even if no such duty is ultimately imposed. That may be the most important sentence in the entire book for student affairs administrators to read and comprehend.

It is increasingly advisable for student affairs administrators to shift their attention and efforts to providing reasonable care as opposed to attempting to avoid legal duty. No-duty arguments are for lawyers, not student affairs administrators. Student affairs administrators can have a high level of confidence that the strategy of pursuing reasonable efforts is likely to be protected in litigation.[28] Student affairs administrators should realize that operating with reasonable care does not itself create legal duty where none otherwise exists; nor does operating as if duty were owed trigger courts to determine that duty exists because of that hypothesis. Thinking about elephants will not conjure them. You do not "assume a duty" simply by being reasonable or reasonably operating under the assumption that you may be held accountable for your actions. It is theoretically possible that affirmative steps taken by student affairs administrators could be the predicate for assuming a duty; however, again, it is almost impossible for student affairs administrators to know which affirmative steps will be the ones that create duty. Indeed, in many situations where duty has been "assumed," student affairs administrators have already taken enough steps in combination with their institutions to create legal duty. To put it another way, legal lines of demarcation regarding the existence of duty are not workable for student affairs administrators in day-to-day practice. Moreover, there is a very real danger of guessing incorrectly and behaving unreasonably in trying to avoid a legal duty: that *will* get you sued.

---

(4) an employer with its employees who are: (a) in imminent danger; or (b) injured and thereby helpless.
Restatement (Third) of Torts: Liab. Physical Harm § 40 (2007).
Some courts find a special relationship between the university and its students. *See, e.g., Furek v. Univ. of Delaware*, 594 A.2d 506, 519–20 (Del. 1991) (finding a duty imposed upon the university when student protection is needed against dangerous acts by third parties or "where there is direct university involvement in, and knowledge of, certain dangerous practices of its students. . . ." However, the court acknowledged that the university does not have a duty to control its students "based *merely* on the university-student relationship."). In *Furek*, a student received severe burns during a hazing when the fraternity poured oven cleaner over his head. *Id.* See Cheryl M. Bailey, *Tort Liability of College, University, Fraternity, or Sorority for Injury or Death of a Member or Prospective Member by Hazing or Initiation Activity*, 68 A.L.R. 4th 228 (1989) for additional cases.
[28] Ironically, avoiding legal duty can sometimes be the predicate for a court to find it. *See, e.g., Nero v. Kansas State Univ.*, 861 P.2d 768 (Kan. 1993); *Tarasoff v. Regents of Univ. of Cal.*, 551 P.2d 334 (Cal. 1976).

Affirmative Duty Law and Compliance for Student Affairs Administrators

The law of affirmative duty has become singularly significant for institutions of higher education and student affairs administrators. Administrators are at a distinct disadvantage in this area of the law because it is so complex, and the law has not kept pace with changing expectations about higher education safety.

Affirmative duty law is the "black diamond slope" of safety law. As we shall see, institutions of higher education have no duty to protect students, except when they do. The complexity of duty law misdirects student affairs administrators; currently, student affairs administrators live in an age of *accountability* without significant *liability* risk, except in unusual circumstances. The existence (or not) of duty is a lawyer's challenge and should not be a major concern of student affairs practice, as it might have been in another generation (see bystander case law, discussed below). Many families and political leaders believe that institutions of higher education should make it their mission to provide a reasonably safe higher education learning environment. From a business model perspective, it is difficult to sell anything less, especially to parents who have raised their children in highly protective ways. A very large proportion of the college students of today grew up in a parenting/educational milieu in which safety expectations were at an all-time high. Most of them always wore safety helmets when they rode their bicycles, always wore safety belts in cars, and never ate anything but well-done hamburgers. Expectations for college safety, which often generate accountability for institutions and student affairs administrators, frequently outstrip legal requirements for safety—a tense dissonance and a politically volatile one.

Knowledge and foreseeability alone do not create duty. The first precept of the law of affirmative duty is that knowledge that another person is endangered does not itself create an affirmative duty to act for that person's benefit; that is, foreseeability alone is not enough.[29] Foreseeability is a necessary condition for duty but not a sufficient one; other factors must combine with foreseeability to create duty. Closely related to this precept is the axiom that the mere fact of an accident is not a sufficient predicate for the existence of duty—there must be more.[30]

---

[29] *See Restatement (Second) of Torts* § 314 (2010).
[30] *See, e.g., Gift v. Palmer*, 141 A.2d 408, 410 (Pa. 1958) (holding the defendant not liable for

The exceptions: Times when there is affirmative duty. Although mere knowledge of danger is not sufficient to create duty, courts will impose a duty under certain circumstances. Certain exceptions to the no-duty-to-rescue rule transform the institution of higher education from bystander to potentially responsible party. Many commentators believe that the exceptions have been eating up the rule.[31]

SPECIAL RELATIONSHIPS

Special relationships can create affirmative duty; however, what is legally special is quite complex and counterintuitive. Special relationships in the law are primarily certain kinds of *business* relationships.

In modern K–12 law, the student/school relationship is a special relationship, often referred to by the terms *in loco parentis.* This has never been the law of higher education, except when higher education institutions run special programs for K–12 students.[32] Courts consistently hold that college/student relationships are not legally special in and of themselves.

College students do enjoy certain legally special relationships with their institutions that do not arise from the college/student relationship *per se* but from other legally recognized relationships they have with their institutions. For instance, such relationships are usually present when a student is in a university-operated facility or a residential facility. The law recognizes a "business invitee" as a special relationship. When students come to campus facilities to pursue legitimate educational objectives, they are in a special relationship; the same is true when they are in a landlord/tenant relationship with the institution.[33] More or less, students enjoy the same legal protections on campuses that customers at shopping malls or hotels enjoy. The concept of a business relationship has been extended to those aspects of the college experience that are recognizably similar to other non-educational business activities as well; for example, climbing walls.

---

negligence when his car struck and killed a child in daylight, as no duty was owed).

[31] *See* Diamond, *supra* note 19, at § 8,02, 108 n. 7; *see also Restatement (Third) of Torts* § 37.

[32] "*Gott* directly analogized the powers to regulate and discipline college students to the authority vested in school boards over K–12 students." Peter F. Lake, *Beyond Discipline–Managing the Modern Higher Education Environment* 67 (Hierophant Enterprises, Inc. 2009) (citing *Gott v. Berea College*, 161 S.W. 204 (Ky. 1913)).

[33] *E.g., Mullins v. Pine Manor College*, 449 N.E.2d 331 (Mass. 1983).

Once a special relationship attaches, an institution of higher education typically owes a legal duty and, therefore, must provide reasonable care.[34] Most commonly in institution of higher education litigation cases, controversies arise over hidden or non-readily-observable defects or dangers on property that cause injury (such as improper maintenance[35]), or in providing reasonable security to prevent foreseeable criminal or unlawful behavior that can cause physical injury to students.[36]

Regarding the latter, the seminal and leading case *Mullins v. Pine Manor*[37] held that colleges must use reasonable care to protect students from foreseeable criminal assault on campus and in residential facilities.[38] This is now an almost universally accepted precept, but legal duties to provide safe campuses are relatively new.[39] Always keep in mind that it was only in the 1990s that the mission of campus safety began to shift nationally to protecting students instead of simply protecting campus property. Many jurisdictions consider foreseeability to be crucial in the imposition of such safety duties, often requiring the existence of previous similar incidents as a proxy for foreseeability.[40] Additionally, an institution of higher education might be in a position to foresee danger from knowledge that specific persons or groups have previously engaged in violent or highly dangerous actions.[41]

Nonetheless, the responsibility of an institution of higher education in this section arises from the business relationship with the victims. There must be at least a sufficient nexus between the commercial premises (e.g., campus,

---

[34] *E.g., id.*

[35] *E.g., Sandoval v. Bd. of Regents of New Mexico St. Univ.*, 403 P.2d 699, 700–1 (N.M. 1965).

[36] *Knoll*, 601 N.W.2d at 764–65.

[37] 449 N.E.2d 331 (Mass. 1983).

[38] *Id.* at 337.

[39] In addition, the Clery campus crime reporting act has increasingly shifted from a crime reporting bill to an omnibus campus safety act. See *infra*.

[40] *See Kline v. 1500 Massachusetts Ave. Apartment Corp.*, 439 F.2d 477 (D.C. Cir. 1970) (finding that the landlord has the duty to protect a tenant from third party criminal assaults in common areas of an apartment building; for example, with regard to previous criminal acts in the building); *see also Thompson v. Skate America, Inc.*, 540 S.E.2d 123 (2001) (business operator has a duty to protect patrons from known dangerous individual who presents an imminent threat of attack); *cf. Bash*, 22 Mass. L. Rptr. 84 (university owes no duty in noncommon area of apartment building where there is no foreseeable risk to students).

[41] See note 40, *supra*.

residential living facility) and the injury.[42] These responsibilities attach to the "possessory" interest of the institution of higher education as a business. This means that duty follows the exercise of some regulatory power over some property. Mere ownership of a piece of property is not sufficient to create landowner duties.[43] The most challenging cases for courts to decide are those involving premises safety/security in situations in which an event or incident straddles a geographic boundary in some way.[44] Danger does not respect physical boundaries, and wicked people often take advantage of seams in responsibility. The law recognizes that danger near a premises might foreseeably cause danger on the premises, and that a danger might incept on the premises but complete elsewhere. Moreover, in some cases, a danger may straddle geographic boundaries, and the landowner owes no duty to a victim.[45]

Student affairs administrators are not usually in a position to predict the ultimate outcome of such "straddle situations," where danger is moving across property lines. Administrators should project reasonable safety and risk management efforts into foreseeable zones of danger and move from a *landscape* focus to a conceptual *riskscape* focus based on foreseeability of risk and the potential for reasonable efforts to mitigate risk. Institutions of higher education imperil themselves legally when they resist this approach for fear of assuming duties. In almost all instances, this concern is unwarranted in light of how modern courts approach assuming duties, and the law of duty generally. Institutions of higher education typically face much larger risk—physically and legally—from overreliance on bright-line geophysical interdiction strategies.[46]

---

[42] *See, e.g., Knoll*, 601 N.W.2d 757 (1999); *but see Rhodes v. Ill. Central Gulf Railroad*, 665 N.E.2d 1260 (Ill. 1996) (In that case, a college student who had received head injuries, presumably in an altercation in Chicago, collapsed on a train platform in Chicago. His head injuries were not readily detectible, and train personnel did not call for immediate assistance. The Illinois Supreme Court held that an individual who brings injuries from off premises to a business location does not trigger a business owner's duty to provide a rescue).

[43] "A more persuasive explanation for the common law rules that limited land-occupier duty arises from the importance placed on the ownership, possession, and use of land in the seventeenth and eighteenth centuries." Diamond, *supra* note 19, at 132–44.

[44] *See, e.g., Knoll*, 601 N.W.2d 757; *Pawlowski v. Delta Sigma Phi*, 2007 WL 2363146 (Conn. Super. 2007); *Guest v. Hansen*, 2007 WL 4561104 (N.D. N.Y. 2007).

[45] *See, e.g., Rhodes v. Ill. Central Gulf Railroad*, 665 N.E.2d 1260 (Ill. 1996); *Guest v. Hansen*, 2007 WL 4561104 (N.D. N.Y. 2007).

[46] Counsel for an institution of higher education may be more risk-averse to litigation than student affairs administrators. Moreover, landowner responsibility laws evolved rapidly in the past

In rare instances, institutions of higher education may acquire special relationships other than from business-premise-based relationships.

Custodial care relationships can serve as a predicate for the existence of duty; for example, K–12 is a special relationship because it is custodial. Custodial care is the exercise of substantial physical control over people that may include depriving them of freedom of movement. This is a rare level of control for an institution of higher education or a student affairs administrator to exercise over a student. An arrested student is in a custodial state, but students who are being disciplined are not. Limiting access to an area is also *not* custodial control of an individual: one may be the custodian of a space but not the people in it, or using it.

Employment relationships are legally special and can give rise to duties of care; however, many (but not all) injuries in the employment context are covered by workers' compensation laws and are not subject to the type of litigation other special relationships may cause. Workers' compensation laws also significantly limit the amount of damages an aggrieved party can receive.

In *therapeutic/medical relationships*, health care providers may have special relationships with their patients sufficient to create legal duties to protect them, even off campus. This is commonly known as a *Tarasoff* situation.[47] However, these duties are almost always limited to the therapeutic context, most often when a patient is under custodial control of the health care provider.[48] A few states impose duty somewhat more broadly on health care providers.[49] However, as a limit on the risk of liability, the law usually requires that a potential victim be either known or readily identifiable or the like; often, the health care provider can discharge responsibility with a timely warning to the endangered

---

20 years, and many institutions of higher education lawyers were educated primarily using materials that reflected more bright-line geographical boundary responsibility. Finally, at times, good legal advice conflicts directly with good business practice. The decision to extend reasonable risk management efforts into the educational environment riskscape is a business choice and should be made with due consideration for a variety of factors, including potential legal responsibility. Nonetheless, the distinct trend is to manage so-called "off-campus behavior," and courts are aware of, and encourage, this. *See, e.g., Pawlowski v. Delta Sigma Phi*, 2007 WL 2363146 (Conn. Super. 2007).

[47] *Tarasoff v. Regents of Univ. of California*, 551 P.2d 334 (Cal. 1976); *Restatement (Third) of Torts: Liab. Physical Harm* § 7 (2005).

[48] *Fraser v. United States*, 674 A.2d 811 (Conn. 1996); *Santana v. Rainbow Cleaners*, 969 A.2d 653 (R.I. 2009).

[49] *See, e.g.*, Mont. Code Ann. § 27-1-1102 (2010).

person.[50] Student affairs administrators will most likely encounter these issues if they work on care or threat assessment teams with health care providers, if they are health care providers themselves, or if they supervise health care providers. *Tarasoff* duties are almost never accepted for the clergy (unless the clergyperson is also a health care provider), family, friends, or coworkers.[51] Moreover, *Tarasoff* rules typically apply only if a patient endangers others, not just him- or herself. For example, *Tarasoff* has not been widely accepted in suicide situations; in fact, some courts have rejected *Tarasoff* duties outright in the suicide context.[52]

Finally, some courts and commentators have discovered special relationships in *rare ad hoc circumstances*. Such situations are most likely to occur when persons in need of protection/rescue find themselves in isolated circumstances in which only a discrete few persons or a single person is in a position to offer assistance at no or very little risk to the rescuer.[53] Remoteness may play a role in the duty to rescue,[54] but the law has yet to speak clearly on this issue.

Assuming Duties

It is possible for institutions of higher education or student affairs administrators to take on a responsibility they did not previously or otherwise have by assuming a duty. American tort law includes a great deal of debate over the precise contours of assumption of duty, and this is another area of tort law that is usually far too complex for student affairs administrators to make competent *legal* decisions about. It is tempting but dangerous, both physically and legally,

---

[50] *See* Ohio Rev. Code Ann. § 2305.51 (2010) (The amended statute cites to OH Legis. 26 § 3, which states, "In amending section 5122.34 and in enacting section 2305.51 of the Revised Code, it is the intent of the General Assembly to respectfully disagree with and supersede the statutory construction holdings of the Ohio Supreme Court relative to section 5122.34 of the Revised Code as set forth in *Estates of Morgan v. Fairfield Family Counseling Ctr.* (1997), 77 Ohio St. 3d 284, under heading G of section I at 304–5, and, thereby, to supersede the second, third, and fourth syllabus paragraph holdings of the Court in that case.") In Ohio, the Ohio Supreme Court first adopted a formulation of *Tarasoff* duties but the legislature later amended the law.

[51] *Restatement (Third) of Torts: Liab. Physical Harm* § 7 (2005).

[52] *Nally v. Grace Church*, 763 P.2d 948 (Cal. 1988); *but see Eisel v. Board of Educ. of Montgomery County*, 597 A.2d 447 (Md. 1991).

[53] *See Farwell v. Keaton*, 240 N.W.2d 217 (Mich. 1976).

[54] *See generally* Peter F. Lake, *Recognizing the Importance of Remoteness to the Duty to Rescue*, 46 DePaul L. Rev. 315 (1997). The latest *Restatement of Torts (Third)* has acknowledged this possibility, too.

to adopt a very litigation-avoidance-oriented posture vis-à-vis assuming duties. Our lawyers might sometimes wish we were working in a cave, sitting very still in the dark, doing nothing—an excellent way not to get sued, but no way to run a campus. But we do not have that luxury. Student populations demand very high levels of engagement in the learning environment, and many of their parents certainly have this expectation. Student affairs administrators experience the push and pull of trying to do their jobs professionally and responsibly without creating undue legal responsibility for themselves and their institutions in the process.

Before student affairs administrators try to figure out whether they have assumed duties, they should consider the following points:

1. Duty may already exist because the activities of an institution of higher education or student affairs administrator are considered misfeasance, not nonfeasance. For example, duty exists in the programmatic context.[55] In many ways, we "manufacture" an institution of higher education experience, and the law recognizes that duty and responsibility follow in the footsteps of what we create. It would be legally incorrect to view this as assuming duties; rather, we create responsibility along with our programs.

2. As discussed below, other exceptions to traditional no-duty rules may apply, such as special relationships or contractually assumed duties. Duty can arise in several different ways simultaneously. You may have a duty even if you did not assume it.

3. Business realities of the institution of higher education may require student affairs administrators to engage students in the learning environment in new ways. Esoteric legal discussions of whether student affairs administrators are assuming duties are sometimes philosophical luxuries; in the end, we have to do what we have to do. Student affairs administrators should not be oblivious to creating legal risk; however, we have lawyers for a reason. It is hard for a student affairs administra-

---

[55] *Davidson v. Univ. of North Carolina Chapel Hill*, 543 S.E.2d 920 (N.C. Ct. App. 2001); *Nova Southeastern Univ., Inc. v. Goss*, 758 So. 2d 86 (Fla. 2000).

tor to play administrator and lawyer simultaneously. It is sort of like Peyton Manning or Brett Favre: Only a few quarterbacks can coach and play at the same time, and the result can be spectacular success and spectacular failure.

4.   Sometimes we must balance litigation risk avoidance and risk management strategies. This can be a complex calculation. Choosing not to become involved in a potentially dangerous situation may be preferable in terms of immediate litigation avoidance; however, from a risk management perspective, it may be the wrong choice. Some strategies that have appeal for short-term litigation avoidance can backfire in the long run, creating greater risk management and litigation risks. For example, choosing not to send a staff member to an off-campus event might reduce the risk of litigation over incidents arising from that event. However, long-term disengagement may allow an off-campus residential facility to fester and grow into a massive source of campus risk that will mature into serious litigation danger. Moreover, litigants often choose to sue based on a variety of factors including their sense of whether or not a defendant institution of higher education showed care, compassion and acted of genuine concern. Deliberate disengagement can sometimes send exactly the wrong message and bait the oppositional attitudes that are the seeds of future litigation.

5.   Reasonable care is always an excellent defense (although it is not technically an *affirmative* defense); no one who acts reasonably in higher education loses negligence cases. Lawyers may not prefer this protection strategy, because litigation costs associated with establishing reasonable care can be high and unpredictable. Jury assessments of reasonable care can vary and, as we will see, the standard of reasonable care is designed to be eternally flexible. Institutions of higher education and student affairs administrators can take comfort in the fact that published judicial opinions holding that an institution or administrator behaved unreasonably are exceedingly rare; at most, some opinions set the determination of whether reasonable care was delivered for trial, and many cases find no basis for negligence whatsoev-

er.[56] Sometimes we play like timid pitchers who have wicked fast balls but are afraid to throw them.

6. Colleges must recognize that certain policy-based interdiction approaches can actually create risk. Thus, draconian policies may drive students to riskier behavior. While courts consistently hold that having a policy is not an assumption of duty, an institution of higher education can be held responsible if enforcement of a policy *enhances* risk or danger to a community. This is simply an application of longstanding principles of misfeasance.

7. It looks as though accrediting bodies and government regulations may ultimately connect student safety to demonstrable academic achievement and assessment. In time, the existence of duty in tort law could be supplemented—even supplanted—by direct federal or state regulation and/or accreditation standards. For example, the Clery Act, which began as a campus crime reporting bill, has steadily matured into an omnibus campus crime prevention bill. (See below.)

8. Often, the question of whether a duty has been assumed is, legally speaking, moot. There is a class of cases in which legal duty has not been assumed, but it is nearly impossible to identify such situations *a priori* from the operational standpoint of student affairs practice. The focus on avoiding assumption of duty is a vestige of a bygone era, in which the status of an institution of higher education was enough to block litigation. We live in an age of accountability, and no-duty arguments are much less fashionable, even as no-liability results persist.

9. The trickiest litigation involves student groups (usually registered student organizations) and individuals who are injured (usually via alcohol or drugs, or in a transportation/vehicle event) off-campus or in private spaces on campus.[57] This legal conceptual grey space is

---

[56] *See, e.g., Bash,* 22 Mass. L. Rptr. 84; *Robertson v. State ex rel. Department of Planning and Control,* 747 So. 2d 1276 (La. Ct. App. 1999).
[57] Study abroad and externship responsibility is much simpler in some ways because it is programmatic. *See Davidson,* 543 S.E.2d 920; *Nova Southeastern Univ., Inc.,* 758 So. 2d 86 (Fla. 2000).

penumbral to core areas of university responsibility but easily distinguishable from obvious no-duty situations, such as the situation in which a student living at home for the summer is injured in the family bathroom. In this penumbral space, institutions of higher education engage student populations with program rules, risk management strategies, and the like, and often can foresee danger from previous similar incidents. This penumbral space is perhaps the great last legal battleground for the existence of legal duty via assumption of duty in higher education. The law of torts is interested in this space and how legal issues resolve in it.[58] Institutions of higher education and student affairs administrators typically win on this battleground owing to the ways courts define the nature of assuming a duty, the way they analyze other elements of the prima facie case of negligence, and the subtle ways they partner in the management of college student risk.[59] We tend to win *legally* here; but accountability remains high.

Courts are not always consistent in the way they articulate and apply rules of assumed duty, making it difficult for student affairs administrators to craft compliance strategies.[60] Most courts agree that negligently or de-

---

[58] *See Restatement (Third) of Torts* (2005).

[59] *See, e.g., Pawlowski v. Delta Sigma Phi*, 2007 WL 2363146 (Conn. Super. 2007).

> While [the court] ha[s] attempted to draw definitional distinctions between the terms willful, wanton, or reckless, in practice the three terms have been treated as meaning the same thing. The result is that willful, wanton, or reckless conduct tends to take on the aspect of highly unreasonable conduct, involving an extreme departure from ordinary care, in a situation where a high degree of danger is apparent. . . . It is at least clear . . . that such aggravated negligence must be more than any mere mistake resulting from inexperience, excitement, or confusion, and more than mere thoughtlessness or inadvertence, or simply inattention.

Id. at *3 (quoting *Craig v. Driscoll*, 781 A.2d 440, 445 (Conn. App. 2001) (citations omitted)).

[60] *See Blackburn v. Dorta*, 348 So. 2d 287 (Fla. 1977) ("At the outset, [the court notes] that assumption of risk is not a favored defense. There is a puissant drift toward abrogating the defense. The argument is that assumption of risk serves no purpose which is not subsumed by either the doctrine of contributory negligence or the common law concept of duty. It is said that this redundancy results in confusion and, in some cases, denies recovery unjustly. The leading case in Florida dealing with the distinction between the doctrines recognizes that '(a)t times the line of demarcation between contributory negligence and assumption of risk is exceedingly difficult to define.'" *Blackburn*, 348 So. 2d at 289 (quoting *Byers v. Gunn*, 81 So. 2d 723, 727 (Fla. 1955)). "The issue

liberately interfering with a putative rescuer is a form of misfeasance that can create liability.[61] Many courts insist that once a person or institution has taken steps to help someone by taking charge and control, the effort may not be abandoned if it leaves the imperiled person worse off.[62] There is some disagreement about what makes someone "worse off,"[63] but many courts take the view that once a rescuer/intervener has taken significant steps, he or she must use reasonable care going forward.[64]

Courts have been very sensitive to placing burdensome responsibility on institutions of higher education. They have made it crystal clear that merely having rules or policies is not in itself an assumption of duty.[65] This is crucial for student affairs administrators to understand: Institutions of higher education are free to regulate off-campus behavior, for instance, without the fear that such regulation will be the predicate for a duty not otherwise owed. (However, other factors may create duty.) As one court stated, making rules and attempting to enforce them is far from controlling a situation.[66] Institutions of higher education are empowered to influence the greater educational environment. Influence is different from taking charge and control: you are not Dean Wormer, the tyrannical dean of the fictional Faber College in the movie "Animal House."

Courts seem to be aware that the application of assumed duty rules for colleges requires special adaptation. Most states have Good Samaritan laws; most Good Samaritan laws do not require rescuers to aid someone in danger but im-

---

is most salient in states which have enacted comparative negligence legislation. Those statutes provide that the common law defense of contributory negligence no longer necessarily acts as a complete bar to recovery. The effect of these statutes upon the doctrine of assumption of risk has proved to be controversial. Joining the intensifying assault upon the doctrine, a number of comparative negligence jurisdictions have abrogated assumption of risk. Those jurisdictions hold that assumption of risk is interchangeable with contributory negligence and should be treated equivalently. Today [the Florida Supreme court is] invited to join this trend of dissatisfaction with the doctrine. For the reasons herein expressed, we accept the invitation." *Id.* at 289–90).

[61] *See* Diamond, *supra* note 19, at 112.

[62] *See Restatement (Second) of Torts* §§ 314, 323–24 (2005); *Farwell v. Keaton*, 240 N.W.2d 217 (Mich. 1976).

[63] *See Farwell*, 240 N.W.2d 217.

[64] The threshold of how much effort the rescuer or intervener must expend is also somewhat unclear. See *Furek v. The Univ. of Delaware*, 594 A.2d 506 (Del. 1991); *Coghlan v. Beta Theta Pi Fraternity*, 987 P.2d 300 (Idaho 1999).

[65] *Pawlowski v. Delta Sigma Phi*, 2007 WL 2363146 (Conn. Super. 2007); *Fitzpatrick v. Universal Technical Institute, Inc.*, 2009 WL 2476639 (E.D. Pa. 2009).

[66] *Fitzpatrick*, 2009 WL 2476639, at *4.

munize them for ordinary negligence if they attempt to do so.[67] Emergency rescue personnel usually have similar legal protection.[68] The way most state statutes are written shows that legislatures imagine rescues in which a motorist comes to the aid of another on the roadside after a horrific accident or the like: most statutes would have to be tortured to stretch to institution of higher education interdiction, which primarily involves preventive efforts designed to avoid or reduce the need for a rescue in the first place. Good Samaritan statutes are typically not written to protect this special class of Good Samaritans. Thus, colleges and student affairs administrators are uniquely legally vulnerable to preventive rescue/assumed duty responsibility, largely because policymakers have not viewed preventive risk management efforts as similar to rescue attempts by professional rescue personnel such as EMTs. Courts implicitly detect this oversight and are much less likely to see assumed duty in the college context. For the sake of parity, the law should hold institutions of higher education and student affairs administrators responsible for gross negligence or worse only when they intervene proactively and potentially assume duties, if ever. The law has not yet made this explicit leap, although it functions much as though it had. Some of the cases we "lose" on duty issues feature facts that might show deliberate indifference to risk to students—a key feature of recklessness or gross negligence.

Courts also implicitly recognize that there are significantly different causation issues in preventive efforts versus actual rescue situations, in which a rescuer harms a victim or set of victims, or a putative rescuer starts to engage in a rescue and stops. It is difficult to impossible to calculate what would have happened without some of the preventive efforts by institutions of higher education and their administrators. Students would probably be much worse off without preventative efforts, making it hard to argue for the usual predicate of assumed duty that someone was made worse off. Thus, courts encourage institutions of higher education to actively engage the educational environment and do not create rules of liability that dissuade institutions and student affairs administrators from doing so.

---

[67] *See, e.g.*, Vt. Stat. Ann. 12 § 519 (1967) (Vermont requires that affirmative duty to rescue in some situations).

[68] Police, EMTs, and hospital emergency rooms usually enjoy protection from ordinary negligence claims in emergency situations.

This is precisely what the court in *Pawlowski*[69] was doing, in a rare and candid glimpse into the judicial world's attempt to encourage accountability without imposing liability:

> Thus recognizing a[n] [assumed duty] under the circumstances presented by this case poses a risk of a university engaging in either over enforcement, i.e. excessive control or under enforcement towards, i.e. no control, of its students' private off-campus recreational activities. Neither of these are desirable outcomes. As desirable as it may be to address the serious problem of students' underage drinking and its adverse consequences courts recognize that it is "[hard] . . . to eradicate alcohol ingestion," Baldwin v. Zoradi, supra, at 123 Cal. App. 3d 290. As a practical matter, it may be impossible for a university to police students' off-campus alcohol consumption. The practical limitations on the proactive measures a university may be able to undertake combined with the attendant cost of such measures further militates against finding any duty on the part of the university. . . . [A] conclusion that a duty arises based on policies contained in the student handbook and past practices of the university in enforcing those policies could potentially discourage institutions of higher education from having policies and implementing enforcement practices that govern such things as students' alcohol consumption and students' unlawful behavior. If the absence of a policy means the absence of any duty, a rational institution could opt for . . . [lax] enforcement to the detriment of the student population.[70]

The message of *Pawlowski* is emblematic of the age of accountability: The very fact that we engage the wider institution of higher education environment with safety policies reduces the risk of liability.

Reasonable and responsible efforts are superior to bunkering or deliberate nonengagement. This is particularly true in our college business world when you consider that the police have no general duty to protect individuals from crime unless they assume a duty to that individual or a discrete class of individu-

---

[69] *Pawlowski v. Delta Sigma Phi*, 2007 WL 2363146 (Conn. Super. 2007).
[70] *Id.*

als.[71] For better or worse, the tort responsibility to create safe business environments has become a cost of doing business. College environments are somewhat unique among businesses, as few businesses offer so many services, a living/learning environment, and open business premises. (Consider some of the closest alternatives to colleges—theme parks, cruise ships, nursing homes, and casinos—and you will see that there is nothing quite like a college "business.")

Instrumentality or Conduct Causing Harm

The law recognizes a duty to rescue if an actor's conduct or instrumentality causes harm, even innocently.[72] This is an unusual avenue for institutions of higher education to owe a duty, and even if a duty is owed under this exception, it is only a postinjury responsibility to call for help. In practice, this exception drives student affairs administrators in institutions of higher education to train staff to respond reasonably, both in time and in relation to the cause of an accident, if a person is harmed, for instance, in a classroom fall or a collision with a school vehicle.[73]

Promises, Reliance, and Contract

Contracts are rarely the predicate for tort responsibility.[74] This feature of American law protects institutions of higher education even when they make

---

[71] This is ironically known as the public duty doctrine. *See Davidson v. City of Westminster*, 649 P.2d 894, 895–900 (Cal. 1982). This case involved a public laundromat that was under surveillance by the police due to recent stabbings at and near the laundromat. *Id.* The police knew the plaintiff was inside the laundromat, and the police watched a man resembling the attacker of the previous evening enter the laundromat. *Id.* The police never warned the plaintiff of this man's presence. *Id.* The plaintiff, Yolanda Davidson, was stabbed four times by this man. *Id.* The court held that the police officers were under no duty to warn the plaintiff of the possibility of becoming the next victim, and therefore no cause of action for negligence could result. *Id.*

[72] *Restatement (Second) of Torts* § 322.

[73] Closely related is the concept of negligent entrustment—a form of misfeasance by which someone furnishes a dangerous instrumentality to another person negligently, as in handing a gun to a person who is about to commit suicide. The most common form of negligent entrustment in a college environment is negligent provision of alcohol. However, most states regulate that form of entrustment with dram shop acts, that typically limit such liability to very specific classes of entrustment—commonly, serving minors who are visibly intoxicated or on-premises consumption in a commercial setting. However, there is significant variation from state to state; some states do provide for social host responsibility, although many immunize it. Most states still provide little or no liability for social hosts. Liability is often limited to transactional entrustment of alcohol. There may be broader criminal penalties, but civil remedies are circumscribed by statute in many states.

[74] *Cf. Restatement (Second) of Torts* §§ 356–57.

promises to students or parents. A student handbook itself, for instance, does not create negligence-based responsibility to protect students.

The close cousin of a contract or promise is *reliance*. It is possible to lure students into a false sense of security and to do so negligently;[75] however, reliance itself is not a sufficient basis to create a tort duty in the vast majority of situations.[76] The existence of a legal duty is much more likely to arise not from reliance but because a defendant's behavior negligently enhanced the risk to another—a form of misfeasance.[77] There are many complex reasons why the legal system has hesitated to make reasonable reliance the basis for duty in tort.[78] The net result is reliance, promise or contract rarely forms a basis of responsibility for negligence except insofar as it may show foreseeability of danger (which, on its own, is not sufficient to create affirmative duty).

BREACH

Even if a student affairs administrator or institution of higher education has legal duty, liability is far from certain; a plaintiff must also show breach of duty. If a duty is owed, some standard of care is always owed. Duty necessarily implies standard of care; breach of duty is, therefore, not acting in accordance with the standard of care implied by the existence of duty.

This all sounds complex and technical, but it is usually very simple: In almost every instance, the standard of care owed (if there is a duty) is the reasonable person standard. A common formulation is as follows:

Negligence is the failure to use reasonable care. Reasonable care is the degree of care a reasonably careful person would use under similar circumstances. Negligence may consist either in doing something that a reasonably careful person would not do under similar circumstances or in failing

---

[75] Robert Bickel, Susan Brinkley & Wendy White, *Seeing Past Privacy: Will the Development and Application of CCTV and Other Video Security Technology Compromise an Essential Constitutional Right in a Democracy, or Will the Courts Strike a Proper Balance?* 33 Stetson L. Rev. 299, 340–45 (2003).

[76] *Cf. Florence v. Goldberg*, 375 N.E.2d 763 (N.Y. 1978).

[77] *Restatement (Second) of Torts* § 321; *Pacht v. Morris*, 489 P.2d 29 (Ariz. 1971).

[78] *Thorne v. Deas*, 1809 N.Y. Lexis 164 (N.Y. Feb. 1809) (holding a defendant's failure to obtain insurance on a vessel jointly owned by plaintiff and defendant did not allow the plaintiff to obtain his share of the insurance proceeds when the vessel was destroyed, as the promise was unsupported by consideration); E. Allan Farnsworth, *Contract* (4th ed., Aspen Publishers 2004).

to do something that a reasonably careful person would do under similar circumstances.[79]

The reasonable person standard is an objective standard rather than a subjective one. Compliance with the standard does not entail what a specific person subjectively believes is reasonable; compliance with the standard is determined from the point view of an objectively reasonable person.

The following are among the key aspects of the legal standard for student affairs administrators:

Mandates/Compliance

The reasonable person standard is an unusual legal mandate. Student affairs administrators, like most legally untrained people, are usually more comfortable with legal mandates that are concrete or specific; for example, a numeric speed limit. The reasonable person is a conceptual standard that varies with the circumstances, so it often provides little *a priori* comfort to a student affairs administrator. Reasonable care can be in the eye of the beholder (a jury, usually); worse yet, an adversary might attempt to paint a picture of a student affairs administrator or institution of higher education as objectively unreasonable. Every little mistake or oversight can be magnified. The process of discovery can feel like being smeared in a tabloid.

Student affairs administrators try to cope with this in two predictable ways. First, they may become very risk-averse or susceptible to risk-averse arguments and positions (sometimes generated by their own lawyers). Uncertainty and indeterminacy breed hypervigilance. Second, they may be tempted to invent bright-line compliance approaches, even if they are legal placebos. A common one is discourse about "best practices," which we might assume would be better than minimal or reasonable care. Or student affairs administrators might become enamored of forms, such as waiver forms (discussed below), hoping that a signed form will block negligence cases. Student affairs administrators should accept the fact that they rarely have the power to reduce the indeterminacy of the reasonable person standard to simple, certain compliance steps that will be like Deep Woods Off for legal mosquitoes.

---

[79] Supreme Court of Florida Committee on Standard Jury Instructions, *Florida Standard Jury Instructions in Civil Cases* § 4.1 (Fla. B. 2001), *available at* http://www.flcourts18.org/PDF/civil.pdf.

Does that mean student affairs administrators are doomed to a Kafkaesque legal hell, waiting to be damned under standards that refuse to be comprehensible until it is too late? Hardly. In fact, the picture is far rosier. The U.S. Supreme Court recently announced that higher education administrators are owed "decent respect" in their day-to-day operations, and courts and juries are still quite deferential to higher education.[80] Our adversaries may try to paint us as devils, but the law sees us differently most of the time.

The Reasonable Person: Rationality, Reasonableness, and Foreseeability

The reasonable person is neither a saint nor a god. The reasonable person is rational and reasonable, and attends to that which is foreseeable. The reasonable person is not expected to ensure or guarantee anyone's safety, or to be clairsentient. A reasonable person is merely asked to do what is reasonable. Many accidents will occur despite reasonable efforts.[81]

The famous federal judge Learned Hand posited a formula for negligence that is a good place to start. He said that a reasonable person will consider the burden (B) of precautions (P) and balance them against the weighted risk of loss (L). The B < PxL formula (probability times severity of harm) is known as the Hand formula. If B is less than P times L, a reasonable person will naturally choose to take precautions. If B is more than P times L the reasonable person will not choose to take the safety step. As my Dad used to say, "There's no point in putting a $20 saddle on a $10 mule." Hand's formula is a shorthand way of saying that the reasonable person is usually rational and will engage in cost-benefit analysis when making decisions.[82] It might be desirable to post security guards in front of every student residence facility on or off-campus, 24 hours a day. But the cost would be prohibitive. A reasonable person will not do *everything* possible to avoid harm; budgets and personnel constraints are very real,

---

[80] *See Christian Legal Society at Hastings College of the Law v. Martinez*, 130 S. Ct. 2971 (2010).

[81] *See Gift v. Palmer*, 141 A.2d 408 (Pa. 1958).

[82] Hand's formula was not intended to be a formula, but that has not stopped math geeks from grabbing on to it as one. If you are a math geek, you will figure out that the B < PxL formula does not work well as an arithmetical formula. In fact, one must actually develop a calculus formula to make the B < PxL formula plausible. *See* Richard A. Posner, *The Economic Analysis of Law* (7th ed., Aspen Publishers 2007). But if you are not someone who speaks regularly at math conventions, you do not need to know this.

and reasonable people work with the available resources. Reasonable people will weigh the real dangers and prioritize resources accordingly.[83]

Another feature of rationality is captured in the requirement of foreseeability. Reasonable persons only attend to reasonably foreseeable risks. This is the "one-bite rule": The dog is not usually foreseeably dangerous until after it bites someone, or if it is a dangerous breed.[84] This is also an admonition against being Niles Crane, Neville Chamberlain, or Evel Knievel. Niles Crane in the television series "Frasier" is a risk ninny—he is so pathologically risk-averse that he is comically unreasonable. Evel Knievel was a well-known daredevil. Reasonable people do not try to jump over school buses with motorcycles; in fact, such a stunt can probably not be performed using reasonable care—it is ridiculously dangerous. Neville Chamberlain, prime minister of England, believed that he could make peace with Adolf Hitler. Reasonable people do not put their faith in unicorns, rainbows, leprechauns, or sociopathic monsters.

These are the three deadly sins of unreasonableness:

1. Overemphasis of risk or fear. Risk aversion and concern over low probability events can be paralyzing.

2. Reckless disregard for risk. "I've gotta be me" worked for Sammy Da-

---

[83] After the events at Virginia Tech, many institutions of higher education—motivated in part by new compliance rules under the Clery Act—created and tested elaborate emergency notification systems to warn campuses about active shooters. The probability of an active shooter event such as the one that occurred at Virginia Tech is extremely low, although the severity of harm is exceedingly high if such events occur. Institutions of higher education have had to balance the allocation of resources to active shooter interdiction with other campus priorities. Psychological studies often show that people place higher priority on low-probability events with very severe consequences than on high-probability events with more predictable consequences. George F. Loewenstein et al., *Risk As Feelings,* 127 Psychological Bulletin 2, 267–86 (2001).

[84] According to New York Law, strict liability for a dog bite arises only if the dog has vicious propensities, and the owner knew or should have known about them. *Collier v. Zambito*, 807 N.E. 2d 254, 256 (N.Y. 2004); *Brooks v. Parshall*, 806 N.Y.S.2d 796, 797 (N.Y. App. Div. 3d Dept. 2006); *Calabro v. Bennett*, 737 N.Y.S. 2d 406, 407 (N.Y. App. Div. 3d Dept. 2002). Vicious propensities are acts that endanger the safety of persons or property. *Collier*, 807 N.E. 2d at 256. One must prove that the dog has a disposition to cause harm toward others. *Id.* The owner has knowledge or should have knowledge of vicious propensities if the dog has bitten someone before, or if it is a guard dog, or if the owner restrains the dog because he fears it may attack. *Id.* "'Proof of a previous attack is unnecessary where other factors are indicative of knowledge.'" *Calabro*, 737 N.Y.S. 2d at 407 (quoting *Brophy v. Columbia County Agricultural Society*, 498 N.Y.S. 193, 195 (N.Y. App. Div. 3d Dept. 1986)).

vis Jr. and Frank Sinatra; however, they were not judged under the reasonable persons standard. "Me" may be good for you but not for other people. The most reckless, otherwise lawful thing you should ever do in higher education is wear your CBGB T-shirt under a blazer to the Monday morning staff meeting.

3. Pollyannaism. Denial of real risk is extremely dangerous. Danger, risk, and the dark side flourish when people refuse to confront them.

Legally speaking, don't be those guys. The irony of the hyper-risk-averse personality is that risk-averse people often end up being the most at risk. It took Niles Crane seven seasons to close the deal with his beloved Daphne; it should have taken no more than two.[85] For student affairs administrators, the great risk of risk aversion is that they will not do the very job they were hired to do. Student affairs administration is a risky business, and a certain amount of danger comes with the job.

Student affairs administrators are not known for recklessness in the daredevil sense, but they have a tendency to run ahead of their resources. Fear of not being reasonable can bait a student affairs administrator into trying to do things that are unreasonable. For instance, we may be tempted to use the highest security, state-of-the-art locking systems available for doors on our dorms. But our personnel and our populations may not support the use of such systems. We might be better off using lower-tech solutions that we can manage with reasonable care. We also have a tendency to grind our personnel into stumps with overwork—that leads to error.

Student affairs administrators can be tempted into see-no-evil approaches, in which they merely react to risk. A reasonable person does a certain amount of due diligence to determine whether things are as safe as they appear to be. The enormous amount of activity that a student affairs administrator must manage often leads to a high level of reactivity, but doing too much can be dangerous; sometimes less is more. It is hard to find time to be proactive in an environment that is like playing the Whack-a-Mole game, but the reasonable person will be proactive, because an ounce of prevention is worth a pound of cure. A reasonable student affairs administrator will set aside a reasonable amount of time to be preventive.

---

[85] *Frasier* (NBC 1993–2004) (TV series).

Finally, the reasonable person is more than just rational and calculating about foreseeability of risk, and there is more to reasonable care than the Hand formula. Reasonableness implies the human element. Reasonable people are not risk computers, and no such machine could ever exist. Reasonable people—especially in education—act with care and compassion, in good faith, and with commitment to their populations. Often, this is what distinguishes student affairs administrators from potentially responsible actors in other fields and provides a valuable layer of legal protection. Reasonable care implies the use of intuition, judgment, and even empathy.

Reasonable Care: A Process, Not a Point

Reasonable care is best understood procedurally. In a legal procedural sense, what is or is not reasonable care emerges through the process of litigation—especially at summary judgment or through jury verdicts.

Student affairs administrators often get the clearest glimpse of what reasonable care might be when judges make rulings on summary judgment. If material facts are not in dispute, a judge may be in a position to rule on the law applicable to those facts or determine that reasonable jurors could reach only certain results on agreed-upon material facts. Verdicts from juries are usually less helpful; juries do not always explain their verdicts in useful terms. Gathering helpful information about patterns of jury verdicts is difficult, and the results are often highly debatable. Occasionally, the judge will play the role of fact finder; in that case, the student affairs administrator gets the benefit of (almost) looking into the jury room. But relatively few such reported decisions occur in higher education law.[86] In theory, settlements might provide a window into what reasonable care looks like in a given situation; however, the terms of settlement are often highly confidential, and the information parties release may be designed to posture, not inform.

Legal procedures can give student affairs administrators some insight into what reasonable care may be for future situations. However, the legal system is not designed primarily as an advisory or guidance system but as a dispute resolution system with an eye toward facilitating settlements.

---

[86] In certain areas of the law (such as admiralty law) where there are no juries, judges are allowed to be fact finders. *See U.S. v. Carroll Towing*, 159 F.2d 169 (2d Cir. 1947).

From a compliance standpoint, it is helpful to think of the reasonable person standard as encouraging a process of reaching safety-related positions rather than commanding specific directives. Often, a few reasonable care solutions are acceptable/desirable—not just one specific compliance step that would be *the* reasonable thing to do. And student affairs administrators typically operate with some uncertainty even about the *range* of potential reasonable solutions to a safety challenge.

Usually, the best decisions are made when student affairs administrators collaborate, share information, consider alternatives, use due diligence to determine the strategies of others who are similarly situated, and engage in cost-benefit analysis and constructive discourse about pros and cons. A good process depends on well-educated people committed to career-long professional development. Decision making that is most likely to be considered reasonable after the fact leaves decision makers feeling a little uncomfortable with the choices they have made. Reasonable care is connected to the exercise of good judgment, and good judgment is not always clear-cut. Judges and juries are influenced by *how* decisions are made, not just which decisions are made.

It is possible for a well-trained and experienced student affairs administrator to go through this process alone. Some professionals are very good at constructive self-assessment of their own decision making or due diligence. However, the modern educational environment places such heavy demands on administrators that the practice of working in teams and collaboratively has become emblematic of modern student affairs practice. Student affairs administrators work in teams just like most other professionals, including those in law, K–12 education, and medicine. The lone wolf/Dean Wormer administrator is a dying breed. The catch phrase for good decision making for student affairs administrators is "careful and deliberative."

One final note: Student affairs administrators work in a business that is very left-brain oriented. Reasonable decision makers should watch the tendency to make hyper-rational decisions that may not be, or even appear to be, reasonable. Careful, deliberative decision making usually involves a balance of right- and left-brain functioning—a balance of intuition and instinct against "harder" forms of cognitive reasoning, such as inductive reasoning from facts.

Real-time Decision Making/Monday Morning Quarterbacking

In an age of accountability, student affairs administrators will experience criticism—often harsh—of real-time decision making from the perspective of the armchair. The reports on the events at Virginia Tech make an interesting case study of this phenomenon.[87] However, the reasonable person legal standard is not an armchair standard; it can take into account factors such as emergency circumstances, the need for decision making with imperfect information, and lack of previous experience with the particular situation. Reasonable people make mistakes—the reasonable person is a human being, not an angelic construct. Reasonable people sometimes make snap decisions under great pressure because they have to.[88] Student affairs administrators have well-developed abilities to make excellent—even heroic—decisions under extreme pressure.[89]

The Reasonable Person and Record Keeping Procedures

Student affairs administrators often inquire about record keeping. The law regarding record keeping can be influenced by privacy law (see below and the discussion of FERPA and other privacy laws) and by the reasonable person standard. Record keeping procedures should be driven by ordinary course of business concerns and not out of concern for liability, except when litigation has already commenced. During litigation, persons who have over-recorded or under-recorded information out of fear of litigation can look as though they were apprehensive about their own course of action or frightened that others would know too much. Record keeping practices should grow out of the reasonable needs of day-to-day tasks. The reasonable person standard itself generates no specific mandate for record keeping.

---

[87] *See e.g.,* Virginia Tech Review Panel, *Mass Shootings at Virginia Tech, April 16, 2007—Report of the Review Panel Presented to Governor Kaine, Commonwealth of Virginia* 40–53 (2007), *available at* http://www.vtreviewpanel.org/report/index.html.

[88] *Cordas v. Peerless Transportation Co.,* 27 N.Y.S.2d 198 (N.Y. Ct. Cl. 1941).

[89] Consider the heroic actions of Liviu Librescu, who barricaded a door during the Virginia Tech shootings to save the lives of others, knowing full well that it would cost him his own life. Or consider the coolheadedness of faculty marshals at Kent State, who intervened after the first volley was fired at unarmed students and prevented further bloodshed. See Stetson College of Law, *Three Educators Receive Stetson Law's Facilitator Award* (March 2, 2009), http://www.law.stetson.edu/tmpl/news/article/aspx?id=5954.

Reasonable Care: Statutes and Regulations

A reasonable person is typically presumed to know safety law generally and act accordingly. That expectation is not reasonable, but it is the law, and ignorance of the law is no excuse.[90] The presumption that reasonable people have read the constitution and every statute and regulation is utterly unrealistic, but statutes and regulations can and will be used against you in a court of law.

To provide some modicum of relief to those of us who live in an overwhelmingly juridical world, courts have devised fairly complex schematics for when a statute or regulation applies in negligence and when violations of statutes and regulations are excused.[91]

Compliance with other legal rules is sometimes necessary to show reasonable care. Plaintiffs often attempt to use regulatory and statutory compliance issues and litigation against institutions of higher education. Laws designed to set physical safety standards to protect a discrete class of people from a certain type of harm are most likely to be used effectively against student affairs administrators and institutions of higher education.[92] Excuses for noncompliance are usually very limited in the institution of higher education context.[93] However some statutes are not designed as the type of safety statute that applies in a negligence action or other civil action.[94]

Lawyers refer to this area of the law under the heading "negligence per se." As the famous jurist Benjamin Cardozo once wrote, if a safety statute requires that a buggy have buggy lights, a reasonable person will have buggy lights on his buggy.[95]

---

[90] *See Restatement (Second) of Torts* § 288D (2010).

[91] *See id.* at § 288A.

[92] *See id.* §§ 500–01.

[93] *Id.* at § 288A.

[94] *See Gonzaga v. Doe,* 536 U.S. 273 (2002).

[95] *Martin v. Herzog,* 126 N.E. 814 (N.Y. 1920). There are a variety of circumstances in which student affairs administrators may encounter negligence per se arguments. A common situation involves statutes and regulations aimed at traffic and pedestrian safety. Rules of the road (remember that handbook you read when you took your drivers' license test?) are applicable in negligence actions generally. Speeding on campus may not garner a ticket in every instance, but if a pedestrian is struck, exceeding the posted speed limit is negligence per se. Usually plaintiffs will generate separate counts in a complaint for each separate claim of negligence per se, in addition to a general count alleging general negligence.

The Reasonable Person in a Silo

The reports that came out after the events at Virginia Tech in April 2007 drew attention to the problems of information collection, collation, and transfer. One of the reports used the term *silo*,[96] which has become shorthand for referring to this problem. Most student affairs administrators are surprised to learn that the law usually expects an institution of higher education to know what its student affairs administrators know, and is presumed to collect and collate that information in a reasonable amount of time and take appropriate, reasonable action.[97] However, historically, institutions of higher education have not crunched data this way, and our information collection systems are still primitive in comparison with those of some other industries.[98] Siloing information is potentially very dangerous and can generate litigation risk.[99] Institutions of higher education should be careful not to put too much emphasis on information gathering alone; it is easy to overload student affairs administrators or teams with more information than they can reasonably process. A reasonable person thinks, "What information do I need?"; "With whom will I share that information?"; "How will I collate and synthesize the data I collect?"; "What additional steps will be taken, by whom, with the data I collect and synthesize?"

The reasonable person standard is both individual and collective—an institution of higher education is considered akin to a person. Compliance can

---

[96] Michael O. Leavitt, Margaret Spellings & Alberto R. Gonzalez, *Report to the President on Issues Raised by the Virginia Tech Tragedy* (June 13, 2007), *available at* http://www.hhs.gov.vtreport.html.

[97] *Restatement (Second) of Agency* § 265 (2010).

[98] *See* Sara Lipka, *U. of Virginia Abandons Proposed Student Background Checks in Favor of Stricter Self-Disclosure*, Chronicle of Higher Education (Aug. 10, 2010), *available at* http://chronicle.com/article/U-of-Virginia-Abandons-Pro/123870/. While the proposal for continuous background checks on students at the University of Virginia recently died owing to impossible logistics, the university is exploring other methods to remain informed about current students' criminal background to avoid threats on campus. *Id.* One solution, a notification system from state law-enforcement agencies, also seemed logistically challenging and "would have required a major investment to change national recording standards." *Id.* Cost and logistics are not the only concerns. *Id.* The university strives to avoid intrusiveness regarding students' personal affairs. *Id.* "This fall the university plans to start an online safety-education program to train students to identify unsafe situations, threatening behavior, and peers in need of help." *Id.*

[99] *See Garofalo v. Lambda Chi Alpha Fraternity*, 616 N.W.2d 647 (Iowa 2000). In this case, students at a fraternity house chose to attempt to self-manage a severely intoxicated student's risk. *Id.* at 651–655. They did not promptly share information that the student was in serious physical risk with emergency medical professionals or campus authorities. *Id.* After the student died, some of the students involved faced serious criminal and civil charges. *Id.*

be assessed at both the individual and institutional level. What might be reasonable for a student affairs administrator might not be reasonable for an institution, or vice versa. Remember that the standard of care is reasonable care and that it is tested in real time. Student affairs administrators must expect to operate, to a certain extent, in the fog of war; they will be forced to make decisions with incomplete, even inaccurate, information from time to time, as in the *Lloyd* case.[100] In that case, a student initially said that his injuries were not related to hazing. Later, the reality of the plaintiff's victimization as a hazing target came to light. The court in *Lloyd* was sensitive to the fact that institutions of higher education must work with information they reasonably have; when a student misrepresents information, it may be difficult or impossible to make ideal decisions.

The Reasonable Person: Custom and Best Practices

The reasonable person must observe all widely accepted relevant and reasonable safety customs in an industry.[101] In making decisions, the reasonable person must use his or her special skills, knowledge, education, experience, training, and intellect.[102] Otherwise, the term *best practice* is not a term of art in the law of negligence.

Much of what is bandied about as "best practice" in higher education would fail to achieve the status of "custom" under evidentiary standards in court. Safety customs must be broadly accepted and must demonstrate the relevance to a particular risk-generating activity—and they must be reasonable.

---

[100] *See Lloyd v. Alpha Phi Alpha Fraternity,* 1999 WL 47153 (N.D.N.Y. 1999).

[101] *See* Clarence Morris, *Custom and Negligence*, 42 Columbia L. Rev. 1147 (1942). "In determining whether the defendant had a duty to be careful, we look to existing social values and customs, as well as to appropriate social policy." *Davis v. Westwood Group*, 652 N.E.2d 567, 569 (Mass. 1995). In the case of *Roberts v. Indiana Gas and Water Co.*, the court cites a custom (the gas company practice of odorizing natural gas) and the negligent result for failure to abide by this custom, even though due care would not require this action. 218 N.E.2d 556 (Ind. App. 1966).

[102] *See Restatement (Second) of Torts* § 298; *BG&E v. Flippo*, 684 A.2d 456, 462 (Md. Spec. App. 1996) (explaining that the defendant, an electrical services company, was under a duty to exercise the utmost degree of care and attention regarding the electrical distribution system and, therefore, was under a duty to ensure that climbable trees close to high-tension wires were removed, trimmed, or cut to avoid access to the electrical wires); *Lunar v. Ohio Dept. of Transp.*, 572 N.E. 2d 208, 210 (Ohio App. 10th Dist. 1989) (holding the engineers' conduct reasonable, as it complied with accepted engineering practices).

Industries often have customs that are not safety customs, or habits that are not customs either; neither proves much about what a reasonable person would do. Student affairs administrators should beware of the allure of best practice discourse. Acting in accordance with some practices is not necessarily evidence of reasonable care and may actually lull an administrator into not taking actions that reasonable care demands. Good student affairs administrators will use their knowledge and training in making decisions—this is a good practice in accord with the reasonable person standard. A lot of valuable information may not be known throughout the industry or widely put into practice but, as a reasonable person, a student affairs administrator might use this information . . . and might even be required to do so.[103]

Student Affairs Administrators and Professional Standards

Student affairs professionals are moving forward toward defining the necessary skills and competencies for student affairs practice;[104] however, the law generally does not recognize student affairs as a profession for purposes of applying professional standards of care. Articulated competencies may be relevant to determine what is reasonable, but not necessarily dispositive. In negligence law, professional standards of care (which differ from the reasonable person standard) are usually reserved for the so-called "learned professions" (e.g., law, medicine, architecture, engineering, and accountancy), which feature self-regulation and self-discipline systems, licensing, and clearly defined professional standards.[105]

The Reasonable Person and Nonstudents on Campus

How should student affairs administrators approach risks associated with nonstudents on campus?

First, many people who come to campus but are not matriculated students in the traditional curriculum are owed reasonable care during their time on campus. This usually includes vendors and others who come to campus for

---

[103] *See T. J. Hooper,* 60 F.2d 737 (2d Cir. 1932) (holding that even though the tug company implemented the industry standard of no required radio receiver on board, the company was still liable, as the general practice of the tug industry was not the standard of care).

[104] ACPA and NASPA, *Professional Competency Areas for Student Affairs Practitioners* (July 24, 2010) *available at* http://www.naspa.org/programs/prodev/Professional_Competencies.pdf.

[105] Diamond, *supra* note 19, at § 7.01, 91–92.

business purposes, police and emergency personnel, persons visiting campus or staying overnight for campus tours, and guests of students, even if they come for purely social purposes.[106] In some jurisdictions, social guests on campus are owed less than reasonable care.[107] Campuses may also owe a duty of reasonable care to small children who are drawn to campus for a foreseeable reason, such as an open swimming pool area.[108] Many determinations of duty and standard of care in this situation turn on complex legal analysis of so-called entrant status classification.[109] Institutions of higher education will owe little or no care to trespassers, particularly criminal trespassers, or to persons (including students) who deviate into unforeseeable areas or in unforeseeable ways.[110]

Campus responsibility for so-called "open and obvious dangers" arising from conditions on campus is also limited, and in many cases there is negligible legal risk relating to injuries arising from open and obvious dangers.[111] People are usually expected to observe readily identifiable conditions and avoid them—or else. The law essentially presumes that open and obvious dangers, in contrast with hidden dangers, give warning of danger ahead. At times, however, dangers that are open and obvious cease to be so; for example, when a person is distracted, or heavily laden with books or other materials.[112]

---

[106] *Id.* at 136–40.

[107] *See, e.g., Chatham v. Larkins,* 216 S.E.2d 677, 679 (Ga. App. 1975). "A licensee is a person who is neither a customer, nor a servant, nor a trespasser, and does not stand in any contractual relation with the owner of the premises, and who is permitted expressly or impliedly to go thereon merely for his own interest, convenience or gratification." *Id.*

[108] *See* Diamond, *supra* note 19, at 134–36, which explains the duty owed to children even when they trespass on another's property owing to a luring attraction on the land, such as a swimming pool.

[109] *See* Dan B. Dobbs, *The Law of Torts,* 591–624 (West Group 2000). However, the law has moved to impose the responsibility to reasonable care to a broad class of entrants, with the exception of adult trespassers who come for unlawful or illegal purposes. There is, however, a significant state-to-state variation in precisely how the law relates to nonstudents on campus, and student affairs administrators may detect subtle differences between adjacent jurisdictions.

[110] *Robertson v. State ex rel. Dept. of Planning & Control,* 747 So. 2d 1276, 1280 (La. App. 2d Cir. 1999) (explaining that "[t]he owner of a building cannot be held responsible for all injuries resulting from any risk posed by his building, only those caused by an unreasonable risk of harm to others. The defect must be of such a nature as to constitute a dangerous condition that would reasonably be expected to cause injury to a prudent person using ordinary care under the circumstances"(citations omitted).).

[111] *See Ward v. K-Mart Corp.,* 554 N.E.2d 223 (Ill. 1990).

[112] *See, e.g., id.* at 232. "The inquiry is whether the defendant should reasonably anticipate injury to those entrants on his premises who are generally exercising reasonable care for their own safety, but who may reasonably be expected to be distracted, as when carrying large bundles, or forgetful

In many instances, the responsibility to exercise care for persons on campus can be discharged with reasonable warning signs; however, sometimes a campus must do more than that, and some situations must be managed with forms of care other than warnings. Colleges often face problems when a condition on campus requires limited access to an area or closing off an area completely. In some cases, the college can permit access under supervision. An institution of higher education must usually create some system to gather and reasonably respond to information regarding dangerous conditions that arise on campus. If someone drops blackened banana peels on a dark macadam parking lot, so-called *constructive notice rules* apply. These rules require an institution of higher education that is aware, or *should be aware*, of this danger to act in a reasonable amount of time to respond to the dangerous condition.[113] However, if a fresh yellow banana peel is dropped on a white tile floor, the condition may be considered open and obvious—at least to most entrants.[114]

Many institutions of higher education simply were not designed the way other high-traffic, high-density businesses are designed today. Supermarkets, shopping malls, etc., are architecturally designed to reduce risk to business patrons; for example, it is virtually impossible to wander into the slippery meat-cutting area at a supermarket the way one could back in the 1960s. Premises management is a constant and difficult concern for student affairs administrators. The charm and beauty of our campuses—and their open nature—are emblematic features of higher education, but they create challenges for delivering

---

of the condition after having momentarily encountered it. If in fact the entrant was also guilty of negligence contributing to his injury, then that is a proper consideration under comparative negligence principles." *Id.*

[113] *See Goddard v. Boston & Maine R.R. Co.*, 60 N.E. 486 (Mass. 1901) (finding the railroad company not liable when a passenger slipped on a noticeable banana peel); *Anjou v. Boston Elevated Railway Co.*, 94 N.E. 386 (Mass. 1911) (finding the railway company liable when a women slipped on a banana peel that was "black, flattened out and gritty"); *Joy v. Great Atlantic and Pacific Tea Co.*, 405 F.2d 464 (4th Cir. 1968) (the grocery store was not liable when a customer slipped on a banana peel and injured himself, as there was not enough evidence to determine how long the peel may have been on the floor); *Jasko v. F.W. Woolworth Co.*, 494 P.2d 839 (Colo. 1972) (finding the store liable when a customer slipped on a piece of pizza; selling pizza by the slice with customers standing to eat it is dangerous).

[114] *See* note 113, *supra.* However, a situation in which students, particularly in high-traffic areas, are rushing to class, burdened with books or otherwise distracted, might vitiate the open and obvious rule, making the institution responsible for managing the dangerous condition. *See Ward,* 554 N.E.2d 223.

reasonable care. Many features of typical college campuses generate risk. Slip-and-fall hazards and the constant threat of criminal intrusion are particularly difficult to manage on older, open campuses. The good news is that the law has not demanded that we redesign our campuses from the ground up. For the most part, we are legally permitted to work with our long-term architectural footprints. So far, no clear architectural negligence case in higher education has ruled that an entire building or area on campus must be redesigned. However, as we apply the long-term planning process to our architectural footprint, it behooves us to build and renovate in ways that create a more reasonably safe environment. Enterprise risk management (ERM) efforts should be part of all long-term campus planning. The law permits American higher education to evolve, but evolve we must. The law does impose retrofitting responsibilities, and retrofitting becomes more difficult and even impossible over long periods of time.

CAUSATION

A plaintiff must prove causation in fact and proximate cause to prove a prima facie case of negligence. This is in addition to the other essential elements of the prima facie case; and liability is yet another matter.

Causation in fact is not usually a difficult conceptual topic for student affairs administrators. If an institution of higher education or a student affairs administrator (or the institution's agent or instrumentality) contributes to harm in a substantial and demonstrable way, the institution or administrator is a cause in fact of harm. In very simple cases of causation (like slip-and-fall cases), courts may apply the so-called *but for* test,[115] which tests counterfactually whether the injury to the plaintiff would have occurred "but for" the negligence of the defendant.[116] It is not the defendant's conduct as a whole that is tested; it is the *negligent* conduct that must be the cause in fact of harm.[117]

In complex cases of causation—in which the *but for* test does not work—courts will use so-called *substantial factor analysis* and insist that a plaintiff provide more than mere statistical evidence or conjecture regarding causation.[118]

---

[115] *Jordan*, 257 S.E.2d at 763.
[116] *See Nichols v. Northeast Louisiana Univ.*, 729 So. 2d 733 (La. App. 2d Cir. 1999); *see also Saelzler v. Advanced Group 400*, 25 Cal. 4th 763 (Cal. 2001).
[117] *See Jordan*, 257 S.E.2d at 763.
[118] *See Restatement (Second) of Torts* § 423(2).

Courts have been hesitant to impose affirmative duties of care for reasons related to causation. Who is to say that a putative rescuer would have changed the course of events? In many instances, arguments that an institution of higher education should or should not have acted for the benefit of students or others amount to statistical guesses at best.

A more challenging aspect of causation is legal or proximate cause. Proximate cause analysis is not causal, really, and the term *proximate* is extremely misleading. Proximate cause analysis is the junk drawer of negligence analysis. There are all sorts of things in there and many explanations for how they got there; some things are just there, and it is a mess. Understanding proximate cause is also like understanding your mother: It can take years and then, just when you think you have her figured out, she surprises you. Negligence law is the law of accidents and the unpredictable. Proximate cause is the winking gnome of chaos in the negligence formula.

Student affairs administrators would be wise to reduce proximate cause to a few simple features and rules, like the following ones.

Foreseeability and the Get Out of Jail Free Card

A judge and a jury have their go at foreseeability in a negligence case. Proximate cause is a question of fact for a jury, and a jury can usually consider foreseeability in determining proximate cause (except when it cannot, discussed below).[119]

---

[119] *See also McCain v. Fla. Power Corp.,* 593 So. 2d 500 (Fla. 1992*).*

> [F]oreseeability relates to duty and proximate causation in different ways and to different ends. The duty element of negligence focuses on whether the defendant's conduct foreseeably created a broader 'zone of risk' that poses a general threat of harm to others. The proximate causation element, on the other hand, is concerned with whether and to what extent the defendant's conduct foreseeably and substantially caused the specific injury that actually occurred. In other words, the former is a minimal threshold *legal* requirement for opening the courthouse doors, whereas the latter is part of the much more specific *factual* requirement that must be proved to win the case once the courthouse doors are open. As is obvious, a defendant might be under a legal duty of care to a specific plaintiff, but still not be liable for negligence because proximate causation cannot be proven.

Id. at 502–03 (citations omitted). Under *McCain,* the question of foreseeability as it relates to duty is determined by the judge, as a matter of law; whereas the question of foreseeability as it relates to proximate cause is determined by the jury, based on the facts. *Id.* Not every state is as clear as Florida on its division of responsibilities between judges and juries.

Sometimes proximate cause operates like a get out of jail free card. Technically, proximate cause is not a defense; it relates to the prima facie case of negligence, so it is the plaintiff's burden to carry proof of proximate cause forward. However, a jury may decide that an accident is so unusual that it exonerates the defendant, or it may believe that other defendants are so at fault that their faulty behavior trumps the fault of the defendant. In both situations, the jury determines that other forces or persons were "intervening" or "superseding" or "supervening" causes (terms of art in proximate cause analysis) that absolve one defendant of responsibility at the expense of others. In practice, this is fairly rare—juries are far more inclined to determine relative shares of fault under comparative fault rules (discussed below), under which defendants are found to be jointly responsible for harm or at least responsible for a share of harm.

Alcohol

Once upon a time, the voluntary drinker was considered the sole proximate cause of harm as a matter of law.[120] The law has moved away from this bright-line rule, and juries can now consider some other actors as concurrent causes of harm if a voluntary drinker causes injury. Primarily, the law has been extended to vendors of alcohol for on-premises consumption who serve either the visibly or noticeably intoxicated, or minors.[121] The expansion of liability for alcohol risk has timed out with the decline of the proximate cause rule. Do you see now why the quintessential bystander era cases (*Beach* and *Bradshaw*) were decided the way they were?

Suicide

The law once believed that a suicidal person was always the sole proximate cause of harm.[122] That rule of proximate causation has also been relaxed, opening up the possibility of another's liability for the suicide.[123] However, the law

---

[120] *Fleckner v. Dionne*, 210 P.2d 530 (Cal. 1949); *Parsons v. Jow*, 480 P.2d 396 (Wyo. 1971).

[121] Dobbs, *supra* note 109, at 899; *see* Mothers Against Drunk Driving, http://www.madd.org/Drunk-Driving/Drunk-Driving/Laws.aspx (last visited Aug. 5, 2010) (under "Laws," provides relevant DUI laws in a clickable state-by-state menu.).

[122] Peter F. Lake, *Still Waiting: The Slow Evolution of the Law in Light of the Ongoing Student Suicide Crisis*, 34 J.C. & U.L. 253 (2008).

[123] Peter Lake & Nancy Tribbensee, *The Emerging Crisis of College Student Suicide: Law and Poli-*

has been reluctant to impose liability for suicide on institutions of higher education that do not fit into the narrow exceptions to the old proximate cause rule.[124] There is some room for debate, however, regarding an institution's negligently permitting access to lethal means or means causing suicidal ideation.[125]

Intentional Wrongs of Others

The law once held that intentional wrongdoers were the sole proximate causes of harm, even if the negligent conduct of others facilitated the intentional harm.[126] This older proximate cause rule has also been relaxed, and juries may consider negligent defendants as concurrent proximate causes of harm if their negligence foreseeably enhanced the risk to the plaintiff. The prime examples are in negligent hiring, supervision, training, and retention of employees, and negligence with respect to preventing criminal assault on campus. Institutions of higher education and student affairs administrators must use reasonable care in employment practices and to protect students on campus from foreseeable criminal danger. These rules apply to fellow students as well. If an institution of higher education or student affairs administrator can reasonably foresee that a certain person, who has shown dangerous propensities, will repeat a crime or escalate into a more serious crime (or pick a new target of violence), courts and juries may find proximate cause and duty.[127]

Weird or Unusually Extensive Injuries

The rules of law regarding proximate cause state that if the type of injury is foreseeable, the manner or extent of injury need not be.[128] Lawyers know this

---

cy Responses to Serious Forms of Self-Inflicted Injury, 32 Stetson L. Rev. 125 (2002).

[124] *Id.; see Jain v. Iowa*, 617 NW.2d 293 (Iowa 2000); *cf. Shin v. Mass. Inst. of Tech.*, 2005 WL 1869101 (Mass. 2005).

[125] *See The JED Foundation*, http:// www.jedfoundation.org (last visited Aug. 14, 2010).

[126] *Watson v. Duerr,* 379 So. 2d 1243 (Ala. 1980). Thus, in the olden days, failure to repair a lock on a dormitory room would not be considered the proximate cause of harm if a rapist entered through the door and attacked a female tenant.

[127] *See Nero v. Kansas State Univ.*, 861 P.2d 768 (Kan. 1993); *Sharkey v. Bd. of Regents of Univ. of Nebraska,* 615 N.W.2d 889, 900–02 (Neb. 2000), abrogated by *A.W. v. Lancaster Cnty. Sch. Dist. 001,* 784 N.W.2d 907 (Neb. 2010).

[128] Dobbs, *supra* note 110, at § 180, 443–45.

as the *eggshell-thin skull* rule,[129] which is a dated, Coen-brothers-esque way of explaining the concept. Basically, in modern negligence law you take your victims the way you find them: if you injure Bill Gates, it could cost you billions of dollars. The *eggshell-thin skull* rule explains why colliding with a "beater" is preferable in most instances to colliding with a Mercedes Benz.[130]

When accidents happen in unusual Rube Goldberg ways, defendants may try to squirm out of responsibility, but they rarely succeed. Only if a different *type* of injury occurs from that which is foreseeable can defendants successfully argue that they are not the proximate cause of harm.[131]

It can be very difficult to determine type of injury versus manner/extent of injury. Complex policy factors often militate in favor of one or the other determination, and the line is not very bright. There are, however, two situations in which injury is foreseeable as a matter of law, even when it truly sometimes is not.

First, rescuers are considered foreseeable victims, even if they are hiding in the bushes and no one could have known they were present. As one judge said, "Danger invites rescue."[132] Fellow college students, student affairs administrators, and volunteers may rush to the aid of an injured student and themselves become victims of harm arising from the original negligent act or omission.

Second, subsequent medical negligence is considered foreseeable as a matter of law. It is reasonable in the real world to assume that doctors will not routinely make injured victims worse off. However, the law presumes foreseeability of medical negligence following a negligently caused injury. This is very important for student affairs administrators to understand, because emergency services and first responders often have emergency care immunities that protect them from liability for ordinary medical negligence claims.[133] Thus, the institution

---

[129] *Id.*

[130] The urban dictionary defines a beater as "a car used for daily transport to avoid damage or wear and tear on a nicer car. 'I drove my beater to work today, it is raining too hard to take the Z.'" Urban Dictionary, www.urbandictionary.com/define.php?term=beater (1999–2010).

[131] If you are blasting near a mink farm, it is foreseeable that concussion waves or debris could harm minks; however, if minks choose not to reproduce because they dislike the commotion of blasting, this type of damage is not considered foreseeable. *See Foster v. Preston Mill Co.*, 268 P.2d 645 (Wash. 1954). Leave the minks alone.

[132] *Wagner v. International Ry.*, 133 N.E. 437, 437–38 (N.Y. 1921).

[133] Fla. Stat. Ann. § 768.13 (West 2004); *see also* Jonathan Turley, *Torti Tort: California Supreme Court Rules Against Good Samaritan* (Dec. 19, 2008), *available at* http://jonathanturley.org/2008/12/19/torti-tort-california-supreme-court-rules-against-good-samaritan.

of higher education or the student affairs administrator could be the target of litigation over injuries caused by medical malpractice when health care providers themselves are not. First response may be subject to workers' compensation law requirements if a covered employee is injured in the scope of employment, but that is only one class of potential victims. This example shows that student affairs administrators may be more vulnerable than their counterparts in other employment sectors to emergency injury cases.

The subsequent medical malpractice rule is a special application of a broader rule known as the *second injury* rule.[134] Accidents often create other accidents. For example, when two vehicles collide, other vehicles might pile up with them.[135] For student affairs administrators, postaccident management is critical, because putative rescuers may appear, emergency services may fail, or the initial incident may create new hazards. Risk of liability ends when risk-rippled waters have calmed.[136] Not all second injuries are automatically foreseeable, but many are.

Closely related (although not technically a proximate cause issue) is the duty of an injured plaintiff to mitigate injuries or damage reasonably after an accident.[137] This usually plays out in two practical ways. First, the victim must seek appropriate medical assistance in a reasonable amount of time. Injured college students have a dangerous tendency to hide or obscure their injuries, which can make things worse for them.[138] Students should realize that the law does not compensate for enhanced harm of this type. Second, the mitigation rule may come into play if students or others fail to use necessary safety equipment, such as seat belts and helmets, which can result in enhanced injuries. Some courts view this as a form of contributory negligence to factor into comparative fault (see below). Failure to use safety devices can severely limit an injured person's claims for negligence.

DAMAGES

Plaintiffs often sue for damages. There is no actionable negligence without damage. Negligence in the air (breach of duty where no one gets hurt, as in your

---

[134] Dobbs, *supra* note 109, at § 249, 650–52.

[135] *See White v. Burns*, 567 A.2d 1195 (Conn. 1990). In *White*, a truck collided with several cars at a toll plaza in Stratford, causing multiple deaths and injuries. *Id.* at 1197.

[136] Again, this a matter of some dispute: When does an accident end?

[137] Diamond, *supra* note 19, at § 14.04, 238; *Restatement (Second) of Torts* § 918.

[138] *See Lloyd v. Alpha Phi Alpha Fraternity, supra* note 100, at *7.

morning commute when you were driving fast, eating, and talking on your cell phone) is not actionable, which is very good, because most of us are frequently unreasonable. We are usually just plain lucky that no one gets hurt. In negligence, no harm, no foul.

Negligence lawsuits are usually for either bodily injury or property damage.[139] Bodily injury is physical injury to a person including any emotional distress that flows from having a physical injury.[140] Property damage is physical damage to tangible property.[141] For a variety of extremely complex reasons, few lawsuits are brought for economic loss unless bodily injury or property damage occurs first. Lawsuits such as those for educational malpractice—in which no one has been physically injured—are disfavored in part for this reason. There is a great deal of media attention to punitive damages, but they are very unlikely in higher education.[142] First, punitive damages are usually prohibited under state sovereign immunity rules when institutions of higher education or officials are sued.[143] Second, punitive damages are sometimes only available if a defendant has acted intentionally or maliciously, and most states preclude insurance coverage of such damages. Third, punitive damages are rarely, if ever, available for simple negligence. Fourth, the standard to prove punitive damages has risen since tort reform. These days, plaintiffs often must prove punitive damages with clear and convincing evidence—a very high standard.[144] The major risk of punitive damages arises in lawsuits alleging vicarious liability (discussed below).

Student affairs administrators are not likely to see many large physical/tangible property damage cases. We do not routinely risk large physical property losses, as a major petrochemical company might. It is also possible to sue colleges for *intangible* property damage. Institutions of higher education are increasingly

---

[139] John L. Diamond, *Cases and Materials on Torts* (2d ed., Thompson/West 2008).

[140] Robert H. Jerry, II, *Understanding Insurance Law*, § 65(a), 440–41 (2d ed., Matthew Bender 1996).

[141] *Id.* at 441–42.

[142] Huffington Post, *Nancy Grace Interview Contributed to Melinda Duckett Suicide, Professor Says* (Dec. 6, 2009), *available at* http://www.huffingtonpost.com/2009/12/06/nancy-grace-inter-veiw-con_n_381846.html.

[143] "[P]unitive damages are not available against government entities." *Hooper v. North Carolina*, 379 F. Supp. 2d 804, 811–12 (M.D.N.C. 2005); *see also Clay v. Texas Women's University*, 728 F.2d 714, (5th Cir. 1984); *Marrapese v. State of R.I.*, 500 F. Supp. 1207 (D.R.I. 1980)

[144] Fla. Stat. Ann. § 429.297 (West 2006). The American Tort Reform Association (ATRA) outlined statutory tort reform regarding punitive damages; *see* ATRA, *Punitive Damages Reform* (2007), http://www.atra.org/issues/index.php?issue=7343.

in fights over such things as licenses and other intangible rights, but this is not a major part of student affairs practice.[145] Student affairs administrators and their institutions are more commonly implicated in lawsuits alleging bodily injury.[146]

Reading a newspaper about bodily injury cases can scare student affairs administrators to death. "So and so seeks X million dollars in damages from Y university." The reality of damages is far different from that reflected in the media.[147]

In their complaints, plaintiffs often choose extravagant numbers and so-called *ad damnum clauses*.[148] This is a feature of our litigation system; the numbers in a complaint are rarely realistic.[149] Large judgments or settlements are possible but unlikely against institutions of higher education or student affairs administrators.[150] This is why:

First, sovereign immunity law often caps damages, setting upper limits of potential responsibility.[151]

Second (discussed below), a plaintiff's damages can be diminished considerably by comparative fault rules and other defenses.

Third, a plaintiff has a responsibility to mitigate damages (discussed earlier).

Fourth, plaintiffs' lawyers have incentives to pursue cases that are routine or those that have a high potential for damages. Litigation is costly (most personal injury lawyers bear the brunt of litigation costs themselves, particularly if a case is not successful), and personal injury lawyers usually work on a con-

---

[145] Student affairs administrators may get caught in the middle if they have to work with the recording industry. It is increasingly important for institutions of higher education to teach students to respect intangible property rights of others, including reputation.

[146] William A. Kaplin & Barbara A. Lee, *The Law of Higher Education*, §§ 6.5, 13.2.5.4.1, 13.2.5.5, at 522–28, 1346–50 (4th ed., Jossey-Bass 2006).

[147] The media often reports the inflated damage figures in a plaintiff's complaint; few stories connect these numbers to later settlements or ultimate judgments to illustrate how inflated the original demands were.

[148] *Ad damnum* is Latin word for "to the damage." *Black's Law Dictionary* 15 (8th ed., Thompson/West 2004). It is defined as "[a] clause in a prayer for relief stating the amount of damages claimed." *Id.*

[149] Fed. R. Civ. P. 8 (2007).

[150] Nonetheless, they do occur from time to time. For example, Arizona State recently settled a case for $850,000 involving a student who was allegedly sexually assaulted. Tessa Muggeride, *ASU Settlement Ends in $850,000 Payoff* (Feb. 3 2009), http://www.statepress.com/archive/node/4020.

[151] Md. State Govt. Code Ann. §§ 12-104 to 12-110 (2010). Some states cap the amount of damages awarded against private institutions under "charitable immunity." *See* Tex. Civ. Prac. & Rem. Code § 84.006 (2010).

tingency fee basis, which means that small, non-routine cases are not valuable to pursue.[152] Litigation is likely in large cases in which injuries are very severe (e.g., death, need for long-term medical care), but thankfully, such cases are rare. Routine cases with modest (by litigation standards) damages are bread and butter cases—like slip and fall cases.

Fifth, even if an institution of higher education or a student affairs administrator is negligent in a serious injury case, student affairs administrators are rarely the only ones who are potentially negligent and responsible. As discussed below, institutions and administrators will likely split the bill with others under comparative fault rules. Other responsible actors may be much more culpable than any institution of higher education or student affairs administrator.

Sixth, large damage awards by juries are often reduced by judges. Judges can review jury verdicts and reduce them via what is known as *remittitur*.[153] A judge always has the power to trim a verdict, because it is the judge's job to turn a *verdict* into a *judgment*.[154]

Seventh, rules for calculation of damages do not always favor plaintiffs in litigation with student affairs administrators and institutions of higher education. Very large medical bills, very long periods of pain and suffering, or the grief of close family members occasioned by death would be the most likely causes of an extremely large verdict. Consider the following:

- Damages for bodily injury include compensation for medical costs pursuing cure. Traditional-age college students probably heal more quickly than others in the population at large. Also, many injuries have low

---

[152] Contingency fees are fees based on (contingent on) the outcome of the case. However, some matters, such as a divorce, prohibit contingency fee agreements. According to the Florida Rules of Professional Conduct, "[a] contingent fee agreement shall be in writing and shall state the method by which the fee is to be determined, including the percentage or percentages that shall accrue to the lawyer in the event of settlement, trial, or appeal, litigation and other expenses to be deducted from the recovery, and whether such expenses are to be deducted before or after the contingent fee is calculated." Florida Bar Association, *Rules Regulating the Florida Bar: Rule 4-1.5 Fees and Costs for Legal Services* (Feb. 1, 2010), http://www.floridabar.org/divexe/rrtfb.nsf/FV/A8644F215162F9DE85257164004C0429.

[153] *See, e.g., Johnston v. Joyce*, 596 N.Y.2d 625, 626 (N.Y.A.D. 4th Dept. 1993) (reducing the jury's award of $1,000,000 for future pain and suffering in a medical malpractice suit, owing to the excessiveness of the award and its deviation from what would be "reasonable compensation").

[154] Fed. R. Civ. P. 58(b)(1)(A) (2007).

medical health costs. In addition, some jurisdictions allow offsets for collateral sources in certain cases, meaning that damages will be reduced by the amount of health care coverage available (however, government programs may have rights to recoup these costs[155]). Medical damages will be greatest when long-term care is necessary. Severe head and spinal cord injuries, for example, are usually the most costly and generate the largest damage awards. Somewhat perversely, and for hyper-technical legal reasons, accidents causing instantaneous death do not usually generate the largest medical costs or the largest damage awards.

- Damages for bodily injury can include lost wages and impaired future earnings; however, many college students will recover only modest damages on this dimension, as few are high earners in college, and many make full recovery before they graduate and enter the workforce. Permanent, debilitating injuries are a different matter, but here plaintiffs often struggle because future earning capacity can be speculative. Damages are more likely to be high and demonstrable in programs that lead to specific profitable careers such as law and medicine. But these damages are likely to be the highest only when a plaintiff suffers severe head or spinal cord injuries or other very debilitating, career threatening injuries. But even many of those injuries do not preclude all future earnings and may only partially *impair* a person's ability to earn a living in the future.

- Damages for bodily injury include compensation for pain and suffering, emotional distress, and grief occasioned by death. Pain and suffering is often the largest quantum of damage in a college injury case. However the law provides no compensation for pain and suffering upon instantaneous death, however horrific, because it is presumed that there was no conscious interval of pain and suffering. Otherwise, pain and suffering is often calculated on a daily basis: Juries are sometimes asked to quantify each day's pain and suffering, add it up, and reduce it to present value.[156] This can be a very large sum. Terrible scar-

---

[155] Jerry, *supra* note 140, at § 96[d], 605–11.
[156] Pain and suffering is measured on a per diem basis. *Beagle v. Vasold*, 417 P.2d 673, 681–82 (Cal. 1966).

ring or disfigurement, constant back or neck pain, or loss of a function such as eyesight can generate a significant award. However, in some instances, pain and suffering diminishes with time, and a plaintiff is usually expected to cope with the normal overall lousy feeling that is a permanent feature of life after childhood.[157]

- Pain and suffering can also include mental suffering: emotional distress. Courts often discuss emotional distress in elaborate terms, such as hedonic damages or the loss of enjoyment of life.[158] These damages can be substantial. American courts usually require that the person seeking emotional distress damages was physically injured or very close to an accident that could have injured him or her.[159] If a student is killed in an accident, the law will permit certain relatives to maintain claims for their emotional distress, grief, or loss of consortium.[160] Close relatives—usually defined as "survivors" in wrongful death statutes—can potentially recover pecuniary loss.[161] For most

---

[157] "Mr. Waturi: *And what's this about a doctor's appointment? You're always going to the doctor.* Joe Banks: *I don't feel good.* Mr. Waturi: *So what? You think I feel good? Nobody feels good. After childhood it's a fact of life. I feel rotten. So what? I don't let it bother me. I don't let it interfere with my job.*" *Joe Versus the Volcano* (Warner Bros. Pictures 1990) (motion picture).

[158] Dobbs, *supra* note 109, at § 378, 1053. "Hedonic comes from the Greek word referring to pleasure. . . . [I]t suggest[s] a recovery for lost pleasures" and even "lost pleasures of which the plaintiff was not aware." *Id.*; *Sterner v. Wesley College, Inc.*, 747 F. Supp. 263, 272 (D. Del. 1990).

[159] *See Dillon v. Legg*, 441 P.2d 912 (Cal. 1968) (holding that a mother who does not fear imminent physical harm but who witnessed the negligent infliction of injury or death on her child may state a claim and recover for emotional distress). *Dillon* essentially expanded the general rule of emotional distress to include not only the victim but also bystanders who are close in relation to the victim, present at the scene of injury, and suffer from observing the accident. *Id.* However, this extension is only followed by a minority of states. *Diamond, supra* note 139 at 325; *Thing v. La Chusa*, 771 P.2d 814 (Cal. 1989) (upholding *Dillon* with the addition that the bystander must not only be present for the injury producing event, but also must be aware that the event that is causing injury to the victim). In *Thing*, the mother was not present when her son was struck by a car, nor was she aware that her son had been injured, whereas in *Dillon*, the mother witnessed the injury to her child. *Id.* In *Thing*, the mother could not recover for emotional distress, whereas in *Dillon*, the mother could recover. *Id.*

[160] A cause of action for loss of "consortium" is an action brought by a married person when his or her spouse is injured as a result of a third party's negligence. *Rodrigues v. Bethlehem Steel Corp.*, 525 P.2d 669 (Cal. 1974). Loss of consortium is defined as "the loss of conjugal fellowship and sexual relations" . . . include[ing] the loss of love, companionship, society, sexual relations, and household services. *Borer v. American Airlines, Inc.*, 563 P.2d 858 (Cal. 1977) (citations omitted).

[161] Diamond, *supra* note 139, at 349. Dobbs, *supra* note 109, at § 294, 804.

college students, however, this calculation is low because of the way courts define pecuniary loss.[162]

• Damages for bodily injury also include so-called special foreseeable damages—such as the cost of a rental car—but these damages are rarely extensive in and of themselves.

Overall, student affairs administrators should realize that (a) a great deal of negligence is pragmatically not actionable; (b) damages (and hence the likelihood of actionable cases) must arise from routine cases or be serious for lawsuits to eventuate; (c) only a small fraction of incidents will have injuries serious enough (e.g., death, serious head or spinal cord injury, disfigurement) to generate significant compensable damages; (d) the media hype about spectacular tort remedies is not reality; and (e) institutions of higher education and student affairs administrators should expect litigation when damages are particularly high, because injured plaintiffs may need to sue to cover their medical costs, and plaintiffs' lawyers will have a greater incentive to take such cases forward.

Whether a student affairs administrator has insurance or not is usually a minor consideration. Damages must first be significant, and institutions of higher education usually have sufficient insurance or resources to pay judgments. At best, the existence of student affairs administrator insurance is just a small part of a complex calculation of whether a matter goes forward.

One final note: Studies have shown that a major factor determining whether plaintiffs go forward with cases against institutions of higher education, student affairs administrators, and others is bedside manner. When people believe that they were poorly treated after an incident or injury, the temptation to become oppositional litigants grows. Very often in serious injury matters, plaintiffs and families are more interested in meaning and closure than in money damages.

---

[162] *See* Wex Malone, *The Genesis of Wrongful Death*, 17 Stanford L. Rev. 1043 (1965); *Greene v. Texeira*, 505 P.2d 1160, 1171–74 (Haw. 1973) (holding that the survival statute granted damages for potential future earnings reflecting what the person was making before his death, despite the fact that the decedent was 19 years old and a college freshman).

AFFIRMATIVE DEFENSES

Not long ago (in the 1970s in many states), affirmative defenses to negligence were largely all or nothing defenses. If a defendant institution of higher education or a student affairs administrator could prove a valid legal immunity, or that the plaintiff was contributorily negligent or assumed the risk, the claim would be completely defeated, with very few exceptions.[163] Today, immunities have been relaxed or abolished in whole or in part, and comparative negligence systems have replaced the old all-or-nothing systems. This major change in American tort law has opened the door for wider accountability on the part of institutions of higher education and student affairs administrators.

What Is Contributory Negligence?

Contributory negligence is the failure of the plaintiff to use reasonable care for his or her own safety. Think of this as a reverse negligence case: Plaintiffs have a legal duty to protect themselves using reasonable care. This is why it is so important to use crosswalks when you cross the street. Unless you are in a state like California where jaywalking rules are enforced (unlike Boston, my hometown), you probably will not get picked up for jaywalking; but if you are hit by a negligent motorist while jaywalking, it will cost you dearly in tort. Contributory negligence includes contributory negligence *per se*, so plaintiffs must observe safety statutes for their own safety.

What Is Assumption of Risk?

Assumption of risk is consent to a risk (not to harm, just the risk). Voluntarily proceeding in the face of a known danger is tantamount to assuming a risk.[164] There are two types of assumption of risk: express and implied.

---

[163] *See, e.g., Davies v. Mann*, 152 Eng. Rep. 588, 590 (1842) (holding that where a plaintiff improperly tethered his donkey, the plaintiff's contributory negligence in failing to fetter properly does not bar recovery: The defendant, while driving his team of horses, had the "last clear chance" to avoid the accident and could have if he had acted with ordinary care). The *Davies* case is famous for articulating the so-called "last clear chance" doctrine, which protected helpless plaintiffs from being victimized by defendants. Most jurisdictions have merged last clear chance rules into comparative fault rules, and the doctrine is almost entirely vestigial today. Dobbs, *supra* note 109 at § 200, 499–500.

[164] "Volenti non fit injuria. One who takes part in such a sport accepts the dangers that inhere in

Implied assumption of risk arises from a plaintiff's conduct and circumstances surrounding an injury. If you walk onto a tennis court and begin playing, you have assumed the risk of the ordinary and reasonably discoverable or known dangers of tennis. Tennis is not a particularly dangerous sport, but you can twist an ankle, get hit by a tennis ball, or get sunburned playing outdoors too long at a resort in Arizona.

One of the most tragic examples of assumption of risk and its effect on litigation can be seen in the *Pitre* litigation in Louisiana.[165] In that case, a student "sledded" down a hill into a parking lot on his back, head first.[166] He had watched several other students do the same thing before he chose to proceed.[167] On his ill-fated run, he struck a concrete light pole and suffered a severe spinal cord injury.[168]

The Louisiana Supreme Court held that the student had assumed the risk. He voluntarily sledded down the hill and could observe the risk of colliding with objects or others in the parking lot before he took off.[169] It is interesting that in *Pitre*, the justices were sharply divided on their view of the appropriate result, although ultimately a majority of the justices of the Louisiana Supreme Court struck down the claim. *Pitre* is a very good example of a very close and difficult case.

Implied assumption of risk is often indistinguishable from contributory negligence. Might you not at least argue that going downhill head first on your back is unreasonable? Individuals born in snowy northern states usually know better. Consenting to a risk and acting unreasonably are not always that different, but sometimes they are. For instance, it may be reasonable to attempt rock

---

it so far as they are obvious and necessary, just as a fencer accepts the risk of a thrust by his antagonist or a spectator at a ball game the chance of contact with the ball." *Murphy v. Steeplechase Amusement Co.*, 166 N.E. 173, 174 (N.Y. 1929) (The "Flopper," an amusement park ride that flops patrons, flops a "floppee," who assumed risk of being flopped by voluntarily choosing to take the ride; Diamond, *supra* note 139, at 421.

[165] *Pitre v. Louisiana Tech Univ.*, 655 So. 2d 659 (La. Ct. App. 1995), *rev'd*, 673 So. 2d 585 (La. 1996).
[166] *Id.* at 664.
[167] *Id.*
[168] *Id.*
[169] "It is common knowledge that one must be able to steer to avoid colliding with fixed objects while sledding. Despite his familiarity with the campus and the parking lot, Pitre chose to sled, on his back, head first, down a hill on a device over which he had no control." *Pitre*, 673 So. 2d at 593. [T]he light pole is of great social utility, as it serves important safety interests by providing lighting to pedestrians and users of the parking lot. Furthermore, the likelihood of the harm was minimal since the light pole was obvious and apparent to those sledding on the hill that evening, and the associated risks of colliding with it while sledding were well-known." *Id.*

climbing with the right equipment and supervision. There is nothing unreasonable about taking reasonable risk. However, by participating in rock climbing, you have, by implication, assumed the risks of the sport.[170]

Express assumption of risk arises from words, either out loud or in writing. Signed express assumption of risk forms are often referred to as waivers, releases, exculpatory agreements, or consent forms. The names of the forms are not always used in precisely correct ways. In most states, precision in the name of a form is not as important as it might have been 50 years ago, but it can be decisive in some situations. Your lawyers can tell you exactly how best to comply here.

Signed assumption of risk forms can be complete bars to recovery in many states. In most jurisdictions, express assumption of risk survives comparative fault rules (discussed below). However, these forms are not always valid—some states require the forms to use certain magic words.[171] It is also common to scrutinize forms to see if they agree with good public policy. Believe it or not, some

---

[170] A common problem occurs when one person appears to assume the risk and later recants and claims he or she never agreed to assume the risk. *See O'Brien v. Cunnard S.S. Co., Ltd.*, 28 N.E. 266 (Mass. 1891) (holding that even if the plaintiff did not subjectively consent to a vaccination, her conduct of holding out her arm as others had gave the appearance of consent upon which the defendant was entitled to rely). The law permits a person to proceed as if another person has assumed the risk if it would reasonably appear he or she has done so. *Id.* Moreover, an individual is charged with proceeding reasonably into an activity and will usually be held to know what objective reasonable persons would know before going into that activity. *See Eli v. City of New York*, 901 N.Y.S.2d 899 (N.Y. App. Div. Kings Cnty. 2009) (finding that the plaintiff, while sitting near third base at the game, assumed the risk when a bat flew into the stand); *Pakett v. The Phillies, L.P.*, 871 A.2d 304 (Pa. Cmmw. 2005) (stating that risks are inherent in the game of baseball, particularly when one sits near third base). However, a person who has assumed a risk can withdraw his or her assent.

A student affairs administrator should also know that the analogous defense in intentional torts is consent. While institutions of higher education and student affairs administrators rarely commit intentional torts, students do. Three of the more common patterns that student affairs administrators will encounter are mutual affray, sexual assault, and hazing. Issues of consent and assumption of risk will arise with each of these topics. In many situations, the law does not permit students to either consent to or assume the risk of unlawful behavior. For instance, all states with hazing laws except Alabama eliminate defenses of consent and assumption of risk for hazing, and some states hold that a mutual affray, although perhaps consensual, does not permit either party to raise defenses of consent or assumption of risk. *See, e.g., Lloyd v. Alpha Phi Alpha Fraternity*, 1999 WL 47153 (N.D. N.Y. 1999). Moreover, in sexual assault cases, the alleged victim may be incapable of consent because he or she is incapacitated, intoxicated, or underage. *Tanja H. v. Regents of Univ. of Cal.*, 228 Cal. App. 3d 434, 436–38 (Cal. App. 1st Dist. 1991).

[171] For example, some states require that valid forms include such terms as "negligence." *Gross v. Sweet*, 400 N.E.2d 306 (N.Y. 1979).

colleges have tried to have students sign forms essentially assuming all the risks of college, or residential life, or premises safety. Courts typically strike down such forms because they violate public policy.[172] However, courts usually uphold express assumption of risk forms in a recreational sports setting, particularly if they clearly describe the risks of the activity.[173] Public policy is not likely to protect students when they are voluntarily participating in recreational sports, but with respect to basic safety rights, public policy frowns on the use of signed forms to avoid responsibility. Public policy also dislikes exculpatory language that attempts to excuse reckless or intentional behavior.[174]

With respect to either implied or express assumption of risk, an institution of higher education or student affairs administrator must endeavor to make a recreational sports activity as safe as it reasonably appears to be. There is no assumption of risk for hidden or obscure dangers of an activity that cannot be discovered by participants using reasonable care. For example, a torn-up football field warns of danger ahead, but if the field appears safe but has hidden hazards (such as deep holes patched over with fresh grass), participants do not assume the risks of such hazards, unless, of course, they are clearly spelled out on a written form. It is crucial that recreational sports maintenance be performed with precision; staff must be trained to use reasonable care to observe risks that might not be readily apparent to participants and not to wallpaper over significant defects in fields, courts, or equipment that might cause injury.[175] But some risks are beyond the scope of what has been assumed. It is not one of the risks of tennis that the benches you sit on between sets will be in disrepair with hidden risks.[176] It is possible for specta-

---

[172] *See Tunkle v. Regents*, 383 P.2d 441 (Cal. 1963); *Porubiansky v. Emory Univ.*, 275 S.E.2d 163 (Ga. App. 1980); *Gonzalez v. Univ. System of New Hampshire*, 2005 WL 530806, at *7 (Conn. Super. 2005) (holding that the plaintiff, a quadriplegic from injuries sustained from a fall atop a human pyramid, was not barred from a negligence claim against the university despite the plaintiff's signing of a release of liability to participate in the cheerleading club).

[173] *See Cain v. Cleveland Parachute*, 457 NE.2d 1185 (Ohio 1983).

[174] *Southwestern Public Services Co. v. Artesia Alfalfa Growers' Assn.*, 353 P.2d 62 (N.M. 1960).

[175] *Davidson*, 543 S.E.2d at 927 (explaining that the types of omissions that could constitute negligence on the university for the plaintiff's injury as a result of a cheerleading accident are failure to provide safety equipment, failure to sufficiently train cheerleaders in safety and technique, failure to supervise, failure to evaluate cheerleaders' skill and fitness levels, failure to institute guidelines, and failure regulate the height of human pyramids).

[176] *Morgan v. State*, 685 N.E.2d 202, 210 (N.Y. 1997) (holding the owner of indoor tennis courts liable for injury to a tennis player when he snagged his foot in the torn net, as the player does not assume this risk).

tors to assume risks (as in sitting on the third base line and assuming the risk of a line drive foul ball), but a spectator does not assume all risks.[177] There are some seats at the Gallagher show that are vegetable/fruit-free.[178]

It is also axiomatic that one cannot assume risks one has no chance or choice to avoid. This is the essence of voluntariness: free will and choice. If icy steps are the only way out of a dormitory, it is not fair to tell students that they have "assumed the risk" on the way to scheduled classes.

Finally, assumption of risk of either type assumes the capacity to give voluntary consent to a risk. Age is rarely an issue in college litigation, because college students either have reached the age of maturity for consent or are presumed capable of giving consent to risks appropriate for their age and experience.[179] Alcohol or other drug use can also affect capacity to consent to a risk.

What Is Comparative Fault?

Currently, comparative fault is the dominant approach in the U.S. legal system.[180] Comparative fault systems abolish all-or-nothing rules in favor of comparing the fault of the defendant and plaintiff, and assigning percentage shares of responsibility to each. Juries must weigh the negligence of a defendant (a form of fault) against the plaintiff's contributory negligence (another form of fault). Assumption of risk creates a conceptual challenge: It is not always faulty to make a voluntary choice to encounter a risk. However, implied assumption of risk is so similar to contributory negligence in many situations that courts treat it as a form of fault and allow juries to factor it into that part of the calculus. Express assumption of the risk, however, is usually treated as a complete bar to recovery, even after the adoption of comparative fault rules.[181] Thus, legal battles

---

[177] *Hayden v. Univ. of Notre Dame*, 716 N.E.2d 603 (Ind. App. 1999) (holding that the university owed the spectator who was injured by other spectators lunging for a football owing to a duty to protect her and take reasonable steps to ensure her safety).

[178] "Gallagher's favorite prop is a prehistoric-looking mallet he calls a Sledge-o-matic. In a parody of those old slice-and-dice TV commercials for kitchen appliances, the wacky comedian pounds away at a selection of fruit and vegetables, thoroughly soaking and splattering those sitting in the first few rows of the theater. He calls this section 'death row.'" Gene Stout, *Gallagher Tosses Out Observations While Throwing Food* (Aug. 21, 1987), http://www.seatlepi.com/archives/1987/8701220487.asp.

[179] Dobbs, *supra* note 109, at § 210, 534–38.

[180] Dobbs, *supra* note 109, at § 210, 538–41.

[181] *Jones v. Dressel*, 623 P.2d 370 (Colo. 1981) (illustrating an express assumption of risk associ-

over express assumption of risk are often over the validity of forms, which determines whether a plaintiff has a chance of recovery or not. The search for effective and valid forms is a constant process for student affairs administrators.

So, how do juries (or fact finders) arrive at shares of fault? Many juries come up with simple calculations:

1. It was completely the defendant's or plaintiff's fault—100%:0%

2. The plaintiff and defendant were equally faulty—50%:50%

3. The plaintiff (or defendant) was slightly more faulty than the defendant (or plaintiff)—51%:49%

4. The plaintiff (or defendant) was not entirely innocent—99%:1%

5. The plaintiff (or defendant) was twice as faulty as the defendant (or plaintiff)—67%:33%

Sometimes juries make very complex calculations of relative fault, driven by the facts of the case, the lawyers' arguments, and the law. But the five verdicts in the list above are common, either in themselves or as baselines off of which many lawyers and juries operate.

Lawmakers have been careful in choosing systems of comparative fault for their jurisdictions. A popular approach, favored by the *Restatement of Torts*,[182] is *pure comparative fault*.[183] Under pure comparative fault, if a plaintiff is 99% at fault, that plaintiff can still recover 1% of the total damages from the defendant if the defendant is at fault. Many states dislike this approach and choose so-called *modified comparative fault* systems that bar some plaintiffs from recovering under various standards. States that use modified comparative fault typically bar the plaintiff from recovery if the plaintiff is more at fault than the defendant.[184] Some states bar certain classes of faulty plaintiffs from recovery.[185]

---

ated with skydiving by releasing the provider from liability through a contract).

[182] *Restatement (Third) of Torts: Apportionment of Liability* § 7 (2000). "This Section provides the basic principle of comparative responsibility. It replaces the rule of contributory negligence as an absolute bar to a plaintiff's recovery under *Restatement (Second) of Torts* § 467." *Id.* at cmt a.

[183] *See* Fla. Stat. Ann. § 768.81(West 2006).

[184] This is the so-called "greater fault bar." *See, e.g.,* Minn. Stat. § 604.01 (2010).

[185] *See, e.g.,* Fla. Stat. Ann § 768.36.

Some states are more litigation-prone than others with respect to college responsibility. Location in a state with modified comparative fault rules significantly reduces the risk of litigation against a college, all things being equal. It is difficult to find completely innocent college victims, many of whom became voluntarily intoxicated before they got injured. This type of behavior can significantly reduce recovery for a plaintiff and can even, in some cases, completely bar all chance of recovery.[186] Student affairs administrators should make sure their students understand that voluntary risky or unlawful behavior is both dangerous *and* likely to reduce the likelihood of compensation if they are injured. Many students do not realize, for example, that contributory negligence *per se* can reduce and in some cases eliminate, their potential for recovery. College students are primarily responsible for their own safety; they must always act as if they will be held responsible for their own safety if they are injured. Significant recovery by students against institutions of higher education or student affairs administrators is still relatively rare.

Comparative fault gets trickier when multiple parties are involved in an incident and the jury must assign shares of fault to all of them. In some cases, a jury must calculate the fault of a criminal or intentional wrongdoer, and rules of law such as vicarious liability (discussed below) may make some parties responsible for not only their share of fault but also the share of another actor. Another complex situation arises when some, but not all, parties settle before trial or legal action.[187] These issues fall under the heading of *apportionment*[188] and require expert legal assistance to sort out. Even law professors shudder at the issues that judges and juries must confront in some cases.

What Is Left of the Historical Immunities As They Apply to Institutions of Higher Education?

Except for some government immunity, very little.

In loco parentis—shorthand for a form of quasi-parental immunity—is long and completely gone in higher education.[189] In fact, it is not entirely clear that it

---

[186] *See Robertson*, 747 So. 2d at 1281–85.
[187] *See, e.g., Wells v. City of St. Petersburg*, 958 So. 2d 1076 (Fla. 2d Dist. App. 2007).
[188] *See Restatement (Third) of Torts: Apportionment of Liability* § 16.
[189] *See Lake, supra* note 32, at 27–63.

ever really existed as significant legal doctrine in higher education: *in loco parentis* has been overemphasized by modern writers and courts.[190] No modern American court recognizes any form of quasi-parental immunity for colleges vis-à-vis traditional college-age students or students matriculated in full-time academic programs.

Charitable immunity has been abolished almost universally in the United States.[191] Vestigial charitable immunities linger on in some states, but they are typically not sufficient factors in personal injury litigation against colleges by students.[192] Some protections apply to volunteers only; not to the charitable organization itself or its paid staff.[193]

Sovereign immunity is by far the most significant residual immunity in higher education safety law. As discussed earlier, states have only partially abolished sovereign immunity, although a very large range of routine tort lawsuits (e.g., slip-and-fall, negligence security) are not barred by sovereign immunity rules. Even in states with strong sovereign immunity rules protecting public institutions, liability risk might be lower but accountability expectations might actually be higher. As an arm of the state, public institutions face double scrutiny—as both institutions of higher education and government entities—by the public, the press, parents, students, and legislators. Higher education's two most notorious incidents—Kent State and Virginia Tech—occurred on public college campuses, and the political fallout from both outstripped the litigation.

The other significant tort law immunity student affairs administrators will encounter is workers' compensation—most injuries to workers that occur in the scope of employment are governed by this special statutory and regulatory system.[194] When a worker is covered by workers' compensation, an institution of higher education as employer enjoys an immunity in the tort system for claims arising from injuries sus-

---

[190] *Id.*

[191] Dobbs, *supra* note 109, at § 282, 760–65.

[192] Congress did provide some protection for volunteers of charitable organizations in the Volunteer Protection Act of 1997. 42 U.S.C.A. § 14501 (West 1997).

[193] 42 U.S.C.A. § 14505. "The term 'volunteer' means an individual performing services for a nonprofit organization or a governmental entity who does not receive—(A) compensation (other than reasonable reimbursement or allowance for expenses actually incurred); or (B) any other thing of value in lieu of compensation, in excess of $500 per year, and such term includes a volunteer serving as a director, officer, trustee, or direct service volunteer." *Id.* The Volunteer Protection Act has a limited impact on American higher education.

[194] Fla. Stat. Ann. §§ 440.01–440.60 (West 2010) (Workers' Compensation Law).

tained in the course of employment.[195] Immunity typically extends to student affairs administrators and other supervisors and fellow employees as well.[196] However, not all injuries are covered, and certain defendants may be sued in tort for workplace injuries.[197] The precise contours of what claims are in or out of workers' compensation laws can vary from state to state. A student affairs administrator must consult with the human resource director/legal counsel to understand workers' compensation rights in a given state. Injured workers often are entitled to compensation, although it is rarely as generous as plaintiffs might receive in the tort system. However, in the workers' compensation system, workplace injuries and responsibility are typically easier to prove.[198]

VICARIOUS LIABILITY IN EMPLOYMENT NEGLIGENCE

The law is generally averse to making one person responsible for the actions of another, so *vicarious liability* is limited to special situations in American law. There are two forms of vicarious liability. We are already familiar with one: negligence-based vicarious liability. The other is called strict vicarious liability. Both types of vicarious liability are triggered in one of two situations: employment or entrustment of dangerous items, such as automobiles. Be careful whom you hire and what you give them to work with.[199]

Type 1. Vicarious Liability Based in Negligence Law

An institution of higher education or student affairs administrator can be held responsible for negligently "entrusting" a dangerous instrumentality to a person that causes injury to that person or to a third party. The classic example is lending a car to a drunk driver who later crashes[200] or a gun to a suicidal person who

---

[195] Dobbs, *supra* note 109, at §§ 393, 395, at 1100, 1104–7.

[196] *Id.*

[197] *Id.*

[198] *Id.*

[199] This book does not provide in-depth treatment of all aspects of employment law. Topics such as employment discrimination and workplace disability accommodation law usually require interaction with trained human resource directors and/or lawyers to answer questions. Indeed, student affairs administrators should not attempt human resource management without professional human resource assistance or direct supervision by and interaction with counsel.

[200] *Ingram v. Pettit*, 340 So. 2d 922, 924–25 (Fla. 1976) (holding that an automobile is a "dangerous instrumentality," and such danger is heightened when the person operating the automobile is "incapable of exercising vigilance and caution," particularly when driving under the influence of alcohol; thus, a punitive damages award is proper).

uses it to kill himself. Critically, this form of liability requires that the entrustment be negligent and that the entrustor be the proximate and factual cause of harm.

Negligence-based vicarious liability is also common in the employment context, although many claims of negligence are diverted to the workers' compensation system. Third parties may claim that their injuries arose from negligent hiring, retention, supervision, or training.[201] Negligence-based employment torts do not require paid employment, and the status of an employee does not always determine liability. Moreover, if the employer commits negligence directly, the employee need not have committed negligence for an action to proceed. For instance, it might be reasonable to expect an employer to train employees a certain way in safety procedures, but a reasonable employee might not know exactly what safety training is necessary. Also, you do not have to be an employer to have negligence liability: supervisors can be negligent, as can fellow employees.

Type 2. Strict Vicarious Liability

In a sense, strict vicarious liability is actually semi-strict. It is also essentially limited in higher education to employment law. Under the doctrine of *respondeat superior*,[202] an employer is "strictly liable" for the torts of certain employees (typically referred to archaically as "servants")[203] committed in the scope of employment.[204] On the other hand, employers are usually not responsible for torts

---

[201] *Midwest Knitting Mills, Inc. v. U.S.*, 950 F.2d 1295 (7th Cir. 1991); *Moses v. Diocese of Colo.*, 863 P.2d 310 (Colo. 1993); *Shore v. Town of Stonington*, 444 A.2d 1379 (Conn. 1982); *Island City Flying Service v. General Elec. Credit Corp.*, 585 So. 2d 274 (Fla. 1991).

[202] "Under *respondeat superior*, an employer is vicariously liable for the torts of his employees committed within the scope of the employment." *Rodgers v. Kemper Construction Co.*, 50 Cal. App. 3d 608, 617 (Cal. App. 4th Dist. 1975). "*Respondeat superior* includes liability for an employee's intentional tort as well as negligence." *Id.* at 621.

[203] *Restatement (Second) of Torts* § 317 (2010).

[204] Diamond, *supra* note 19, at § 13.02(c). According to Kentucky law, to determine whether an employer is vicariously liable for the torts of its employees, the court applies the scope of employment test, which determines: (1) "whether 'the conduct was similar to that which the employee was hired to perform'"; (2) "whether 'the action occurred substantially within the authorized special and temporal limits of employment'"; (3) "whether 'the action was in furtherance of the employer's business'"; and (4) "whether 'the conduct, though unauthorized, was expectable in view of the employee's duties.'" *Booker v. GTE.net LLC*, 350 F.3d 515, 518–19 (6th Cir. 2003) (quoting *Coleman v. U.S.*, 91 F.3d 820, 824, 825 (6th Cir. 1996)). "In Indiana, an employee's tortuous act may fall within the scope of employment 'if his purpose was, to an appreciable extent, to further his employer's business.'" *Kemezy v. Peters*, 622 N.E.2d 1296, 1298 (Ind. 1993) (quoting *Stropes v. Heritage Childrens Center*, 547 N.E.2d 244, 247 (Ind. 1989)). "An employee's act is

committed by other types of employees (e.g., independent contractors)[205]—except when they are.[206] Consider the following points.

First, what type of employee do you have? The *Restatement (Second) of Agency*, often cited by courts, provides the following multifactor balancing test to determine which employee is which:

> In determining whether one acting for another is a servant or an independent contractor, the following matters of fact, among others, are considered:
>
> (a) the extent of control which, by the agreement, the master may exercise over the details of the work;
>
> (b) whether or not the one employed is engaged in a distinct occupation or business;
>
> (c) the kind of occupation, with reference to whether, in the locality, the work is usually done under the direction of the employer or by a specialist without supervision;
>
> (d) the skill required in the particular occupation;
>
> (e) whether the employer or the workman supplies the instrumentalities, tools, and the place of work for the person doing the work;
>
> (f) the length of time for which the person is employed;
>
> (g) the method of payment, whether by the time or by the job;
>
> (h) whether or not the work is a part of the regular business of the employer;

---

within the scope of employment if it is incident to some service being performed for the employer or arises out of an emotional response to actions being taken for the employer." *Rodebush v. Okl. Nursing Homes, Ltd.*, 867 P.2d 1241, 1245 (Okla. 1993). "Under Mississippi law, a determination that an employee's conduct falls within the scope of employment under the doctrine of *respondeat superior* requires a finding that the conduct was performed 'incident to the ultimate purpose which constitutes the employee's job.'" *Moran v. Kingdom of Saudi Arabia*, 27 F.3d 169, 173 (5th Cir. 1994) (quoting *Marter v. Scott*, 514 So. 2d 1240, 1242 (Miss. 1987)).

[205] *See Restatement (Second) of Agency* § 220 (2010).
[206] Dobbs, *supra* note 109, at §§ 336–37, at 917–26.

(i) whether or not the parties believe they are creating the relation of master and servant; and

(j) whether the principal is or is not in business.[207]

This seems immensely complicated, but it usually is not. If you pay someone hourly and closely supervise the details of work, the employee is usually a servant. If a person delivers completed projects subject to specifications and is paid by the job, he or she is usually an independent contractor. Most student affairs administrators are servants of their institutions of higher education; so are most of the paid and salaried staff. Roofers, building contractors, and consultants are typically independent contractors.

Second, there *must* be a tort committed by the servant (the employer need not commit a tort). The tort can be negligence or, in some cases, intentional (e.g., assault or battery). Hence, strict vicarious liability is automatically semi-strict because there is fault present.

Third, and crucially, the tort must be committed in the "scope of employment." Prepare to be shocked for two reasons: (1) The law defines scope of employment very broadly, which no student affairs administrator or institution of higher education will like. (2) Employees will steal food or money, get high or drunk at work, sexually harass one another, crash into innocent people (including the police),[208] deviate from work assignments when you send them off-campus to do errands, and generally do exactly what you told them not to do as soon as you leave the room. A certain amount of employee management skill is required in student affairs administration—Dean Wormer's lone wolf administration is a thing of the past. The law defines acting within the scope of employment in a counter-intuitive way to include acting to further the employer's purpose, however attenuated, within reasonable time and space requirements.[209]

Let's discuss reasonable time and space requirements first. Commuting is not ordinarily within the scope of employment under the so-called *going-and-coming rule*.[210] But there are exceptions under which an employee is within the

---

[207] *Restatement (Second) of Agency* § 220 (2010).
[208] *See Kobe v. Industrial Acc. Commission*, 35 Cal. 2d 33, 35 (Cal. 1950).
[209] *See Riviello v. Waldron*, 391 N.E.2d 1278 (N.Y. 1979).
[210] *See Ralphs Grocer Co. v. Workers' Comp. Appeals Bd.* 58 Cal. App. 4th 647, 651–52 (Cal. App. 4th Dist. 1997).

scope of employment, such as a special errand on the way to work or traveling between work locations.[211] Merely paying mileage does not usually bring a drive to work within the scope of employment, but paying travel time may do so.[212] If an employee takes a break from work for personal convenience or hygiene, he or she remains in the scope of employment; major deviations from work—such as using illegal drugs or getting drunk, as when an employee hits the local tavern on the way back from getting office supplies—are considered a *frolic and detour*, and are outside the scope of employment.[213]

Next, acting to further a master's purpose has been very broadly defined. Acts in contravention of policy or orders of superiors remain in the scope of employment if the employee acted to further some master's purpose in their own mind, authorized or not.[214] In one famous case, an employee claimed he had filled out an expense report on the road in a motel while smoking and dozed off (he had been drinking heavily); the employer was held responsible for the fire that burned down the motel. Filling out the expense report was considered a benefit to the employer, even though virtually everything else in this situation was not.[215]

Fourth, employers are not usually responsible for the torts of independent contractors, with two notable exceptions: (1) If an employer exercises close control over an independent contractor's work, that can transform the independent contractor into a servant.[216] (2) An employer will be responsible for torts committed in the scope of employment if there is a nondelegable duty. This exception is important to student affairs administrators because premises safety and security are notable nondelegable duties.[217] Thus, outsourcing student affairs tasks may not work as a litigation-avoidance technique, because nondelegable duties may be in the mix. And remember, it is possible to be negligent in hiring and retaining an independent contractor.

---

[211] *Id.*

[212] *See Caldwell v. A.R.B., Inc.*, 176 Cal. App. 3d 1028 (Cal. App. 5th Dist. 1986) (holding that merely paying a travel allowance without showing a benefit to the employer does not permit the exception to the coming and going rule).

[213] *See* explanation of "scope of employment," *supra* note 204.

[214] *Riviello*, 391 N.E.2d at 1281.

[215] *Edgewater Motel, Inc. v. Gatzke*, 277 N.W.2d 11 (Minn. 1979).

[216] *See Restatement (Second) of Agency* § 220; *N.L.R.B. v. Maine Caters, Inc.* 654 F.2d 131, 133 (1st Cir. 1981).

[217] Dobbs, *supra* note 109, at § 337, 920–26.

RISK MANAGEMENT AND CAMPUS SAFETY AND WELLNESS

Institutions of higher education and student affairs administrators work within a broad conceptual framework of potential legal responsibility and accountability. The law does not specifically mandate what a responsible campus must look like, so administrators must integrate good student affairs practice with general legal guidance. Since at least the 1980s, student affairs practice has steadily evolved to be more proactive with respect to many issues of safety and wellness; it is no longer widely acceptable to simply try to reduce the risks of litigation. Indeed, student affairs administrators have come to agree that the best litigation-avoidance strategy of all is to create campus environments in which injuries and risks to students are reduced.

Rise of Risk Management Culture in Student Affairs

Risk management culture in higher education has its origins on the business side of institutional operations. Employees with the title "risk manager" often spend a significant amount of time helping place and procure necessary insurances and working with insurance companies on risk management projects—especially workers' compensation and building safety. Risk management was not considered a primary student affairs responsibility until after the tragic collapse of the bonfire at Texas A&M University in 1999.[218] Student affairs administrators have always performed many functions that can be described as risk management efforts, but an overt risk management culture developed rapidly after this event. Today, administrators consider risk management an important part of student affairs practice.[219]

---

[218] Nancy Tribbensee, *Faculty Adviser, Beware: You May Be Liable*, Chronicle of Higher Education (June 25, 2004), *available at* http://chronicle.com/article/Faculty-Advisor-Beware-Yo/29646.

[219] However, progress remains to be made. "Fewer than half of respondents 'mostly agreed' that their institution's risk tolerance is understood (46.6 percent) and guides decision making (43.8 percent). Even fewer (40.7 percent) 'mostly agreed' that risk management is a priority at their institution (Q1)." Association of Governing Bds. of Univ. and Colleges, *The State of Enterprise Risk Management at Colleges and Universities Today* [hereinafter *The State of Enterprise Risk Management*] (June 25, 2009), *available at* http://www.epi.soe.vt.edu/perspective/policy_news/pdf/AGB_RISK.pdf; *see also* Association of Governing Boards of Universities and Colleges, http://www.agb.org (last visited January 31, 2011).

What Is Risk Management in Higher Education?

Over the past decade, models for risk management in higher education have proliferated.[220] Risk management in higher education is essentially the adaptation of principles developed for other businesses, although the field of risk management itself has been growing.[221]

A recent white paper, published by the Association of Governing Boards and United Educators, raised the following concerns arising from a survey of colleges and universities:

> Sixty percent of respondents said their institutions do not use comprehensive, strategic risk assessment to identify major risks to mission success.
>
> Fewer than half of the respondents said they "mostly agreed" with this statement: "Board members and senior administrators actively engage in discussions regarding institutional risks."
>
> Five percent of respondents said their institutions had exemplary practices for management of major risks to mission success.[222]

The white paper recommended the following best practices:

1. Define risk broadly. Traditionally, institutions focused on financial risks covered by insurance. Current thinking defines "risk" as any impediment to accomplishing institutional goals. In a 2000 report, the National Association of College and University Business Officers (NACUBO) discussed the "new language of risk" and identified five types of risk: strategic, financial, operational, compliance, and reputational.

---

[220] *See, e.g., The State of Enterprise Risk Management, supra* note 219.

[221] *Id.*; Committee of Sponsoring Organizations of the Treadway Commission, *Enterprise Risk Management —Integrated Framework: Executive Summary* (Sept. 2004), *available at* http://www. coso.org/Publications/ERM/COSO_ERM_ExecutiveSummary.pdf; *see also* National Association of College and University Business Officers and the Association of Governing Boards of Universities and Colleges, *Meeting the Challenges of Enterprise Risk Management in Higher Education* (2007), *available at* http://www.uncop.edu/riskmgt/erm/documents/agb_nacubo_hied.pdf.

[222] *See The State of Enterprise Risk Management, supra* note 219.

2. Recognize both the opportunities and downsides of risk. Many colleges focus only on the downsides of risk. In addition they should weigh risks against potential rewards. All successful organizations take risks, and the most promising opportunities often involve heightened risk.

3. Develop a culture of evaluating and identifying risk at multiple levels. Presidents and board members rarely see the first warnings of risk. Institutions need to identify and assess risks regularly at multiple levels so that the most critical ones filter up to top decision makers.

4. Look at the total cost of risk. Risk is not just about dollars and cents; institutions must consider all the consequences of risk. For example, in a lawsuit over denial of tenure, there are litigation costs, but there are also non-monetary costs [such as] . . . lost productivity, distraction from mission, and negative publicity.

5. Boards and presidents should collaborate. They need to engage in candid discussions at the strategic level. By working together presidents and boards can fulfill their shared responsibility for insuring the success of the mission and stability of the institution.[223]

The report also lists nine action steps designed to help institutions of higher education enhance their risk management culture.[224]

---

[223] *See The State of Enterprise Risk Management, supra* note 219, at 2.
[224] *See The State of Enterprise Risk Management, supra* note 219, at 3.
    Action Steps:
    1. Develop a disciplined process to consider risk in strategic discussions. . . .
    2. Designate an owner of the risk identification process. . . .
    3. Require all top administrators to prioritize risk. . . .
    4. Sift through the prioritized risks to decide which ones warrant attention at the highest level. . . .
    5. Require annual written reports on each high-priority risk being monitored. . . .
    6. Reassess priority risks at the board level at least once a year. . . .
    7. Look for blind spots. . . .
    8. Move risk identification deeper into the institution each year. . . .

Student affairs administrators must recognize that best business practices and legal compliance with tort law may be different things. Nonetheless, the process of proactive environmental risk management is something a reasonable actor would at least consider in managing a modern institution of higher education environment. Risk management has the promise of reducing risks that lead to lawsuits.

Identify Core and Common Risks: Major Challenges of a Modern University

Risks to college students change, and certain safety and wellness challenges have recently emerged as salient.

Alcohol and other drugs.

High-risk alcohol use by college students (sometimes referred to as "binge drinking")[225] or drug use correlates highly with negative outcomes on campus over a broad spectrum of risk, from vehicular accidents to academic performance.[226] Alcohol and other drug prevention efforts are a key component of good risk management and can potentially reduce the frequency, cost, and severity of student risk.

The science of alcohol and drug prevention has evolved rapidly in the past three decades, and has recently been cited and referred to in reported legal decisions.[227] Courts of the 1970s and 1980s were more likely to take "judicial notice" of "facts" about college alcohol use. Today, courts are more likely to refer to modern "prevention science." Alcohol and other drug prevention was once an amateur field; now leading prevention scientists may find themselves called

---

9. Keep repeating the process.

[225] Henry Weschler, et al., *Underage College Students' Drinking Behavior, Access to Alcohol, and the Influence of Deterrence Policies,* 50 J. Am. College Health 227 (2002); Henry Weschler, et al., *College Binge Drinking in the 1990s: A Continuing Problem, Results of the Harvard School of Public Health 1999 College Alcohol Study,* 48 J. Am. College Health 5 (March 2000); Henry Weschler, et al., *Trends in College Binge Drinking During a Period of Increased Prevention Efforts: Findings From 4 Harvard School of Public Health College Alcohol Study Surveys: 1993–2001,* 50 J. Am. College Health 5, 203–17 (2002).

[226] See United Educators website, https://www.ue.org/home/aspx, which provides to its members summaries of student loss.

[227] *See, e.g., McClure v. Fairfield Univ.*, 2003 WL 21524786 (Conn. Super. 2003) (alleging that the university was negligent for not enforcing its alcohol policy and failing to provide adequate transportation to and from off-campus locations, and denying the grant of summary judgment to the university when a student was injured while returning from a beach party where alcohol was consumed).

as experts in litigation, much like experts in other industries. Alcohol and drug prevention is coming of age, so to speak, legally.

Modern prevention strategies are increasingly science-based.[228] Thanks in part to the pioneering public health work of William DeJong, former director of the U.S. Department of Education's Higher Education Center for Alcohol, Drug Abuse, and Violence Prevention,[229] environmental management strategies are now widely accepted.[230]

Federal intervention in alcohol and other drug issues has been somewhat limited. For example, there is no broad legal mandate to use or develop evidence-based strategies on campus, although many grants ask institutions of higher education to do so. Institutions must have policies in place that prohibit unlawful use and possession of alcohol and drugs,[231] but having a policy and enforcing it are just one part of an environmental management strategy.[232]

---

[228] National Center on Addiction and Substance Abuse at Columbia University (CASA), *Wasting the Best and the Brightest: Substance Abuse at America's Colleges and Universities* (Mar. 2007), *available at* http://www.casacolumbia.org/absolutenm/articlefiles/380-WastingtheBestandtheBrightest.pdf; National Institute on Alcohol Abuse and Alcoholism (NIAAA), *A Call to Action: Changing the Culture of Drinking at U.S. Colleges* (NIH Pub. No. 02-5010, 2002), *available at* http://www.collegedrinkingprevention.gov/NIAAACollegeMaterial/TaskForce/TaskForce_Toc.aspx.

[229] "Student alcohol and other drug abuse and violence (AODV) still reign as the most serious social problems faced by U.S. institutions of higher education." William DeJong, *Problem Analysis: The First Step in Prevention Planning* (2009), *available at* http://www.higheredcenter.org/files/product/problem-analysis.pdf. "Coalitions are more successful when they are backed by a college president who publicly expresses support and invests staff and resources and money to solve the problem, and when the coalition leader has strong skills in program development, community organizing, coalition building, and advocacy." Linda Langford & William DeJong, *Strategic Planning for Prevention Professionals on Campus* 2 (2008), *available at* http://www.higheredcenter.org/services/publications/stategic-planning-prevention-professionals-campus. The first step in "environmental management" is problem analysis, which involves "(1) gathering objective data on the nature and scope of the problem at both national and local levels; (2) examining available resources and assets in the campus community; and (3) analyzing and summarizing this information to clarify needs and opportunities." DeJong, *Problem Analysis: The First Step to Prevention Planning*, at 1. "National surveys typically have found that about two in five U.S. undergraduates engage in heavy episodic drinking, which is usually defined as 'having five or more drinks in a row at least once in a two-week period.'" William DeJong, *Experience in Effective Prevention* 5 (2007), *available at* http://higheredcenter.org/files/product/effective-prevention.pdf.

[230] National Institute on Alcohol Abuse and Alcoholism (NIAAA), *A Call to Action: Changing the Culture of Drinking at U.S. Colleges* (NIH Pub. No. 02-5010, 2002), *available at* http://www.collegedrinkingprevention.gov/NIAAACollegeMaterials/TaskForce/TaskForce_TOC.aspx.

[231] Safe and Drug Free School Act , 20 U.S.C. § 7101 (2000).

[232] M. D. Wood, W. DeJong, A. M. Fairlie, D. Lawson, A. M. Lavigne, & F. Cohen, *Common Ground: An Investigation of Environmental Management, Alcohol Prevention Initiative in a Col-*

Suicide and wellness.

Mental health issues have increased in significance on college campuses.[233] Some, but not all, mental health issues involve serious physical risks to students, and student mental health issue management has become a major activity for student affairs administrators. The JED Foundation[234] accurately surveyed the law in this area in a recent report.[235] As that report correctly stated:

> The potential for an IHE [institution of higher education] to be held liable for student suicide is a recent phenomenon. For decades, suicide was considered to be a wrongful act, solely the fault of the suicidal individual. Therefore, IHEs historically faced no significant risk of litigation regarding a student suicide. Recently, a few courts have begun to consider lawsuits alleging that an institution of higher education has a responsibility to find some level of care to prevent suicide or to mitigate suicide risk. However, the law in its current state is largely inconclusive regarding such responsibility. Note that most cases settle before courts are afforded the opportunity to make pronouncements of law.

> There is no immediate legal movement to impose broad-based suicide prevention responsibilities on colleges, despite the fact that there have been several highly publicized lawsuits. . . .

> The law does provide some guidance for IHEs, which could conceivably be held legally responsible in the following situations:

---

lege Community, 16 J. Stud. on Alcohol & Drugs, Supplement 96–105 (2009); *see* NIAAA, *supra* note 230.

[233] Lake & Tribbensee, *supra* note 123.

[234] The JED Foundation, http://www.jedfoundation.org (last visited Jan. 31, 2011). The JED Foundation is an organization that specializes in the reduction of emotional distress and the prevention of suicide among college students by raising awareness of issues surrounding these topics, such as the stigma surrounding emotional disorders, symptoms of emotional disorders, and warning signs of suicide. The foundation offers a collaborative approach, using leaders in higher education, mental health, and research to strengthen campus environments, including mental health services, polices, and programs.

[235] *Student Mental Health and the Law: A Resource for Institutions of Higher Education* 25–26 (JED Found. 2008).

- The IHE causes the suicide or serious injury of a student by illegally or negligently prescribing, dispensing, or giving access to medication.

- The IHE causes emotional distress and suicide through some exceptionally abusive and deliberate process, such as knowingly and maliciously prosecuting a clearly innocent student under the discipline code.

- The IHE caused physical trauma that resulted in physical and mental health consequences, including suicide (e.g., a negligent-causes vehicular accident that results in pain, depression, and suicidal ideation).

- The IHE failed to use reasonable care to prevent the suicide of an individual under "suicide watch" (i.e., the constant monitoring of a person known to be a significant risk for suicide in order to prevent suicidal behavior). Occasionally, the police have been held responsible when individuals under arrest have caused themselves harm, but it is clear that merely providing non-negligent health/mental services or other intervention short of custodial suicide watch will not trigger liability. . . .

[T]here has been recent litigation claiming that IHEs have an independent duty to notify parents of a student's dangerous, suicidal, and/or self-destructive behavior. To date, the courts have not offered consistent guidance about this, but the proposed amendments to the FERPA regulations may help clarify an IHE's discretion in notifying parents in emergency situations. It is clear, however, that the law does not require an IHE to warn parents about what it does not know nor could not reasonably have known. . . .

In sum, the scope of an IHE's legal responsibility for the prevention of violence toward others is clearer than for the prevention of suicide. Unfortunately, such legal uncertainty hinders the development of best practices, as there can be an inclination not to shoulder responsibility that might fall elsewhere. It also fuels concern by some IHEs that, by engaging in suicide prevention or intervention activity, they are assuming legal duties. This concern is likely unwarranted. . . . [236]

The JED Foundation report developed several "good practices" for institutions of higher education,[237] and other major reports have also recommended practices.[238]

Mental health, wellness, and suicide liability issues are not as prominent in student affairs practice as privacy law issues (discussed below). Negligence law almost always requires physical injury to a student to trigger liability. Most mental health issues do not present significant physical risk of the kind that negligence law typically addresses, although a few do.

When students are injured by a mental health, wellness, or suicide risk, institutions of higher education and student affairs administrators are usually not the responsible parties. Often, the only legally responsible party is the mentally ill student. Some jurisdictions have altered the traditional suicidal person as sole proximate cause rule.[239] Or the mentally ill person may self-harm in a way that no reasonable person could have prevented.[240] Duties to warn others of a dangerous, mentally ill person's intentions to harm others are often limited to mental health professionals,[241] although knowledge of a specifically dangerous person on campus can trigger duties to provide reasonable security on campus.[242] (Of course, student affairs administrators *may* warn others even if they are not legally *required* to do

---

[236] JED Foundation, *supra* note 234; *see also* Lake & Tribbensee, *supra* note 123.

[237] *Student Mental Health and the Law*, *supra* note 235, at 7, 9, 11, 15–17, 19–24, 26.

[238] *See* Judge David L. Bazelon Center for Mental Health Law, *Supporting Students: A Model Policy for Colleges and Universities* (May, 15 2007), *available at* http://bazelon.org.gravitatehosting.com/LinkClick/aspx?fileticket=2sA8atOxlT0%3d&tabid=225.

[239] *See Student Mental Health and the Law*, *supra* note 235, at 25–26.

[240] *See Bash v. Clarke Univ.*, 2007 WL 1418528 (Mass. Super. 2007) (finding no special relationship between the college student and her parents in order to impose upon them liability for negligent care; additionally, reiterating that no special relationship exists between the student and university); *see Bash*, 22 Mass. L. Rptr. 84 (holding that the university was not liable for a student's overdose in a dorm room with no forewarning of serious drug abuse).

[241] *See Tarasoff*, 551 P.2d 334.

[242] *See Sharkey v. Bd. of Regents of Univ. of Nebraska*, 615 N.W.2d 889, 900–2 (Neb. 2000).

so.[243]) There is a responsibility not to enhance the risks of mental illness that might cause physical injury; for example, carefully managing access to prescription drugs.[244]

Student affairs administrators can hardly be oblivious to mental health and wellness issues on campus. These issues affect classroom management, residential life management, retention, and so on. Mental health issues are core enterprise risks for the institution of higher education, even if they are not prominent sources of legal risk in tort. Perhaps no other modern college challenge better illustrates the difference between accountability and liability.

Virginia Tech, silos, and threat assessment/care teams.

Institutions of higher education have always had some responsibility for threat assessment under the reasonable person standard, so it is no surprise that many campuses conducted threat assessment before the shootings at Virginia Tech in April 2007.[245] The law of agency presumes that what is known to agents of a business is usually known to the business at about the same time and the business is responsible for synthesizing that information into reasonable action in a reasonable amount of time.[246] Moreover, employees of an institution of higher education owe a fiduciary duty to the institution, typically not to students.

Many of the major reports following Virginia Tech[247] identified pre-

---

[243] *See* FERPA discussed *infra.*

[244] *See Brennan v. Bd. of Trustees for Univ. of Louisiana Systems,* 691 So. 2d 324 (La. App. 1st Cir. 1997); *Wallace v. Broyles,* 961 S.W.2d 712 (Ark. 1998).

[245] *See* Gene Deisinger, *Best Practices in Campus Threat Assessment & Management,* 1, 3–5, 8, 12–13 (2009) (conference materials from 2010 National Conference on Law and Higher Education, Feb. 20–23, Orlando, Florida, available to conference participants on CD); Gene Deisinger et al., *The Handbook for Campus Threat Assessment & Management Teams* (2008).

[246] *See, e.g., Lara v. Saint John's Univ.,* 735 N.Y.S.2d 578 (N.Y. App. Div. 2d Dept 2001); *Bearman v. Univ. of Notre Dame,* 453 N.E.2d 1196 (Ind. App. 3d Dist. 1983); *Wartski v. C.W. Post Campus of Long Island Univ.* 882 N.Y.S.2d 192 (N.Y. App. Div. 2d Dept. 2009).

[247] Michael O. Leavitt, Margaret Spellings, & Alberto R. Gonzales, *Report to the President on Issues Raised by the Virginia Tech Tragedy* (June 13, 2007), *available at* http://www.hhs.gov/vtreport.html#key.

   Key Findings
   • **Critical information-sharing faces substantial obstacles** Education officials, health care providers, law enforcement personnel, and others are not fully in-

ventive actions that should have been widely embraced before the incident; however, the law, understanding of the law, expectations of accountability, and the culture of higher education clashed in some ways. The reports have changed higher education culture, even though the reports are not themselves legal mandates.

The following are the three major culture changes brought about by events at Virginia Tech and the subsequent reports:

(1) Rise in rapid response and warning systems. In response to the federal mandate under the Clery Act,[248] campuses quickly developed rapid response and warning systems to deal with active shooter situations and warn everyone on campus of the presence of a shooter. This aspect of the Virginia Tech reports has translated into a national legal mandate: Colleges must have an emergency

---

formed about when they can share critical information on persons who are likely to be a danger to self or others, and the resulting confusion may chill legitimate information-sharing.

- **Accurate and complete information on individuals prohibited from possessing firearms is essential to keep guns out of the wrong hands** State laws and practices do not uniformly ensure that information on persons restricted from possessing firearms is appropriately captured and available to the National Instant Criminal Background Check System (NICS).
- **Improved awareness and communication are key to prevention** It is important that parents, students, and teachers learn to recognize warning signs and encourage those who need help to seek it, so that people receive the care they need and our communities are safe.
- **It is critical to get people with mental illness the services they need** Meeting the challenge of adequate and appropriate community integration of people with mental illness requires effective coordination of community service providers who are sensitive to the interests of safety, privacy, and provision of care.
- **Where we know what to do, we have to be better at doing it** For the many states and communities that have already adopted programs, including emergency preparedness and violence prevention plans, to address school and community violence, the challenge is fully implementing these programs through practice and effective communication. *Id.*

[248] Jeanne Clery Disclosure of Campus Security Policy and Campus Crime Statistics Act (Clery Act), 20 U.S.C. § 1092(f) (2006). The Clery Act requires "[a] statement of current campus policies regarding immediate emergency response and evacuation procedures, including the use of electronic and cellular communication . . . which policies shall include procedures to—

(i) immediately notify the campus community upon the confirmation of a significant emergency or dangerous situation involving an immediate threat to the health or safety of students or staff occurring on the campus . . .

(iii) test emergency response and evacuation procedures on an annual basis.
Id. at § 1092(f)(1)(J)(i–iii).

plan and procedures for immediate notification of everyone on campus and must conduct at least an annual drill to evaluate their emergency plan.[249]

(2) Threat assessment and case management. The rise of threat assessment teams has been notable; they are responsible for a variety of duties, from threat analysis and assessment to interdiction.[250] So far, only a few states have mandated such teams;[251] and there is, as yet, no specific federal mandate.

(3) Silos. Student affairs administrators are increasingly conscious of the hazards of information siloing, in which one person knows a piece of information but—for whatever reason—has not shared, synthesized, or acted on it. Institutions of higher education have had a hard time changing this situation. Most institutions and student affairs administrators rely heavily on their threat assessment or care teams to combat information siloing.[252]

Recreational athletics.[253]

Recreational sports involve risk and, thus, potential liability.

Participants in recreational sports are presumed to assume the ordinary risks of the sports in which they engage. Some courts have gone so far as to

---

[249] *Id.* at § 1092(f); 34 C.F.R. § 668.46 (2010).

[250] *See* Deisinger et al., *supra* note 245; *The State of Enterprise Risk Management, supra* note 219; D. Drysdale, W. Modzeleski, & A. Simons, *Campus Attacks: Targeted Violence Affecting Institutions of Higher Education* (2010), *available at* http://www2.ed.gov/admins/lead/safety/campus-attacks.pdf.

[251] *See, e.g.*, Va. Code Ann. § 23-9.2:10 (2008); Ill. Admin. Code tit. 29, pt §§ 305.10–305.110 (2010).

[252] Threat Assessment is "[a] systematic process that is designed to: 1) [i]dentify persons of concern, 2) [g]ather information/investigate, 3) [a]ssess information and [the]situation, 4) [m]anage the situation. Threat Assessment is an objective process." The functional authority and role of a threat assessment team is to "[u]nderstand threats/concerns; [e]valuate legitimacy of concerns; [i]dentify motivation for violence; [a]ssess likelihood of physical harm; [d]evelop strategies for risk reduction; [g]uide implementation of strategies; [r]e-evaluate threat; [e]valuate needs of [the] community." Deisinger, *Best Practices in Campus Threat Assessment and Management, supra* note 247 at 4, 8; *The State of Enterprise Risk Management, supra* note 219. The College of Davidson and Davie Counties (DCCC) institutes a "care team" to assess campus safety. "The team's goal is to address concerns as early as possible and offer needed assistance to students in distress." DCCC, http://www.davidsonccc.edu/studentlife/campus_security.htm (last visited Aug. 21, 2010).

[253] Some of the information here applies equally to intercollegiate athletics. However, intercollegiate athletics have special legal issues associated with them and are beyond the scope of this Book. Intercollegiate athletic management is a specialized practice.

say that there is no duty in such situations.[254] Institutions of higher education and student affairs administrators must be especially sensitive to hidden or unknown risks. Institutions have programmatic responsibility to ensure that the proper equipment is available, safety monitoring is in place, and participants are not permitted to move beyond their skill levels in dangerous ways, at least not without understanding the risks involved.[255] Participants should not be permitted to use equipment in an inappropriate way; for example, a resistance pool is not a children's splash pool. Visibly intoxicated persons present legal dangers of negligent entrustment. Student affairs administrators should be sensitive to restricting access and use of facilities where high-risk alcohol or drug use are involved. Alcohol and other drug use significantly enhances the risk of injury and the potential severity of injury, along with the risk of legal liability. Proper equipment, proper maintenance of facilities, and proper management of use are the cornerstones of reasonable care in recreational sports.

Earlier, we considered the law relating to written forms that cover express assumption of risk. If properly used, these forms can alert participants to dangers of a sport or activity that novices might not be aware of or know how to minimize. Good forms educate participants; forms work best in combination with training to cement safety lessons. Students tend to sign standard forms without reading or internalizing them, unless forms are accompanied with training. Paperwork alone is not good risk management. Combining proper paperwork with proper instruction and training can combat risk and reduce potential legal exposure.

VIOLENCE IN A LEARNING ENVIRONMENT

Student affairs administrators work hand-in-hand with campus police/security and law enforcement to reduce violence. Violence prevention is a very broad topic.[256] This section treats salient issues where law interacts with violence prevention on campus.

---

[254] *E.g. Univ. of Denver v. Whitlock*, 744 P.2d 54 (Colo. 1987).
[255] *See Davidson*, 543 S.E.2d at 927–28.
[256] *See* Linda Langford, *Preventing Violence and Promoting Safety in Higher Education Settings: Overview of a Comprehensive Approach* (Feb. 2004), *available at* http://www.higheredcenter.org/services/publications/preventing-violence-and-promoting-safety-higher-education-settings-overview-co.

Reasonable Care and the Learning Environment

For most purposes, students and many others are considered to be in a special relationship on campus or in residential facilities; thus, they are owed reasonable care. Institutions of higher education must use reasonable care to prevent foreseeable danger, including violence. Foreseeability can arise from consideration of the "totality of the circumstances" relating to a building or location on campus, or knowledge of potential danger from known violent persons on campus.[257] This includes violence risk created by students or intruders.[258] The responsibility for reasonable care extends off campus to externship programs and even to study abroad.[259]

Campuses often struggle with whether to regulate or intervene in off-campus behavior that is not programmatic, and whether regulations transform off-campus behavior to programmatic behavior (see the earlier discussion on assuming duty). Danger does not respect campus boundaries and often transports onto or off of the campus.[260] Institutions of higher education may owe reasonable care in some riskscape situations[261] but not in others, even on campus.[262] Institutions of higher education and student affairs administrators do not assume duties simply by regulating behavior,

---

[257] *Sharkey*, 615 N.W.2d at 901–2.

> [I]n a landowner-invitee setting, it is the totality of the circumstances, not solely the number or location of prior incidents, that must be considered in determining foreseeability. The evidence adduced at trial shows that violent altercations were not unknown at that particular location on the UNO campus, and thus, acts such as Clark's violent attack on Sharkey are reasonably foreseeable. . . . The University, as a matter of law, owed such a duty to Sharkey in the instant case. *Id.* Recently, the Nebraska Supreme Court superceded *Sharkey* and held that foreseeability is a question of fact for the jury when determining whether the university owes a duty to the student. *A.W.*, 784 N.W.2d 907.

[258] Judith Areen, *Higher Education and the Law: Cases and Materials* 822–28 (Foundation Press 2009).

[259] *See, e.g.*, *Nova Southeastern Univ.*, 758 So. 2d at 88–89; *Bloss v. Univ. of Minn.*, 590 N.W.2d 661 (Min. App. 1999); John T. Hall & Rowan Fergunson, *Case Study: University of Anyplace: Strategic Legal Risk Review*, 27 J.C. & U.L. 119 (2000); William P. Hoye & Gary M Rhodes, *An Ounce of Prevention Is Worth the Life of a Student: Reducing Risk in International Programs*, 27 J.C & U.L. 151 (2000); Beth McMurtrie, *College Settles Suit by 3 Students over '98 Attack in Guatemala*, Chronicle of Higher Education (July 5, 2002), *available at* http://chronicle.com/daily/2002/07/2002070502n.htm.

[260] *See Knoll*, 601 N.W.2d at 760–61.

[261] *See id.* at 764.

[262] *Id; see Bash*, 22 Mass. L. Rptr. 84 (finding no special relationship between the university and the student).

nor is underenforcement a basis for creating duty.[263]

Safety training and student empowerment are the cornerstones for using reasonable care to create a reasonably safe higher education learning environment. Students are typically the best first agents of their own safety.

Architecture and Premises Maintenance

Violence risk depends heavily on architecture and proper maintenance. Courts have not been willing to ask institutions of higher education to fundamentally redesign their campuses or abandon the open campus model,[264] but they may need to retrofit buildings and modernize safety equipment such as door locks. Maintenance issues can be a source of liability risk; for example, when an intruder is able to enter because a broken door lock was not repaired in a reasonable amount of time.[265] Student affairs administrators should be careful about deploying safety technology that does not function well within reasonable resource limitations or making areas of campus appear safer than they actually are.[266] In addition, student affairs administrators must use reasonable care to ensure that promised safety systems are available and operational when needed.[267]

---

[263] *See Davies v. Barnes*, 503 A.2d 93 (Pa. Cmwlth 1986); *Gragg v. Wichita State*, 934 P.2d 121 (Kan. 1997). Indeed, some violence will occur despite reasonable care, and an institution of higher education will not be responsible. *See Gragg,* 934 P.2d at 128–29.

[264] *See Robertson*, 747 So. 2d at 1281–85.

[265] *See* 20 U.S.C. § 1092(f); *Delaney v. Univ. of Houston*, 835 S.W.2d 56 (Tex. 1992) (holding that the university's negligent failure to fix the broken lock provided the opportunity for criminal intrusion).

[266] Bickel et al., *supra* note 75, at 333–42.

[267] As Bickel & Lake state:

> The cases indicate how simple acts of maintenance—such as locking doors, quickly fixing broken locks, trimming bushes, and challenging observed dangerous behavior—can forestall crime and send a message that order, not conditions of criminality, exists on the campus. Implicitly, courts have begun to accept the Kelling/Coles/Wilson/Bratton notion that order maintenance measures prevent serious crime. Courts do not view inadequate maintenance as a vindication of a student's liberty interest. On the contrary, safe premises are a condition under which student freedom can be exercised and foreseeably dangerous persons can be thwarted.

* * * *

> The conclusions to be drawn from the recent explosion of cases involving a dangerous person on campus are at one level very simple. Universities consistently have a legal duty to provide reasonable protection for students on campus and in dormitories. Duty is not liability, however. To hold a university liable under negligence law, a student victim must establish that the danger was foreseeable in more than a general sense.

These duties are nondelegable—using third-party vendors will not insulate an institution of higher education from its responsibility to provide a safe campus.

Campus Police/Security

The following schematic shows the development of the campus police and security mission since World War II:

The danger must be reasonably apparent (like overgrown bushes near an isolated dormitory entrance), or a pattern of behavior must establish and define the risks. Moreover, the risks must be capable of being mitigated by reasonable efforts on the part of the university. Student-victim misconduct is relevant, especially when that conduct is disorderly or indicated improper uses of alcohol.

Robert D. Bickel & Peter F. Lake, *Rights and Responsibilities of the Modern University: Who Assumes the Risks of College Life?* 146–49 (Carolina Academic Press 1999); *see, e.g., Johnson v. State,* 894 P.2d 1366 (Wash. App. 1995); *Peterson v. San Francisco Community College,* 685 P.2d 1193 (Cal. 1984) (finding that the university can be liable for an intruder hiding in untrimmed foliage near a stairway if a student is sexually assaulted).

MISSION 1— Buildings (1960s–1970s) ———————————▶	Protect buildings, physical property, and plant; Manage entry to and exit from property; Report to business office. Law: No duty
MISSION 2— Crime Prevention (Began in mid-1980s) ———————————▶	Protect campus, especially students, from foreseeable third party criminal physical danger/risk; Focus on violent assault, rape, etc., by nonstudents; Report to business office or student affairs. Law: *Mullins* case
MISSION 3— Student Life (mid-1990s–2000s) ———————————▶	Interdict in student life issues: alcohol and other drugs, peer violence, residential life, behavioral issues; Report to or collaborate with student affairs vice president. Law: *Knoll* case
MISSION 4— Wellness/Active Shooter (Post-Virginia Tech (2007)) ———————————▶	Prevent and interdict active shooters; Assess dangerous students and others; Manage emergency notification systems; Assist in managing populations of mentally ill students and others; Significant coordination of all operatives on campus, and police and emergency responses off campus; Serve on threat assessment teams; Report to or collaborate with all student affairs vice presidents; Accountable to president and board. Law: *Gross* case, Virginia Tech Report, Clery Act

The changes in mission have been driven by changes in law and social expectations. The missions have been cumulative: Campus safety/police have all the responsibilities of Mission 1 forward, although they may not have reached Mission 4 at some institutions. The role of campus security/police has expanded steadily since World War II—often, they are the first employees contacted when no one knows what to do about a situation.

Reasonable care in the campus safety world often turns on mission identification, clear delineation of police responsibilities, proper and sufficient personnel, necessary training and resources, and collaboration with campus constituencies and law enforcement in the community.

Two other issues are common in campus security: background checks and the Clery Act.

The law has not evolved to require extensive background checks of students prior to admission.[268] This posture might be advisable for residential students;[269] however, criminal background checks do not always provide sufficient information to assess a student's potential threat level, and some information regarding previous criminality is not evidence of future danger. A focus on background checks misses the mark; campuses would be better served if key information in a student's K–12 files was transmitted to campus and translated for college use.

The Clery Act requires campuses to make annual reports;[270] it requires "colleges and universities that participate in federal financial aid programs to notify their [campuses] of certain reported crimes."[271] Professor Judith Areen has summarized the history of the act:

> On April 5th, 1986, Jeanne Clery "was tortured, raped, sodomized and murdered in her dormitory room at Lehigh University." After

---

[268] *See* Lipka, *supra* note 98. "Colleges say they cannot predict when a troubled student will turn violent. In a one-month span in 2004, two University of North Carolina Wilmington students were murdered by other students who hid their criminal backgrounds on admissions applications. A report by the University of North Carolina found a pattern of applicants with criminal backgrounds lying on applications and suggested better scrutiny of applications." Thomas Frank, *Campus Security Flaws a Pattern in Slayings*, USA Today (June12, 2007), *available at* http://www.usatoday.com/news/nation/2007-06-12-campus-security-flaws_N.htm.

[269] *Id.*

[270] 20 U.S.C. § 1092(f)(1)–(18); 34 C.F.R. § 668.46 (2010).

[271] *Havlik v. Johnson & Wales*, 509 F.3d 25 (1st Cir. 2007).

discovering that there had been numerous other unreported crimes on the campus, Jeanne Clery's parents took action. After more than three years of lobbying, the Jeanne Clery Disclosure of Campus Security Policy and Campus Crime Statistics Act was signed into law in 1990. . . . Originally named "Crime Awareness and Campus Security Act of 1990," the act requires that colleges report violent crimes that occur on or near campus. The information is also made available to prospective students and families through the Department of Education website.[272]

The Act started out as a campus crime reporting act and has been amended several times to increase reporting requirements.[273] Over time, the reach of the Clery Act has expanded, and it has taken on aspects of an omnibus campus crime control/response bill. For example, recent amendments mandate emergency response systems.[274]

Clery Act reporting requirements fall heavily on campus security/police, but recent mandates have brought student affairs administrators into an assisting role. In fact, several new reporting requirements are directly related to student affairs practice; for example, disciplinary proceedings and incidents involving registered student organizations.[275] As Clery Act compliance grows beyond reporting requirements into the realm of campus crime prevention, student affairs administrators will be drawn nearer to the center of compliance.[276]

Disturbingly, a person might be able to bring a claim for damages against student affairs administrators and campus police/security arising out of failures in Clery Act compliance.[277] The position of the U.S. Supreme Court under FERPA suggests that the Court may disagree;[278] however, the threat of private lawsuits arising from alleged Clery Act noncompliance could increase exponen-

---

[272] Areen, *supra* note 258, at 987 (citations omitted).

[273] *See Havlik*, 509 F.3d at 29–32.

[274] *See id.* at 32.

[275] *See* 20 U.S.C. § 1092(f)(1)(F)(i)(IX).

[276] *See, e.g.*, Security on Campus, Inc., *Campus Sexual Assault Free Environment (SAFE) Blueprint – 2010: Proposed Enhancements to the Federal Jeanne Clery Act and Title IX*, *available at* http://www.securityoncampus.org/pdf/SAFEblueprint.pdf; 34 C.F.R. § 668.46 (2010).

[277] *See Havlik,* 509 F.3d at 35–36 (holding that section 1983 immunity bars suit, but suggesting that other claims could be viable).

[278] *See Gonzaga, supra* note 94.

tially as the act evolves from a campus crime reporting act into a crime prevention bill. It would be very difficult for plaintiffs to show damages from simple reporting errors; however, noncompliance with safety-specific directives could be a different matter.

CHAPTER 4

MANAGING THE INSTITUTION OF HIGHER EDUCATION ENVIRONMENT

PART II: PROMOTING AND PROTECTING THE CORE ACADEMIC MISSION

Modern institutions of higher education have developed complex systems to manage their educational environments, in addition to risk management efforts directed at physical safety and well-being. The centerpieces of most campus management strategies are student codes—usually broken down into codes of conduct and codes for academic offenses. Codes are typically printed in student handbooks, which in most states are components of the contract with the student.[1]

From the era of power, prerogative, and legal insularity before World War II to the present, the law has acknowledged the wide latitude of institutions of higher education to govern their own affairs. The law defers less to academic

---

[1] *See Havlik v. Johnson & Wales Univ.*, 509 F.3d 25 (1st Cir. 2007).

institutions today than it did fifty-plus years ago, but the Supreme Court has recently reiterated that administrators are due "decent respect."[2] Consider the following language in Justice John Paul Stevens' concurring opinion in *Christian Legal Society*:

> Public universities serve a distinctive role in a modern democratic society. Like all specialized government entities, they must make countless decisions about how to allocate resources in pursuit of their role. Some of those decisions will be controversial; many will have differential effects across populations; virtually all will entail value judgments of some kinds. As a general matter, courts should respect universities' judgments and let them manage their own affairs. [3]

This sort of deference is reflected even in cases discussing contract law theories:

> A student's relationship to his university is based in contract. . . .
>
> The relevant terms of the contractual relationship between a student and a university typically include language found in the university's student handbook. We interpret such contractual terms in accordance with the parties' reasonable expectations, giving those terms the meaning that the university reasonably should expect the student to take from them. Thus, if the university explicitly promises an appeal process in disciplinary matters, that process must be carried out and aligned with the student's reasonable expectations. . .
>
> [A]mong other things, . . . parties to a contract act pursuant to an implied duty of good faith and fair dealing. Good faith and fair dealing cannot be separated from context, however, and in evaluating those covenants in the educational milieu, courts must accord a school some measure of deference in matters of discipline. See *Schaer v. Brandeis Univ.*, 432 Mass. 474,735 NE.2d 373, 381 (2000) (stating that universities must be given broad discretion in disciplining students).[4]

---

[2] *Christian Legal Society at Hastings College of the Law v. Martinez*, 130 S. Ct 2971 (2010).
[3] *Id.* at 2997–98 (Stevens, J., concurring).
[4] *Havlik*, 509 F.3d at 35.

Interestingly, the law does not provide specific mandates on how best to approach the management of an institution of higher education's learning environment. We have seen a similar phenomenon with respect to risk management efforts in compliance with the duty to use reasonable care. Some parameters arise from the application of due process principles, some from contract law, and some from specific legislative or regulatory directives. For example, the Clery Act may eventually require institutions of higher education to use a particular burden of proof—"preponderance of the evidence"—in matters involving sexual misconduct.[5]

Nonetheless, even in the absence of mandates, most colleges take a remarkably similar approach to the tasks of managing their environments. A broad grant of liberty to use educational discretion has not translated into a highly diverse ecosystem of educational environmental management techniques. Indeed, many institutions of higher education operate under the assumption that they are following a legal mandate and that uniformity is preferable to diversity. Legal mandates can arise from constitutions, legislation, regulation, or contract; by far the dominant source of "mandate" is contract law, which means that much of what passes as a mandate arises, somewhat ironically, from what we have promised students in the first place.[6] The law defers to us; we defer to the law; the law enforces that deference. It is all a little strange, and courts are sometimes perplexed at how we have responded to juridical light-handedness.

DUE PROCESS AND PUBLIC LAW MANDATES

The U.S. Supreme Court has never squarely held that college students are owed due process, even though consumers, some faculty, K–12 students, criminals, public employees, and others are owed due process.[7] This is remarkable in light of the fact that many other constitutional rights of college students are settled.[8] It seems inevitable that someday soon the Supreme Court will finally resolve the basic question of due process rights (if any) in college. There is significant variation in the way lower federal courts manage the absence of a direct

---

[5] *See* Security on Campus, Inc., http://www.securityoncampus.org (last visited August 18, 2010).
[6] *See Havlik*, 509 F.3d at 34.
[7] *See, e.g., Goss v. Lopez*, 419 U.S. 565 (1975); *Fuentes v. Shevin*, 407 U.S. 67 (1972); *Perry v. Sindermann*, 408 U.S. 593 (1972); *Gideon v. Wainwright*, 372 U.S. 335 (1963).
[8] *See* Chapter 3, *supra*.

Supreme Court directive: Some courts, like the Sixth Circuit,[9] simply assume that due process must exist, while other lower federal courts are more hesitant.[10]

Nonetheless, there is no U.S. constitutional mandate coming from the highest court of the land requiring due process at public colleges. The Supreme Court has hesitated to march into higher education with legalistic due process requirements because due process rights of students, if any, must be weighed against academic freedom and other constitutional freedoms of institutions. If cases like *Southworth* and *Christian Legal Society* (discussed in Chapter 5) are any indication, the Supreme Court will have to undertake a delicate balancing process to protect the rights of students while ensuring that American higher education does not become a student discipline litigation nightmare. It is a delicious legal ponderable to try to imagine what process is "due" in the higher education context.

In the two leading cases on due process in higher education, the Supreme Court merely "postulated" that sufficient legal interests exist to support student due process rights.[11] We have two key, essentially hypothetical, cases from the Supreme Court. How are student affairs administrators supposed to work with that?

For a person to have due process rights, state action must deprive him or her of life, liberty, or property—so-called *protected interests*.[12] Colleges do not take "life." However, property or liberty interests could be at stake in higher education. K–12 education presents a much easier avenue of analysis, because states guarantee the right to a basic K–12 education as a significant property right. However, there is no such right to higher education. Liberty interests are compromised when government entities stigmatize individuals.[13] To the extent that higher education starts mirroring criminal prosecutions, it may create a stigmatizing effect that will, in turn, be the predicate for the creation of due process requirements. Turning educational process into handing out scarlet letters is dangerous constitutional business.

In the two key cases in which the Supreme Court "postulated" necessary predicate interest to support due process requirements, the Court held that the institutions of higher education provided more than enough process by engaging in a

---

[9] *Flaim v. Medical College of Ohio*, 418 F.3d 629 (6th Cir. 2005).

[10] *See e.g.*, *Williams v. Wendler*, 530 F.3d 584 (7th Cir. 2008).

[11] *See* note 14, *infra*.

[12] *E.g.*, *Coalition of Clergy, Lawyers, and Professors v. Bush*, 310 F.3d 1153 (9th Cir. 2002).

[13] *Boston v. Webb*, 783 F.2d 1163 (4th Cir. 1986).

careful and deliberative analysis of student issues.[14] The Supreme Court clearly envisioned the kind of evaluative process that is emblematic of decision making in the academy. It is not too much to ask institutions of higher education to check basic facts to ensure that manifest error has not gone unnoticed[15] or to make careful and deliberative decisions when evaluating a student's performance on a broad spectrum of indicators. As the two key cases—*Horowitz* and *Ewing*—both observed, higher education already does this and probably does more of it than is necessary.[16]

Leading up to the *Horowitz* and *Ewing* decisions, some lower federal courts aligned themselves with the groundbreaking *Dixon v. Alabama* case.[17] *Dixon* was the first American case to impose traditional procedural due process requirements on higher education. It required that students receive notice and an opportunity to be heard before expulsion—basic aspects of procedural fairness under the due process clause.[18] Some courts have taken *Dixon* even further and imposed a wide variety of traditional legal due process requirements on colleges.[19] However, the Supreme Court did not ratify this approach and made a point of warning against the perils of legalistic due process in higher education:

> The University's refusal to allow Ewing to retake the NBME [National Board of Medical Examiners] Part I [Examination] is thus not actionable in itself. It is, however, an important element of Ewing's claim that his dismissal was the product of arbitrary state action, for under proper analysis the refusal may constitute evidence of arbitrariness even if it is not the actual legal wrong alleged. . . .
>
> Ewing's claim, therefore, must be that the University misjudged his fitness to remain a student in the Interflex program. The record unmistak-

---

[14] *Board of Curators of the Univ. of Missouri v. Horowitz*, 435 U.S. 78 (1978); *Regents of the Univ. of Michigan v. Ewing*, 474 U.S. 214 (1985).

[15] *Goss*, 419 U.S. at 583–84.

[16] Peter F. Lake, *Beyond Discipline–Managing the Modern Higher Education Environment* 101–14 (Hierophant Enterprises, Inc. 2009)

[17] "We are confident that precedent as well as a most fundamental constitutional principle support our holding that due process requires notice and some opportunity for hearing before a student at a tax-supported college is expelled for misconduct." *Dixon v. Alabama State Board of Education*, 294 F.2d 150, 158 (5th Cir. 1961); See Lake, *supra* note 16, at 64–78.

[18] *Goss*, 419 U.S. at 579; *Dixon*, 294 F.2d at 158–59.

[19] *See Esteban v. Central Missouri State College*, 277 F. Supp. 649 (W.D. Mo. 1967).

ably demonstrates, however, that the faculty's decision was made conscientiously and with careful deliberation, based on an evaluation of the entirety of Ewing's academic career. When judges are asked to review the substance of a genuinely academic decision, such as this one, they should show great respect for the faculty's professional judgment. Plainly, they may not override it unless it is such a substantial departure from accepted academic norms as to demonstrate that the person or committee responsible did not actually exercise professional judgment.[20]

These sentiments are echoed in recent Supreme Court cases treating issues other than due process. For instance, in the *Christian Legal Society* case, which upheld an "all-comers policy" in registered student organization systems, the Court referred to the unique role of American higher education and the need for deference toward administrators.[21]

Despite the fact that the Supreme Court twice purposefully refused to impose due process requirements on higher education, legalistic due process requirements have made a return in a number of lower federal courts—both substantively and procedurally[22]—and even in state court application of due process requirements.[23] The state of federal decisional law on due process leaves student affairs administrators in a tenuous position. Many administrators are constrained by the law in their federal circuits, because even if the decisions of lower federal courts are ultimately held not to be constitutional (and some are visibly inconsistent with Supreme Court decisions), these rulings are voidable but not

---

[20] *Ewing*, 474 U.S. at 224–25 (citations omitted); *see also Horowitz*, 435 U.S. at 90; *Goss*, 419 U.S. at 583.

[21] *Christian Legal Society*, 130 S. Ct. at 2994.

[22] "Substantive" due process differs slightly from procedural due process. Typically, governmental entities must refrain from arbitrary and capricious action under substantive due process standards. *See, e.g., Concerned Citizens of Lake Milton, Inc. v. Mahoning County*, 1995 WL 574217, at *3 (Ohio App. 7th Cir. 1995) (explaining that "[i]n order to establish a claim of a violation of substantive due process, it must be shown that the act or omission. . . . was unreasonable, arbitrary or capricious and that it bore no real or substantial relation to the object sought to be obtained)." Distinctions between substantive due process and procedural due process are for lawyers—with little practical effect in higher education to date.

[23] *See, e.g., Flaim*, 418 F.3d 629; *Gorman v. Univ. of Rhode Island*, 837 F.2d 7 (1st Cir. 1989); *Univ. of Texas Medical School at Houston v. Than*, 901 S.W.2d 926 (Tex. 1995).

void.[24] Moreover, it is not readily apparent to student affairs administrators that many of the new due process cases are a direct result of promising such process to students in contract.[25] Lower federal court decisional law has become a blend of contract-like/constitutional law that blurs the line relating to pure constitutional mandates. The academic choice of due-process-like requirements invites the application of *constitutional* due-process-like requirements; however, the Supreme Court will likely recognize that this "choice" may have been made with the mistaken belief that it was mandated. How will the Supreme Court sort this out?

Due-process-like proceduralism has crept up on higher education from other directions as well. Several states have ruled that their administrative procedure acts—which are highly legalistic—apply to "adjudication" in the college context. Translated, this means that extensive legalistic process may be required in campus disciplinary proceedings to comply with administrative procedure acts.[26] Moreover, some federal laws mandate specific content for student codes (e.g., the Safe and Drug Free School and Communities Act),[27] and new laws may require certain standards of proof (see potential Clery Act amendments) and certain procedures for implementation of statutory provisions (e.g., Title IX, FERPA).[28] Indeed, the growing influence of disability law in student affairs practice comes at a time when

---

[24] In some instances, one can ignore facially unconstitutional laws. However, some laws, while they may be unconstitutional, are not facially unconstitutional, and therefore need to be followed. *Compare Shuttleworth v. City of Birmingham*, 394 U.S. 147 (1969) (illustrating a facially unconstitutional law), *with Poulos v. State of New Hampshire*, 345 U.S. 395 (1953) (upholding a conviction and illustrating the consequence of violating an ordinance that is aligned with the Fourteenth Amendment). In *Shuttleworth*, citizens peacefully marched in protest. *Shuttleworth*, 394 U.S. at 149. The marchers were arrested for violating a city ordinance that forbade parades/processions without a valid permit. *Id.* The ordinance gave unbridled discretion to allow or deny permits. *Id.* at 150. The Supreme Court explained that "a person faced with such an unconstitutional licensing law may ignore it and engage with impunity in the exercise of the right of free expression. . . . The Constitution can hardly be thought to deny to one subjected to the restraints of such an ordinance the right to attack its constitutionality, because he has not yielded to its demands." *Id.* at 151.

[25] *Havlik*, 509 F.3d at 34–35; Lake, *supra* note 16, at 141.

[26] *See, e.g., Southwest Fla. Water Mgmt. Dist. v. Save the Manatee Club, Inc.* 773 So. 2d 594, 597 (Fla. 1st Dist. App. 2000) (explaining the test applied to determine whether agency rulemaking constitutes "an invalid exercise of delegated legislative authority" as that term is defined in section Florida Statutes § 120.52(8)).

[27] No Child Left Behind Act, Title IV, Part A, 20 U.S.C § 6319 (2006); Safe and Drug Free School and Communities Act, U.S.C. §§ 7101–7104 (2006).

[28] Education Amendments of 1972 ("Title IX"), 20 U.S.C. § 1681 (2006).

federal agencies and courts enforcing disability law believe that due-process-like requirements may be appropriate in disability matters.[29]

The Supreme Court will almost inevitably be drawn back to questions of due process as conflicts among federal courts grow and the weeds of federal and state regulation clutter the academic garden. The Court has expressed its concern over the prospect of substituting federal judges for college administrators and about the potential for a flood of litigation relating to due process in higher education. We can assume that any mandate on due process from the Supreme Court will have the potential to conflict with educational self-determinacy and academic freedom. The Court will face the daunting task of sorting out the complex interests at stake in the looming due process wars, especially as many institutions of higher education and student affairs administrators have embraced legalistic due-process-like systems to manage their environments, in some cases under the mistaken belief that they must do so. One intriguing possibility is that promising more process than one can reasonably deliver may actually violate due process principles: Too much process, or the wrong type of process, might be as "undue" as too little.[30]

CONTRACT LAW: THE PRIVATE LAW "MANDATE"

Numerous cases interpreting college contracts deal with discipline issues.[31] A number of public law due process cases essentially set the standards for following an institution of higher education's own published rules.[32] These cases blur the line between public and private law (which is not entirely unusual in due process cases).[33] The cases do not readily distinguish between constitutional floors and promised process ceilings, although some cases have asserted significant rules for institutions of higher education and shown institutions that certain criminal law procedures are not owed to students.[34]

The courts have held consistently that contract law principles require institutions to provide substantial fairness and not act in an arbitrary or capricious

---

[29] See *infra* Chapter 5 for a discussion of disability law.

[30] *See* Lake, *supra* note 16.

[31] *Schaer v. Brandeis Univ.*, 735 N.E.2d 373 (Mass. 2000).

[32] *See, e.g., Univ. of Texas Medical School at Houston v. Than*, 901 S.W.2d 926 (Tex. 1995); *see also* William A. Kaplin & Barbara Lee, *The Law of Higher Education* 917 (4th ed. 2006).

[33] *See, e.g., Perry*, 408 U.S. 593; *Board of Regents of State Colleges v. Roth*, 408 U.S. 564 (1972).

[34] *See, e.g., Gomes v. Univ. of Maine System*, 365 F. Supp. 2d 6 (D. Me. 2005).

manner.[35] However, substantial fairness does not mean strict compliance with all promises or zero compliance error. Contract law principles are still generally deferential to institutions of higher education, and the institutions still typically win under contract law theories in discipline cases.

However, the following five points are worth emphasizing. First, courts will usually require only substantial compliance with promised practices. As with other contract cases, a breach must be material to generate legal rights.[36] Thus, routine compliance error in a discipline system that does not subvert the substantial fairness of the process is not actionable.[37]

Second, unlike the era in which *Anthony v. Syracuse* endorsed double se-cret probation, institutions of higher education do not automatically win all breach of contract cases simply because they are institutions of higher educa-tion.[38] Failing to deliver specific process promises that are a material breach of the college contract can cause successful legal action against an institution of higher education.[39] But the breach must be material, as in very significant. Billy Idol sang, "There is nothing pure in this world,"[40] and courts agree.

Third, for some courts, contract law is different when it is applied to institutions of higher education. Consider the following from *Ross v. Creighton University*:

> It is held generally in the United States that the "basic legal relation between a student and private university or college is contractual

---

[35] *See, e.g., Schaer*, 735 N.E.2d 373; *Slaughter v. Brigham Young*, 514 F.2d 622 (10th Cir. 1975).
[36] *See, e.g., Schaer*, 735 N.E.2d 373.
[37] *Cf. Schaer*, 735 N.E.2d at 381–83 (Cowin, J., dissenting). "In short, if the university puts forth rules of procedure to be followed in disciplinary hearings, the university should be legally obligated to follow those rules. To do otherwise would allow Brandeis to make promises to its students that are nothing more than a 'meaningless mouthing of words.' While the university's obligation to keep the members of its community safe from sexual assault and other crimes is of great importance, at the same time the university cannot tell its students that certain proce-dures will be followed and then fail to follow them. In a hearing on a serious disciplinary mat-ter there is simply too much at stake for an individual student to countenance the university's failure to abide by the rules it has itself articulated. I would therefore not affirm the dismissal of Schaer's complaint so hastily." *Id.* at 382–83 (citations omitted).
[38] *See, e.g., Ross v. Creighton Univ.*, 957 F.2d 410 (7th Cir. 1992); *Paladino v. Adelphi*, 89 A.D.2d (N.Y. App. Div. 1982); *Zumbrun v. Univ. of Southern California*, 25 Cal. App. 3d 1 (Cal. App. 1972).
[39] *See Ross, supra* note 38.
[40] Billy Idol, *White Wedding* (Chrysalis Records 1982).

in nature. The catalogs, bulletins, circulars, and regulations of the institution made available to the matriculant become a part of the contract." *Zumbrun v. Univ. of Southern California*, 25 Cal. App. 3d 1, [10 (Cal. App. 5th Dist. 1972)]. It is quite clear, however, that Illinois would not recognize all aspects of a university-student relationship as subject to remedy through a contract action. . . "[C]ourts are not qualified to pass an opinion as the attainment of a student . . . and . . . courts will not review a decision of the school authorities relating to . . . the qualifications of the students."[41]

Even under private law, a clear judicial attitude of deference to the academy is readily discernable. This attitude skews outcomes of contract cases in favor of institutions of higher education—at least for now. Acting in the spirit of good faith with care and compassion for students is a crucial element in maintaining protection from excessive judicial interference. The message of many of the contract cases is simply "Do not be like Dean Wormer."

Fourth, many colleges have discipline procedures that are very similar to those available to defendants in criminal court. In fact, many rules of conduct precisely mirror legal standards for crimes in the criminal system. However, courts have been reluctant to impose on educational institutions the procedural requirements of criminal trials;[42] courts will not impose full criminal due process requirements simply because institutions promise some criminal-*like* proceedings.[43] Courts allow public institutions of higher education to serve cupcakes without icing because it is college. This has meant, among other things, that students have limited rights to counsel and may not have the pretrial discovery rights of a criminal defendant.[44]

This is dangerous territory for institutions of higher education to walk through. Courts of law and lawyers are intimately familiar with criminal procedure, and if institutions of higher education promise criminal-like proceedings,

---

[41] *Ross*, 957 F.2d at 416 (quoting *DeMarco v. Univ. of Health Sciences*, 352 N.E.2d 356, 362 (Ill. App. 1ˢᵗ Dist. 1976)).

[42] *Gorman*, 877 F.2d at 16; *see also Gomes*, 365 F. Supp. 2d at 20 ("*Gorman* has reminded us not to 'impose on educational institutions all the procedural requirements of a common law criminal trial.'"(quoting *Gorman*, 877 F.2d at 16)).

[43] *Id.*

[44] *See, e.g., Gomes*, 365 F. Supp. 2d 6.

some judges will be willing to impose criminal law standards of review.[45] There is a risk that courts may not just make due process coterminous with promised process but may require institutions of higher education to ice the cupcake and provide nearly complete criminal law protections.[46] Moreover, as discussed below, the promise of a highly legalistic process can lead to protracted litigation; the institution may ultimately win, but it may pay a heavy price in litigation costs.[47]

Finally, some judges are clearly concerned that institutions of higher education are promising to deliver criminal-like procedures.[48] Criminal courts themselves struggle with delivering criminal process; it is even more difficult for institutions of higher education to manage such systems, and error seems inevitable. Oppositional legalistic systems of discipline that mimic the attempt to prove crimes may not be suitable or desirable for managing an institution of higher education environment. Institutions may be trying to make legalistic discipline systems do things the legal system itself struggles with. Institutions of higher education must be careful not to allow unrealistic expectations of intervention to drive them to adopt unmanageable systems.

CODES AND CODE ADMINISTRATORS

There is no federal due process or state contractual law mandate that institutions of higher education must have discipline codes as such.[49] Some states empower their public institutions of higher education to create codes, and a handful of federal laws create specific requirements that institutions of higher education adopt certain rules or procedures.[50] Even in states where courts have held that public institutions of higher education must comply with state administrative procedure requirements, there is no specific requirement that the institutions must adopt codes.

Nonetheless, code culture is ubiquitous in higher education, even if it arises from choice rather than legal mandate. Discipline codes became popular

---

[45] *See Schaer*, 735 N.E.2d at 381–83 (Cowin, J., dissenting).
[46] *See, e.g., Than*, 901 S.W.2d 926.
[47] *See* Lake, *supra* note 16, at 208–9 (discussing the costs of primary litigation avoidance).
[48] *See, e.g., Schaer*, 735 N.E.2d 373; *Than*, 901 S.W.2d 926.
[49] However, some laws do require that institutions of higher education adopt certain policies. *See* No Child Left Behind Act, 20 U.S.C § 6319.
[50] *See, e.g.,* Title IX, 20 U.S.C. § 1681.

in the wake of the tumultuous 1960s and early 1970s.[51] Institutions of higher education and student affairs administrators elected to adopt or expand the role of discipline codes out of a desire to achieve legal compliance and out of the belief that code systems are so compliant.[52] Institutions tend to pattern their codes after various model codes; some models are more popular than others.[53]

Codes, like Mr. Potato Head, have multiform possibilities. Some institutions of higher education have separate conduct and academic codes; others have one uniform code; and still others have honor codes.[54] In addition, colleges also often have mini-codes running around—like traffic codes, etc. Most codes have three key moving parts: rules, procedures, and sanctions.[55]

Rules

Typical rules include prohibitions against hazing, cheating, plagiarism, sexual misconduct, and unlawful alcohol and drug use.[56]

College codes invariably prohibit hazing. As discussed in Chapter 3,

---

[51] *See* Lake, *supra* note 16, at 65 ("*Dixon* also presaged the campus revolutions of the 1960s, which culminated in the event at Kent State and other campuses in May of 1970. *Dixon* was Scene I in Act I of a multi-act college student rights revolution play. Law, violence, oppositionalism, and protest would become more prominent in higher education after 1961. It is easy to overlook, however, that campus unrest of the precise *Dixon* period was noticeably distinct from the campus unrest of the late 1960s and especially 1970. *Dixon's* students fought, peaceably, against Southern segregationist policies. Students of the late 1960s and 1970s were protesting the war in Vietnam and the draft, primarily, and were often more violent and forcibly confrontational than their early 1960s/late 1950s counterparts.").
[52] *Id.*
[53] *Id.* at 179–81.
[54] *See id.* at 187–88
[55] *See, e.g.*, Edward N. Stoner II & John Wesley Lowery, *Navigating Past the "Spirit of Insubordination": A Twenty-First Century Model Student Conduct Code with a Model Hearing Script*, 31 J.C. & U.L. 1 (2004).
[56] Professor Judith Areen summarized the challenges of hazing and legal responses:
  Hazing is common at many universities, both in Greek organizations and in sports. One survey found that 80% of college athletes had been subject to some form of hazing. Joshua A. Sussberg, Note, *Shattered Dreams, Hazing in College Athletics*, 24 Cardozo L. Rev. 1421, 1427 (2003). Anti-hazing laws have been passed in almost every state and some students have been formally charged in hazing incidents. Massachusetts, for example has made hazing punishable by a fine up to three thousand dollars and/or one year in prison. The [Massachusetts] statute defines hazing as "any conduct or method of initiation into any student organization ... which willfully or recklessly endangers the physical or mental health of any student or other person" and removes consent as a defense to prosecution. ... Massachusetts has also made failure to report hazing punishable ...Florida has enacted one of the toughest anti-hazing laws, making hazing resulting in serious physical injury a felony punishable by up to five years in prison ...
  Judith Areen, *Higher Education and the Law: Cases and Materials* 776–77, n. 1 (Thompson/West 2009).

foreseeability of the risk of hazing may be critical in determining university responsibility to prevent hazing incidents, although foreseeability alone is not sufficient to create duty.[57] Moreover, it is increasingly common to see individual students successfully sued in serious hazing incidents.[58] In an exceptional situation, administrators at Rider University were criminally charged with neglect in relation to a fraternity hazing incident, although those charges were later dropped.[59] Hazing is closely related to another phenomenon: bullying. Higher education institutions are toeing into the world of regulating bullying, which brings with it some significant free speech and association challenges under the law. Many legal initiatives aimed at stopping bullying have been initially targeted to the K–12 system.[60]

Plagiarism and cheating are common on college campuses.[61] Because of the serious potential stigmatizing effects to a student of being deemed a plagiarist, campuses should be careful to draw their academic misconduct rules carefully. An area of great debate is whether plagiarism requires a certain state of mind: intention, recklessness, mere negligence, or even "strict" liability. Institutions of higher education should be cautious about branding individuals with labels that imply levels of culpability they did not have. Plagiarism is a scarlet letter in high-

---

[57] *See, e.g.*, *Lloyd v. Alpha Fee Alpha Fraternity*, 199 W.L. 47153 (N.D.N.Y. 1999).

[58] *See, e.g.*, *Garofalo v. Lambda Chi Alpha Fraternity*, 616 N.W.2d 647 (Iowa 2000); *see also Parents Win Settlement for Son's Death in Hazing*, Chronicle of Higher Education (July 10, 1991); *Criminal Charges Filed in Alleged Fraternity Hazing at Penn*, Chronicle of Higher Education (Aug. 31, 2006); Areen, *supra* note 56, at 778 n. 3.

[59] *Compare* Paula Wasley, *Rider U. Official Indicted in Student's Death*, Chronicle of Higher Education (Aug. 17, 2007), *available at* http://chronicle.com/article/Rider-U-Officials-Indicted/25138/ (discussing the criminal indictment of Rider University officials for the death of a student after a fraternity hazing), *with* Paula Wasley, *Judge Dismisses Hazing Charges Against 2 Rider U. Officials*, Chronicle of Higher Education (Aug. 28, 2007), *available at* http://chronicle.com/articl/Judge-Dismisses-Hazing-Char/39465/ (discussing the dismissal of charges for hazing death against Rider University officials).

[60] See Peter Monaghan, *Dealing With Bullies*, The Chronicle of Higher Education (Sept. 12, 2006), *available at* http://chronicle.com/article/Dealing-wth-bullies/117964; Deval Patrick, *Governor Patrick Signs Landmark Anti-Bullying Legislation* (May 3, 2010) http://www.mass.gov/?pageID=gov3pressrelease&L=1&L0=Home&sid=Agov3&b=pressrelease&f=050310_anti_bullying&csid=Agov3; Raven Clabough, *Anti-Bullying Legislation in Massachusetts*, New American (May 4, 2010), *available at* http://www.thenewamerican.com/index.php/culture/education/3468-anti-bully-legislation-in-massachusetts.

[61] Areen, *supra* note 56, at 735 n. 4; *see also* Stanley Fish, *The Ontology of Plagiarism: Part Two*, N.Y. Times (Aug. 16, 2010), *available at* http://opinionator.blogs.nytimes.com/2010/08/16/the-ontology-of-plagiarism-part-two/?hp.

er education and should be treated carefully. Despite the substantial efforts and resources that have been devoted to creating a culture of academic integrity, millennial students apparently bring different values to campus regarding the ownership and use of information. Turning educational battles over the appropriate use of academic resources and information into fights about discipline and code application may miss the mark with this generation and bait litigation.[62]

College populations face significant risks related to sexual misconduct. Recent studies have shown that as many as one in five college-age females may be subject to sexual assault or harassment at school. Increased awareness of sexual assault issues on campus has led Congress to consider expanding the rules under the Clery Act relating to sexual misconduct. Colleges struggle with disciplining sexual misconduct, because predatory violence on females has increased and become more sophisticated, and because many other allegations of sexual misconduct arise among individuals who know each other and have voluntarily consumed alcohol. In the latter situation, justiciability of misconduct issues is extremely tricky; it includes complex issues of evidence and consent.

Colleges also struggle with the close cousin of sexual assault: sexual harassment. Peer-on-peer sexual harassment is a serious issue.[63] Students are entitled to some legal protection from student-on-student sexual harassment.[64] Peer-on-peer harassment can create complex issues. As one court has stated, "'[W]hether gender-oriented conduct rises to the level of actionable "harassment" thus "depends on a constellation of surrounding circumstances, expectations, and relationships," including but not limited to the ages of the harasser and the victim and the number of individuals involved. To have a "systemic

---

[62] *See, e.g.*, Lake, *supra* note 16, at Ch. 5.

[63] Interview with David Lisak & Peter Lake, *Myths That Make It Hard to Stop Campus Rape*, NPR (Mar. 4, 2010), transcript *available at* http://www.npr.org/templates/transcript/transcrip.php?storyId=124272157; Bonnie S. Fisher, Francis T. Cullen, & Michael G. Turner, *The Sexual Victimization of College Women*, National Institute of Justice (2000), *available at* http://www.ojp.usdoj.gov/nij; David Lisak, *Understanding the Predatory Nature of Sexual Violence* 5–9 (Univ. of Mass. 2008), *available at* http://www.middlebury.edu/media/view/240951/original/PredatoryNature.pdf. Dr. Lisak cites numerous reports in his article. *See, e.g.*, M. P. Koss, C. A. Gidycz,, & N. Wisniewski, *The Scope of Rape: Incidence and Prevalence of Sexual Aggression and Victimization in a National Sample of Higher Education Students*, 55 Journal of Consulting and Clinical Psychology 162–70 (1987).

[64] *See, e.g.*, Title IX, 20 U.S.C. § 1681; *Williams v. Board of Regents of Univ. System of Georgia*, 477 F.3d 1282 (11th Cir. 2007).

effect" of denying the victim equal access to an educational program or activity, gender discrimination must be more widespread than a single instance of one-on-one peer harassment.'"[65] To succeed in a claim against an institution, the claimant must show deliberate indifference on the part of the institution to known sexual harassment.[66] The standard is much more deferential to higher education institutions than similar laws applied in the workplace.[67]

Procedures

Typical procedures usually include visible attempts to meet perceived minimum due process/substantial fairness requirements. For example, codes usually include procedures for giving "notice" of charges and elaborate rules for a fair "hearing."[68] Honor code procedures usually depend largely on students to manage and run processes. Other code systems tend to rely more heavily on professional staff, although student involvement is very common. Most systems offer at least one level of "appeal."

Sanctions

Typical sanctions include oral and written warnings, fines, suspension, and expulsion. Some campuses have developed systems that aim to create corrective justice. Few systems use rewards as a motivator; older systems of merit/demerit have given way to more punitive and restorative consequences.

---

[65] *See* Areen, *supra* note 56, at 834 (quoting *Williams*, 477 F.3d at 1297 and *Hawkins*, 322 F.3d at 1289). Also see Chapter 5 for a discussion of Title IX.

[66] Heather M. Karjane, Bonnie S. Fisher, & Francis T. Cullen, *Sexual Assault on Campus: What Colleges and Universities Are Doing About It* 12–14, National Institute of Justice (Dec. 2005), *available at* www.ojp.usdoj.gov/nij.

[67] The U.S. Supreme Court set forth "actual knowledge" and "deliberate indifference" standards to assess responsibility for student harassment by faculty members, but the Court failed to explicitly state whether these standards would apply to peer-on-peer sexual assault. *Gebser v. Lago Vista Independent School Dist.* 524 U.S. 274 (1998). However, in *Davis v. Monroe County Bd. of Education,* the Supreme Court explicitly discussed and defined the applicability of these standards when determining the extent of the university's responsibility for peer-on-peer sexual assaults. 526 U.S. 629 (1999); *see generally* William A. Kaplan & Barbara A. Lee, *The Law of Higher Education* §§ 5.2.3, 8.1.5, 386–89, 747–52 (2006).

[68] In many ways, modern codes try to embody the spirit of *Dixon v. Alabama*, 594 F.2d 150 (5th Cir. 1961), which first announced notice and hearing requirements for higher education.

Some More Observations About Codes

Modern codes tend to be:

1. Legalistic: They use legal terms and mimic legal concepts.

2. Objective: Statements of rules outnumber statements of values.

3. Supported by or referential to other systems: Institutions of higher education typically have many parallel codes. Codes are often deferential to specialized proceedings such as disability accommodation, Title IX, or FERPA.

4. Difficult and slow to change: Most codes are subject to revision, but in many cases revision is a time-consuming process. Student affairs administrators rarely have sole, direct, and final supervision over the content of codes. Student behavior changes faster than most codes can.

5. Managed by specialists: Increasingly, discipline is evolving into a distinct subspecies of student affairs administration. Student affairs administrators who work in discipline have their own organization (the Association for Student Conduct Administration)[69] and training opportunities (e.g., the Gehring Institute and the NASPA Certificate Program in Student Affairs Law and Policy).

6. Divided: Most colleges differentiate between academic and conduct processes. The received wisdom is that academic dismissals are due more deference than conduct proceedings.[70]

---

[69] Lake, *supra* note 16, at 193–198.

[70] Kaplin & Lee, *supra* note 32, at §§ 9.4, 972–93. There are some serious issues in drawing the academic/conduct line, and received wisdom may not be consonant with directives from the Supreme Court.

Recently, there has been a flurry of interest in discipline codes and their management, and in protecting campuses from dangerous persons.[71] Some momentum exists to make discipline systems less legalistic, more educationally focused, and less reliant on academic/conduct distinctions. As institutions of higher education move into the 21st century without a definitive answer from the U.S. Supreme Court on due process for colleges, the task of managing the higher education environment will require more than the use of codes. Efforts aimed at better mentoring, better planning to avoid disciplinary infractions, proactive environmental intervention, expanded educational programs, and more parent/family involvement promise to join in a combined arms operation to drive out the negative aspects of the higher education environment.[72]

---

[71] *See* Sara Lipka, *Discipline Goes on Trial at Colleges*, Chronicle of Higher Education (March 27, 2009), *available at* http://chronicle.com/article/Discipline-Goes-on-Trial-at/30030/; Sara Lipka, *Ties Between Colleges and Students Increasingly Look Like Contracts*, Chronicle of Higher Education (June 29, 2010), *available at* http://www.chronicle.com/article/Ties-Between-Col-legesS/66088/; Sara Lipka, *U. of Virginia President Meets With Governor to Push for Access to Law-Enforcement Records*, Chronicle of Higher Education (May 12, 2010), *available at* http://chronicle.com/article/A-Call-for-Access-To-Studen/65482; Sara Lipka, *Watchdog Group Proposes Stricter Disclosure Requirement for Sexual-Assault Cases*, Chronicle of Higher Education (April 15, 2010), *available at* http://chroncile.com/article/Watchdog-Group-Proposes-Str/65143; *see* Stoner & Lowery, *supra* note 55; *see* Lake, *supra* note 16. *See also* sources on corrective justice in student discipline, e.g., Susan R. Komives & Dudley Woodward, *Student Services: A Handbook for the Profession* (4th ed., Jossey-Bass 2003).
[72] Lake, *supra* note 16, at 217–20.

CHAPTER 5

STUDENT EMPOWERMENT, CIVIL
RIGHTS, INCLUSION, AND DIVERSITY

eginning in the 1960s, American college students won sweeping civil rights.
The Supreme Court rewrote the law of higher education in fundamental
ways, broadly applying constitutional civil rights principles to students in higher
education.[1] Congress passed civil rights legislation that fundamentally altered
the legal landscape of higher education in American society. Under the aegis of a
grant of authority from Congress, the Department of Education (DOE)—with
its civil rights enforcement arm, the Office for Civil Rights (OCR)—followed
constitutional and congressional action with broad regulatory responses.

THE SUPREME COURT AND THE FIRST AMENDMENT

The First Amendment[2] protects freedom of speech, press, religion, association, academic freedom, and privacy; and prohibits the establishment of a

---

[1] In many instances, states have erected parallel systems of rights, occasionally going beyond
federal civil rights mandates. *See, e.g.*, *State v. Schmid*, 423 A.2d 615, 624 (N.J. 1980). This
Book focuses primarily on federal law mandates.
[2] "Congress shall make no law respecting an establishment of religion, or prohibiting the free exercise thereof; or abridging the freedom of speech, or of the press; or the right of the people peaceably
to assemble, and to petition the Government for a redress of grievances." U.S. Const. amend I.

national religion. Through a doctrine known as *selective incorporation*, the First Amendment applies to the states via the Fourteenth Amendment.[3] In addition, the First Amendment has both explicit and penumbral protections—in other words, some specific freedoms, such as academic freedom, are not enumerated in the amendment but are implied by other, explicitly enumerated freedoms. (Some freedoms are penumbral because more than one constitutional amendment or clause combines to create other rights, such as privacy).[4]

The U.S. Supreme Court has squarely held that the First Amendment protects students in the educational context.[5]

Freedom of Speech

In protecting speech, the Supreme Court has recognized that certain forms of conduct also convey ideas, images, or symbols worthy of First Amendment protection. Thus, in *Tinker*, when students wore black armbands to high school to protest the Vietnam war, the Court recognized this as protected speech.[6]

However, not all purported speech receives First Amendment protection. Obscenity,[7] fighting words,[8] and other speech designed to incite imminent lawless behavior[9] do not qualify. The Supreme Court has also held that "true threats" are not protected[10] and has repeatedly made it clear that speech or conduct that is materially disruptive to legitimate educational functions may be regulated.[11]

Nonetheless, the reach of the First Amendment is broad, and often exceed-

---

[3] *Griswold v. Conn.,* 381 U.S. 479, 527 (1965).
[4] U.S. Const. amends. I, IV.
[5] *Tinker v. Des Moines*, 393 U.S. 503, 506 (1969); *Healy v. James*, 408 U.S. 169, 180 (1972). "State colleges and universities are not enclaves immune from the sweep of the First Amendment." *Healy*, 408 U.S. at 180.
[6] *Tinker*, 393 U.S. at 505–6.
[7] *Roth v. U.S.*, 354 U.S. 476, 484 (1957) (finding that obscenity is "utterly without redeeming social importance" and therefore is unprotected by the First Amendment).
[8] *Chaplinski v. New Hampshire*, 315 U.S. 568, 572 (1992).
[9] *Brandenburg v. Ohio*, 395 U.S. 444, 447 (1969).
[10] *Hess v. Indiana*, 414 U.S. 105, 109 (1973).
[11] *See, e.g.*, *Healy*, 408 U.S. at 180; *Christian Legal Society at Hastings College of the Law v. Martinez*, 130 S. Ct. 2971 (2010); *Widmar v. Vincent*, 454 U.S. 263, 268 n. 5 (1981) ("[a college] has the authority to impose reasonable regulations").

ingly distasteful or unpopular speech must be tolerated.[12] Much that is hateful, rude, and repulsive has constitutional protection. The typical remedy for bad speech is more speech, not rules and punishment. Public colleges cannot punish hate speech (except in specific circumstances such as fighting words, incitement, or true threats),[13] but hateful motivation evidenced by hate speech can be used to enhance punishment if other wrongs are committed.[14] An institution of higher education can regulate conduct so long as the regulations or rules are viewpoint-neutral and not aimed at punishing ideas or beliefs. An institution of higher education can also act to stop imminent disruption of material academic functions if such disruption can be reasonably anticipated or forecast.[15] Student affairs administrators need not wait until a building is burning to disburse a protest rally, for instance.

However, the Supreme Court is aware of the Dean Wormers of the past. As the Court stated in *Tinker v. Des Moines*:

> The District Court concluded that the action of the school authorities was reasonable because it was based upon their fear of a disturbance from the wearing of the armbands. But, in our system, undifferentiated fear or apprehension of disturbance is not enough to overcome the right to freedom of expression. Any departure from absolute regimentation may cause trouble. Any variation from the majority's opinion may inspire fear. Any word spoken, in class, in

---

[12] *See, e.g., United States v. Stevens,* 130 S. Ct. 1577 (2010); *Village of Skokie v. National Socialist Party of America,* 373 N.E.2d 21, 23 (1978) (Neo-Nazi march in a town with a high concentration of Holocaust survivors must be permitted to proceed, however pernicious. First Amendment protects abhorrent speech and expressive conduct.); *see also Virginia v. Black,* 538 U.S. 343 (2003); *Texas v. Johnson,* 491 U.S. 392 (1989).

[13] *Rav v. St. Paul,* 505 U.S. 377, 391 (1992).

[14] *Wisconsin v. Mitchell,* 508 U.S. 476, 488 (1993).

[15] "[T]he record does not demonstrate any facts which might reasonably have led school authorities to forecast substantial disruption of or material interference with school activities, and no disturbances or disorders on the school premises in fact occurred. . . . [The petitioners'] deviation consisted only in wearing on their sleeve a band of black cloth, not more than two inches wide. They wore it to exhibit their disapproval of the Vietnam hostilities and their advocacy of a truce, to make their views known, and, by their example, to influence others to adopt them. They neither interrupted school activities nor sought to intrude in the school affairs or the lives of others. They caused discussion outside of the classrooms, but no interference with work and no disorder. In the circumstances, our Constitution does not permit officials of the State to deny their form of expression." *Tinker,* 393 U.S. at 514.

the lunchroom, or on the campus, that deviates from the views of another person may start an argument or cause a disturbance. But our Constitution says we must take this risk, and our history says that it is this sort of hazardous freedom—this kind of openness—that is the basis of our national strength and of the independence and vigor of Americans who grow up and live in this relatively permissive, often disputatious, society."[16]

Tinker made two key points. First, a public college must tolerate a certain degree of incivility and conflict south of material and substantial disruption.[17] The law does not permit public colleges to force students to operate as if they were an audience at a classical music concert in every facet of their educational experience. Second, *Tinker* emphasized (along with *Healy v. James*) that proactive intervention requires some reasonable basis; "I am afraid" or "they might..." do not cut it under *Tinker*. The Supreme Court made the mistake of permitting the denial of fundamental rights to citizens in the *Korematsu* case.[18] Although the Court has never formally overruled the *Korematsu* case, Congress has apologized for the internment of Japanese Americans following the attack on Pearl Harbor.[19] *Healy* and *Tinker* clarify for higher education that Dean Wormer could not return and that *Korematsu* "logic" cannot be used to deny First Amendment rights on campus.

---

[16] *Id.* at 508–9 (citations omitted).

[17] *See also Shamloo v. Mississippi State*, 620 F.2d 516, 521–22 (explaining that the test to determine whether the students' First Amendment activities conflict with the university's adopted regulations depends on whether the demonstration was disrupting and distracting). The district court concluded that "'the demonstration had a disruptive effect with respect to other students' rights.' But this is not enough to conclude that the demonstration was not protected by the First Amendment. The court must also conclude (1) that the disruption was a material disruption of classwork or (2) that it involved substantial disorder or invasion of the rights of others. It must constitute a material and substantial interference with discipline." *Id.* at 522.

[18] *Toyosaburo Korematsu v. U.S.*, 323 U.S. 214, 217–20 (1944). Following the attack on Pearl Harbor, Japanese Americans were discriminated against on the basis of race. *Id.* The Supreme Court, in a highly unusual case, held that such discrimination was legally permissible. *Id.* The government argued that the fact that there had been no Japanese American subversive activities leading up to the attack on Pearl Harbor could be used as evidence of a potential Japanese American conspiracy to attack the United States. *Id.* You read that correctly—that kind of "logic" deserves an F.

[19] *Justice Delayed 43 Years*, Extension of Remarks, 99th Cong. 1st Sess., 131 Cong. Rec. E468 (Feb. 19, 1985).

It is also fairly well accepted that the "heckler's veto" argument will fail.[20] Otherwise, a speaker could be squelched because an audience chose to act out on its own initiative. This would allow people to shout down speakers with whom they disagree and silence them. The line is sometimes a fine one—a speaker inciting imminent lawlessness versus an audience choosing to riot because they hate the speaker's ideas. For a classic example of the heckler's veto, watch the scene in "Blues Brothers" in which Jake and Elwood encounter neo-Nazi protestors. The protestors are protected under *Village of Skokie v. National Socialist Party of America*,[21] and the city cannot stop their stupid, evil, neo-Nazi demonstration simply because Jake and Elwood might react the way they do. (Although some crimes may be worth committing.[22]) Justice John Paul Stevens' concurring opinion in *Christian Legal Society at Hastings College of the Law v. Martinez* reasons correctly that the Constitution may protect speech, but no one is required to like or respect that speech. There is no constitutional requirement that student affairs administrators respect the views of neo-Nazis. The only obligation is to respect the First Amendment.

The First Amendment gives broad protection to ideas, however expressed, but it does set limits. Some putative "speech" is not really speech at all (such as true obscenity)—or deserving of protection—and an institution of higher education has First Amendment rights, too. Colleges are primarily designed to be educational institutions. The Supreme Court has consistently and vigorously protected core mission delivery and made it clear that speech rights must nod to the college's right to deliver core mission without substantial and material disruption. In part, this protection is based on the right of public universities to create "reasonable time, place, and manner restrictions"[23] (discussed below). In part, it arises from general deference to institutions of higher education. The

---

[20] *See, e.g.*, *Lewis v. Wilson*, 253 F.3d 1077, 1082 (2001).

[21] 373 N.E.2d 21 (1978)

[22] Occasionally breaking the law using peaceable means promotes justice and ultimately serves the law. When Dr. Martin Luther King, Jr. was convicted on March 22, 1956, of organizing a bus boycott in Montgomery, Alabama, he said, "Ordinarily, a person leaving a courtroom with a conviction behind him would wear a somber face. But I left with a smile. I knew that I was a convicted criminal, but I was proud of my crime." Martin Luther King, Jr., *The Autobiography of Martin Luther King, Jr.* 87–88 (Warner Books 1998).

[23] *Lamb's Chapel v. Center Moriches Union Free School Dist.*, 508 U.S. 384, 395 (1993); *Madison, Joint School Dist. v. Wisconsin Employment Relations Commission,* 429 U.S. 167, 176 (1976).

Supreme Court has not just acknowledged the power of an institution of higher education to set reasonable time, place, and manner restrictions or simply treated higher education as an amalgam of different fora. (A shopping mall is nothing more than the sum of its stores, but a public university is more than the sum of its fora.) A public university is a speaker and a constitutionally significant association itself, not simply a vehicle for other people's speech.

In the recent *Citizens United* case,[24] the Supreme Court held that corporations have First Amendment rights.[25] In another line of cases since the landmark *Pickering* decision,[26] the Court has made it clear that a government entity has rights, too, and can restrict the speech of employees under some circumstances.[27] An institution of higher education is not just its constituencies: students, lawful protesters, faculty, and so on. The institution itself has First Amendment "is-ness" and the right (balanced against the rights of others) to its own agenda and its own views.[28] Institutions of higher education are not mere placeholders for other people's rights or vehicles for First Amendment–protected passengers.

---

[24] *Citizens United v. Federal Election Commission,* 130 S. Ct. 876, 899 (2010).

[25] "Corporations and other associations, like individuals, contribute to the "discussion, debate, and the dissemination of information and ideas" that the First Amendment seeks to foster." *Pacific Gas & Elec. Co. v. Public Utilities Comm. of California*, 475 U.S. 1, 8 (1986) (quoting *First Natl. Bank of Boston v. Bellotti*, 435 U.S. 765, 783 (1978)).

[26] *Pickering v. Bd. of Ed. of Tp. High School*, 391 U.S. 563 (1972) (holding that the high school teacher's letter to the newspaper criticizing the school board's financial plan addressed "a matter of legitimate public concern" and thus was protected); *Connick v. Myers*, 461 U.S. 138 (1983) (holding that the public employee who circulated a questionnaire throughout the district attorney's office regarding office management was not protected by the First Amendment, as the questionnaire minimally addressed "matters of public concern"); *Garcetti v. Ceballos*, 547 U.S. 410 (2006) (holding that the First Amendment did not protect a district attorney from being disciplined for testifying against the state regarding a memorandum he wrote discussing his professional duties).

[27] *See* note 26, *supra.*

[28] *See Christian Legal Society*, 130 S. Ct. at 2988–89. "'First Amendment rights,' we have observed, 'must be analyzed in light of the special characteristics of the school environment. *Widmar*, 454 U.S. at 268 n.5. This Court is the final arbiter of the question whether a public university has exceeded constitutional constraints, and we owe no deference to universities when we consider that question. . . . Cognizant that judges lack the on-the-ground expertise and experience of school administrators, however, we have cautioned courts in various contexts to 'resist substitut[ing] their own notions of sound educational policy for those of the school authorities which they review.' *Bd. of Educ. of Hendrick Hudson Central School Dist., Westchester Co., v. Rowley*, 458 U.S. 176, 206 (1982). . . .
Schools, we have emphasized, enjoy 'a significant measure of authority over the type of officially recognized activities in which their students participate.'" *Id.* at 2988, 2989.

They are along on the ride *and* are the vehicles, too.

There is no constitutional right to make a university speak for you or adopt your message.[29] The Supreme Court has always been very careful to protect speakers from being forced to adopt a point of view. The Court also protects associations by affirming that they have the right to have members and the right not to have members.[30] They have a job to do and the right to do it. Admittedly, institutions of higher education are unusual corporate and government speakers, because they often invite collaborative determination of an institutional message from a broad spectrum of individuals and entities in and outside the institution. However, having

---

[29] *Id.* at 2978. "The First Amendment shields CLS against state prohibition of the organization's expressive activity, however exclusionary that activity may be. But CLS enjoys no constitutional right to state subvention of its selectivity." *Id.*

[30] *See Wooley v. Maynard*, 430 U.S. 705, 714, 717 (1976) (finding that a person could not be punished by the Granite State for blocking out New Hampshire's motto— "Live free or die"—on his license plate and explaining that "the right of freedom of thought protected by the First Amendment . . . includes both the right to speak freely and the right to refrain from speaking at all"); *Boy Scouts v. Dale*, 530 U.S. 640, 648 (2000) (state cannot force membership in a private association); *Bd. of Regents of Univ. of Wisconsin v. Southworth*, 529 U.S. 217 (2000). The issue of forced speech arose clearly in the *Southworth* case. Students were not literally forced to condone or adopt any speech *per se* as was the case in the *Wooley v. Maynard*, but some students complained that a portion of their mandatory student activity fee was used to fund speech they disliked. *Southworth*, 529 U.S. at 221. The Supreme Court was concerned with indirectly forcing speech via forced subsidization but was also respectful of an institution of higher education's desire to create a vibrant student activity system as part of its learning experience. Striking a balance, the Supreme Court held, with caveats, that a public institution of higher education can force students to pay into a mandatory activity fee system and can have an opt-out provision for objecting students if the institution so chooses, but need not have an opt-out provision to remain constitutionally compliant. *Id.* However, the Supreme Court insisted that an institution of higher education have a viewpoint-neutral system. *Id.* at 233–34. Further, the Court insisted that, to actualize this, an institution of higher education should have a student activity fee system that will "facilitate a wide range of speech" and encourage the "free and open exchange of ideas" on campus. *Id.* at 229, 231. In an unusually specific directive to campuses, the Supreme Court also told institutions of higher education to design systems that treat minority and majority views with equal respect. *Id.* at 233–35. As a result, the Court specifically disapproved of making student fee allocation decisions based on grandfathering or referendum. *Id.* at 235. Either practice could taint the viewpoint-neutrality of the process and skew it toward majoritarianism. *Id.* In addition, paralleling developments in tort law, the Supreme Court noted that the viewpoint-neutrality principle must guide allocation decisions on *and* off campus. The Court essentially acknowledged that a campus environment is a speech-scape broader than boundaries or geographic or spatial restrictions. "We find no principled way, however, to impose upon the University, as a constitutional matter, a requirement to adopt geographic or spatial restrictions as a condition for RSOs' entitlement to reimbursement." *Southworth*, 529 U.S. at 234.

a fluid, dynamic, and collaborative identity is not tantamount to having no constitutional identity as a speaker at all. Moreover, it is true that a public institution of higher education cannot force its community to accept or adopt ideas as their own. But forced speech is very different from the right to create an institution of higher education environment in its own image.[31] There may be times, places, and spaces on campus when the balance of rights tips more favorably to students and others, but that should not mislead student affairs administrators into thinking that the First Amendment only works out the rights of students, faculty, and other speakers.

Time, place, and manner.

Recently, the Supreme Court has been interpreting reasonable time, place, and manner restrictions more favorably to government entities.[32] Content or viewpoint regulations are different in kind and warrant more serious judicial oversight, in most instances.

The Court has deferred to reasonable time, place, and manner restrictions when they are "narrowly tailored"[33] to "promote a substantial governmental interest that would be achieved less effectively absent the regulation."[34] Reasonable restrictions must also be content-neutral, although they may affect some speakers more than others.[35] The government need not choose the "least restrictive or intrusive regulation."[36] A regulation is also not reasonable if it closes off "ample alternative channels for communication."[37]

One of the most common issues that raises reasonable time, place, and manner questions is the speech zone conundrum.[38] The Supreme Court has not directly determined whether such designated zones are permissible or, if so, under what conditions. Speech zones are facially content-neutral and may serve a

---

[31] *Christian Legal Society*, 130 S. Ct. at 2988–89.

[32] *See Clarke*, 468 U.S. at 299; *Ward v. Rock Against Racism*, 491 U.S. 781, 800 (1989); *U.S. v. Albertini*, 472 U.S. 675, 688–89.

[33] *See Albertini*, 472 U.S. at 689.

[34] *See id.*

[35] *See Ward*, 491 U.S. at 791. "'[A] regulation that serves purposes unrelated to the content of expression is deemed neutral, even if it has an incidental effect on some speakers or messages but not others.'" *See Christian Legal Society*, 130 S. Ct. at 2994 (quoting *Ward*, 491 U.S. at 791).

[36] *See Christian Legal Society*, 130 S.Ct. at 2994.

[37] *See, e.g., Clarke*, 468 U.S. at 293; *Ward*, 491 U.S. at 791.

[38] *See* Thomas J. Davis, *Assessing Constitutional Challenges to University Free Speech Zones under Public Reform Doctrines*, 79 Indiana L.J. 267 (2004).

substantial government interest, although articulating exactly what that is can be tricky, because a speech zone can be like a junk drawer: a tidy space for untidy things. Most problematic of all may be that squeezing speakers into a speech zone can feel a little bit like being on a full flight—an experience vaguely reminiscent of modern flying. It is not entirely clear how "big" a speech space must be to give diverse views a chance to breathe.

Leading higher education law authors William Kaplin and Barbara Lee have raised a variety of other concerns about speech zones:

> Free speech zones sometimes have been implemented by requirements that students reserve the zone in advance . . . or that students obtain prior approval for any use outside the hours specified in the institutional policy. . . . In addition, even if the institution does not employ any prior approval requirement, the free speech zone must meet the requirements of the U.S. Supreme Court's public forum cases. . . . Free speech zones will raise serious difficulties under these requirements in at least two circumstances. *First*, if the institution's regulations allow free speech only in the approved zone or zones, and if other parts of the campus that are unavailable for certain speech activities are considered traditional public forums, serious issues will arise because traditional public forum property cannot be entirely closed off to expressive uses. *Second,* if some but not all of the other campus areas that are public forums (besides the free speech zone or zones) are left open for some or all expressive activity, other serious issues may arise. . . . Specifically, there could be problems concerning (1) whether the institution selected other areas to be open and closed, or limited the expressive activity in the other open areas, on a content-neutral basis; (2) whether the closings of certain forum areas (or the limitation imposed on certain areas) were narrowly tailored to serve substantial interest of the institution; and (3) whether the areas that remain open are sufficient to provide "ample alternative channels for communication."[39]

---

[39] William A. Kaplin & Barbara Lee, *The Law of Higher Education* Vol. II, 1006 (4th ed., Jossey-Bass 2006) (citations omitted and emphasis in original).

Kaplin and Lee correctly point out that a campus probably cannot use a speech zone as an excuse to close off First Amendment rights in other fora on campus.

Chill, overbreadth, and vagueness.

The First Amendment is concerned not only with direct attacks on freedom of speech but also with *chill*.[40] Freedom of speech can be scared off by rules that *might* bring penalties, even if they do not; the threat of prosecution may be enough to chill speech.[41] Rules can be problematic in at least two ways. First, a rule can be so unclear or vague as to be open to just about any interpretation. Dean Wormer was fond of nonspecific threats. Second, a rule can be overkill and squelch protected speech while trying to eliminate unprotected speech—overbreadth.

Attacks on vagueness and overbreadth are common in First Amendment litigation.[42] Student affairs administrators should anticipate that controversial regulations will routinely be challenged on these grounds.

The Supreme Court has essentially endorsed a meta-process to arrive at preferable regulations in contested situations. First, student affairs administrators should almost always engage lawyers in the process of developing and defining regulations. Second, organized watchdog groups will often challenge regulations with First Amendment implications.[43] Third, the process of arriving at preferable regulations typically involves not just receiving initial legal advice but a dialectical process with opponents and opposing beliefs, and a "partnership" with the courts. Student affairs administrators should expect litigation— even embrace it. In striking down a regulation, courts often offer roadmaps for successful redrafting. Accountability under law sometimes blurs into judicial partnership and collaboration in finding solutions. First Amendment principles are so precious in a constitutional democracy that student affairs administrators should appreciate the value of contested process refereed by courts, not resist it. Other industries—the mass media, in particular—have learned this lesson.

---

[40] *See, e.g., Smith v. California*, 361 U.S. 147, 151 (1959); *Heinz v. Mayer*, 425 U.S. 610, 616 (1976).

[41] *See White v. Davis*, 533 P.2d 222, 227 (Cal. 1975) (explaining that presence of undercover police in classrooms can chill the free exchange of ideas).

[42] "A law is unconstitutionally vague if a reasonable person cannot tell what speech is prohibited and what is permitted." Erwin Chemerinsky, *Constitutional Law: Principles and Policies* 491 (3rd ed., Aspen Publishers 2006).

[43] *See, e.g.,* Foundation for Individual Rights in Education, *FIRE: Defending Individual Rights in Higher Education*, http://www.thefire.org/spotlight (last visited Aug. 27, 2010).

Indeed, without Supreme Court intervention in *New York Times v. Sullivan*,[44] mass media in the United States would likely be operating in a completely different way, minus significant legal protection. This is one area of the law in which controversy and litigation serve the First Amendment. Try to be right, but join the fight.

FORUM ANALYSIS

A college learning environment is not one uniform space for purposes of constitutional First Amendment analysis. Some spaces are more constitutionally sensitive than others; there are places where we can channel our inner Dean Wormer and tell people to shut up and other places where we cannot. "Forum" analysis, which can be maddeningly complex and usually requires expert legal guidance, determines when, if, and how an institution of higher education can intervene with respect to content or viewpoint. Forum analysis involves two things—identifying who is the speaker, and then what is the forum.

There are four types of speakers: (1) the institution of higher education itself, (2) its personnel (such as student affairs administrators), (3) students, and (4) everyone else. Imagine these four types of speakers trying to shout each other down and compete for talking space, like characters in MTV's "Real World."[45] (The Supreme Court has made some key pronouncements on the rights of personnel to speak on topics an institution of higher education may wish to discourage, but that discussion is beyond the scope of this Book.)[46] Needless to say, some fora are better than other fora for some "teams" (like the old home of the Celtics, the Boston Garden, may it rest in peace).[47]

The Supreme Court appears to believe (at least for now) in the existence of four constitutionally significant fora (three plus a nonforum, if you must):

---

[44] 376 U.S. 254 (1954).

[45] *Real World* (MTV 1992–2010) (TV series). Everyone has some rights, but some rights vis-à-vis others are stronger—it was so much simpler in "Animal House." Think of the fora as their fields of play, like a sport. We are not going to consider every form of gladiatorial speech-combat here, just the ones with the biggest impact on student affairs practice.

[46] *See, e.g., Pickering*, 391 U.S. at 574; *Connick*, 461 U.S. at 154; *Garcetti*, 547 U.S. at 423.

[47] Wikipedia, *Boston Garden,* http://wn.wikipedia.org/wiki/Boston_Garden (last visited Aug. 27, 2010).

(1) a traditional or designated public forum, (2) a limited public forum, (3) a non-public forum, and (4) a nonforum. An institution of higher education has some control over which forum is which (more control over some than others), but it cannot just announce all fora by fiat; some evolve on their own. And (for more legal and pragmatic reasons than I can count) a public institution of higher education cannot simply say, "There are no fora here," and shut out all speech it finds undesirable. Moreover, a college can stake out preferred speech spaces for itself, but cannot drive unwanted speech underground. To use a sports analogy, "home cooking" is common when a team cashes in on home field advantage,[48] but you cannot shower the field with shards of glass moments before play starts. The law of free speech does have rules of fair play.

Limiting our analysis primarily to students,[49] the next step is to understand what the forum is and what rights speakers in that forum receive. Keep in mind that fora are conceptual spaces, so they can exist in the physical or nonphysical world. (Also keep in mind that not all justices have used forum analysis terms to mean exactly the same thing—confusing!)

Traditional Public Forum

A traditional public forum is a neutral field, like the Super Bowl.[50] As long as the speech is protected speech, these spaces are free from content/viewpoint censorship. They include public thoroughfares and green spaces that are traditionally open to the public, such as parks. A space may not always have existed, or always existed as a traditional public forum, but it can gain equivalency to a traditional public forum.[51] Just because an institution of higher education includes a space that is a traditional public forum or its equivalent does not mean

---

[48] *See, e.g.,* Wikipedia, *Celtics-Lakers Rivalry* http://en.wikipedia.org/wiki/Celtics-Lakers_rivalry (last visited Aug. 27, 2010). The so-called "Heat" game in 1985 at Boston Garden stands out as a signature moment in home field advantage. Eyewitnesses have claimed that the Celtics closed the windows, turned up the heat, and shut off water in the Lakers' locker room. (Conversation with Robert Orsi, Esq., Sept. 2010).

[49] Faculty and other personnel are another matter. *See Garcetti*, 547 U.S. at 423.

[50] No, not really. Technically, there is a home team in the Super Bowl, which is fairly ridiculous. Moreover, NFL football teams look to host the Super Bowl and then fantasize about home field advantage in that Super Bowl. Weirdly, there is no particular reason to believe that a team playing in its home stadium would be the home team in the Super Bowl.

[51] *See International Society for Krishna v. Lee*, 505 U.S. 672, 678 (1992).

that it has the plenary power to control speech, as it might have if it had never created (or tolerated the creation of) such a space in the first place long ago.[52]

In traditional public fora, regulation is usually limited to reasonable time, place, and manner restrictions. (Note that *Rosenberger* acknowledged a different type of forum—a limited public forum in which more restrictions are permissible. See below.) The Supreme Court *theoretically* permits regulation of content in a traditional public forum, but only if regulation is "necessary to serve a compelling state interest."[53] Regulation must also be "narrowly tailored" to serve a compelling state interest, in order to avoid overbreadth, vagueness, po-

---

[52] *See Widmar*, 454 U.S. at 268. *See also Rosenberger v. Rector & Visitors of Univ. of Va.,* 515 U.S. 819 (1995). In the *Rosenberger* case, the Supreme Court discussed the limits of content and viewpoint discrimination:

> It is axiomatic that the government may not regulate speech based on its substantive content or the message it conveys . . . Other principles follow from this precept. . . . [G]overnment regulation may not favor one speaker over another . . . Discrimination against speech because of its message is presumed to be unconstitutional . . . These rules informed our determination that the government offends the First Amendment when it imposes a financial burden on certain speakers based on the content of their expression . . . When the government targets not subject matter, but particular abuse taken by speakers on a subject, the violation of the First Amendment is all the more blatant . . . Viewpoint discrimination is thus an egregious form of content discrimination. The government must abstain from regulating speech when the specific motivating ideology or the opinion or perspective of the speaker is the rationale for the restriction.
>
> These principles provide the framework forbidding the State to exercise viewpoint discrimination, even when the limited public forum is one of its own creation. In a case involving a school district's provision of school facilities for private uses, we declare that "there is no question that the district, like the private owner of property, may legally preserve the property under its control for the use to which it is dedicated." *Lamb's Chapel v. Center Moriches Union Free School District*, 508 U.S. 384, 390 (1993). The necessities of confining a forum due to limited and legitimate purposes for which it was created may justify the State in reserving it for certain groups or for the discussion of certain topics . . . Once it is opened [as] a limited forum, however, the State must respect the lawful boundaries it has itself set. The State may not exclude speech, or its discussion is not "reasonable in light of the purpose served by the forum," *Cornelius* [*v. NAACP Legal Defense & Educ. Fund, Inc.*, 473 U.S. 788, 804–6 (1985)], nor may it discriminate against speech on the basis of its viewpoint . . . Thus, in determining whether the state is acting to preserve the limits of the forum it has created so that the exclusion of a class of speech is legitimate, we have observed a distinction between, on the one hand, content discrimination, which may be permissible yet it preserves the purposes of that limited forum, and on the other hand, viewpoint discrimination, which is presumed impermissible when directed against speech otherwise within the forum's limitations." *Id.* at 828–30 (citations omitted).

[53] *See Cornelius*, 473 U.S. at 800; *Arkansas v. Forbes*, 523 U.S. 666, 677 (1998).

tential squelching of protected speech, or chilling of other protected speech.[54] Needless to say, successful *content* regulation in a traditional public forum is difficult to justify.[55]

---

[54] Overbreadth is a doctrine the Supreme Court has created to illustrate a situation in which a regulation may properly regulate some speech but affects protected speech too broadly and is therefore unconstitutional. *See, e.g., Virginia v. Hicks,* 539 U.S. 113 (2003). Crafting regulations requires legal artfulness and is sometimes a complex process that requires several trips to court to succeed.

[55] *See, e.g., Chicago Police Department v. Mosley,* 408 U.S. 92, 99 (1972) (court strikes down an ordinance prohibiting all picketing near schools because it was a content-based restriction aimed at labor protests); *Boos v. Barry,* 485 U.S. 312 (1988) (law forbidding signs with specific messages struck down). However, success under the standard is not impossible. In *Ward v. Rock Against* Racism, 491 U.S. 781, 790 (1989), the Supreme Court handed down a decision of particular interest to persons putting on events. The Court upheld a law that required performances in a municipal theater to use the municipality's sound equipment. The Court believed that the regulation was indeed "narrowly tailored," because it protected the municipality from the potential for excessive noise emanating from an event. *Id.* at 791.

The Supreme Court has protected speech from overbroad, vague and chilling regulatory schemes. Imagine the Supreme Court imagining Dean Wormer. He was fond of heavy-handedness (over-breadth), threatening innuendo (vagueness) and generally sought to eliminate and chill speech and association he did not approve of. (Keep in mind that we never are entirely certain whether Faber College is public or private, although one might presume that Faber is private from the founders' statue, which prominently displays "Knowledge is good." If Faber was private then Dean Wormer might have been free to continue many of his practices under the First Amendment because he was not a state actor; however, some states might have prohibited his behavior under a state constitution and other laws).

The Supreme Court has also been concerned about a related phenomenon in higher education—clearly this is the Dean Wormer doctrine. The Supreme Court has been concerned that governmental regulators could use broad *discretion* to systematically promote speech they agree with and discourage speech they disagree with. There is however a difference between license and discretion: Discretion is the exercise of judgment within limits, license is being Dean Wormer and doing whatever you choose without accountability. The Supreme Court has repeatedly struck down systems of regulation that create Dean Wormer-like powers in regulatory bodies—license, not discretion. *See, e.g., Forsythe County, Georgia v. Nationalist Movement,* 505 U.S. 123, 133 (1992) (the Supreme Court struck down a Dean Wormer-like system that permitted a regulator to change the price of a permit for a parade march or rally based on the subject of same). The Supreme Court has been so insistent on playing "death mobile" to Dean Wormer that the Court has instructed citizens that they may disregard Dean Wormer-like systems of regulation entirely and exercise their First Amendment rights. *See, e.g., Lovell v. City of Griffin,* 303 U.S. 444, 452–53 (1938). Dean Wormeresque systems create a form of pernicious prior restraint. Therefore, although citizens usually must treat voidable laws as valid until they are held void or voided, the First Amendment protects and even encourages a certain degree of civil disobedience in the face of unbridled power. *See, e.g., Shuttlesworth v. Birmingham,* 394 U.S. 147, 151 (1969); *City of Lakewood v. Plain Dealer Publishing Co.,* 486 U.S. 750, 755–56 (1988). "Recognizing the explicit protection accorded speech and the press in the text of the First Amendment, our cases have long held that when a licensing statute allegedly vests unbridled discretion in a government official over whether to permit or deny expressive activity, one who is subject to the law may challenge it facially without the necessity of first

Limited Public Forum

Censorship battles on campus tend to rage with the most vigor in limited public fora (sometimes referred to as designated public fora). A limited public forum is one created by an institution of higher education.[56] In the act of creation, the institution imbues a limited public forum with certain qualities that make it different from other fora: "the necessities of confining a forum to the limited and legitimate purposes for which it was created may justify the state in reserving it for certain groups or the discussion of certain topics."[57] Limited public fora include systems of student publications, registered student organizations (RSOs), student activity systems, some Internet functions, and certain billboards.[58]

Broader regulation of limited public fora is permissible and the standard of scrutiny is lower. An institution of higher education must "respect the lawful boundaries it has itself set."[59] *Viewpoint* discrimination is not permissible,[60] but *content* can be regulated if the regulations are "reasonable in light of the purpose served

---

applying for, and being denied, a license." *City of Lakewood*, 486 U.S. at 755.

Finally, institutions of higher education and student affairs administrators should be aware of one interesting pattern in Supreme Court cases: The Court has typically shown deference to regulators who prohibit loud or excessive noise. *See, e.g.*, *Kovacs v. Cooper*, 336 U.S. 77, 81–82 (1949); *Ward v. Rock Against Racism*, 491 U.S. 781, 796 (1989). This is not terribly surprising when one considers the composition of the Court, even though most of the justices were of age during the rock-n-roll revolution. But while they might have aged gracefully to prefer quiet classical music and jazz, the justices apparently have not totally forgotten their generational aversion to "the Man." Thus, in *Saia v. New York*, 334 U.S. 558, 562 (1948), the Court struck down an ordinance that gave too much discretion to officials to determine who was permitted to use sound trucks, and it is likely that the Supreme Court would endorse this principle again today.

Needless to say, citizens cannot willy-nilly ignore government regulations; if a regulatory law contains reasonable standards managing the discretion of a regulatory body, a citizen must use the court system to challenge the validity of the regulation. *Poulos v. New Hampshire*, 345 U.S. 395, 409 (1953). Supreme Court jurisprudence offers a wonderful opportunity for student affairs administrators to teach their students about the power and limits of civil disobedience and the legal limits on governmental disobedience—abusing power over citizens.

[56] *See Rosenberger*, 515 U.S. at 829. Of course, a university can also create, if it chooses, a space equivalent to a traditional public forum.

[57] *See id.*

[58] The line between fora is not always entirely clear, and the Supreme Court itself in various opinions has discussed fora in somewhat inconsistent ways. The Roberts Court appears to be very interested in advancing First Amendment jurisprudence. Student affairs administrators should carefully watch all First Amendment cases that emerge as the Supreme Court crafts and refines its ontology of the First Amendment—and the boundaries of disputes among Justices.

[59] *See id.*

[60] *See id.*; *Christian Legal Society*, 130 S. Ct. at 2987–90.

by the forum."[61] The Supreme Court discriminates between *content* censorship and *viewpoint* censorship.[62] That distinction is not always easy to see, or justify.

In *Rosenberger*, the Court struck down a system of funding for student publications that singled out religious publications for less favorable treatment; the regulations were held to be viewpoint-discriminatory.[63] However, in *Christian Legal Society*, the Court held that an all-comers policy for membership in RSOs was viewpoint-neutral and that the policy was reasonable in light of the purposes of the RSO.[64]

---

[61] *See Rosenberger* 515 U.S. at 828 (citations omitted); *see also Lamb's Chapel*, 508 U.S. at 392–3.

[62] *See Rosenberger* 515 U.S. at 844–45. "Were the dissent's view to become law, it would require the University, in order to avoid a constitutional violation, to scrutinize the content of student speech, lest the expression in question—speech otherwise protected by the Constitution—contain too great a religious content. The dissent, in fact, anticipates such censorship as crucial in distinguishing between works characterized by the evangelism of Wide Awake and writing that merely happens to express views that a given religion might approve. That eventuality raises the specter of governmental censorship, to ensure that all student writings and publications meet some baseline standard of secular orthodoxy. To impose that standard on student speech at a university is to imperil the very sources of free speech and expression. As we recognized in *Widmar*, official censorship would be far more inconsistent with the Establishment Clause's dictates than would governmental provision of secular printing services on a religion-blind basis." *Id.* (citations omitted).

[63] *See id.* at 832.

[64] As stated in *Christian Legal Society*:

We next consider whether Hastings' all-comers policy is viewpoint-neutral.

Although this aspect of limited-public-forum analysis has been the constitutional sticking point in our prior decisions, as earlier recounted . . . we need not dwell on it here. It is, after all, hard to imagine a more viewpoint-neutral policy than one requiring *all* student groups to accept *all* comers. In contrast to *Healy, Widmar,* and *Rosenberger,* in which universities singled out organizations for disfavored treatment because of their points of view, Hastings' all-comers requirement draws no distinction between groups based on their message or perspective. An all-comers condition on access to RSO status, in short, is textbook viewpoint-neutral.

Conceding that Hastings' all-comers policy is "nominally neutral," CLS attacks the regulation by pointing to its effect: The policy is vulnerable to constitutional assault, CLS contends, because "it systematically and predictably burdens most heavily those groups whose viewpoints are out of favor with the campus mainstream." This argument stumbles from its first step because "[a] regulation that serves purposes unrelated to the content of expression is deemed neutral, even if it has an incidental effect on some speakers or messages but not others." [*Ward*, 491 U.S. at 791.]

Even if a regulation has a differential impact on groups wishing to enforce exclusionary membership policies, "[w]here the [state] does not target conduct on the basis of its expressive content, acts are not shielded from regulation merely because they express a discriminatory idea or philosophy." [*R.A.V.*, 505 U.S. at 390.]

Hastings' requirement that student groups accept all comers, we are satisfied, "is justified without reference to the content [or viewpoint] of the regulated speech." [*Ward*, 491 U.S. at 791.] The Law School's policy aims at the *act* of rejecting would-be group members without

Both cases, however, had vigorous dissents.[65]

Student affairs administrators should recognize that much of their work is directed toward the management of limited public fora: activities, clubs, RSOs, Greek life, and even recreational athletics. The mantra of wide viewpoint access and reasonable regulation in light of the purposes of a forum should perpetually reverberate in student affairs practice. (This would make an excellent bumper sticker, except that it is too long to fit on a bumper.)

The actual process of illuminating the educational and developmental nature and purposes of a forum is critical in any legal challenge to regulations under the First Amendment. Analysis of the genuine educational and developmental purposes of a forum factored very heavily into the *Christian Legal Society* case. All the justices—majority concurrences and dissenters—were deeply committed to analyzing the reality of the RSO system at Hastings Law School. Consider the language of the Court's opinion on this point: "[T]he Law School reasonably adheres to the view that an all-comers policy, to the extent it brings together individuals with diverse backgrounds and beliefs, 'encourages tolerance, cooperation, and learning among students.'"[66]

Or consider Justice John Paul Stevens' destined-to-be-foundational concurrence:

> The campus is, in fact, a world apart from the public square in numerous respects, and religious organizations, as well as other organizations, must abide by certain norms of conduct when they enter an academic community. Public universities serve a distinctive role in a modern democratic society. Like all specialized government

---

reference to the reasons motivating that behavior: Hastings' "desire to redress th[e] perceived harms of exclusionary membership policies provides an adequate explanation for its [all-comers condition] over and above mere disagreement with [any student group's] beliefs or biases." *Wisconsin v. Mitchell*, 508 U.S. 476, 488 (1993). CLS's conduct—not its Christian perspective—is, from Hastings' vantage point, what stands between the group and RSO status. "In the end," as Hastings observes, "CLS is simply confusing its *own* viewpoint-based objections to . . . nondiscrimination laws (which it is entitled to have and [to] voice) with viewpoint *discrimination*. . . ."

Finding Hastings' open-access condition on RSO status reasonable and viewpoint-neutral, we reject CLS' free-speech and expressive-association claims. 130 S.Ct. 2993–95 (citations omitted).

[65] *Rosenberger* 515 U.S. at 863; *Christian Legal Society*, 130 S. Ct. at 3000.
[66] *Christian Legal Society*, 130 S. Ct. at 2997 (Stevens, J., concurring).

entities, they must make countless decisions about how to allocate resources in pursuit of their role. Some of those decisions will be controversial; many will have differential effects across populations; virtually all will entail value judgments of some kind. As a general matter, the court should respect universities' judgments and let them manage their own affairs.

The RSO forum is no different. It is not an open and common forum Hastings happens to maintain. It is a mechanism through which Hastings confers certain benefits and pursues certain aspects of its educational mission. Having exercised its discretion to establish an RSO program, a university must treat all participants evenhandedly. But the university need not remain neutral—indeed it could not remain neutral—in determining which goals the program will serve and which roles are best suited to facilitate those goals. These are not legal questions but policy questions; they are not for the court but for the university to make. When any given group refuses to comply with the rules, the RSO sponsor need not admit that group at the cost of undermining the program and the values reflected therein. On many levels the university administrator has a "greater interest in the content of student activities than the police chief has in the content of a soapbox oration." *Widmar v. Vincent*, 454 U.S. 263, 280 (1981) (Stevens, J., concurring in judgment).[67]

Justice Anthony Kennedy, in concurrence, also discussed the nature of Hastings Law School's RSO system as a limited public forum:

In the instant case, however, if the membership qualification were enforced, it would contradict a legitimate purpose for having created the limited forum in the first place. Many educational institutions, including respondent, Hastings College of Law, have recognized that the process of learning occurs both formally in a classroom setting and informally outside it . . . students may be shaped as profoundly by their peers as by their teachers. Extracurricular activities,

---

[67] Id. at 2997–98 (Stevens, J., concurring).

such as those in the Hastings "Registered Student Organization" program, facilitate interactions between students, enabling them to explore new points of view, to develop interests and talents, to nurture a growing sense of self . . . the Hastings program is designed to allow all students to interact with their colleagues across a broad, seemingly unlimited range of ideas, views and activities. . . .

Law students come from many backgrounds and have but three years to meet each other and develop their skills. They do so by participating in a community that teaches them how to create arguments in a convincing, rational, and respectful manner and to express doubt and disagreement in a professional way. A law school furthers these objectives by allowing broad diversity in RSOs. But these objectives may be better achieved if students can act cooperatively to learn from and teach each other through interactions and social intellectual context. A vibrant dialog is not possible if students wall themselves off from opposing points of view.

The school's objectives thus might not be well served if, as a condition to membership or participation in a group, students were required to allow particular personal beliefs or to disclose private, off-campus behavior. Students whose views are in the minority at the school would likely fare worse in that regime. Indeed, were those sorts of requirements to become prevalent, it might undermine the principle that in a university community—and in a law school community specifically—speech is deemed persuasive based on its substance, not the identity of the speaker. The era of loyalty oaths is behind us. [Not entirely.] A school quite properly may conclude that allowing an oath or belief-affirming requirement, or an outside conduct requirement, could be divisive for student relations and inconsistent with the basic concept that a view's validity should be tested through free and open discussion. The school's policy therefore represents a permissible effort to preserve the value of its forum.[68]

The dissent in *Christian Legal Society* was deeply concerned that the "all-comers policy is not viewpoint neutral because it was announced as a pretext to justify viewpoint discrimination."[69] The vitriolic dissent—essentially calling out Hastings Law School on its stated objectives—illustrates that members of the Court will not simply accept asserted rationales of the purposes of a limited public forum on their face alone. The justices are concerned about the return of Dean Wormer and will insist on a certain amount of authenticity and perlucidity in forum creation and management. This is, after all, the age of accountability. The Supreme Court will be concerned that political correctness can masquerade as legitimate educational policy. Courts will be watching to see if what we *say* substantially coincides with what we *do*. Power comes with responsibility; discretion is not license. The law is watching, carefully, as it should.

There is no doubt that the era of *Anthony v. Syracuse* is dead in limited public forum analysis. While the majority in *Christian Legal Society* talked of owing "decent respect"[70] to administrative regulations in the higher education context, the entire Court made it clear that deceptive or insincere attempts to justify regulation will draw its heavy judicial scrutiny and even ire. There is nothing more pernicious in a constitutional democracy than entrusting academic freedom to someone who would use it to wear a false mask of righteousness and purport to promote speech while actually seeking to deny it. In Chapter 3, I discussed the importance of good faith and proper motivation in serious injury litigation; the same principles apply here.

In the inimitable words of The Who, "We won't get fooled again."[71] Decent respect is not blind acquiescence. There is accountability under law, brought to us

---

[68] *Id.* at 2999–3000 (Kennedy, J., concurring). The Supreme Court has permitted the federal government to require public officers and some public employees to take certain loyalty oaths under certain circumstances. *Connell v. Higgenbotham*, 403 U.S. 207, 208 (1971); *Cole v. Richardson*, 405 U.S. 676, 679 (1972). However the Supreme Court has protected public employees who are simply members of a group from discrimination qua membership in a group. *See Keyishian v. Board of Regents*, 385 U.S. 589, 606 (1967).

[69] *Christian Legal Society*, 130 S.Ct. at 3000 (Alito, J., dissenting).

[70] *Id.* at 2997.

[71] The Who, *We Won't Get Fooled Again* (Arista Records 1970).

by Supreme Court justices who may or may not have marched in the streets in the 1960s but who do remember higher education of the era of Dean Wormer, President Trenholm (*Dixon v. Alabama*), and Kent State. The Supreme Court will not tolerate clowns of intolerance masquerading as educational leaders. *Christian Legal Society* may be the first Supreme Court case to have rock n' roll as its soundtrack. There has never been a time in student affairs practice when intentionality and careful and deliberative educational policymaking has been so closely tied to legal standards.

Developing a sense of accountability under law is a *concept*; it takes a certain amount of "feel," not the memorization of rules. Student affairs administrators should make a point of reading and discussing cases such as *Christian Legal Society* to process them. The spirit of the law is as important as its letter. The law is not a machine, nor does it regulate machines. Those who fail to appreciate the spirit of the law are doomed to violate it again and again. Student affairs administrators who learn to appreciate the spirit of the law will find the experience of working with and living in a juridical world more positive and fruitful. Administrators often seek bright-line rules, clear compliance steps, and outlines with neatly organized sequences of accurate legal statements. These are a critical feature of understanding the law, but it is equally essential in student affairs practice to conceptualize the law and engage it. The student affairs practitioner who does not do this will be doomed to operate in a sea of legal uncertainty and will miss the opportunity to appreciate a partnership with the law. Get to the show; don't just read about it!

Nonpublic Forum

Some fora are not open to the public generally but are open only for very select purposes. An institution of higher education can permit "selective access for individual speakers rather than general access for a class of speakers."[72] These fora are subject to a slightly lower standard of scrutiny than limited public fora.[73] It may be that nonpublic fora are a very special example of limited public fora, except that they are more narrowly created.

---

[72] *Forbes*, 523 U.S. at 679.
[73] *See Krishna v. Lee*, 505 U.S. 672, 678 (1992).

Nonforum

Some spaces are not fora at all.[74] Some fora are not open to the public generally; some are not even open for speech. In such places, the freedom of speech/association of the institution of higher education itself (or the student affairs administrator or other employee) may be at stake, and allowing forum analysis would squelch speech or association and/or the dedicated use of the property for a nonspeech purpose. A board meeting is such a place; institutions of higher education and student affairs administrators are free to choose among content and viewpoint as well as time, place, and manner. The Monday morning administrative meeting might seem like a limited public forum, but in constitutional analysis it is not.

Forum analysis requires legal expertise, and even then courts may surprise a campus in how they characterize a space. Although forum analysis is presented here in a clear-cut way, the reality is not always so clear. The Supreme Court has slowly evolved its own forum analysis, and the justices do not all agree on exactly how to characterize fora.

Student affairs administrators should be aware of one other "forum." As illustrated in the famous *State v. Schmid*[75] case, there may be times when parts of a *private* campus are so infused with the characteristics of traditional public fora that state constitutions can treat those areas more or less as such.[76] This situation varies from state to state; a student affairs administrator at a private college must consult legal counsel to determine what, if any, public law rights accrue on private college campuses.

Rights of Association

Rights of speech and association are closely linked on college campuses. In one sense, an institution of higher education is a large, multidimensional communication machine, running on the fuel of countless educational interactions—a learning team.

---

[74] *See Forbes*, 523 U.S. at 677.

[75] 423 A.2d 615 (N.J. 1980). In some states, like New Jersey, portions of a private campus (like Princeton's, at issue in the case) have been open to the public in ways that imbue at least that part of a private campus with public rights.

[76] *See id.* at 619; *see also Pruneyard Shopping Center v. Robins*, 447 U.S. 74, 88 (1980).

The Supreme Court protects the rights of groups connected to campus to associate and balances those rights against the First Amendment rights of the institution itself, both as a speaker/association and as an entity with the power to regulate fora it has created within constitutional limits.

Dean Wormer made a practice of summarily running students and groups he disliked off campus.[77] The Supreme Court halted this practice in the landmark case, *Healy v. James*.[78] In that case, students sought to form a chapter of Students for a Democratic Society (SDS) on campus and the institution refused to allow them to do so.[79] (SDS organizations were notorious in their day and struck fear in the hearts of administrators.[80]) The Supreme Court held that such prior restraint of the freedom of association undermines academic freedom and is not constitutional:

> At the outset we note that state colleges and universities are not enclaves immune from the sweep of the First Amendment. "It can hardly be argued that either students or teachers shed their constitutional rights to freedom of speech or expression at the school house gate." *Tinker v. Des Moines Independent School District*, 393 U.S. 503, 506 (1969). Of course, as Mr. Justice Fortas made clear in *Tinker*, First Amendment rights must always be applied "in light of the special characteristics of the . . . environment" in the particular case. *Id.* And where state-operated educational institutions are involved, this Court has long recognized "the need for farming the comprehensive authority of the States and of school officials, consistent with fundamental constitutional safeguards, to prescribe and control conduct in the schools." *Id.* at 507. Yet, the precedents of this Court leave no room for view that, because of the acknowledged need for order, First Amendment protection should apply with less force on college campuses then in the community at large. Quite to the contrary, "[t]he vigilant protection of constitutional freedoms is

---

[77] *Animal House* (National Lampoon 1978) (motion picture).
[78] 408 U.S. 169 (1972).
[79] *See id.* at 170–80.
[80] Students for a Democratic Society (SDS) was a national organization with local chapters. During the late 1960s and early 1970s, SDS was a "catalytic force" on college campuses for issues related to civil disobedience. *Id.*

nowhere more vital than in the community of American schools."
Shelton v. Tucker, 364 U.S. 479, 487 (1960). The college classroom
with its surrounding environments is particularly the "market place
of ideas" and we break no new constitutional ground in reaffirming
this nation's dedication to safeguarding academic freedom.[81]

The Supreme Court was also deeply concerned about negative actions directed by institutions of higher education toward individuals "because of association with unpopular organizations."[82] Nonetheless, *Healy* acknowledged that
associational rights on a college campus are unique:

> As the litigation progressed in the District Court, a third rationale
> for [the president's decision] beyond the questions of affiliation and
> philosophy began to emerge. His second statement, issued after the
> court-ordered hearing, indicates that he based rejection on a conclu-
> sion that this particular group would be a "disruptive influence . . . "

> If this reason, directed at the organization's activities rather than its
> philosophy, were factually supported by the record, this Court's pri-
> or decisions would provide a basis for considering the propriety of
> non-recognition. The critical line heretofore drawn for determining
> the permissibility of regulation is the line between mere advocacy
> "directed to inciting or producing imminent lawless action and . .
> . likely to incite or produce such action." *Brandenberg v. Ohio*, 395
> U.S. 444, 447 (1969). In the context of the "special characteristics of
> the school environment," the power of the government to prohibit
> "lawless action" is not limited to actions of a criminal nature. Also
> prohibitable are actions which "materially and substantially disrupt
> the work and discipline of the school." *Tinker*, 393 U.S. at 513. Asso-
> ciational activities need not be tolerated where they infringe reason-
> able campus rules, interrupt classes, or substantially interfere with
> the opportunity of other students to obtain an education.[83]

---

[81] *Id.* at 180–81.
[82] *Id.* at 186. However, when individuals act in furtherance of the group in engaging in unlawful activity, the Supreme Court does allow them to be punished.
[83] *Id.* at 188–89. The Supreme Court was clearly aware of the killings at Kent State a scant two

The Court has also struck down loyalty oaths in some other contexts,[84] and Justice Kennedy recently reiterated that the general use of loyalty oaths is a dead practice and will stay dead.[85] However, *Healy* essentially ratified the use of an equivalent in higher education:

> [J]ust as in the community at large, reasonable regulations with respect to the time, the place, and the manner in which student groups conduct their speech-related activities must be respected. A college administration may impose a requirement, such as may have been imposed in this case, that a group seeking official recognition affirm in advance its willingness to adhere to reasonable campus law. Such a requirement does not impose an impermissible condition on the students' associational rights. . . . It merely constitutes an agreement to conform with reasonable standards respecting conduct. This is a minimal requirement, in the interest of the entire academic community, of any group seeking the privilege of official recognition."[86]

This principle was essentially endorsed by the Supreme Court in the recent *Christian Legal Society* case: It is still permissible to deny RSO status if an organization has a stated intention not to conform with reasonable rules and regulations.[87]

Thus, a group cannot demand to join an RSO system in overt protest and hope for martyrdom as a tool of change of the overall system. Institutions of higher education and student affairs administrators should realize that except

---

years earlier. Although the *Healy* opinion makes no direct reference to Kent State, it clearly is the Kent State opinion. The Supreme Court unequivocally sent the message that a campus has a right to disburse protests that incite imminent lawless action and behavior that substantially disrupts a campus. *Healy* is written around limitations on institution of higher education prerogative, but it is also a message about the power of institutions of higher education to regulate their environments.

[84] *See, e.g., Keyishian v. Board of Regents*, 385 U.S. 589, 606 (1967); *Wieman v. Updegraff,* 344 U.S. 183, 188 (1952).

[85] *See Christian Legal Society*, 130 S. Ct. at 2998–3000 (Kennedy, J., concurring).

[86] *Healy*, 408 U.S. at 192–93.

[87] *Christian Legal Society*, 130 S. Ct. at 2998–3000 (perhaps, in light of Justice Anthony Kennedy's concurrence in *Christian Legal Society*, higher education would generally be wise not to speak in terms of loyalty oaths).

in public employment—and even there[88]—the power over student association granted in *Healy* is constitutionally unique.

In cases outside higher education since *Healy*, the Supreme Court "has rigorously reviewed laws and regulations that can restrain associational freedom. In the context of public accommodations, we have subjected restrictions on that freedom to close scrutiny; such restrictions are permitted only if they serve 'compelling state interests' that are 'unrelated to the suppression of ideas'—interests that cannot be advanced 'through . . . significantly less restrictive [means].'"[89]

A great deal of time has elapsed since *Healy* (almost forty years—an entire generation of student affairs administrators), and a myriad of new associational rights issues have emerged, with RSO systems as a key battleground.

Recently, in *Christian Legal Society*, the Supreme Court chose to consider First Amendment issues in RSO systems under limited public forum analysis—triggering a more deferential standard of review than that used in other contexts to regulate speech and expressive association. As the Court stated:

> An example sharpens the tip of this point: schools, including *Hastings*, . . . ordinarily, without controversy, limit official student-group recognition to organizations comprising only students—even if those groups wish to associate with non-students. . . . The same ground rules must govern both speech and association challenges in the limited-public-forum context, less strict scrutiny trump a public university's ability to "confin[e] [a] speech forum to the limited and legitimate purposes for which it was created." *Rosenberger*, 515 U.S. at 829.[90]

Using this framework of analysis—reasonableness and viewpoint-neutrality—the Court upheld an all-comers policy requiring any group that wished to join the RSO system to comply with the policy of allowing all comers to become members, participate, and even lead if elected.[91] In passing on the reasonableness of the all-comers policy, the Court showed "decent respect" for the

---

[88] *See Garcetti*, 547 U.S. at 413, *Connick*, 461 U.S. at 142.
[89] *Christian Legal Society*, 130 S. Ct. at 2985.
[90] *Id.* at 2985–86 (citations omitted).
[91] *Id.*

institution of higher education environment and its administrators:

> A college's commission—and its concomitant license to choose among pedagogical approaches—is not confined to the classroom, for extracurricular programs are, today, essential parts of the educational process. . . . Schools, we have emphasized, enjoy "a significant measure of authority over the type of officially recognized activities in which those students participate." *Bd. of Educ. of Westside Community Schools (Dist. 66) v. Mergens*, 496 U.S. 226, 240 (1990). We therefore "approach our task with special caution," *Healy*, 408 U.S. at 171, mindful of Hastings' decisions about the character of its student-group program are due decent respect."[92]

However, the Court made it perfectly clear that deference to school administrator decision making is not the same as jurisdictional deference:

> Our inquiry is shaped by the educational context in which it arises: "First Amendment rights," we have observed, "must be in line with special characteristics of the school environment." *Widmar*, 454 U.S. at 268 n.5. This Court is the final arbiter of the question whether a public university has exceeded constitutional constraints. . . . Cognizant that judges lack the on-the-ground expertise and experience of school administrators, however, we have cautioned courts in various context to resist "[substituting] their own notions of sound educational policy for those of school authorities which they review." *Rowley*, 458 U.S. at 206.[93]

This paragraph is historically significant. In the era of power and prerogative, courts sometimes viewed the power of institutions of higher education to manage their own affairs internally as *jurisdictional*, based on longstanding early American higher education law derived from England. Jurisdictional deference has evolved into deference to the educational context of the First Amendment.

Christian Legal Society is particularly important to Greek letter groups and RSO systems throughout the country. Historically strong relationships among

---

[92] *Id.* at 2988–89.
[93] *Id.*

Greeks in their institutions of higher education deteriorated in the 1970s to 1990s, when the law of responsibility for alcohol risk baited institutions of higher education into playing the role of bystander, or worse.[94] Three decades of strain are evident in modern student affairs practice, as institutions of higher education and Greeks struggle with relationship agreements, expanded Clery reporting requirements, and how best to deal with individual and group misbehavior in Greek letter groups, among other things. The *Christian Legal Society* framework provides significant guidance for the appropriate analysis going forward, although it leaves many issues open.[95]

ESTABLISHMENT/IMPAIRMENT OF RELIGION

The viewpoint-neutrality principle factors heavily in the law. The Supreme Court has made it clear that institutions of higher education may not single out religious groups for disfavorable treatment in public or limited public fora.[96] In *Widmar v. Vincent*, the Court struck down a rule preventing the use of institution of higher education facilities "for the purposes of religious worship or religious teaching."[97] In *Rosenberger*, the Court struck down a student funding system that was open broadly to student groups but excluded "religious activities."[98] Viewpoint-neutral access to funds and facilities is constitutionally required.

Many cases raise the twin issue of establishment: An institution of higher education must be viewpoint-neutral but may not "establish" religion. The Supreme Court has devised a three-prong test (the *Lemon* test[99]) to determine whether a policy passes muster and does not violate the establishment clause. The *Lemon* test permits a government program to continue if it (a) has a secular

---

[94] One of the unintended consequences of cases from the bystander era such as *Beech* and *Bradshaw* was to drive a wedge between Greek letter organizations and institutions of higher education. Cases of that era seemed unaware of this potential effect of casting the institution in the role of bystander: Institutions of higher education could be tempted to point the finger at individual students and Greek letter organizations in the higher education environment. Some recent cases involving alcohol risk have sought to rectify this situation so as not to create a perverse incentive that would pit allies in the education environment against each other.

[95] *See* Webinar Recording: Tim Burke, *Christian Legal Society v. Martinez* (Stetson Univ. Coll. L. May 4, 2009) (on file with Center for Excellence in Higher Education Law and Policy).

[96] *See Widmar*, 454 U.S. at 277; *Rosenberger*, 515 U.S. at 839.

[97] 454 U.S. at 277.

[98] 515 U.S. at 857.

[99] *See Lemon v. Kurtzman*, 403 U.S. 602, 612 (1971).

purpose, (b) has a primary effect that neither advances nor inhibits religion, and (c) does not produce excessive government entanglement.[100] The Court has been comfortable in its application of the *Lemon* test in public higher education when a forum is available to "a broad class of non-religious as well as religious speakers."[101] This is similar to *Southworth's* requirements for student activity fees: That which permits an institution of higher education to collect fees also protects the institution from establishment clause violation claims.

Moreover, neither free exercise nor establishment issues are raised by time, place, or manner restrictions, and an institution of higher education retains the *Healy*-like power to create, protect, and maintain its academic environment.

PRESS

The First Amendment protects freedom of the press on campus. Dean Wormer favored North Korean-style censorship of the *Daily Faberian*.[102] Colleges once routinely patrolled publications for indecency and punished students who transgressed norms.[103] This approach ended for good in 1973, when the Supreme Court handed down *Papish*, which unequivocally affirmed freedom of the press on college campuses and gave student newspapers equal constitutional footing with other print media in society.[104] Content censorship and prior re-

---

[100] *Id.* at 612. Occasionally, the government adopts a program that is specific to some religious sect. In these unusual situations, the Supreme Court applies a strict scrutiny standard. *See Bd. of Educ. v. Grumet*, 512 U.S. 687 (1994).

[101] *Widmar*, 454 U.S. at 271.

[102] *Animal House, supra* note 77.

[103] *See, e.g., Stetson University v. Hunt*, 102 So. 637, 639 (Fla. 1925).

[104] *Papish v. Bd. of Curators of the Univ. of Mo.*, 410 U.S. 667, 670 (1973). The Court stated:
This case was decided several days before we handed down *Healy v. James*, 408 U.S. 169 (1972), in which, while recognizing a state university's undoubted prerogative to enforce reasonable rules governing student conduct, we affirm that "state colleges and universities are not enclaves immune from the sweep of the First Amendment." *Id.* at 180. We think *Healy* makes it clear that the mere dissemination of ideas—no matter how offensive to good taste—on a state university campus may not be shut off in the name alone of "conventions of decency." Other recent precedents of this Court make it equally clear that neither the political cartoon or the headline story involved in this case can be labeled as constitutionally obscene or otherwise unprotected. . . . There is language in the opinions below which suggests that the University's action here could be viewed as an exercise of its legitimate authority to enforce reasonable regulations as to the time, place, and manner of speech and its dissemination. While we have repeatedly approved such regulatory authority . . . the facts set forth in the opinions

straint are constitutional no-nos, as is the pretense of reasonable time, place, and manner restrictions when the real goal is to engage in content censorship. Consider the following points:

1. Student newspapers are subject to and protected by constitutional standards relating to the law of defamation.[105] There is no special college privilege to defame, nor is defamation easier to prove from a constitutional standpoint against a college newspaper. On matters of public concern, college newspapers, like others, are governed by the *New York Times* standard of "actual malice."[106]

2. Electronic media are governed by somewhat different rules in some circumstances, but there is no reason to believe that college electronic media are constitutionally different in kind from noncollege media.

3. Forum and other familiar constitutional analysis applies. This means that an institution of higher education can create a limited public forum for media and even nonpublic fora for communication via media. Bulletin boards in dormitories are different from school newspapers, and institutions of higher education can establish use and access policies for the Internet.[107] Speech that is not protected, such as true threats, also can be regulated.[108]

4. Courts are far more deferential to colleges if a newspaper is produced in a class with academic goals and standards. An institution of higher

---

below show clearly that petitioner was expelled because of the *disapproved content* of the newspaper rather than the time, place, or manner of its distribution.

Since the First Amendment leaves no room for the operation of a duel standard in the academic community with respect to the content of speech, and because the state University's action here cannot be justified as non-discriminatory application and reasonable roles governing conduct, the judgments of the courts below must be reversed. *Id.* at 670–71.

[105] *See New York Times Co.*, 376 U.S. at 266.

[106] *Id.* at 284.

[107] Kaplin & Lee, *supra* note 39 at 996–1001.

[108] The First Amendment does not protect statements or expressive conduct meant to communicate an intent to put a person or group of people in fear of bodily harm. *Virginia*, 538 U.S. at 364–368 (when "intent to intimidate" is proven, the government may prohibit crossburning). Hate speech is otherwise protected. *See R.A.V. v. City of St. Paul*, 505 U.S. 377, 391 (1992) (invalidating an ordinance singling out epithets based on race, religion, or gender; the ordinance only punished certain hateful viewpoints). "True threats," like "fighting words," are different from mere hate speech in that the former generates fear of imminent bodily harm and the latter are highly likely to incite a prompt violent response.

education can teach journalism and "censor" an article by pointing out that it is terrible and deserves an F. In this situation, the class is not a forum but a classroom. However, the mere fact that school newspaper participation is graded for academic credit does not justify content censorship any more than school funding justifies censorship.[109] In the end, courts will examine the motive, purpose, and structure of a newspaper or publication system and apply forum analysis accordingly. Linus believed that sincerity was a virtue that would draw the Great Pumpkin to his patch:[110] Courts will examine genuine motives and real reasons for the structure of a program, not just purported justifications.

PRIVACY

The right to speak implies the right to remain silent. The right to associate implies the right to be left alone or not associate. Except in college, with exceptions. Privacy is a concern of the First Amendment, but it is a concern in other contexts as well; for example, in Fourth Amendment search and seizure law, and under statutory/regulatory rules such as FERPA.[111]

One of the more interesting privacy issues raised in college life is communal living, including so-called *parietal* rules that require certain groups of students (e.g., freshman) to live on campus and under certain conditions. Although the Supreme Court has not addressed this issue directly, it would appear that such rules are not *per se* unconstitutional.[112]

Although college search and seizure cases are rare in reported criminal cases,[113] there is ample reason to believe that Fourth Amendment protections

---

[109] *See Papish*, 410 U.S. 671.

[110] *Charlie Brown's Halloween Special* (Lee Mendelson & Bill Melendez 1966) (TV special).

[111] The Family Educational Rights and Privacy Act (FERPA), 20 U.S.C. § 1232(g) (2006).

[112] *See Prostrollo v. Univ. of South Dakota*, 507 F.2d 775, 780 (8th Cir. 1974).

[113] *See People v. Superior Court*, 49 Cal. Rptr. 3d 831 (Cal. App. 6th Dist. 2006). This case noted, however, "There are surprisingly few cases addressing the constitutional validity of searches of college dormitory rooms. . . . Many of the cases have involved the legality of searches by college officials only, and not addressed whether police searches abridged the Fourth Amendment rights of dormitory room occupants. . . ." *Id.* at 844. Courts usually take the position that the Fourth Amendment applies to tenants in a college dormitory just like those in any other tenancy. *See, e.g., State v. Ellis*, 2006 WL 827376 at *2 (Ohio App. 2006). *Piazzola v. Watkins*, 442 F.2d 284 (5th Cir. 1971); *cf. People v. Kelly*, 195 Cal. App. 2d 669 (1961); *see also Washington v. Chapman*, 455 U.S. 1 (1982) (applying plain view doctrine in search of dormitory

extend to dormitory living, although they must be appropriately tailored to the nature and features of specific residence hall living arrangements, just as in private tenancies.[114]

In general, however, privacy law is not as generous as legally untrained persons believe it to be. Most college students will find that their strongest privacy law arguments come under FERPA or medical privacy laws (see below). FERPA was passed[115] with two main purposes. First, it was a necessary add-on to other civil rights laws (discussed below). FERPA gave students access to and the right to correct their "educational records."[116] Without this right, students could be easy targets for blacklisting by administrators who do not support civil rights laws.[117] Second, FERPA created a new milieu for registrars, requiring a higher level of consumer accountability. Before FERPA, the record keeper might have been a clerk or secretary, and records were not always well managed.

Congress added privacy provisions to FERPA that clear up concerns about the sharing of information without a student's consent.[118] Additional regulations cover three common situations:

First, direct observations and interactions with a student are not themselves education records, so they are not privacy-protected by FERPA.

Second, FERPA permits both academic and nonacademic information to be shared within an institution of higher education on a need-to-know basis—a "legitimate educational interest."[119]

Third, when health or safety issues are involved, institutions of higher edu-

---

room does not create a special exception for college tenancies under the Fourth Amendment).

[114] *See* Eric Hoover, *Police in the Dorms: Student Safety or Privacy Infringement?*, Chronicle of Higher Education (July 28, 2008), *available at* http://chronicle.com/article/Polic-in-the-Dorms-Studen/27059.

[115] *See* FERPA, 20 U.S.C. § 1232(g).

[116] Steve McDonald, *The Fundamentals of Fundamental FERPA* (Feb. 21, 2010), *available at* http://www.law.stetson.edu/tmpl/academics/helps/conf/conf-sub.aspx?id=10813.

[117] *See* Peter Lake, *Student-Privacy Rules Show a Renewed Trust in Colleges*, Chronicle of Higher Education (Feb. 6, 2009), *available at* http://chronicle.com/article/Student-Privacy-Rules-Show-/20332.

[118] There are actually a number of circumstances under which a student's records can be shared. *See* JED Foundation, *Student Mental Health and the Law: A Resource for Institutions of Higher Education* 8–9 (Jed Foundation 2008).

[119] FERPA, 20 U.S.C. § 1232(g); 34 C.F.R. § 75.740 (2010).

cation and student affairs administrators may disclose to "appropriate parties" information necessary to protect a student or others.[120] The health or safety situation must be significant and articulable.[121] Department of Education regulations state that the department will not investigate a potential violation of this standard if an institution of higher education can articulate "a rational basis" for the perceived health or safety situation. Fear is not enough, but the reason for the fear may well be. ("I'm afraid of him." No. "I'm afraid of him because he has a gun that he is brandishing." Yes.) The Department of Education (DOE) clearly lines up with a well-established privacy law principle: Privacy protection wanes when danger rises.[122]

Occasionally, state law provides additional standards for student privacy. Privacy rights can arise from contract and from beliefs and expectations regarding educational privacy. So-called "student-teacher confidentiality," however, is only as real as the Shire is to Frodo. Sorry to kill the fantasy, but the law knows no such thing.[123] Student affairs administrators often must correct misperceptions regarding privacy law.[124]

When a student affairs administrator must balance privacy against risk of harm, he or she would be wise to consider the advice of the music group Black Sheep: In a choice between privacy or tort lawsuits, "You can get with this, or you can get with that."[125] You may just have to pick the type of lawsuit you would rather face. (A friendly suggestion: It usually makes much more sense to argue about privacy rights than risk serious injury.)

---

[120] *Id*; *see* JED Foundation, *supra* note 118 at 8–11.

[121] *Id.*

[122] *See Tarasoff v. Bd. of Regents of the Univ. of Cal.*, 551 P.2d 334, 442 (Cal. 1976).

[123] *Lord of the Rings* (Peter Jackson 2002) (motion picture).

[124] Students, parents, and family members have become well-versed in how to turn an educational dialogue into an oppositional, even legalistic, dialogue. One classic way to shift focus away from educational objectives is to play the law card. Once someone begins arguing about legal rights, educational discourse tends to be less central or effective. Student affairs administrators must be aware of their own potential for baiting people into talking in lawlike and oppositional ways. Parents often lack a language to communicate about student information transfer; in addition, the law tends to disassociate parents and families from college students in this generation. FERPA was passed at a time when baby boomers were headed to college *en masse*, and most baby boomers favored the idea of becoming independent from their parents. Millennial students—a dominant population in today's colleges—are usually the opposite. When a student affairs administrator hears law discourse being used in a dysfunctional way, he or she might consider how to foster a better system of educational discourse.

[125] Black Sheep, *The Choice Is Yours* (Mercury Records 1991).

To add to the incentive to share information when students are at risk, the Supreme Court has ruled that there is no private cause of action under FERPA for monetary damages; the only remedy for FERPA violations is administrative.[126] (The Court has not yet ruled on this issue with respect to the Clery Act.)[127]

Medical privacy laws are a significant source of privacy law for students as well. There are two key features to consider at the outset. First, medical privacy can be protected under state law and, in some instances, under federal law as well.[128] Perhaps even more significant, however, health care providers have professional codes and standards of conduct, and are subject to state law licensure requirements. Violation of medical privacy law can be a predicate for license revocation, discipline, or a professional malpractice suit. Although the law varies from state to state, most health care providers will release information only if a patient consents to such release; they are empowered (and occasionally mandated) to share information with or without consent if a patient presents an imminent risk of harm to self or others.[129] The use of the latter standard is rare, and many health care pro-

---

[126] *See Gonzaga Univ. v. Doe,* 536 U.S. 273 (2002). The Department of Education occasionally hands out fines for FERPA violation. Most fines relate to improper practices in the handling of student academic information. DOE has not been inclined to fine institutions in health and safety situations; however, it did indicate that if it discovers a pattern or practice of abuse of the new regulatory scheme, it may revisit the current favorable regulations.

[127] Jeanne Clery Disclosure of Campus Security Policy and Campus Crime Statistics Act (Clery Act), 20 U.S.C. § 1092(f) (2006).

[128] *See* The JED Foundation, *supra* note 118 at 10.

[129] The Baker Act, Fla. Stat. § 394.451–394.4789 (2010). The involuntary examination portion of the Baker Act states:

(1) Criteria. —A person may be taken to a receiving facility for involuntary examination if there is reason to believe that the person has a mental illness and because of his or her mental illness:

(a)1. The person has refused voluntary examination after conscientious explanation and disclosure of the purpose of the examination; or

2. The person is unable to determine for himself or herself whether examination is necessary; and

(b)1. Without care or treatment, the person is likely to suffer from neglect or refuse to care for himself or herself; such neglect or refusal poses a real and present threat of substantial harm to his or her well-being; and it is not apparent that such harm may be avoided through the help of willing family members or friends or the provision of other services; or

2. There is a substantial likelihood that without care or treatment the person will cause serious bodily harm to himself or herself or others in the near future, as evidenced by recent behavior. *Id.* at § 394.463; *see, e.g., Tarasoff,* 551 P.2d at 347.

For an overview of child abuse statues and mandatory reporting requirements, see U.S. Depart-

fessionals say they have never shared information in these circumstances. Medical privacy rules are less likely to permit disclosure than rules under the more relaxed FERPA standard.[130]

INCLUSION AND DIVERSITY: EQUAL PROTECTION AND CIVIL RIGHTS LAWS

Beginning with the landmark constitutional ruling in *Brown v. Board of Education*[131] and subsequent federal legislation (especially portions of the Civil Rights Act of 1964, including Title VI), federal law has prohibited discrimination in education on the basis of race. Title IX prohibits discrimination on the basis of gender.

Titles VI and IX apply to educational institutions that receive federal assistance, which is more or less everyone.[132] Title VI has broad, largely unexceptional applicability in prohibiting race discrimination; Title IX has many exceptions, including several that are key for student affairs administrators:

1. 20 U.S.C. § 1681(a)(6)(A) exempts fraternities and sororities in most instances.

2. 20 U.S.C. § 1681(a)(8) permits most father/son and mother/daughter events.

3. 20 U.S.C. § 1681(a)(5) exempts some admissions practices.

4. 20 U.S.C. § 1681(a)(4) exempts most military academies (although merely being exempt from Title IX does not mean that a practice is per se constitutional under the equal protection clause).[133]

---

ment of Health and Human Services, Administration for Children and Families, *Mandatory Reporters of Child Abuse and Neglect: Summary of State Laws* (2008), *available at* http://www.childwelfare.gove/systemwide/laws_policies/statutes/manda.cfm.

[130] Student affairs administrators often ask about HIPAA, the Health Insurance Portability and Accountability Act of 1996. *See* 42 U.S.C.A. § 201 *et seq.* (2006). However, HIPAA privacy rules do not apply to student treatment records created on campus. *See* JED Foundation, *supra* note 118 at 10. HIPAA only comes into play if the campus actually runs a hospital or medical health facility and maintains records and shares them in a certain way.

[131] 347 U.S. 483 (1954) (igniting the legal desegregation movement by holding that historical policies of *de jure* segregation in K–12 education were unconstitutional).

[132] 20 U.S.C. § 1681 (2006).

[133] *See U.S. v. Virginia,* 518 U.S. 515, 536 (1996) (holding that Virginia Military Institute, an all-male school, violated the constitution by not allowing women to attend the university and

Several complexly interrelated federal laws protect students from discrimination on the basis of disability. Section 504 of the Rehabilitation Act (which applies to federally assisted programs) prohibits discrimination in higher education for most purposes.[134] The Americans with Disabilities Act (ADA) provides slightly broader coverage in some circumstances,[135] and the ADA Amendments Act also affects college student disability rights.[136] Other laws, including state law protections, may have an impact on a student's disability claims.[137]

In marked contrast with civil rights laws protecting against race, disability, and sex discrimination, federal law does not provide students with significant protection against other forms of discrimination, including discrimination on the basis of sexual orientation. Some states and local governments protect sexual orientation discrimination and employment, but that is hardly universal. In higher education, LGBT (lesbian, gay, bisexual, and transgender) rights are far more likely to arise from contract law rights.[138] Moreover, students have only limited protection on the basis of economic status/class; there is no constitutional right to a college education. College is not an entitlement. Moreover, as discussed in Chapter 4, neither the U.S. Constitution nor federal legislation guarantees due process generally in higher education.

Race

The equal protection clause of the Fourteenth Amendment prohibits racial discrimination; so does Title VI. The Supreme Court has essentially held that Title VI and the equal protection clause are coextensive.[139]

---

participate in adversarial training). "'Inherent differences' between men and women, we have come to appreciate, remain cause for celebration, but not for denigration of the members of either sex or for artificial constraints on an individual's opportunity." *Id.* at 533.

[134] Kaplin & Lee, *supra* note 39, at 1464; 29 U.S.C. § 791; *see* 34 C.F.R. § 104–10 (2010).

[135] 42 U.S.C. §§ 12131–12134, 12181–12189; 28 C.F.R. § 35 (2010).

[136] Americans with Disabilities Act Amendments Act of 2008, 42 U.S.C. §§ 12101–12189 (2010).

[137] *See* JED Foundation, *supra* note 118, at 12.

[138] So far, equal protection arguments are possible but not promising for LGBT students. *See, e.g.*, *Miguel v. Guess*, 51 P.3d 89, 99 (Wash. Ct. App.); *see also* Lambda Legal, www.lambdalegal.org (last visited Aug. 28, 2010).

[139] *See Regents of the Univ. of California v. Bakke*, 438 U.S. 265, 287 (1978). "In view of the clear legislative intent, Title VI must be held to proscribe only those racial classifications that would violate the Equal Protection Clause or the Fifth Amendment." *Id.*

However, Congress realized, and the courts agree, that the effectiveness of federal civil rights law would be limited in higher education if enforcement and development of the law were merely constitutional and legislative. Remember that after Reconstruction and the passage of the Fourteenth Amendment, dominant Supreme Court jurisprudence held that separate treatment of races could be equal.[140] The Court changed this course with *Brown v. Board of Education* in 1954, but it would take more than *Brown* and the Civil Rights Act of 1964 to reverse a century of *de jure* segregation and discrimination.

Thus, Congress has entrusted significant enforcement and regulatory power in the Department of Education (DOE), which has extensive rulemaking authority. In fact, DOE can generate regulations that are more specific and more extensive than minimal constitutional equal protection guarantees.[141] DOE has promulgated numerous regulations dealing with a wide variety of issues, including admissions and financial aid, participation in college programs, and desegregation of facilities.[142] DOE is not the only federal regulatory body enforcing federal civil rights laws, but for student affairs administrators, it is usually the most significant and closely watched. The department could potentially determine that a school is ineligible to receive federal aid or participate in federally assisted programs, which for many schools would mean institutional death. DOE's Office for Civil Rights (OCR) publishes highly influential policy interpretations and guidance regarding civil rights statutes.[143] Institutions of higher education are much more likely to get quick and detailed feedback in OCR letters or publications than from the courts; court cases take much longer to resolve and are less numerous. And although courts are not bound to follow OCR interpretations of the law, an institution of higher education that

---

[140] This attitude persisted well into the 20th century; see *Sweatt v. Painter*, 339 U.S. 629, 635 (1950). The law thus permitted *de jure* discrimination, where laws could be literally written for different races.

[141] *Guardians Ass'n v. Civil Serv. Comm'n*, 463 U.S. 582, 601 (1983) "Congress included an explicit provision in § 602 of Title VI that requires that any administrative enforcement action be 'consistent with achievement of the objectives of the statute authorizing the financial assistance in connection with which the action is taken.'" *Id.* (quoting 42 U.S.C. § 2000d–1 (2006)).

[142] *See generally* 34 C.F.R. §§ 100–6.

[143] *See* U.S. DOE, OCR, *Letter to Woodbury University in California* (June 29, 2001), *available at* http://ahead-lists.org/downloads/training/lissner_handouts/J-psych)%20Woodbury%20University.rtf; 34 C.F.R. § 104.43.

complies with OCR directives is not likely to be crucified in court. Good-faith attempts at regulatory compliance bring certain advantages in litigation in most cases. Even individual officers of public institutions may find some solace under immunity law for acting in good faith and attempting to comply with even presumptively valid regulations.

An area of great concern in higher education is race-conscious admissions. Creating a diverse, inclusive student body begins with admissions, and one of the hallowed four academic freedoms is "whom to teach."[144] However, neither the equal protection clause, nor Title VI, countenances racial discrimination in admission or retention policies.[145] Recently, the Supreme Court decided twin cases—*Grutter v. Bolinger*, 539 U.S. 306 (2003) and *Gratz v. Bolinger*, 539 U.S. 244 (2003)—on the issue of race-conscious admissions.

Race-conscious admissions cases not only raise issues of equal protection and Title VI compliance but may also raise issues under a somewhat less well-known federal law: 42 U.S.C. § 1981. Section 1981 provides, in part:

> All persons within the jurisdiction of the United States shall have the same right in every State and Territory to make and enforce contracts, to sue, be parties, give evidence, and to the full and equal benefit of all laws and proceedings for the security of persons and property as is enjoyed by white citizens. . . .
>
> [T]he term "make and enforce contracts" includes the making, performance, modification, and termination of contracts, and the enjoyment of all benefits, privileges, terms, and conditions of the contractual relationship. . . .
>
> The rights protected by this section are protected against impairment. . . . under color of State law."[146]

In *Gratz*, the Supreme Court reviewed Michigan's undergraduate admissions program and held:

---

[144] *See Sweezy v. New Hampshire*, 354 U.S. 234, 263 (1957).
[145] The growing field of enrollment management—which heavily involves student affairs administrators—is subject to the same principles.
[146] 42 U.S.C. § 1981 (a)–(c).

To withstand our strict scrutiny analysis, respondents must demonstrate that the University's use of race in its current admissions program employs "narrowly tailored measures that further compelling governmental interests." *Adarand Constructors, Inc. v. Peña*, 515 U.S. 200, 227 (1995). Because "racial classifications are simply too pernicious to permit any but the most exact connection between justification and classification," *Fullilove v. Klutznick*, 448 U.S. 448, 537 (1980) (Stevens, J., dissenting), a review of whether such requirements have been met must entail "'a most searching examination.'" *Adarand*, 515 U.S. at 223 (quoting *Wygant v. Jackson Bd. of Educ.*, 476 U.S. 267, 273 (1986) (Powell, J., plurality)). We find that the university's policy, which automatically distributes 20 points, or one-fifth of the points needed to guarantee admission, to every single "under-represented minority" applicant solely on the basis of race, is not narrowly tailored to achieve the interest in educational diversity that respondents claim justifies their program.[147]

In contrast, in *Grutter*, the Court upheld a law school admissions program at the University of Michigan:

> Since *Bakke*, we have had no occasion to define the contours of the narrow-tailoring inquiry with respect to race-conscious university admissions programs. That inquiry must be calibrated to fit the distinct issues raised by the use of race to achieve student body diversity in public higher education. . . .
>
> To be narrowly tailored, a race-conscious admissions program cannot use a quota system—it cannot "insulate each category of applicants with certain desired qualifications from competition with all other applicants." *Bakke*, 438 U.S. at 315. Instead, a university may consider race or ethnicity only as a "'plus' in a particular applicant's file" without "insulating the individual from comparison with all other candidates for the available seats." *Id.* at 317.[148]

---

[147] *Gratz v. Bollinger*, 539 U.S. 244, 270 (2003).
[148] *Grutter v. Bollinger*, 539 U.S. 306, 333–34 (2003).

Unlike unconstitutional quota systems, the Michigan law school admissions process was "highly individualized":

> Here, the Law School engages in a highly individualized, holistic review of each applicant's file, giving serious consideration to all the ways an applicant might contribute to a diverse educational environment. The Law School affords this individualized consideration to applicants of all races. There is no policy, of either de jure or de facto, of automatic acceptance or rejection based on any single "soft" variable. Unlike the program at issue in *Gratz v. Bollinger*, 539 U.S. 244, the Law School awards no mechanical, predetermined diversity "bonuses" based on race or ethnicity.... Like the Harvard Plan, the Law School's admissions policy is "flexible enough to consider all pertinent elements of diversity in light of the particular qualifications of each applicant, and to place them on the same footing for consideration, although not necessarily according them [the] same weight." *Bakke*, 438 U.S. at 317.

> We also find that, like the Harvard Plan Justice Powell references in *Bakke*, the Law School's race conscious admissions program adequately ensures that all factors that may contribute to student body diversity are meaningfully considered alongside race and admissions decisions. With respect to the use of race itself, all underrepresented minority students admitted by the Law School have been deemed qualified. By virtue of our nation's struggle with racial inequality, such students are both likely to have experiences of particular importance to the Law School's mission, and less likely to be admitted in meaningful numbers and criteria that ignore those experiences."[149]

Interestingly, the Supreme Court took the unusual step of placing a time stamp on race-conscious admissions in America—mark your calendars for 2028:

> We are mindful, however that "a core purpose of the Fourteenth Amendment was to do away with all governmentally imposed dis-

---

[149] *Id.* at 337–38.

crimination based on race." *Palmore v. Sidoti*, 466 U.S. 429, 432 (1984). Accordingly, race-conscious admissions policies must be limited in time. This requirement reflects the [fact that] racial classifications, however compelling their goals, are potentially so dangerous that they may be employed no more broadly than the interest demands. Enshrining a permanent justification for racial preferences would offend this fundamental equal protection principle. We see no reason to exempt race conscious admissions programs from the requirement that all governmental use of race must have a logical end point. The Law School, too, concedes that "all race conscious programs must have reasonable durational limits. . . . "

We expect that twenty-five years from now, the use of racial preferences will no longer be necessary to further the interest of proof today.[150]

The Supreme Court rulings on race-conscious admissions reverberate throughout student affairs practice. Creating and maintaining a diverse, vibrant, and inclusive student population turns on highly individualized assessment. Students are not categories or boxes they check; categorical information might help, but inclusion and diversity require the use of judgment and individualized student assessment.

Higher education "passed" the Court's application of strict scrutiny. The only other case to pass strict scrutiny for racial classifications was *Korematsu*; in that case, the United States had just come under attack from a foreign power and entered World War II. Surviving strict scrutiny is constitutionally remarkable.

So why did higher education pass such a high legal hurdle? Simple:

Our holding today is in keeping with our tradition of giving a degree of deference to a university's academic decisions, within constitutionally prescribed limits. . . .

We have long recognized that, given the important purpose of public education and the expansive freedoms of speech and thought

---

[150] *Id.* at 341–42, 343.

associated with the university environment; universities occupy a special niche in our constitutional tradition. . . . In announcing the principle of student body diversity is a compelling state interest, Justice Powell invoked our cases recognizing the constitutional dimension, grounded in the First Amendment, of educational autonomy: "The freedom of a university to make its own judgments as to education includes the selection of its student body." *Bakke*, 438 U.S. at 312. From this premise, Justice Powell reasoned that by claiming "the right to select those students who will contribute the most to the 'robust exchange of ideas,' a university 'seeks to achieve a goal that is of paramount importance in the fulfillment of its mission." *Id.* at 313 (quoting *Keyishian*, 385 U.S. at 603). Our conclusion that the Law School has a compelling interest in a diverse student body is informed by our view that obtaining a diverse student body is at the heart of the law school's proper institutional mission, and that "good faith" on the part of the university is "presumed" absent a "showing to the contrary."

As part of its goal of "assembling . . . a class that is both exceptionally academically qualified and broadly diverse," the Law School seeks to "enroll [a] 'critical mass' of minority students. . . . " The Law School's interest is not simply "to assure within its student body some specified percentage of a particular group merely because of its race or ethnic origin." *Id.* at 307. That would amount to outright racial balancing, which is patently unconstitutional. . . . Rather the Law School's concept of critical mass is defined by reference to the educational benefits that diversity is designed to produce.

These benefits are substantial.[151]

The Supreme Court has carved out special constitutional space for institutions of higher education, asking only that they do what they do best— conduct careful and deliberative individualized assessment of all students with an eye toward creating empowered citizens in a constitutional democracy. The

---

[151] *Id.* at 328–30 (citations omitted).

core values of the Constitution's equal protection clause and Title VI are those of modern student affairs practice. The law simply uses a slightly different language system.

Gender/Sexual Orientation

Gender discrimination is not subject to strict scrutiny, and it is analyzed under a different framework from race discrimination. Discrimination based on sexual orientation is not the same under law as discrimination based on sex and to date, has received little protection under federal law. (Drawing lines between sex discrimination and discrimination based on sexual orientation is bound to become more problematic in federal law in the future.) The following are the four primary aspects of the gender discrimination framework:

1. The Supreme Court applies intermediate, not strict, scrutiny in sex discrimination cases arising under the equal protection clause, although there is some disagreement on the Court about the exact standard being used.[152] Under the intermediate standard of review, an institution of higher education must proffer an "exceedingly persuasive justification" for discrimination based on gender.[153] Institutions of higher education have succeeded in meeting that burden on a number of occasions.[154]

2. Equal protection analysis only applies to state action; essentially, public institutions of higher education. Private institutions of higher

---

[152] *See Virginia,* 518 U.S. at 571 (Scalia, J., dissenting); *see also Mississippi Univ. for Women v. Hogan,* 458 U.S. 718, 723 (1982).

[153] *See Hogan,* 458 U.S. at 724–25.

Although the test for determining the validity of gender-based classification is straightforward, it must be applied free of fixed notions concerning the roles and abilities of males and females. Care must be taken in ascertaining whether the statutory objective itself reflects archaic and stereotypic notions. Thus, if the statutory objective is to exclude or 'protect' members of one gender because they are presumed to suffer from an inherent handicap or to be innately inferior, the objective itself is illegitimate. . . . *Id.*

[W]e next determine whether the requisite direct, substantial relationship between objective and the means is present. The purpose of requiring that close relationship is to assure that the validity of a classification is determined through reasoned analysis rather than through the mechanical application of traditional, often inaccurate assumptions about the proper roles of men and women. *Id.* at 725–26.

[154] Judith Areen, *Higher Education and the Law: Cases and Materials* 614–16 (Foundation Press 2009).

education are free to discriminate on the basis of sex/gender except insofar as discrimination is prohibited by Title IX or state antidiscrimination law.[155] Title IX has exceptions not recognized by equal protection, and Congress cannot exempt public institutions from the application of constitutional principles. Thus, the public/private distinction is important in gender discrimination.

3. Title IX applies to public and private institutions that receive federal funds and assistance. Title IX has many exceptions, some of which have been promulgated via regulations emanating from the Department of Education.[156] For instance, religious institutions of higher education are exempt.[157]

4. If Title IX is applicable, an institution of higher education may not discriminate on the basis of gender in employment of staff, hiring, housing fees, services, or benefits. It is permissible to have separate bathrooms/locker room facilities, but they must be comparable. Access to academic/health care and many other services must be discrimination-free as well.[158]

5. Violations of Title IX can be subject to private suits for money damages and can also subject an institution of higher education to potential fines and sanctions from the U.S. Department of Education.[159]

---

[155] Thus, although Title IX would protect historically single-sex-admission institutions by virtue of specific exemption, the equal protection clause applied in *U.S. v. Virginia* to public Virginia Military Institute (VMI). 518 U.S. at 519. The VMI governing board nearly took VMI private after that decision.

[156] 20 U.S.C. § 1681(a)(1) (2006); 34 C.F.R. § 106.15(d) (2010).

[157] 20 U.S.C. § 1681(a)(3).

[158] *See* Areen, *supra* note 154, at 961–73.

[159] *See Franklin v. Gwinnett Cnty. Public Schools*, 503 U.S. 60, 75–76 (1992). Faculty-on-student harassment and peer-on-peer harassment issues can create significant risk of private litigation for colleges. *See Gebser v. Lago Vista Independent School District*, 524 U.S. 274 (1998), and *Davis v. Monroe County Board of Education*, 526 U.S. 629 (1999). Title IX requires campuses to have grievance processes in place to address sexual assault and harassment issues; both are considered forms of gender discrimination if left unaddressed. *See* 34 C.F.R. § 106. A college must take "prompt and equitable" steps, to address harassment. *Id.* Procedures required by DOE have increasingly mirrored employment procedures; in dealing with harassment issues, student affairs administrators should consult human resource personnel. In addition to legal requirements for special Title IX procedures required by DOE, which set standards for administrative enforcement, the Supreme Court has crafted substantive rules that apply in private claims for damages that are different from those used in employment harassment claims, and more deferential to

Thus, Title IX is a significant source of litigation risk for institutions of higher education, and close compliance with DOE regulations and guidelines is warranted.

Disability

Preliminary observations.

A few preliminary points about disability law and compliance are in order:

1. Compliance with disability law is sufficiently complex that many decisions should be made in consultation with persons who have special training in disability law and accommodation. Disability law is swift-moving water; it is constantly evolving and is not a subject for novices.

2. The law of accommodation changes as students move from K–12 to higher education, but parents and students are often only dimly aware of the difference. Many expect K–12 levels of accommodation and disability law compliance, and are surprised to learn that the law has shifted. Institutions of higher education can help with this major transition through training, education, and mentoring.

---

higher education. *Gebser* and *Davis* limited a college's exposure for private damage claims under Title IX by erecting a difficult set of standards for a plaintiff to prove. Once a college receives actual (not constructive) knowledge of harassment, it must do more than show "deliberate indifference," which essentially means acting in a patently or "clearly unreasonable" way. *Davis*, 526 U.S. at 648. The Court also requires that a plaintiff demonstrate control over the harasser and the context in which the harassment occurs. *Id.* at 645. Harassment must be more than an isolated incident or a condition that exists solely in the eyes of the beholder; It must be "severe, pervasive, and objectively offensive...." *Id.* at 651. It appears that a plaintiff might also have to prove that the harassment caused deprivation of equal access/protection under Title IX—in essence, causation. *Id.* Subsequent to *Gebser* and *Davis*, OCR has revised its compliance guidance to colleges. *See* Office of Civil Rights, *Dear Colleague Letter* (April 4, 2011), *available at* http://www2.ed.gov/about/offices/list/ocr/letters/colleague-201104.pdf. *See also* Lauren Sieben, *Education Dept. Issues New Guidance for Sexual-Assault Investigations*, Chronicle of Higher Education (April 4, 2011), *available at* http://chronicle.com/article/Education-Dept-Issues-New/127004/?sid=at&utm_source=at&utm_medium=en#. Administrative standards of enforcement may differ significantly from standards applicable in actions for civil damages. This is an area of the law in which student affairs administrators must continually engage in high-quality, branded continuing education, particularly regarding the interplay between DOE/OCR guidelines and regulations under Title IX and the Clery Act. Harassment, like disability law, is increasingly a subspecialty of the specially trained and is usually not a beginner-level competency.

3. The law prohibits disability discrimination in admissions.[160] It can be problematic to inquire about disability before admission, although limited exceptions exist.[161] Of course, students can self-identify at any time, and there is nothing unlawful *per se* about providing a mechanism for students to do so after matriculation.

4. Often, the focus in higher education is on whether the institution is *obligated* to accommodate a student with a disability. The law typically requires a student to self-identify and request accommodation before the institution has such an obligation. The emphasis should be on facilitating self-disclosure. An undisclosed disability can be a major problem for an institution of higher education, student affairs administrators, and a student. Institutions cannot force disclosure, but offering a system for self-disclosure is a good idea.[162] The disability law gaps between K–12 and preadmission/matriculation are cracks in the system that cause many headaches down the road for student affairs administrators; this is fixable to a certain extent. Student affairs administrators should try to create as seamless an experience for students and families as possible, shifting the focus from legal obligation to provide accommodation minimums to creating opportunities for success.

5. From a disability law compliance standpoint, managing college student populations is weird. K–12 students work in an Individualized Education Program (IEP) framework.[163] Employers usually have job descriptions that require demonstrated competencies. Higher education typically has neither. Many of the issues student affairs administrators encounter arise from the fact that, from the disability law compliance standpoint, the management of student populations is fluid and unde-

---

[160] *See* 34 C.F.R. § 104.42(a)–(b) (2010).

[161] *See* 34 C.F.R. § 104.42(b)(4)–104.42(c) (allowing preadmission inquiries to combat past discrimination).

[162] *See* U.S. DOE, OCR, *The Civil Rights of Students with Hidden Disabilities under Section 504 of the Rehabilitation Act of 1973* (Jan. 1, 1995), *available at* http://www2.ed.gov/about/offices/list/ocr/docs/hq5269.html.

[163] For an explanation of IEPs, see U.S. DOE, Office of Special Education and Rehabilitative Services, *Questions and Answers on Individualized Education Programs (IEPs), Evaluation, and Reevaluations* (June 2010), *available at* http://www2.ed.gov/policy/speced/guid/idea/iep-qa-2010.pdf.

fined. If institutions of higher education were to specify true competencies for students (essentially, a college student job description), disability issues would be easier to handle.[164] Many difficult challenges of
accommodation arise from the simple fact that institutions have historically not spelled out general competencies for programs.[165] Institutions
typically ask students to conform their conduct to certain standards,
which do not themselves constitute a statement of competencies. Disability law permits regulation of student conduct within limits;[166] however, failing to define core higher education student competencies has
made legal compliance more difficult than it needs to be.

6.   Institutions of higher education can intervene proactively with students
      with disabilities if a student creates a "significant risk to health or safety."[167]
      This includes risk to the student him- or herself and risk to a third party.[168]

---

[164] Some institutions actually do this. *See* Brown University, *Brown University Program in Liberal Medical Education, Academic Affairs Policies Handbook* (1994), *available at* http://bms.brown.edu/plme/current/handbook/PLME_Handbook_prior_2007.pdf. Brown University's Program in Liberal Medication Education "has introduced several innovations in medical education, including a competency-based curriculum that defines nine abilities and a core knowledge base expected of all graduates in the MD Class of 2000 and beyond." *Id.* at 2 (emphasis omitted).

[165] *Id.*

[166] Discipline cannot be a pretext for discrimination. Moreover, a conduct rule that has a dispro-portionate impact on disabled students is suspect. *See Letter to Woodbury University, supra* note 143; *see also* U.S. DOE, OCR, *Letter to Bluffton University in California* (Dec. 22, 2004), *available at* http://www.bazelon.org/LinkClick.aspx?fileticket=LWFnT1VirFU%3D&tabid=313. For a further explanation of the question "Can a student with a disability be disciplined or placed on a leave of absence?" see JED Foundation, *supra* note 118, at 14. "A student with a disability is expected to comply with all essential academic standards and requirements of the student code of conduct. Therefore, a student does not need to meet direct threat criteria for an IHE to hold him/her accountable." *Id.*

[167] *See Letter to Woodbury University, supra* note 143, at 3 n. 6. "A 'direct threat' is a significant risk of causing substantial harm to the health or safety of the student or others that cannot be eliminated or reduced to an acceptable level through the provision of reasonable accommoda-tions." Determination of whether the student's behavior constitutes a direct threat should take into account the nature, duration, and severity of the risk; the likelihood or imminence of the harmful behavior; and whether the threat to the student can be reduced sufficiently by reason-able accommodation. *School Bd. of Nassau Cty. v .Arline,* 480 U.S. 273, 288 (1987); *Chalk v. Orange Cty. Superintendent of Schools,* 840 F.2d 701, 707–8 (9th Cir. 1988). A "significant risk" is a high probability of substantial harm, not just a slightly increased, speculative. or remote risk. *Bragdon v. Abbott,* 524 U.S. 624, 649–50 (1998).

[168] *Id.*

Significant risk means "a high probability of substantial harm."[169] Institutions of higher education that engage in threat assessment have been told to follow these guidelines.[170]

7. Disability law strongly favors treating students as individuals. A student is not the sum of his or her GPA and disability profile. Each student has unique abilities and disabilities in a unique combination. Disability law strives to create a world in which people no longer see "disabled" or "abled" students but rather a world from which labeling has disappeared. When you look at your population and see students—individuals—and not disabled or abled persons, you have taken a great step forward in complying with disability law.

Fundamentals of disability law.

The law forbids discrimination against "qualified/otherwise qualified" students.[171] A student in an educational program is qualified if he or she meets the academic or technical standards for admission or participation in the education program or activity.[172] A student must be able to meet academic and technical standards, with or without accommodation.[173] In a letter to Woodbury College, OCR stated that "technical requirements include those essential provisions found in the college's code of conduct as well as the ability to not represent a 'direct threat' to self or others."[174] For an example of technical requirements, see *An Educational Blueprint for Brown Medical School* and its "nine abilities."[175]

---

[169] *See* JED Foundation, *supra* note 118, at 13 n. 90.

[170] *See id.* at 113–14.

[171] 42 U.S.C. § 12132 (2006); 29 U.S.C. § 794(a) (2006).

[172] 34 C.F.R. § 104.3(1)(3). The test for other services is slightly different, 34 C.F.R. § 104.3(1)(4), and employment is another matter entirely, 34 C.F.R. § 104.3(1)(3).

[173] 42 U.S.C. § 1213.1(2) (2006); 28 C.F.R. § 35.104; 34 C.F.R. § 104.3(k)(3).

[174] *Letter to Woodbury University*, *supra* note 143, at 5.

[175] *See* Brown University, *supra* note 164, at 1. "As stated in *An Educational Blueprint for Brown Medical School,* 'Brown's nine abilities encompass a broad range of expectations for future physicians, ranging from traditional clinical skills to the more elusive aspects of the art of medicine. Each of the abilities includes a list of specific criteria that the student is expected to master at a certain level of achievement, depending upon the student's stage of professional development'" *Id.* The nine abilities are as follows:
1. Effective Communication
2. Basic Clinical Skills
3. Using Basic Science in the Practice of Medicine

Disability law defines protected disabilities quite broadly. Students who have "physical or mental requirements that substantially limit one or more major life activities" or are "regarded as having such" are covered.[176] The legal definition of recognized disabilities is constantly in flux; student affairs administrators should not attempt to guess what is or is not covered but should seek assistance from counsel or campus disability services. A certain level of technical training or understanding is necessary to appreciate and work with disabilities. For example, to be entitled to a reasonable accommodation for a disability, the student must be otherwise qualified for admission. An otherwise qualified student with a disability is usually entitled to reasonable accommodations, which are designed to give such students the opportunity to meet academic and technical standards. Determining which accommodations are reasonable is often one of the most difficult issues in disability law.[177] Disability law does not guarantee success in a program, just equal opportunity. Moreover, an institution of higher education is not required to "fundamentally alter its programs or make accommodations that result in undue burdens on the institution. . . . "[178] As the Supreme Court stated in *Southeastern Community College v. Davis:*

> [T]his is the first case in which this Court has been called upon to interpret § 504 [of the Rehabilitation Act of 1973] . . . [s]ection 504 by its terms does not compel educational institutions to disregard the disabilities of handicapped individuals or to make substantial modifications in their programs to allow disabled persons to participate. Instead, it requires only that an "otherwise qualified handicapped individual" not be excluded from participation in a federally funded program "solely by reason of his handicap," indi-

---

4.   Diagnosis, Management, and Prevention
5.   Lifelong Learning
6.   Professional Development and Personal Growth
7.   Social and Community Contexts of Health Care
8.   Moral Reasoning and Clinical Ethics
9.   Problem Solving

Id.
[176] 34 C.F.R. § 104.3(j)
[177] Laura Rothstein, *Disability Law Issues for High Risk Students: Addressing Violence and Disruption*, 35 J.C. & U.L 3 (2009); *see also U.S. v. Davis*, 442 U.S. 397 (1979).
[178] *Davis*, 442 U.S. at 405.

cating only that mere possession of a handicap is not a permissible ground for assuming an inability to function in a particular context.

The court below, however, believed that the "otherwise qualified" persons protected by § 504 include those who would be able to meet the requirements of a particular program in every respect as to limitations imposed by their handicap. Taken literally this holding would prevent an institution from taking into account any limitation resulting from the handicap, however disabling. It assumes, in effect, that a person need not meet the legitimate physical requirements in order to be "otherwise qualified." We think the understanding of the District Court is closer to the plain meaning of the statutory language. An otherwise qualified person is one who is able to meet all of a program's requirements in spite of his handicap.[179]

Nonetheless, institutions of higher education have been lawfully asked to modify existing procedures and existing physical plant to meet the needs of disabled students.[180]

One of the most consistent messages from OCR has been that disability determination should be made on an individual basis—and the courts appear to back this idea.[181] Negative categorical action directed at all students who are suicidal because they are suicidal is not acceptable.[182] It may be that a given individual student who is suicidal cannot be reasonably accommodated or is not qualified, but that must be determined on an individual basis. Note the similarity to race-conscious admissions in the clear legal preference for individuation in intervention and other actions.

OCR has taken the position that disabled students are entitled to due process,[183] but the Supreme Court has not addressed this issue directly. OCR

---

[179] *Id.* at 405–6.
[180] *See, e.g.,* 28 C.F.R. § 36.301–36.310; 28 C.F.R. § 36.401–36.406.
[181] *See Letter to Woodbury University, supra* note 143; JED Foundation, *supra* note 118, at 10; *Nott v. George Washington Univ.,* No. 05-8503 (D.C. Super. Ct. Oct. 2005), *available at* http://www.bazelon.org/issues/education/incourt/nott/nottcomplaint.pdf.; Va. Code Ann. § 23-9.2:8 (Lexis 2007).
[182] *See Nott, supra* note 181.
[183] *See Letter to Woodbury University, supra* note 143, at 3–4 n. 7. "Lawful actions require

also has expressed a preference for disability systems operated by experienced disability personnel; as a result, many institutions of higher education provide dual-process discipline systems. This area is not entirely devoid of legal murkiness, and institutions of higher education await further guidance from the Supreme Court on how to interpret disability law in the higher education context.

RIGHTS RELATED TO ECONOMIC STATUS/CORE MISSION DELIVERY

As we have seen, race, gender, and disability discrimination are subject to exacting, if slightly different, levels of scrutiny in the law. However, the Supreme Court has hesitated to apply any kind of equivalent equal protection scrutiny to government action that results in demonstrable inequities in the cost/value of education or access to education itself. Economic discrimination is not the same in Supreme Court doctrine as race or gender discrimination. In a well-known case—*San Antonio Independent School District v. Rodriguez*, 411 U.S. 1 (1973)—the Supreme Court upheld a system of school funding based on property taxation that led to wealthy school districts providing much better funded education systems for their neighborhoods. The tax/funding system

---

proceedings with due process." *Id.* at 3. "In exceptional circumstances, a student who represents an immediate direct threat to him/herself may have to have his/her conduct addressed through State procedures for emergency commitment or through criminal law enforcement procedures. As long as such actions are not a pretext for discrimination, nothing in the ADA or Section 504 prevents resort to such external resources and procedures. Conduct that is criminal or 'egregious' may not have to be treated in the same manner as the kind of conduct addressed in this letter." *Humphrey v. Memorial Hospital*, 239 F.3d 1128 (9th Cir. 2001). "Serious misconduct or direct threat behavior may also create exigent circumstances where initial minimal due process is provided before short-term sanctions are imposed, followed by more complete due process at a subsequent point in time." *Id.* at n. 7. "OCR recognizes that, when an educational institution responds to a student's actions that are believed to present a 'direct threat' to health and safety or to actions that appear to breach an essential code of conduct provision, post-secondary institutions are generally entitled to a significant degree of deference. *Regents of the Univ. of Michigan v. Ewing*, 474 U.S. 214, 225, 106 S. Ct. 507 (1985). The degree of deference owed by OCR should be greatest when colleges and universities establish and implement due process procedures well-calculated to conscientiously consider all pertinent and appropriate information. *Wong v. Regents of Univ. of California*, 192 F.3d 807, 817, 819, 823 (9th Cir. 1999); *Wynne v. Tufts Univ. School of Medicine I*, 932 F.2d 19, 25 (1st Cir. 1991). However, this deference is not unlimited. *P.G.A. v. Martin*, [532] U.S. [661], 121 S. Ct. 1879 (2001)." *Id.* at 3–4.

did not violate equal protection, and the Supreme Court applied a much lower standard of review (rational basis) to the alleged discriminatory system. The Court stated:

> However described, it is clear that appellees' suit asks this Court to extend its most exacting scrutiny to review a system that allegedly discriminates against a large, diverse, and amorphous class, unified only by the common factor of residence in districts that happen to have less taxable wealth than other districts. The system of alleged discrimination and the class it defines have none of the traditional indicia of suspectness: the class is not saddled with such disabilities, or subjected to such a history of purposeful unequal treatment, or relegated to such a position of political powerlessness as to command extraordinary protection from the majoritarian political process.[184]

Class/wealth discrimination is simply not the same as race or gender discrimination in the eyes of the Supreme Court. Moreover, the Court has rejected the notion that education is a fundamental right guaranteed by the U.S. Constitution:

> The lesson of these cases in addressing the question now before the Court is plain. It is not the province of this Court to create substantive constitutional rights in the name of guaranteeing equal protection of the laws. . . .
>
> Education, of course, is not among the rights afforded explicit protection under our Federal Constitution. Nor do we find any basis for saying it is implicitly so protected. As we have said, the undisputed importance of education will not alone cause this Court to depart from the usual standard for reviewing a State's social and economic legislation. It is the appellees' contention, however, that education is distinguishable from other services and benefits provided by the State because it bears a peculiarly close relationship to other rights and liberties accorded protection under the Constitution. Specifically, they insist that education is itself a fundamental

---

[184] *Rodriguez*, 411 U.S. at 28 (citation omitted).

personal right because it is essential to the effective exercise of First Amendment freedoms and to intelligent utilization of the right to vote. In asserting a nexus between speech and education, the appellee urges that the right to speak is meaningless unless the speaker is capable of articulating his thoughts intelligently and persuasively. The "marketplace of ideas" is an empty forum for those lacking basic communicative tools. Likewise they argue that the corollary right to receive information becomes little more than a hollow privilege when the recipient has not been taught to read, assimilate, and utilize available knowledge. . . .

We need not dispute any of these propositions. . . . [b]ut they are not values to be implemented by judicial intrusion into otherwise legitimate state activities."[185]

Of course, state constitutions and other laws might create such rights—as they do with regard to K–12 education—but at best that would only create protected (property) interests for due process purposes,[186] not a general U.S. constitutional right to an education. Student affairs administrators should understand that college students have civil rights, but the Supreme Court has hesitated on due process rights and rights to economic equality in education, and on rights to an equal higher education experience for all purposes. Essentially, an education cannot be denied for race, gender, or disability reasons, but one of the major determinants of access to and success in college—economic status/ class—receives no equivalent antidiscriminatory treatment. Higher education no longer benefits from privilege doctrines barring suits over discrimination and other constitutional rights; however, privilege in a broader sense remains legally intact. Higher education is no longer stuck in "Animal House"; but John Hughes's movies illustrating the impact of class and economic opportunity in education still resonate.[187]

There is a risk of a great millennial educational irony. In the 1950s, *Brown*

---

[185] *Id.* at 33–35, 36.
[186] *See Goss v. Lopez*, 419 U.S. 565, 572–73 (1975).
[187] *E.g., Pretty in Pink* (Lauren Shuler 1986) (motion picture); *The Breakfast Club* (Gil Friesen 1985) (motion picture).

v. Board of Education announced that separate is not equal. At the time, higher education was largely stratified along the lines illustrated in "Animal House." Currently, higher education is at risk of returning to that era in some, but not all, ways. College today is mostly for the wealthy, the lucky few who receive scholarships, part-timers who work and go to school, and the new indentured educated class. Perhaps the biggest changes since the 1950s may be that access is no longer barred by race, gender, or disability, but we have created the largest class of indentured persons since the 1800s: College loan debt now surpasses credit card debt.[188] A new economic class has emerged just in the past decade: the highly educated economic underclass, working to emancipate itself from college debt and join the ranks of other economic classes.

This phenomenon will continue to play out in a number of ways, perhaps even with respect to the historically disfavored educational malpractice claim. Until recently, the law has been unwilling to directly address issues of core mission delivery via educational malpractice claims. However, recently, courts have been willing to address breach of contract claims that relate to specific educational services promised or improper mentoring/advice regarding degree completion requirements or professional certification.[189] DOE has been involved in several highly visible initiatives to improve core mission accountability, as well.

Student affairs administrators work in a field in which the economics of higher education increasingly drive legal doctrine. Higher education is big business—not just for institutions of higher education, but for the federal and state governments, and the banks and supplementary loan markets. Civil rights battles of the 20th century will take on increasing tones of class struggle. A powerful economic class of educated persons, many of whom have shouldered large education debt, will shape and inform policy in the decades to come.

---

[188] Mary Pilon, *Student-Loan Debt Surpasses Credit Cards*, Wall Street Journal (Aug. 9, 2010), *available at* http://blogs.wsj.com/economics/2010/08/09/student-loan-debt-surpasses-credit-cards.
[189] *See, e.g., Ross v. Creighton Univ.*, 957 F.2d 410, 416–17 (1992).

CHAPTER 6

A BRIEF OVERVIEW
OF POWERS AND GOVERNANCE

The law of higher education places great emphasis on responsibility and accountability for student safety and student civil rights, among other things, and much less emphasis on the powers and authority of student affairs administrators. This emphasis on responsibility and accountability is interesting in a business in which risk of physical injury is relatively low (college is not like car manufacturing or pharmaceuticals in terms of physical risk to consumers); many outcomes are determined primarily by the choices of consumers themselves (almost no one chooses to crash a car and few people drive truly recklessly, but students often knowingly engage in high-risk behavior, or choose to skip studying, or use extremely dangerous drugs with almost certain results); and consumers and the government have not been as interested in core mission delivery as they are in other industries (e.g., casinos are highly controlled, cars must be manufactured to strict standards, much of the food supply is significantly regulated). Moreover, at no time in human history have college students been educated in an environment with so much fairness, inclusion, and diversity. It is interesting that most of the law of higher education emphasizes accountability and responsibility, yet little is directed toward powers and authority. Why is this?

The answer is simple. From an authority/governance perspective (the corporate way of looking at higher education), Dean Wormer's failings were mostly in the dimension of not caring for student well-being and treating students un-fairly. Except for the Deltas and Omegas at Faber College, other students seemed to be getting a decent education. Institutions of higher education never lost cred-ibility in core mission delivery, and they still enjoy much of the deference toward their corporate powers that they received in the era of power and prerogative.[1]

There is a murkiness to the law of governance in higher education that is a direct result of centuries of legal deference. Student affairs administrators are of-ten vested with critical decision-making power, yet very few have a clear sense of either the origins or the limits of this power. Moreover, in higher education one is likely to find behaviors that are unusual in other businesses. For example, the college president may spend time approving menus for a board dinner; trustees might call student affairs administrators directly to express their views on how to perform a particular task; and individual student affairs administrators might act for their in-stitutions in ways they are not authorized to act. Sometimes higher education runs a little bit like the cavalry in "F Troop."[2] Weaknesses in the organizational structure of an institution of higher education become apparent in a crisis. Forty years ago, Kent State illustrated the enormous physical/safety risks associated with the breakdown of a command structure in higher education.[3] Four years ago, the shootings at Vir-ginia Tech showed the need for higher education information systems to evolve to protect student safety. But there has been no large-scale meltdown in corporate gov-ernance in higher education, although we may be on the cusp of a bursting bubble.

Although a great deal remains to be done in the evolution of management and organizational theory for nonprofit businesses and their equivalents, higher education does operate with *some* structure.

THE INSTITUTION OF HIGHER EDUCATION AS AN ENTITY

Legal authority to exist or operate as an institution of higher education essentially comes from a few discrete sources or events. Some public institutions

---

[1] Peter Lake, *What's Next for Private Universities? Accountability*, The Chronicle of Higher Education (Dec. 5, 2010), *available at* http://chronicle.com/article/Whats-Next-for-Pri-vate/125599/.

[2] *F Troop: Don't Look Now, One of Our Cannons Is Missing* (Warner Brothers, Sept. 21, 1965) (TV series).

[3] Phillip Thompkins & Elaine Vanden Bout Anderson, *Communication Crisis at Kent State: A Case Study* (Gordon & Breach 1971).

exist via a state constitution; that is, the people of a state literally and directly create the power of an institution of higher education and invest that power in a governing body.[4] However, most public institutions exist by virtue of state statute and legislative action, either directly or indirectly. States also operate commissions or boards (e.g., the Board of Regents in New York) that have general powers over higher education in that state. These boards may have some power over private institutions of higher education; however, their power over public institutions is usually significantly greater. Boards have various amounts of power from state to state. Some, like the New York Board of Regents, are heavily involved in the planning and management of statewide systems.[5] Other boards play a more facilitative role.[6]

Private institutions become entities with corporate power usually through incorporation or "chartering" (a somewhat anachronistic term essentially equivalent to incorporation). In some states, private institutions of higher education operate under rules of incorporation designed for nonprofit corporations in general, but most choose a special form of nonprofit corporate existence that does not have a voting membership class or shareholders and is run by a self-perpetuating board of trustees or similar governing body.[7] Public institutions of higher education also typically have their own governing boards, although the relationship with state oversight groups can be complex and varies significantly from state to state. Private institutions of higher education may form consortia—within legal limits relating to the combinations of businesses—but consortia do not manage individual institutions.

State creation of institutions of higher education via constitution, statute, act of a statewide governing body, or incorporation is separate from state licensing. Accredited institutions of higher education are usually partially or totally exempt from licensing requirements. Proprietary institutions of higher education (for-profits) often face a higher level of state business regulation than public institutions.[8] However, the federal government has recently moved to adopt stricter

---

[4] *See generally* Valerie L. Brown, *A Comparative Analysis of College Autonomy in Selected States* 60 Educ. L. Rptr. 299 (1990).
[5] *Id.*
[6] *Id.*
[7] *See* Lake, *supra* note 1.
[8] *See N.Y. Assn. of Career Schools v. St. Educ. Dept. N.Y.*, 749 F. Supp 1264, 1273 (S.D.N.Y. 1990).

requirements for for-profits whose students seek loans from the federal direct lending program.[9]

TRUSTEES, OFFICERS, AND ADMINISTRATORS

Trustees (sometimes known by other names, such as *visitors*) are, in essence, the collective principals (bosses) of their institutions of higher education. For most purposes, the trustee body is the legal "principal"; the big boss, so to speak. Trustees are charged with a variety of common law and statutory duties, including fiduciary duties, to their institution.[10] In state systems, boards of regents may play a role in trustee selection and supervision. Ideally, boards operate to set policy and strategic objectives/goals; the operational bosses (at least in theory) are administrators and faculty. Trustees in public colleges receive their authority from state constitutions or, more commonly, statutes or directives from the legislature or delegated bodies. Trustees in private colleges derive their power and authority from the incorporating documents or charter of their private institution of higher education.

Boards meet regularly and can adopt rules or set practices that are reflected in the minutes of their meetings. Trustee boards usually meet in closed session, although boards at state universities may be subject to state freedom of information or sunshine laws.[11] Trustees typically make rules relating to the exercise of board power; often, these are found in by-laws. Boards also usually delegate tasks to committees, often with significant grants of authority. Investment and finance committees are particularly powerful subunits of the board. In the case of public institutions, state law may specify certain tasks for delegation.

Boards typically include wealthy people, successful business leaders, alum-

---

[9] *See* Goldie Blumenstyk, *Education Dept. to Delay Issuing 'Gainful Employment' Rules Opposed by For-Profit Colleges*, Chronicle of Higher Education (Sept. 24, 2010), *available at* http://chronicle.com/article/Education-Dept-to-Delay/124617.

[10] For example, trustees are often subject to conflict of interest laws, licensing laws, and so on. However, institutions of higher education are largely exempt from the Sarbanes-Oxley Corporate Accountability Act. *See* Judith Areen, *Higher Education and the Law: Cases and Materials* 895–96 (Foundation Press 2009).

[11] *See Arkansas Gazette Co. v. Pickens*, 522 S.W.2d 350 (Ark. 1975) (holding that members of the board of trustees were required by the Freedom of Information Act to conduct their meetings in public and that members of the media were interested parties at meetings and should therefore be allowed to be present at said meetings).

ni, and the politically powerful. Not many board members have significant classroom or college administrative experience, although former college presidents often serve. Many boards have a student or faculty representative or member; in general, however, students, faculty, and persons with significant administrative experience are not widely represented on boards. College presidents may have significant college teaching/operational experience, but in recent times many presidents have been selected and retained primarily for proven fund raising and capital management skills.

Counsel for an institution of higher education plays a leading role in board management and often works with a board longer than any of the trustees, who usually have limited terms of service. Counsel often outlasts the terms of presidents, too; it is not uncommon for an attorney to work with a number of presidents. Counsel may not be a trustee; however, many achieve a position of great power and respect that rivals the power of individual trustees (think consigliere minus the organized crime overtones[12]).

Some state/public institutions of higher education and their trustee boards have more authority than others; it depends on a variety of factors, including whether the institution was created by state constitution, the role of statewide governing bodies such as the New York Board of Regents, the wealth of the institution and its reliance on state funding, historical practice, and whether the institution is a current or former two-year (so-called *community*) college. Many state/public institutions of higher education are highly dependent on their state legislatures, as illustrated in the recent meltdown of the California public higher education system.[13]

---

[12] *See* Jerry Capechi, *The Complete Idiot's Guide to the Mafia* 9 (Alpha Books 2002).

[13] *See* Josh Keller, *U. of California Budget Crises, Some Faculty Members See a Cover-Up*, Chronicle of Higher Education (Sept. 22, 2009), *available at* http://chronicle.com/article/In-U-of-California-Budget/48571/; Josh Keller, *University of California Panel Offers a Timid Response to Budget Crisis*, Chronicle of Higher Education (Mar. 23, 2010), *available at* http://chronicle.com/article/U-of-California-Panel-Offers/64810/?sid=at&utm_source=at&utm_medium=en; Josh Keller, *Thousands Protest Budget Cuts on University of California Campuses*, Chronicle of Higher Education (Sept. 24, 2009), *available at* http://chronicle.com/article/Thousands-Protest-Budget-Cuts/48611; Josh Keller, *California's Budget Problems Leave Community Colleges Holding IUO's*, Chronicle of Higher Education (Mar. 6, 2009), *available at* http://chronicle.com/article/Californias-Budget-Problem/34143; *see also* Paul Fain, *Budget Cuts Intensify Identity Crisis at Washington's Flagship Campus*, Chronicle of Higher Education (Aug. 29, 2010), *available at* http://jobs.chronicle.com/article/Budget-Cuts-Intensify-Identity/124162.

Private institutions of higher education usually have trustee boards that are self-perpetuating. Most private institutions of higher education have neither shareholders nor members.[14] Private institutions of higher education operate with fairly limited accountability to external authority.[15] In theory, state attorneys general provide oversight of private institutions; however, this arrangement leaves much to be desired, for a variety of reasons.[16] In practice, there is little such oversight.

Institutions of higher education use a fairly anachronistic business model of hierarchical, largely insulated, board management. As a result, institutions are not usually versatile businesses, capable of rapid strategic redeployment; rather, they evolve slowly, and usually in response to a crisis or overwhelming external pressure. Student affairs administrators may find that they have a limited direct connection to strategic leadership. A student affairs administrator's only direct link to the board is typically through the president, who participates in board meetings, However, in an era when presidents are tasked by their boards to emphasize fundraising and financial management, student affairs administrators typically find themselves more commonly in direct contact with *vice* presidents, who themselves have limited direct interactions with boards. Student affairs administrators often feel as though they are traveling through the Land of Oz, where an audience with the all-powerful is rare. Pressure is mounting to change the business model in higher education; in the coming decades, many institutions, both public and private, are likely to experience significant changes in their organizational philosophies.

Trustees delegate power over operational matters to the administrative class. American Association of University Professors (AAUP) guidelines call for significant shared governance with faculty over academic matters;[17] however, colleges vary significantly in how faithfully they adhere to these guidelines.[18] Thus, most student affairs administrators derive their authority through a chain

---

[14] Lake, *supra* note 1.

[15] *See id.*

[16] *See id.*

[17] *See* Areen, *supra* note 10, appendix B, 2–4 ("The variety and complexity of the tasks performed by institutions of higher education produce an inescapable interdependence among governing board, administration, faculty, students, and others. The relationship calls for adequate communication among these components, and full opportunity for appropriate joint planning and effort." *Id.*).

[18] *See id.*

of command, typically from the president to the vice president for student affairs. The organization chart shows the flow of authority and responsibility, but custom and practice can be more informative, especially below the vice presidential level, where the chain of command is far more fluid and dynamic, and usually far less hierarchical (although the organizational mentality of institutions of higher education remains predominantly hierarchical).[19]

Student affairs administrators should recognize certain practical concerns with respect to governance and delegation of authority. First, a clear delineation of authority often dissipates significantly below the vice presidential level. Many student affairs administrators have job descriptions that do not accurately reflect the work they do, nor do they always report to just one boss or work under just one delegation of authority.

Second, trustees in higher education sometimes meddle with, control, and even chill student affairs practice. It is not unusual for a trustee (or a lawyer) to become directly involved in an ongoing student affairs matter. This behavior is more unusual in the for-profit corporate world and is not an ideal management approach in any case. The board and the president are responsible for curtailing such practices, but that does not always happen. Trustees may retain final authority over some institutional operational matters,[20] or state law may direct student affairs operational practice. For example, in many institutions of higher education, revision of discipline codes requires prior approval from trustees.[21] From a business operations perspective, such retained control is a serious flaw, but it is not uncommon in student affairs practice. Finally, hearing "The trustees won't like that" has a chilling effect on student affairs practice. Ideally, trustees should be divorced from operational decision making, but again this is not the case in all instances for all institutions.

Third, student affairs administrators face high risks of negative job action, particularly in comparison with faculty, who tend to have longer term contracts, tenure, and other forms of job security. Student affairs administrators work in

---

[19] An excellent exercise for student affairs administrators is to revisit their own job descriptions on an annual or semi-annual basis to observe and report on actual tasks performed and aspirational job identity. Most administrators will find that their actual performed tasks mutate over time and that job descriptions do not always remain fully representative of tasks performed.
[20] *See* Va. Code Ann. § 23-9.2:8 (Lexis 2010).
[21] *See* Mass. Gen. Laws. ch. 15A, § 22 (2010).

a field with loosely defined job responsibilities; however, the management philosophy is hierarchical. This organizational dynamic causes student affairs administrators to be risk-averse and encourages politicking, positioning, posturing, pandering, the choice of "safe" alternatives, and the pursuit of initiatives to reduce "consumer" complaints. Student affairs administrators are an employment underclass in higher education. Although faculty have not unionized nationally, AAUP fights vigorously for their rights. AAUP's power includes, among other things, the ability to affect accreditation decisions.[22] Student affairs administrators have two major national membership groups, the American College Personnel Association and the National Association of Student Personnel Administrators,[23] but neither group functions exactly like AAUP—as an advocacy group for employment rights. Student affairs administrators have no national union.

Fourth, student affairs administrators do not share governance rights with faculty on an equal basis. When the 1966 AAUP statement[24] was drafted, student affairs administration staffs were not included. Many jobs performed by today's student affairs administrators did not exist in 1966, and those that did were usually performed as service functions by faculty. There was relatively little consciousness of "student affairs administration" as a distinct field, and the AAUP governance concepts were written around "faculty." The 1966 statement is a glaringly dated document from a student affairs administrator's perspective. There is no reason to limit shared governance to employees with academic appointments, and it is increasingly obvious that much of student affairs practice is an educational activity on par with classroom teaching (see, e.g., the *Christian Legal Society at Hastings College of the Law* case). Student affairs administration practice has grown from the provision of auxiliary services to full-blown educational partnership; however, most institutions of higher education remain stuck at a point in their corporate evolution and governance structure that creates challenging dynamics for student affairs administrators.

---

[22] *See* Peter Schmidt, *AAUP Votes to Sanction Antioch U. and Censure Two Other Institutions*, Chronicle of Higher Education (June 13, 2010), *available at* http://chronicle.com/article/AAUP-Votes-to-Sanction-Antioch/65930. Although AAUP is not an accrediting body, its decisions can significantly affect the accreditation process, particularly via censure.

[23] *See* American College Personnel Association, www2.myacpa.org (last visited Aug. 30, 2010); National Association of Student Personnel Administrators, http://www.naspa.org (last visited Aug. 30, 2010).

[24] *See* Areen, *supra* note 10, appendix B.

Fifth, student affairs administrators work in a field with a high degree of accountability, a direct impact on core mission delivery, and a high level of consumer expectation regarding delivery of key services. Fortunately, the law observes many different types of business operations and is not oblivious to this reality, which explains the relative paucity of instances in which a court holds a student affairs administrator *liable* (as opposed to *accountable*). From a business lawyer's perspective, student affairs administrators are a subclass of higher education employees charged with some of the most critical and volatile responsibilities in a hierarchical organizational structure that itself is subject to limited external accountability for core mission delivery. Front-line student affairs administration staff either will or will not succeed in their mission to make higher education a safer, more productive learning experience. As the *Christian Legal Society* case illustrates, courts appreciate and deeply respect student affairs administrators and the heavy responsibilities they shoulder. In other words, the law applies both an institutional protectivism and an operational protectivism. The operational protectivism is evident in cases such as *Pawlowski v. Delta Sigma Phi*,[25] which was clearly sensitive to how specific legal rules might influence student affairs practice.

Sixth, a persistent issue in student affairs administration practice (and for institutions of higher education generally) is inappropriate arrogation of authority, particularly in contractual situations. Student affairs administrators should be vigilant regarding who may and who may not "sign" for an institution of higher education and bind it in contract. As agents of institutions of higher education, some student affairs administrators have what the law calls *actual authority*—either express (in words or writing) or implied (arising from conduct or circumstances)—to bind an institution in contract. However, it may reasonably appear to third parties (in part because a student affairs administrator in good faith believes it to be true) that the administrator has authority that in fact does not exist. The law calls this *apparent authority*; in many instances, apparent authority can make an institution of higher education responsible for otherwise unauthorized acts. When authority by delegation and subdelegation is less than crystal clear, it is easy for student affairs administrators to misunderstand their authority. It is good practice to review actual authority and train staff accord-

---

[25] 2007 WL 2363146 (Conn. Super. 2007).

ingly. When student affairs administrators are in doubt, they can usually resolve authority questions quickly and correctly by broadening the conversation and asking others, including counsel, about appropriate authority and past practices.

Seventh, student affairs administrators will encounter people who talk about teacher-student confidentiality. Many misunderstandings exist about student privacy law. In almost all instances, student affairs administrators work for institutions of higher education, not for students. From a legal perspective, they owe loyalty and a fiduciary duty directly to the institution, not to students. Thus, student affairs administrators should be careful about promising confidentiality or loyalty to students that is inconsistent with their job responsibilities. We are not our students' adversaries; however, we are not their business associates, nor do we work for them. It is fairly common for parents and students to say things like "I pay your salary" or "You work for me." They misunderstand the business relationship they have with the host institution of higher education and project this misunderstanding onto student affairs administrators. Student affairs administrators have some power to manage these expectations, although they do not have complete control over them. One good practice is to develop an overarching philosophy for student affairs administration practice and articulate and disseminate this philosophy.[26]

---

[26] *See* Texas A&M Univ., Dept. of Student Activities, *Letter from the Director*, http://studentac-tivities.tamu.edu/orgmanual/stuact (last visited on Aug. 30, 2010).

CONCLUSION

For a student affairs administrator, reading a book about the foundations of higher education law is part of the process of developing and deepening a relationship with law in day-to-day practice. As in any relationship, it is easy at times to expect too much or too little of the other party, or to approach the relationship with one set of ideas only to discover a different set. The law will be a friend who will challenge—and occasionally beat up on—the student affairs administrator. The law will make student affairs administrators uneasy at times, even make them feel insecure, but it can also create a sense of empowerment. Over time and with experience, the student affairs administrator's relationship with law will mature and grow.

Start with good foundations, and you will find yourself returning to them. After more than 25 years of practicing and teaching law, I still pick up moldy old foundations books to keep my fundamentals fresh. We live in an age of minutiae, but depth of understanding of the law comes from a continuous process of moving from the foundations to details and back again. This process is similar to the process of moral reasoning, which the late, great philosopher John Rawls described as "reflective equilibrium."[1] In that process, a student affairs administrator will experience cognitive resolution: moments of clarity in which everything seems to make sense. But these moments rarely last very long. Just when things start to make sense, you read another case or another regulation and induce cognitive dissonance all over again.

A student affairs administrator's experience of the law is actually very simi-

---

[1] John Rawls, *A Theory of Justice* (Harvard University Press 1970).

lar to that of a highly trained expert in the field of law. Competency in law, especially for student affairs administrators, is a process. There are no shortcuts, and the allure of simplistic solutions is an ever-present menace to real understanding. Lawyers refer to their profession as "the practice of law" for a reason. One of my great mentors, who argued and won the *New York Times v. Sullivan* case in the U.S. Supreme Court, told me, "I expect work to be perfect, even though I know it won't always be."

There are several important themes to pull from this book for your ever-evolving relationship with law in student affairs practice. First, the legal system shows great respect for the work of student affairs administrators. Judges and legal leaders are not the ones who tell parents their children are hurt; or who work on dormitory floors at 3:00 a.m.; or who argue with parents and students who want to avoid the very experiences that make college worthwhile. On the whole, the leaders in law remember their time in college fondly. That thank-you note you get in May might someday turn out to be the autograph of a Supreme Court justice. I can't remember what I had for lunch yesterday, but I vividly remember the best lecture I ever heard and my most important mentor in college.[2] This is the kind of impact law can only dream about.

Second, it is best not to focus on avoiding liability and accountability. Embrace accountability, because legal accountability is there to help student affairs practice. The best approach is proactive, professional, and confident. Enhanced accountability is a compliment; it shows how important our work is.

Third, the law favors a focus on students as individuals. A clear legal preference exists for making higher education as personalized a process as it is educationally sound, from admissions to careful and deliberative evaluation of progress to the management of disabilities. It can be very frustrating to spend hours working on one student's issues, but that is often where the law is most protective and praiseworthy of student affairs practice.

Fourth, always try to discern the spirit of the law that applies as best you can. Law exists in rules but also in the principles and policies it seeks to promote. The "untidiness" at that level of analysis can sometimes be unnerving, but there is no reason to think that the soul of the law is any less complicated than

---

[2] Martha Nussbaum, Lecture, *Plato's Symposium*, Harvard University; Hugh Flick (serving as Dean of Silliman College at Yale University for more than 20 years).

your own! Laws have all the strengths and character flaws that human beings do, and a heavy dose of human inconsistency to boot. But look a little deeper and you will find profound and validating principles that student affairs administrators share with the law.

Finally, remember that student affairs practice as we know it today arose from the violence and opposition of the civil rights era, and much of the law we live with today formed in that time. Every day, another student affairs administrator with direct experience of the civil rights period retires, taking a piece of meta-institutional history with him or her. Today's student affairs administrators are the liminal generation: Someday we will tell the next generation what others told us about seeing Led Zeppelin and Janis Joplin live.

The first generation of lawyers, legalists, and student affairs administrators in the civil rights era created the concept of civil disobedience in law and higher education, essentially inventing a field that did not exist before their courageous work. As the late Senator Edward Kennedy said in his eulogy for his assassinated brother Bobby, "Some men see things as they are and say *why?* I dream things that never were and say *why not?*"[3] This was the spirit of those who challenged and ended the doctrine of privilege and ousted Dean Wormer. This spirit animated those who attacked separate but equal and exposed it as an educational lie. It was the spirit of a generation of student affairs administrators who fought for a panoply of rights that, a hundred years ago, would have been utterly unthinkable in higher education. The entire fabric of modern student affairs practice is permeated with the revolutionary successes of this period.

Look around and you will see ramps leading into campus buildings, students from all walks of life and backgrounds living and learning together, a generation of students that answers "other" when asked their race, a student press that speaks its mind, and a thriving student activities system. The great magic of achievement in student affairs administration practice is that when we succeed, often either nothing happens or our work dissolves into invisibility. It is the kind of success that only student affairs administrators can truly understand. It makes most lawyers drool with envy.

There is a temptation in student affairs practice to accept the idea that

---

[3] Edward M. Kennedy, *Address at the Public Memorial Service for Robert F. Kennedy* (June 8, 1968), *available at* http://www.americanrhetoric.com/speeches/ekennedytributetorfk.html.

all the legal masterworks have been painted. The law comes at administrators hard—some days, all you can do is comply. The great challenge is to avoid being crushed by the law and its harshest consequences, and just get a little room to do what student affairs administrators do best: educate and develop student populations. It is tempting to accept the law as it is (or appears to be) and believe that the best we can do is only a little.

But the law continues to beckon student affairs administrators to participate in its evolution in higher education. The law does more than protect higher education; it encourages higher education, and student affairs administrators in particular, to exert academic freedom and the unique role of higher education in a constitutional democracy.

Thus, the generation of student affairs administrators that followed the civil rights era must recast the spirit of civil disobedience. We have no less an obligation than previous generations to confront the law and its weaknesses. We must constantly resist fear of law, avoidance of legal consequences and accountability, and sheeplike acceptance of the legal status quo. For student affairs administrators, courage has new and more subtle characteristics; it involves challenging systems and structures of the law and their relationship to our communities. If the law does not make sense, the student affairs administrator must keep asking *why*? If you catch yourself simply ticking off compliance steps, try to understand why you are being asked to do something in the first place. If the law does not make sense, ask how you can change it. Demand high-quality information about the law, and look for diverse viewpoints.

The great danger of law in modern student affairs practice is apathy, acceptance, and blind obedience. A previous generation created the conditions under which student affairs administrators have enormous power to influence the educational experience of students and the law of higher education itself. This power is all too easy to forget in the day-to-day hum of student affairs practice—and easy to lose through acquiescence. Understanding and appreciating the profound respect that student affairs administrators have earned in the eyes of the law is the primary building block in understanding the foundations of the law of higher education for student affairs administrators.

BIBLIOGRAPHY

TEXTS AND MONOGRAPHS

Judith Areen, *Higher Education and the Law: Cases and Materials* (Foundation Press 2009).

Association of Legal Writing Directors & Darby Dickerson, *ALWD Citation Manual,* (3d ed., Aspen 2006).

John Austin, *The Province of Jurisprudence Determined* (Wilfred E. Rumble ed., 1995).

Robert D. Bickel & Peter F. Lake, *Rights and Responsibilities of the Modern University: Who Assumes the Risks of College Life?* (Carolina Academic Press 1999).

Black's Law Dictionary (8th ed. 2004).

Jerry Capechi, *The Complete Idiot's Guide to the Mafia* (Alpha Books 2002).

Erwin Chemerinsky, *Constitutional Law: Principles and Policies* (3d ed., Aspen 2006).

Gene Deisinger et al., *The Handbook for Campus Threat Assessment & Management Teams* (Applied Risk Management 2008).

John L. Diamond, *Cases and Materials on Torts* (2d ed., West 2008).

John L. Diamond, Lawrence C. Levine & M. Stuart Madden, *Understanding Torts* (3d ed., Lexis 2007).

Dan B. Dobbs, *The Law of Torts* (West 2000).

Ronald Dworkin, *Taking Rights Seriously* (Harvard University Press 1978).

E. Allan Farnsworth, *Contracts* (4th ed. 2004).

E. Allan Farnsworth, *Contracts* (2d ed. 1990).

Neil Howe & William Strauss, *Millennials Go to College: Strategies for a New Generation on Campus* (LifeCourse Associates 2003).

JED Foundation, *Student Mental Health and the Law: A Resource for Institutions of Higher Education* (Jed Foundation 2008).

Robert H. Jerry, II, *Understanding Insurance Law* (2d ed., Matthew Bender 1996).

William A. Kaplan & Barbara A. Lee, *The Law of Higher Education* (Jossey-Bass 2006).

Page Keeton, Robert E. Keeton, Lewis D. Sargentich & Henry J. Steiner, *Tort and Accident Law* (2d ed., West 1989).

Martin Luther King, Jr., *The Autobiography of Martin Luther King, Jr.* (Clayborne Carson ed., Warner Books 1998).

Susan R. Komives & Dudley Woodward, *Student Services: A Handbook for the Profession* (4th ed., Jossey-Bass 2003).

Stefan H. Krieger & Richard K Neumann, Jr., *Essential Lawyering Skills* (3d ed., Aspen 2007).

Peter F. Lake, *Beyond Discipline: Managing the Modern Higher Education Environment* (Hierophant Enterprises, Inc. 2009).

Richard A. Posner, *The Economic Analysis of Law* (7th ed., Aspen 2007).

John Rawls, *A Theory of Justice* (Harvard University Press 1970).

Restatement (Second) of Agency.

Restatement (Second) of Torts.

Restatement (Third) of Torts: Liab. Physical Harm.

Restatement (Third) of Torts: Apportionment of Liability.

J. K. Rowling, *Harry Potter and the Chamber of Secrets* (Scholastic 1999).

Bibliography

J. K. Rowling, *Harry Potter and the Deathly Hallows* (Scholastic 2007).

J. K. Rowling, *Harry Potter and the Goblet of Fire* (Scholastic 2000).

J. K. Rowling, *Harry Potter and the Half-Blood Prince* (Scholastic 2005).

J. K. Rowling, *Harry Potter and the Order of the Phoenix* (Scholastic 2003).

J. K. Rowling, *Harry Potter and the Prisoner of Azkaban* (Scholastic 1999).

J. K. Rowling, *Harry Potter and the Sorcerer's Stone* (Scholastic 1998).

Benjamin Sells, *The Soul of the Law* (Element 1994).

Bradford Stone & Kristin David Adams, *The Uniform Commercial Code in a Nutshell* (7th ed., West 2008).

Phillip Thompkins & Elaine Vanden Bout Anderson, *Communication Crisis at Kent State: A Case Study* (Gordon and Breach 1971).

CASES

Allen v. Cox, 942 A.2d 296 (2008).

Anjou v. Boston Elevated Railway Co., 94 N.E. 386 (Mass. 1911).

Anthony v. Syracuse Univ., 224 A.D. 487 (N.Y. App. Div. 4th Dept. 1928).

Arkansas v. Forbes, 523 U.S. 666 (1998).

Arkansas Gazette Co. v. Pickens, 258 Ark. 69 (Ark. 1975).

Atria v. Vanderbilt Univ., 142 Fed. Appx. 246 (6th Cir. 2005).

A.W. v. Lancaster County. Sch. Dist. 0001, 601 N.W.2d 757 (Neb. 2010).

Baldwin v. Zoradi, 123 Cal. App. 3d 275 (Cal. Ct. App. 1981).

Balk v. Austin Ford Logan, Inc., 221 A.D.2d 795 (N.Y. App. Div. 1995).

Bash v. Clark Univ., 22 Mass. L. Rep. 84 (Mass. Super. 2006).

Bash v. Clark Univ., 2007 WL 1418528 (Mass. Super. 2007).

Beach v. Univ. of Utah, 726 P.2d 413 (Utah 1986).

Beagle v. Vasold, 417 P.2d 673, 681–682 (Cal. 1966).

Bearman v. Univ. of Notre Dame, 453 N.E.2d 1196 (Ind. App. 3d Dist. 1983).

Benner v. Oswald, 592 F.2d 174 (3d Cir. 1974).

Beth Rochel Seminary v. Bennett, 825 F.2d 478 (D.C. Cir. 1987).

BG&E v. Flippo, 684 A.2d 456 (Md. Ct. Spec. App. 1996).

Blackburn v. Dorta, 348 So.2d 287 (Fla. 1977).

Bloss v. Univ. of Minn., 590 N.W.2d 661 (Minn. Ct. App.1999).

Bd. of Curators of the Univ. of Missouri v. Horowitz, 435 U.S. 78 (1978).

Bd. of Educ. v. Grumet, 512 U.S. 687 (1994).

Bd. of Regents of State Coll.s v. Roth, 408 U.S. 564 (1972).

Bd. of Regents of Univ. of Wisconsin Sys. v. Southworth, 529 U.S. 217 (2000).

Boccone v. Eichen Levinson LLP, 301 Fed. Appx. 162 (3d Cir. 2008).

Booker v. GTE.net LLC, 350 F.3d 515 (Ky. 2003).

Boos v. Barry, 485 U.S. 312 (1988).

Borer v. American Airlines, Inc., 563 P.2d 858 (Cal. 1977).

Boston v. Webb, 783 F.2d 1163 (4th Cir. 1986).

Bowen v. Comstock, 2008 WL 2209722 (Tex. App. Waco Dist. 2008).

Boy Scouts v. Dale, 530 U.S. 640 (2000).

Bradshaw v Rawlings, 612 F.2d 135 (3d Cir. 1979).

Brandenburg v. Ohio, 395 U.S. 444 (1969).

Brennan v. Bd. of Trustees for Univ. of Louisiana Systems, 691 So.2d 324 (La. App. 1st Cir. 1997).

Brooks v. Parshall, 806 N.Y.S.2d 796 (N.Y. App. Div. 3d Dept. 2006).

Brown v. Bd. of Educ., 347 U.S. 483 (1954).

Burton v. Wilmington Parking Auth., 365 U.S. 715 (1961).

Byers v. Gunn, 81 So.2d 723 (Fla. 1955).

Cain v. Cleveland Parachute, 457 N.E.2d 1185 (Ohio 1983).

Calabro v. Bennett, 737 N.Y.S. 2d 406 (N.Y. App. Div. 3d Dept. 2002).

Caldwell v. A.R.B., Inc., 176 Cal. App. 3d 1028 (Cal. App. 1986).

Carson v. Springfield Coll., 2006 WL 2242732 (Del. Super. 2006).

Chalk v. Orange County Superintendent of Schools, 840 F.2d 701 (9th Cir. 1988).

Chaplinsky v. New Hampshire, 315 U.S. 568 (1992).

Chatham v. Larkins, 216 S.E.2d 677 (Ga. Ct. App. 1975).

Chicago Police Dep't v. Mosley, 408 U.S. 92 (1972).

Christian Legal Soc'y at Hastings Coll. of the Law v. Martinez, 130 S. Ct. 2971 (2010).

Citizens United v. Fed. Election Comm'n, 130 S. Ct. 876 (2010).

City of Lakewood v. Plain Dealer Publ'g Co., 486 U.S. 750 (1988).

Clark v. Cmty. for Creative Non-Violence, 468 U.S. 288 (1984).

Clay v. Texas Women's Univ., 728 F.2d 714 (C.A. Tex. 1984).

Coal. of Clergy, Lawyers, and Professors v. Bush, 310 F.3d 1153 (9th Cir. 2002).

Coghlan v. Beta Theta Pi Fraternity, 987 P.2d 300 (Idaho 1999).

Cole v. Richardson, 405 U.S. 676 (1972).

Collier v. Zambito, 807 N.E.2d 254 (N.Y. 2004).

Colorado Nat. Bank of Denver v. Friedman, 846 P.2d 159 (Colo. 1993).

Commodari v. Long Island Univ., 62 Fed. Appx. 28 (2d Cir. 2003).

Commodari v. Long Island Univ., 89 F. Supp.2d 353 (E.D.N.Y. 2000).

Concerned Citizens of Lake Milton, Inc. v. Mahoning County, 1995 WL 574217 3 (Ohio App. 7th Cir. 1995).

Connell v. Higgenbotham, 403 U.S. 207 (1971).

Connick v. Myers, 461 U.S. 138 (1983).

Cordas v. Peerless Transp. Co., 27 N.Y.S.2d198, (N.Y. Ct. Cl. 1941).

Cornelius v. NAACP Legal Def. and Educ. Fund, 473 U.S. 788, 800 (1985).

Crosby v. Florida State Bd., 506 So.2d 490 (1987).

Daniel v. American Bd. of Emergency Med., 988 F. Supp. 127 (W.D.N.Y. 1997).

Davidson v. City of Westminster, 649 P.2d 894 (Cal. 1982).

Davidson v. Univ. of North Carolina Chapel Hill, 543 S.E.2d 920 (N.C. Ct. App. 2001).

Davies v. Barnes, 503 A.2d 93 (Pa. Commw. 1986).

Davies v. Mann, 152 Eng. Rep. 588 (1842).

Davis v. Monroe County Bd. of Educ., 526 U.S. 629 (1999).

Davis v. Southerland, 2004 WL 1230278 (S.D. Tex. 2004).

Davis v. Westwood Group, 652 N.E.2d 567 (Mass. 1995).

Delaney v. Univ. of Houston, 835 S.W.2d 56 (Tex. 1992).

De Stefano v. Wilson, 233 A.2d 682 (N.J. Super. L. Div. 1967).

Dillon v. Legg, 441 P.2d 912 (Cal. 1968).

Dixon v. Alabama State Bd. of Educ., 294 F.2d 150 (5th Cir.1961).

Edgewater Motel, Inc. v. Gatzke, 277 N.W.2d 11 (Minn. 1979).

Eisel v. Bd. of Educ. of Montgomery County, 597 A.2d 447 (Md. 1991).

Bibliography

Eli v. City of New York, 901 N.Y.S.2d 899, (N.Y. App. Div. Kings Cnty. 2009).

Elgin v. Dist. of Columbia, 337 F.2d 152 (D.C. App. 1964).

Englert, Inc. v. LeafGuard USA, Inc., 659 S.E.2d. 496 (S.C. 2008).

Erie R.R. Co. v. Tompkins, 304 U.S. 64 (1938).

Estates of Morgan v. Fairfield Family Counseling Ctr., 77 Ohio St.3d 284 (1997).

Esteban v. Cent. Missouri State Coll., 277 F. Supp. 649 (W.D. Mo. 1967).

Ewing v. California, 538 U.S. 11 (2003).

Farwell v. Keaton, 240 N.W.2d 217 (Mich. 1976).

Feldman v. Ho, 171 F.3d 494 (7th Cir. 1999).

Fitzpatrick v. Universal Technical Inst., Inc., 2009 WL 2476639 (E.D. Pa. 2009).

Flaim v. Med. Coll. of Ohio, 418 F.3d 629 (6th Cir. 2005).

Fleckner v. Dionne, 210 P.2d 530 (Cal. 1949).

Florence v. Goldberg, 375 N.E.2d 763 (N.Y. 1978).

Forsythe County, Georgia v. Nat'l ist Movement, 505 U.S. 123 (1992).

Foster v. Preston Mill Co., 268 P.2d 645 (Wash. 1954).

Franklin v. Gwinnett County. Public Sch.s, 503 U.S. 60 (1992).

Fraser v. United States, 674 A.2d 811 (Conn. 1996).

Frye v. United States, 421 U.S. 542 (1978).

Fuentes v. Shevin, 407 U.S. 67 (1972).

Furek v. The Univ. of Delaware, 594 A.2d 506 (Del. 1991).

Garcetti v. Ceballos, 547 U.S. 410 (2006).

Garofalo v. Lambda Chi Alpha Fraternity, 616 N.W.2d 647 (Iowa 2000).

Gebser v. Lago Vista Indep. Sch. Dist., 524 U.S. 274 (1998).

Gideon v. Wainwright, 372 U.S. 335 (1963).

Gift v. Palmer, 141 A.2d 408 (Pa. 1958).

Goddard v. Boston & Maine R.R. Co., 60 N.E. 486 (Mass. 1901).

Goldbarth v. Kansas State Bd. of Regents, 9 P.3d 1251 (Kan. 2000).

Gomes v. Univ. of Maine System, 365 F. Supp. 2d 6 (D. Me. 2005).

Gonzalez v. Univ. System of New Hampshire, 2005 WL 5308067 (Conn. Super. 2005).

Gordon v. Bridgeport Housing Auth., 544 A.2d 1185 (Conn. 1988).

Gorman v. Univ. of Rhode Island, 837 F.2d 7 (1st Cir. 1988).

Gonzaga Univ. v. Doe, 536 U.S. 273 (2002).

Goss v. Lopez, 419 U.S. 565 (1975).

Gott v. Berea Coll., 161 S.W. 204 (Ky. 1913).

Gragg v. Wichita State, 934 P.2d 121 (Kan. 1997).

Gratz v. Bollinger, 539 U.S. 244 (2003).

Greene v. Texeira, 505 P.2d 1160 (Haw. 1973).

Greenya v. GWU, 512 F.2d 556 (D.C. Cir. 1975).

Griswold v. Conn. 381 U.S. 479 (1965).

Gross v. Family Serv.s Agency and Nova Southeastern Univ., Inc., 716 So.2d 337 (Fla. App. 1998).

Gross v. Sweet, 400 N.E.2d 306 (N.Y. 1979).

Grutter v. Bollinger, 539 U.S. 306 (2003).

Guardians Ass'n v. Civil Serv. Comm'n, 463 U.S. 582 (U.S. 1983).

Guest v. Hansen, 2007 WL 4561104 (N.D.N.Y. 2007).

Hack v. President and Fellows of Yale Coll., 237 F.3d 81 (2d Cir. 2000), *cert. denied,* 534 U.S. 888 (2001).

Bibliography

Hacker v. Hacker, 522 N.Y.S.2d 768 (1987).

Hall v. Hawaii, 791 F.2d 759 (9th Cir. 1986).

Hall v. Med. Coll. of Ohio, 742 F.2d 299 (6th Cir. 1984).

Hamilton v. Regents of the Univ. of California, 293 U.S. 245 (1934).

Hanna v. Plumer, 380 U.S. 460 (1965).

Harlow v. Fitzgerald, 457 U.S. 800 (1982).

Harris v. Showcase Chevrolet, 231 S.W.3d 559 (Tex. App. Dallas 2007).

Havlik v. Johnson & Wales Univ., 509 F.3d 25 (1st Cir. 2007).

Hawkins v. Sarasota County Sch. Bd., 322 F.3d 1279, 1289 (11th Cir. 2003).

Hayden v. Univ. of Notre Dame, 716 N.E.2d 603 (Ind. App. 1999).

Healy v. James, 408 U.S. 169 (1972).

Heigl v. Bd. of Educ., 587 A.2d 423 (Conn. 1991).

Heinz v. Mayer, 425 U.S. 610, 616 (1976).

Hess v. Indiana, 414 U.S. 105, 109 (1973).

Ho v. Univ. of Texas at Arlington, 984 S.W.2d 672 (Tex. App. Amarillo 1998).

Hooper v. North Carolina, 379 F. Supp. 2d 804, 811-812 (M.D.N.C. 2005).

Hu v. American Bar Assn., 568 F. Supp. 2d 959 (N.D. Ill. 2008).

Humphrey v. Memorial Hosp., 239 F.3d 1128 (9th Cir. 2001).

In re Name Change of Handley, 736 N.E.2d 125 (Ohio Prob. 2000).

Ingram v. Pettit, 340 So.2d 922 (Fla. 1976).

InterNat'l Soc'y for Krishna v. Lee, 505 U.S. 672 (1992).

Island City Flying Serv. v. General Elec. Credit Corp., 585 So.2d 274 (Fla. 1991).

Jackson v. Metro. Edison Co., 419 U.S. 345 (1974).

Jain v. Iowa, 617 NW.2d 293 (Iowa 2000).

Janzen v. Atiyeh, 743 P.2d 765 (1987).

Jasko v. F.W. Woolworth Co., 494 P.2d 839 (Colo. 1972).

Johnston v. Joyce, 596 N.Y.2d 625 (N.Y.A.D. 4th Dept. 1993).

Johnson v. Lincoln Christian Coll., 501 N.E.2d 1380 (Ill. App. 4th Dist. 1987).

Johnson v. State, 894 P.2d 1366 (Wash. Ct. App. 1995).

Jones v. Dressel, 623 P.2d 370 (Colo. 1981).

Jordan v. Jordan, 257 S.E.2d 761 (1979).

Joseph v. Bd. of Regents of the Univ. of Wisconsin System, 432 F.3d 746 (7th Cir. 2005).

Joy v. Great Atlantic and Pacific Tea Co., 405 F.2d 464 (4th Cir. 1968).

Kashmiri v. Regents of the Univ. of Calif., 156 Cal.App.4th 809 (Cal. App. 1st Dist. 2007).

Katzenbach v. Morgan, 384 U.S. 641 (1966).

Kemezy v. Peters, 622 N.E.2d 1296 (Ind. 1993).

Keyishian v. Bd. of Regents of Univ. of N.Y., 385 U.S. 589 (1967).

Kimps v. Hill, 546 N.W.2d 151 (1996).

Kline v. 1500 Massachusetts Ave. Apartment Corp., 439 F.2d 477 (D.C. Cir. 1970).

Knoll v. Bd. of Regents of Univ. of Nebraska, 601 N.W.2d 757 (Neb. 1999).

Kobe v. Indus. Acc. Comm'n, 35 Cal. 2d 33 (Cal. 1950).

Kolaniak v. Bd. of Educ., 610 A.2d 193 (Conn. App. 1993).

Kovacs v. Cooper, 336 U.S. 77 (1949).

Lamb's Chapel v. Ctr. Moriches Union Free Sch. Dist., 508 U.S. 384 (1993).

Lara v. Saint John's Univ., 735 N.Y.S.2d 578 (N.Y. App. Div. 2d Dept 2001).

Bibliography

Lemon v. Kurtzman, 403 U.S. 602 (1971).

Lewis v. Wilson, 253 F.3d 1077 (2001).

Lloyd v. Alpha Phi Alpha Fraternity, 1999 WL 47153 (N.D.N.Y. 1999).

Lovell v. City of Griffin, 303 U.S. 444 (1938).

Lunar v. Ohio Dept. of Transp., 572 N.E.2d 208, 210 (Ohio App. 10th Dist. 1989).

Madison, Joint Sch. Dist. v. Wisconsin Employment Relations Comm'n, 429 U.S. 167 (1976).

Marbury v. Madison, 5 U.S. 137 (1803).

Marcus v. St. Paul Fire and Marine Ins. Co., 651 F.2d 379 (5th Cir. 1981).

Marrapese v. State of Rhode Island, 500 F. Supp. 1207 (D. R.I. 1980).

Martin v. Bd. of Instn. of Higher Learning, 933 So.2d 833 (Miss. App. 2008).

Martin v. Herzog, 126 N.E. 814 (N.Y. 1920).

McCain v. Fl. Power Corp., 593 So.2d 500 (Fla. 1992).

McClure v. Fairfield Univ., 2003 WL 21524786 (Conn. Super. 2003).

Midwest Knitting Mills, Inc. v. United States, 950 F.2d 1295 (7th Cir. 1991).

Miguel v. Guess, 51 P.3d 89 (Wash. Ct. App. 2002).

Mississippi Univ. for Women v. Hogan, 458 U.S. 718 (1982).

Molitor v. Kaneland Community Unit Dist., 163 N.E.2d 89 (Ill. 1959).

Monell v. N.Y.C. Dept. of Social Servs., 436 U.S. 658 (1978).

Moody v. Pepsi-Cola Metro. Bottling Co., Inc., 915 F.2d 201 (6th Cir. 1990).

Moran v. Kingdom of Saudi Arabia, 27 F.3d 169 (5th Cir. 1994).

Moransais v. Heathman, 744 So.2d 973 (Fla. 1999).

Morgan v. State, 685 N.E.2d 202 (N.Y. 1997).

Moses v. Diocese of Colo., 863 P.2d 310 (Colo. 1993).

Mullins v. Pine Manor Coll., 449 N.E.2d 331 (Mass. 1983).

Murphy v. Steeplechase Amusement Co., 166 N.E. 173 (N.Y. 1929).

Nally v. Grace Church, 763 P.2d 948 (Cal. 1988).

Nero v. Kansas State Univ., 861 P.2d 768 (Kan. 1993).

New York Assn. of Career Sch.s v. St. Educ. Dept. N.Y., 749 F. Supp 1264 (S.D.N.Y. 1990).

New York Times Co. v. Sullivan, 376 U.S. 254 (1954).

Nichols v. Northeast Louisiana Univ., 729 So. 2d 733 (La. App. 2d Cir. 1999).

Nixon v. Mr. Property Mgmt. Co., Inc., 690 S.W.2d. 546 (Tex. 1985).

N.L.R.B. v. Maine Caterers, Inc. 654 F.2d 131 (1st Cir. 1981).

Nott v. George Washington Univ., No. 05-8503 (D.C. Super. Ct. Oct. 2005), *available at* http://www.bazelon.org/issues/education/incourt/nott/nottcomplaint.pdf.

Nova Southeastern Univ. v. Gross, 758 So.2d 86 (Fla. 2000).

O'Brien v. Cunard S.S. Co., Ltd., 28 N.E. 266 (Mass. 1891).

Oregon v. Mitchell, 400 U.S. 112 (1970).

Pacht v. Morris, 489 P.2d 29 (1971).

Pacific Gas and Elec. Co. v. Public Utils. Com'n of California, 475 U.S. 1, 8 (1986).

Pakett v. The Phillies, L.P., 871 A.2d 304 (Pa. Commw. 2005).

Paladino v. Adelphi, 89 A.D.2d (N.Y. App. Div. 1982).

Palsgraf v. Long Island R.R. Co., 162 N.E. 992d (N.Y. 1928).

Papish v. Bd. of Curators of the Univ. of Mo., 410 U.S. 667 (1973).

Parker v. Bd. of Sup'rs Univ. of Louisiana-Lafayette, 296 Fed. Appx. 414 (5th Cir. 2008).

Bibliography

Parsons v. Jow, 480 P.2d 396 (Wyo. 1971).

Pawlowski v. Delta Sigma Phi, 2007 WL 2363146 (Conn. Super. 2007).

People v. Kelly, 195 Cal. App. 2d 669 (1961).

People v. Superior Court, 49 Cal. Rep. 3d 831 (2006).

Perry v. Sinderman, 408 U.S. 593 (1972).

Peterson v. Ohio Cas. Group, 724 N.W.2d 765 (Neb. 2006).

Peterson v. San Francisco Cmty. Coll., 685 P.2d 1193 (Cal. 1984).

P.G.A. v. Martin, 532 U.S. 661 (2001).

Philip Crosby Assn., Inc. v. St. Bd. of Indep. Coll.s, 506 So.2d 490 (Fla. App. 5th Dist. 1987).

Piazzola v. Watkins, 442 F.2d 284 (5th Cir. 1971).

Pickering v. Bd. of Ed. of Twp. High Sch. Dist. 205 Will County, 391 U.S. 563 (1968).

Pitre v. Employers Liability Assurance Corp., 234 So.2d 847 (La. App. 1st Cir. 1970).

Pitre v. Louisiana Tech Univ., 655 So.2d 659 (La. Ct. App. 1995), *rev'd*, 673 So.2d 585 (La. 1996).

Plano v. Fountain Gate Ministries, 654 S.W.2d 841 (1983).

Porubiansky v. Emory Univ., 275 S.E.2d 163 (Ga. App. 1980).

Poulos v. State of New Hampshire, 345 U.S. 395 (1953).

Powe v. Miles, 407 F.2d 73 (2d Cir. 1962).

Prairie View A&M Univ. of Texas v. Mitchell, 27 S.W.3d 323 (Tex. App. 1st Dist. 2000).

Princeton Univ. v. Schmid, 455 U.S. 100 (1982).

Prostrollo v. Univ. of South Dakota, 507 F.2d 775 (8th Cir. 1974).

Pruneyard Shopping Ctr. v. Robins, 447 U.S. 74 (1980).

Purisch v. Tenn. Tech. Univ., 76 F.3d 1414 (6th Cir. 1996).

Ralphs Grocer Co. v. Workers' Comp. Appeals Bd. 58 Cal. App. 4th 647 (Cal. App. 4th Dist. 1997).

R.A.V. v. City of St. Paul, 505 U.S. 377 (1992).

Regents of the Univ. of California v. Bakke, 438 U.S. 265 (1978).

Regents of the Univ. of Michigan v. Ewing, 474 U.S. 214 (1985).

Rendell-Baker v. Kohn, 457 U.S. 830 (1982).

Rhodes v. Illinois Cent. Gulf R.R., 665 N.E.2d 1260 (Ill. 1996).

Riviello v. Waldron, 391 N.E.2d 1278 (N.Y. 1979).

Roberts v. Indiana Gas and Water Co., 218 N.E.2d 556 (Ind. App. 1966).

Robertson v. State ex rel. Dep't of Planning and Control, 747 So.2d 1276 (La. Ct. App. 1999).

Rodebush By and Through Rodebush v. Okla. Nursing Homes, Ltd., 867 P.2d 1241 (Okla. 1993).

Rodgers v. Kemper Constr. Co., 50 Cal.App.3d 608 (Cal. App. 4th Dist. 1975).

Rodrigues v. Bethlehem Steel Corp., 525 P.2d 669 (Cal. 1974).

San Antonio Ind. Sch. Dist. v. Rodriguez, 411 U.S. 1, 28 (1973).

Rosenberger v. Rector and Visitors of the Univ. of Virginia, 515 U.S. 819 (1995).

Ross v. Creighton Univ., 957 F.2d 410 (7th Cir. 1992).

Roth v. U.S., 354 U.S. 476 (1957).

Rowland v. Christian, 443 P.2d 561 (Cal. 1968).

Russel v. Salve Regina Coll., 890 F.2d 484 (1st Cir. 1989).

Saelzler v. Advanced Group 400, 25 Cal.4th 763 (Cal. 2001).

Bibliography

Saia v. New York, 334 U.S. 558 (1948).

Sandoval v. Bd. of Regents of New Mexico St. Univ., 403 P.2d 699 (N.M. 1965).

Santana v. Rainbow Cleaners, 969 A.2d 653 (R.I. 2009).

Schaer v. Brandeis Univ., 735 N.E.2d 373 (Mass. 2000).

Sch. Bd. of Nassau Cty. v. Arline, 480 U.S. 273 (1987).

Shamloo v. Mississippi State, 620 F.2d 516 (5th Cir. 1980).

Sharkey v. Bd. of Regents of Univ. of Nebraska, 615 N.W.2d 889 (Neb. 2000).

Shin v. Mass. Inst of Tech., 19 Mass. L. Rep. 570 (Mass. Super. 2005).

Shore v. Town of Stonington, 444 A.2d 1379 (Conn. 1982).

Shuttleworth v. City of Birmingham, 394 U.S. 147 (1969).

Skokie v. National Socialist Party, 373 N.E.2d 21 (Ill. 1978).

Slaughter v. Brigham Young Univ., 514 F.2d 622 (10th Cir. 1975).

Smith v. California, 361 U.S. 147 (1959).

Southwest Fla. Water Mgmt. Dist. v. Save the Manatee Club, Inc., 773 So.2d 594 (Fla. 1st DCA 2000).

Southwestern Public Servs. Co. v. Artesia Alfalfa Growers' Assn., 353 P.2d 62 (N.M. 1960).

State v. Ellis, 2006 WL 827376 (Ohio App. 2 Dist. 2006).

State v. Schmid, 423 A.2d 615 (N.J. 1980).

Sterner v. Wesley Coll., Inc., 747 F. Supp. 263 (D. Del. 1990).

Stetson Univ. v. Hunt, 102 So. 637 (Fla. 1925).

Sweatt v. Painter, 339 U.S. 629 (1950).

Sweezy v. New Hampshire, 354 U.S. 234 (1957).

Tanja H. v. Regents of Univ. of Cal., 228 Cal.App.3d 434 (Cal. App. 1st Dist. 1991).

Tarasoff v. Bd. of Regents of the Univ. of Cal., 551 P.2d 334 (Cal. 1976).

Texas v. Johnson, 491 U.S. 392 (1989).

Texas A&M Univ. v. Bading, 236 S.W.3d 801 (Tex. App. Waco Dist. 2007).

Than v. Univ. of Tex. Med. Sch., 188 F. 3d 633 (5th Cir. 1999).

The T. J. Hooper v. Northern Barge Corp., 60 F.2d 737 (2d Cir. 1932).

Thing v. La Chusa, 771 P.2d 814 (Cal. 1989).

Thompson v. Skate America, Inc., 940 S.E.2d 123 (Va. 2001).

Thorne v. Deas, 4 Johns. 84 (N.Y. Supp. 1809).

Tinker v. Des Moines Indep. Cmty. Sch. Dist., 393 U.S. 503 (1969).

Toyosaburo Korematsu v. U.S., 323 U.S. 214 (1944).

Tunkle v. Regents, 383 P.2d 441 (Cal. 1963).

Turner v. Staggs, 510 P.2d 879 (Nev. 1973).

Union Pacific R.R. Co. v. Cappier, 72 Pacific 281 (Kansas 1903).

United States v. Albertini, 472 U.S. 675 (1985).

United States v. Carroll Towing, 159 F.2d 169 (2d Cir. 1947).

United States v. Davis, 442 U.S. 397 (1979).

United States v. Fordice, 505 U.S. 717 (1992).

United States v. Virginia, 518 U.S. 515 (1996).

United States v. Stevens, 130 S.Ct. 1577 (2010).

Univ. of Denver v. Whitlock, 744 P.2d 54 (Colo. 1987).

Univ. of Texas Med. Sch. at Houston v. Than, 901 S.W.2d 926 (Tex. 1995).

Vangsguard v. Progressive Northern Ins. Co., 525 N.W.2d 146 (Wis. App. 1994).

Village of Skokie v. Nat'l Socialist Party of America, 373 N.E.2d 21 (1978).

Bibliography

Virginia v. Black, 538 U.S. 343 (2003).

Virginia v. Hicks, 539 U.S. 113 (2003).

Vulcan Eng'g Co. v. XL Ins. America, Inc., 201 Fed. Appx. 678 (11th Cir. 2006).

Wagner v. InterNat'l Ry., 133 N.E. 437 (N.Y. 1921).

Wallace v. Broyles, 961 S.W.2d 712 (Ark. 1998).

Ward v. K-Mart Corp., 554 N.E.2d 223 (Ill. 1990).

Ward v. Rock Against Racism, 491 U.S. 781 (1989).

Wartski v. C.W. Post Campus of Long Island Univ., 882 N.Y.S.2d 192 (N.Y. App. Div. 2d Dept. 2009).

Washington v. Chapman, 455 U.S. 1 (1982).

Watson v. Duerr, 379 So.2d 1243 (Ala. 1980).

Watts v. Wayne Co. Bd. of Educ., 412 S.E.2d 541 (Ga. App. 1991).

Webb v. Bd. of Trustees of Ball State Univ., 167 F.3d 1146 (7th Cir. 1999).

Webb v Univ. of Utah, 125 P.3d 906 (Utah 2005).

Wells v. City of St. Petersburg, 958 So.2d 1076 (Fla. 2d Dist. Ct. App. 2007).

White v. Burns, 567 A.2d 1195 (Conn. 1990).

White v. Davis, 533 P.2d 222, 227 (Cal. 1975).

Widmar v. Vincent, 454 U.S. 263 (1981).

Wieman v. Updegraff, 344 U.S. 183, 188 (1952).

Williams v. Bd. of Regents of the Univ. System of Georgia, 477 F.3d 1282 (11th Ct. App. 2007).

Williams v. Wendler, 530 F.3d 584 (7th Cir. 2008).

Wisconsin v. Mitchell, 508 U.S. 476, 488 (1993).

Wong v. Regents of Univ. of California, 192 F.3d 807, 817, 819, 823 (9th Cir. 1999).

Wood v. Strickland, 420 U.S. 308, 318 (1975).

Wooley v. Maynard, 319 U.S. 624, 633, 642 (1943).

Wynne v. Tufts Univ. Sch. of Med. I, 932 F.2d 19 (1st Cir. 1991).

Yania v. Bigan, 155 A.2d 343 (Pa. 1959).

Yohn v. Coleman, 639 F. Supp. 2d 776 (E.D. Mich. 2009).

Younger v. Harris, 401 U.S. 36 (1971).

Zumbrun v. Univ. of Southern California, 25 Cal.App.3d 1 (Cal. Ct. App. 1972).

Constitutions, Statutes and Regulations

Constitution

U.S. Const. art. I, § 8.

U.S. Const. amends. I, IV, V, VII, XI, XIV, § 5, XXI.

Federal Acts

Administrative Procedure Act (APA), 5 U.S.C. §§ 551 et seq. (2010).

Americans with Disabilities Act Amendments Act of 2008, 42 U.S.C. §§ 12101–12189 (2010).

Civil Rights Act of 1964, Title VI, 42 U.S.C. 2000(d)–2000(d)(1).

Education Amendments of 1972, Title IX, 20 U.S.C. § 1681(2010).

Family Educational Rights and Privacy Act (FERPA), 20 U.S.C. § 1232(g) (2006).

Health Care and Education Reconciliation Act, Pub. L. No. 111-152, §§ 2201–2213, 124 Stat. 1029 (2010).

Health Insurance Portability and Accountability Act of 1996 (HIPAA), 42 U.S.C.A. §§ 201 *et seq.* (1996).

Bibliography

Jeanne Clery Disclosure of Campus Security Policy and Campus Crime Statistics Act (Clery Act), 20 U.S.C. § 1092(f) (2006).

No Child Left Behind Act, Title IV, Part A, 20 U.S.C § 6319 (2010).

Safe and Drug Free School and Communities Act, 20 U.S.C. §§ 7101–04 (2001).

Sherman Antitrust Act, 15 U.S.C. §§ 1–7 (2006).

Volunteer Protection Act of 1997. 42 U.S.C. § 14501 (1997).

U.S. Code

9 U.S.C. § 9 (2010).

20 U.S.C. § 1681 (2010).

20 U.S.C. § 1681(a)(1) (2006).

20 U.S.C. § 1681(a)(3).

20 U.S.C. § 1681(a)(4).

20 U.S.C. § 1681(a)(5).

20 U.S.C. § 1681(a)(6)(A).

20 U.S.C. § 1681(a)(8).

28 U.S.C. § 1331 (2007).

28 U.S.C. § 1332 (2007).

28 U.S.C. § 1367 (2007).

28 U.S.C. §§ 1441 (2007).

28 U.S.C. § 1446 (2007).

29 U.S.C. § 791.

29 U.S.C. § 794(a) (2006).

42 U.S.C. § 1981.

42 U.S.C. § 1983.

42 U.S.C. §§ 12131–12134, 12181–12189.

42 U.S.C. § 12132 (2006).

Code of Federal Regulations

28 C.F.R. Part 35 (2010).

28 C.F.R. § 35.104.

28 C.F.R. § 36.301–10.

28 C.F.R. § 36.401–406.

34 C.F.R. § 75.740 (2010).

34 C.F.R. Parts 100–106.

34 C.F.R. Parts 104–110 (2010).

34 C.F.R. § 104.3(j).

34 C.F.R. § 104.3(k)(3) (2009).

34 C.F.R. § 104.3(*l*)(3) (2009).

34 C.F.R. § 104.3(*l*)(4).

34 C.F.R. § 104.42(a)–(b) (2010).

34 C.F.R. § 104.42(b)(4)–104.42(c).

34 C.F.R. § 104.43.

34 C.F.R. § 106.15(d) (2010).

34 C.F.R. § 106.286.

34 C.F.R. Part 668 (2010).

34 C.F.R. § 668.46 (2010).

Bibliography

Federal Rules of Practice

Fed. R. App. Prac. 4(a).

Fed. R. Civ. P. 3.

Fed. R. Civ. P. 7(a)(1).

Fed. R. Civ. P. 8 (2007).

Fed. R. Civ. P. 8(a)(1)–(3).

Fed. R. Civ. P. 8(b)(1).

Fed. R. Civ. P. 8(c)(1).

Fed. R. Civ. P. 12(b)(6).

Fed. R. Civ. P. 38(a), (d).

Fed. R. Civ. P. 50(a)(2).

Fed. R. Civ. P. 56.

Fed. R. Civ. P. 58.

Fed. R. Civ. P. 58(b)(1)(A) (2007).

Fed. R. Civ. P. 59.

S.Ct. R. 10-16.

1st Cir. R. 36(b)(2).

State Laws and Rules

Colo. Rev. Stat. §§ 201–207 (2010).

F.S.A. §§ 394.451 *et seq.*

F.S.A. § 429.297 (2006).

F.S.A. §§ 440.01–440.60 (2010).

F.S.A. § 627.736(10)(a) (2010).

F.S.A. § 768.13 (2004).

F.S.A. § 768.36 (2002).

F.S.A. § 768.81 (2006).

Fla. Arbitration Code §§ 682.01–682.22 (2003).

Fla. R. Civ. P. 1.710 (2000).

Haw. Rev. Stat. § 662-15 (2010).

Idaho Code Ann. § 6-904 (2010).

Ill. Admin. Code tit. 29, pt. §§ 305.10–305.110 (2009).

Md. Code, State Gov't §§ 12-104–12-110 (2010).

Mass. Gen. Laws ch. 15A, § 22 (2010).

Mass. Gen. Laws ch. 251, §§ 1–19 (2010).

Mass. Gen. Laws ch. 258, § 10 (2010).

Minn. Code § 3.736 (2010).

Minn. Stat. § 604.01 (2008).

Mont. Code § 27-1-1102 (2010).

N.Y. C.P.L.R. 1411.

Ohio Rev. Code § 2305.51 (1999).

Tex. Civ. Prac. & Rem. Code § 84.006 (2010).

Tex. Civ. Prac. & Rem. Code § 102.003 (2010).

Va. Code § 8.01-195.3 (2010).

Va. Code § 23-9.2:8 (2007).

Va. Code § 23-9.2:8 (2010).

Va. Code § 23-9.2:10 (2008).

Bibliography

Vt. Stat. tit. 12 § 519 (1967).

Uniform Laws

U.C.C. §§ 2-102–725 (2002).

LAW REVIEWS, LAW JOURNALS, AND OTHER JOURNALS

Kenneth S. Abraham, *What Is a Tort Claim? An Interpretation of Contemporary Tort Reform*, 51 Md. L. Rev. 172 (1992).

John M. Adler, *Relying Upon the Reasonableness of Strangers: Some Observations About the Current State of Common Law Affirmative Duties to Aid or Protect Others*, 1991 Wis. L. Rev. 867 (1991).

Hazel Beh, *Student versus University: The University's Implied Obligations of Good Faith and Fair Dealing*, 59 Md. L.R. 183 (2000).

Robert Bickel, Susan Brinkley & Wendy White, *Seeing Past Privacy: Will the Development and Application of CCTV and Other Video Security Technology Compromise an Essential Constitutional Right in a Democracy, or Will the Courts Strike a Proper Balance?*, 33 Stetson L. Rev. 299 (2003).

Francis H. Bohlen, *The Moral Duty to Aid Others As a Basis of Tort Liability*, 56 U. Pa. L. Rev. 316 (1908).

Edwin M. Borchard, *Governmental Liability and Tort*, 34 Yale L.J. 129 (1924).

Valerie Brown, *A Comparative Analysis of College Autonomy in Selected States*, 60 West's Ed. L. Rep. 299 (1990).

Cheryl A. Cameron, Laura E. Meyers & Steven G. Olswang, *Academic Bills of Rights: Conflict in the Classroom*, 31 J.C. & U.L. 243 (2005).

Richard A. Epstein, *A Theory of Strict Liability*, 2 J. Leg. Stud. 151 (1973).

John T. Hall & Rowan Ferguson, *Case Study: University of Anyplace: Strategic Legal Risk Review*, 27 J. C. & U. L. 119 (2000).

James A. Henderson, Jr., *Process Constraints in Tort*, 67 Cornell L. Rev. 901 (1982).

William P. Hoye & Gary M Rhodes, *An Ounce of Prevention Is Worth the Life of a Student: Reducing Risk in International Programs*, 27 J.C. & U.L. 151 (2000).

M. P. Koss, C. A. Gidycz,, & N. Wisniewski, *The Scope of Rape: Incidence and Prevalence of Sexual Aggression and Victimization in a National Sample of Higher Education Students*, 55 Journal of Consulting and Clinical Psychology 162 (1987).

Peter F. Lake, *Common Law Duty in Negligence Law: The Recent Consolidation of a Consensus on the Expansion of Analysis of Duty and the New Conservative Liability Limiting Use of Policy Considerations*, 34 S.D. L. Rev. 1503 (1997).

Peter F. Lake, *Recognizing the Importance of Remoteness to the Duty to Rescue*, 46 DePaul L. Rev. 315 (1997).

Peter F. Lake, *Still Waiting: The Slow Evolution of the Law in Light of the Ongoing Student Suicide Crisis*, 34 J.C. & U.L. 253 (2008).

Peter Lake & Nancy Tribbensee, *The Emerging Crisis of College Student Suicide: Law and Policy Responses to Serious Forms of Self-Inflicted Injury*, 32 Stetson L. Rev. 125 (2002).

William M. Landes & Richard A. Posner, *Salvors, Finders, Good Samaritans and Other Rescuers: An Economic Study of Law and Altruism*, 7 J. Leg. Stud. 83 (1978).

George F. Loewenstein et al., *Risk as Feelings* 127 Psychological Bulletin 2, 267 (American Psychological Assn. 2001).

Ian Roderick Macneil, *The Many Futures of Contract*, 47 S. Cal. L. Rev. 691 (1974).

Wex Malone, *The Genesis of Wrongful Death*, 17 Stan. L. Rev. 1043 (1965).

Robert B. Moberly, *Ethical Standard for Court-Appointed Mediators and Florida's Mandatory Mediation Experiment*, 21 Fla. St. U. L. Rev. 702 (1994).

Clarence Morris, *Custom and Negligence*, 42 Colum. L. Rev. 1147 (1942).

Laura Rothstein, *Disability Law Issues for High Risk Students: Addressing Violence and Disruption*, 35 J.C. & U.L 3 (2009).

Michael J. Saks, *Do We Really Know Anything About the Behavior of the Tort Litigation System-And Why Not?* 140 U. Pa. L. Rev. 1147 (1992).

Bibliography

Joseph Sanders & Craig Joyce, *Off to the Races: The 1980s Tort Crisis and the Law Reform Process* 27 Hous. L. Rev. 201 (1990).

Edward N. Stoner II & John Wesley Lowery, *Navigating Past the "Spirit of Insubordination": A Twenty-First Century Model Student Conduct Code with a Model Hearing Script* 31 J.C. & U.L. 1 (2004).

Joshua A. Sussberg, *Shattered Dreams, Hazing in College Athletics*, 24 Cardozo L. Rev. 1421 (2003).

Henry Weschler, et al., *College Binge Drinking in the 1990s: A Continuing Problem, Results of the Harvard School of Public Health 1999 College Alcohol Study*, 48 J. Am. Coll. Health 5 (March 2000).

Henry Weschler, et al., *Trends in College Binge Drinking During a Period of Increased Prevention Efforts: Findings From 4 Harvard School of Public Health College Alcohol Study Surveys: 1993-2001*, 50 J. Am. Coll. Health 5, 203 (2002).

Henry Weschler, et al., *Underage College Students' Drinking Behavior, Access to Alcohol, and the Influence of Deterrence Policies*, 50 J. Am. Coll. Health 223 (2002).

M. D. Wood, W. DeJong, A. M. Fairlie, D. Lawson, A. M. Lavigne, & F. Cohen, *Common Ground: An Investigation of Environmental Management, Alcohol Prevention Initiative in a College Community*, J. Stud. Alcohol & Drugs, Supplement 16, 96-105 (2009).

Other Authority

1940 Statement of principles on academic freedom and tenure, in *AAUP Policy Documents and Reports* (10th ed. 2006), *available at* http://www.aaup.org/AAUP/pubsres/policydocs/contents/1940statement.htm.

AAUP, *Academic Bill of Rights 2006*, http://www.aaup.org/AAUP/GR/Archive/camp/ABOR/aborstateleg.htm (last updated April 2007).

ABA Coalition for Justice, *Judicial Selection: The Process of Choosing Judges* (June 2008), http://www.abanet.org/justice/pdf/judicial_selection_roadmap.pdf.

Accepted (Universal 2006) (motion picture).

American Arbitration Association. *Commercial Arbitration Rules and Mediation*, M-4 (2007), http://www.adr.org/sp.asp?id=22440.

American Bar Association Model Rules of Professional Conduct Model R. Prof. Conduct 3.4(a, b, d) (ABA 2008).

American College Personnel Association, www2.myacpa.org (last visited Aug. 30, 2010).

American College Personnel Association and National Association of Student Personnel Administrators, *Professional Competency Areas for Student Affairs Practitioners* (July 24, 2010) *available at* http://www.naspa.org/programs/prodev/Professional_Competencies.pdf.

American Federation of Teachers, *University Professional of Illinois, Local 4100: About the AFT,* http://www.ilaft.org/041/index/cfm?action=cat&categoryID=4651bda0-3be6-49f9-b7b3-7ee2c2da570e (last visited Aug. 27, 2010).

American Psychiatric Association, *College Mental Health and Confidentiality* (June 2009), http://www.psych.org/Departments/EDU/Library/APAOfficialDocumentsandRelated/ResourceDocuments/200905.aspx.

American Tort Reform Association (ATRA), www.atra.org (last visited Aug. 30, 2010).

Animal House (National Lampoon 1978) (motion picture).

Answers Corp., *Answers.com: Tort*, htt://www.answers.com/topic/tort (last visited Aug. 15, 2010).

Encyclopedia Britannica, *available at* http://www.britannica.com/EBchecked/topic/156569/delict (last visited Aug. 11, 2010).

Association of Governing Bds. of Univ. and Colleges, *The State of Enterprise Risk Management at Colleges and Universities Today* (June 25, 2009), *available at* www.agb.org.

Association for Student Conduct Administration, www.theasca.org (last visited Aug. 20, 2010).

ATRA, *Punitive Damages Reform,* http://www.atra.org/issues/index.php?issue=7343 (last visited Aug. 20, 2010).

Bibliography

Paul Basken, *New Grilling of For-Profits Could Turn Up the Heat for All of Higher Education*, Chronicle of Higher Education (June 22, 2010) *available at* http://chronicle.com/article/New-Grilling-of-For-Profits/66020.

Black Sheep, *The Choice Is Yours* (Mercury/PolyGram 1991).

The Breakfast Club (Universal Studios 1985) (motion picture).

Brown University, *Brown University Program in Liberal Medical Education, Academic Affairs Policies Handbook* (1994), *available at* http://bms.brown.edu/plme/current/handbook/PLME_Handbook_prior_2007.pdf.

Brown University, *An Educational Blueprint for Brown Medical School, available at* http://med.brown.edu/download/curriculum/EducationalBlueprint.pdf.

Webinar Recording: Tim Burke, *Christian Legal Society v. Martinez* (Stetson Univ Coll L. May 4, 2009) (on file with Center for Excellence in Higher Education Law and Policy).

Charlie Brown: It's the Great Pumpkin, Charlie Brown (CBS Oct. 27, 1966).

Chronicle of Higher Education, *Criminal Charges Filed in Alleged Fraternity Hazing at Penn* (Aug. 31, 2006), *available at* http://wiredcampus.chronicle.com/article/Criminal-Charges-Filed-in/37502/.

Chronicle of Higher Education, *Parents Win Settlement for Son's Death in Hazing* (July 10, 1991), *available at* http://chronicle.com/article/Parents-Win-Settlement-for/87535/.

Raven Clabough, *Anti-Bullying Legislation in Massachusetts*, New American (May 4, 2010), *available at* http://www.thenewamerican.com/index.php/culture/education/3468-anti-bully-legislation-in-massachusetts.

The College of Davidson and Davie Counties (DCCC), http://www.davidsonccc.edu/studentlife/campus_security.htm (last visited Aug. 21, 2010).

Committee of Sponsoring Organizations of the Treadway Commission, *Enterprise Risk Management – Integrated Framework: Executive Summary* (Sept. 2004), *available at* http://www.coso.org/Publications/ERM/COSO_ERM_ExecutiveSummary.pdf.

David Horowitz Freedom Center, http://www.horowitzfreedomcenter.org (last visited Aug 20, 2010).

Gene Deisinger, *Best Practices in Campus Threat Assessment & Management* (2009), *available at* http://www.law.stetson.edu/tmpl/academics/helps/conf/conf-sub.aspx?id=7325.

William DeJong, *Experience in Effective Prevention* (2007), *available at* http://higheredcenter.org/files/product/effective-prevention.pdf.

William DeJong, *Problem Analysis: The First Step in Prevention Planning* (2009), *available at* http://www.higheredcenter.org/files/product/problem-analysis.pdf.

Darby Dickerson & Peter F. Lake, *Alcohol and Campus Risk Management.* Campus Activities Programming, Vol. 18 (October 2006), *available at* SSRN: http://ssrn.com/abstract=1097120.

Darby Dickerson, *The Millennial Brain and Risk*, Campus Activities Programming, Vol. 10 (November 2008), *available at* SSRN: http://ssrn.com/abstract=1300625.

Sam Dillon, *Drilling Down on the Budget, Student Loans*, N.Y Times (Feb. 26, 2009), *available at* http://www.nytimes.com/2009/02/27/Washington/27web-edu.html.

Diane Drysdale, William Modzeleski & Andre Simons, *Campus Attacks: Targeted Violence Affecting Institutions of Higher Education* (2010), *available at* http://www2.ed.gov/admins/lead/safety/campus-attacks.pdf.

F Troop: Don't Look Now, One of Our Cannons Is Missing (Warner Brothers, Sept. 21, 1965).

Paul Fain, *Budget Cuts Intensify Identity Crisis at Washington's Flagship Campus*, Chronicle of Higher Education (Aug. 29, 2010), *available at* http://jobs.chronicle.com/article/Budget-Cuts-Intensify-Identity/124162/.

Federal Judicial Center, *How the Federal Courts Are Organized: Federal judges and how they get appointed*, http://www.fjc.gove/federal/courts.nsf/autofram!openform&nav=menu1&page=/federal/courts.nsf/page/183 (last visited Aug. 10, 2010).

Bibliography

Federalist Papers, *available at* http://thomas.loc.gov/home/histdox/fedpapers. html#skip_menu (The Library of Congress).

Stanley Fish, *The Ontology of Plagiarism: Part Two,* N.Y. Times Blog (Aug. 16, 2010), http://opinionator.blogs.nytimes.com/2010/08/16/the-ontology-of-plagiarism-part-two/?hp.

Bonnie S. Fisher, Francis T. Cullen, & Michael G. Turner, *The Sexual Victimization of College Women,* National Institute of Justice (2000), *available at* http://www.ojp.usdoj.gov/nij.

Florida Bar Association, *Rules Regulating the Florida Bar: Rule 4-1.5 Fees and Costs for Legal Services* (Feb. 1 2010), *available at* http://www.floridabar.org/divexe/rrtfb.nsf/FV/A8644F215162F9DE85257164004C0429.

Thomas Frank, *Campus Security Flaws a Pattern in Slayings*, USA Today (June 12, 2007), *available at* http://www.usatoday.com/news/nation/2007-06-12-campus-security-flaws_N.htm.

Frasier (NBC, Sept. 16, 1993–May 13, 2004).

Foundation for Individual Rights in Education, *FIRE: Defending Individual Rights in Higher Education*, http://www.thefire.org/spotlight/ (last visited Aug. 27, 2010).

Ga. Sen. Res. 661 (2003) *available at* http://www.legis.state.ga.us/legis/2003_04/fulltext/sr661.htm.

Scott H. Greenfield, ESQ., *In Defense of the Socratic Method (Update)*, Simple Justice: A New York Criminal Defense Blog, (May 11, 2009), http://blog.simplejustice.us/2009/05/11/in-defense-of-the-socratice-method.aspx.

Justin Hamilton, *Proposed Rule Links Federal Student Aid to Loan Repayment Rates and Debt-to-Earnings Levels for Career College Graduates* (July 23, 2010), http://www.ed.gov/news/press-releases/proposed-rule-links-federal-student-aid-loan-repayment-rates-and-debt-earnings.

Justin Hamilton, *Obama Administration Proposes Student Aid Rules to Protect Borrowers and Taxpayers; Key Elements of Gainful Employment on a Separate Track* (June 16, 2010), http://www.ed.gov/news/student-aid-rules-protect-borrowers-and-taxpayers.

History of the World: Part 1 (Brooksfilms 1981) (motion picture).

Eric Hoover, *Police in the Dorms: Student Safety or Privacy Infringement?*, Chronicle of Higher Education (July 28, 2008), *available at* http://chronicle.com/article/Polic-in-the-Dorms-Studen/27059.

David Horowitz, *After the Academic Bill of Rights*, Chronicle of Higher Education (Nov. 10, 2006), *available at* http://chronicle.com/article/After-the-Academic-Bill-of-/2767.

The Huffington Post, *Nancy Grace Interview Contributed to Melinda Duckett Suicide, Professor Says* (Dec. 6, 2009), http://www.huffingtonpost.com/2009/12/06/nancy-grace-interveiw-con_n_381846.html.

Billy Idol, *White Wedding* (Chrysalis Records 1982).

JEOPARDY (Sony Pictures International 2010).

Interview with David Lisak, Ph.D. & Peter Lake, JD, *Myths That Make It Hard To Stop Campus Rape*, NPR (Mar. 4, 2010), transcript *available at* http://www.npr.org/templates/transcript/transcrip.php?storyId=124272157.

Scott Jaschik, *More Criticism of Academic Bill of Rights,* Inside Higher Ed. (Jan. 9, 2006), http://www.insidehighered.com/news/2006/01/09/resolutions.

The JED Foundation, http:// www.jedfoundation.org (last visited Aug. 14, 2010).

Joe Versus the Volcano (Warner Brothers 1990) (motion picture).

Judge David L. Bazelon Center for Mental Health Law, *Supporting Students: A Model Policy for Colleges and Universities* (May, 15 2007), *available at* http://bazelon.org.gravitatehosting.com/LinkClick/aspx?fileticket=2sA8atOxlT0%3d&tabid=225.

Audrey Williams June, *Southern Association Strips 2 Black Colleges of Accreditation*, Chronicle of Higher Education (Jan. 3, 2003), *available at* http://chronicle.com/article/Souther-Association-Strips/23712.

Justice Delayed 43 Years, Extension of Remarks, 99th Cong. 1st Sess., 131 Cong. Rec. E468 (Feb. 19, 2985).

Heather M. Karjane, Bonnie S. Fisher, & Francis T. Cullen, *Sexual Assault on*

Campus: What Colleges and Universities Are Doing About It, National Institute of Justice (Dec. 2005), *available at* www.ojp.usdoj.gov/nij.

Eric Kelderman, *Credit Hours Should Be Worth the Cost, House Panel Members Say,* Chronicle of Higher Education (June 17, 2010), *available at* http://chronicle.com/article/Credit-Hours-Should-Be-Wort/65986.

Eric Kelderman, *Universities Sue Accreditor for Putting Their Pharmacy Programs on Probation,* Chronicle of Higher Education (Mar. 27, 2009), *available at* http://chronicle.com/article/Universitities-Sue-Accreditor/47138.

Josh Keller, *California's Budget Problems Leave Community Colleges Holding IUO's,* Chronicle of Higher Education (Mar. 6, 2009), *available at* http://chronicle.com/article/Californias-Budget-Problem/34143/.

Josh Keller, *Thousands Protest Budget Cuts on University of California Campuses,* Chronicle of Higher Education (Sept. 24, 2009), *available at* http://chronicle.com/article/Thousands-Protest-Budget-Cuts/48611/.

Josh Keller, *U. of California Budget Crises, Some Faculty Members See a Cover-Up,* Chronicle of Higher Education (Sept. 22, 2009), *available at* http://chronicle.com/article/In-U-of-California-Budget/48571/.

Josh Keller, *University of California Panel Offers a Timid Response to Budget Crisis,* Chronicle of Higher Education (Mar. 23, 2010), *available at* http://chronicle.com/article/U-of-California-Panel-Offers/64810/?sid=at&utm_source=at&utm_medium=en.

Mark Kernes, *Stagliano Obscenity Trial: The Post-Game Wrap-up*, AVN Media Network (Aug. 5, 2010), *available at* http://news.avn.com/articles/Stagliano-Obscenity-Trial-The-Post-Game-Wrap-Up-406388.html.

Peter Lake, *What's Next for Private Universities? Accountability*, Chronicle of Higher Education (Dec. 5, 2010), *available at* http://chronicle.com/article/Whats-Next-for-Private/125599/.

Peter Lake, *Student-Privacy Rules Show a Renewed Trust in Colleges*, Chronicle of Higher Education (Feb. 6, 2009), *available at* http://chronicle.com/article/Student-Privacy-Rules-Show-/20332.

Peter F. Lake, *Will Your College Be Sued for Educational Malpractice?* Chronicle of Higher Education (Aug. 11, 2009), *available at* http://chronicle.com/article/Education-Malpractice-Ma/47980/.

Lambda Legal, www.lambdalegal.org (last visited Aug. 28, 2010).

Linda Langford, *Preventing Violence and Promoting Safety in Higher Education Settings: Overview of a Comprehensive Approach* (Feb. 2004), *available at* http://www.higheredcenter.org/services/publications/preventing-violence-and-promoting-safety-higher-education-settings-overview-co.

Linda Langford and William DeJong, *Strategic Planning for Prevention Professionals on Campus*, 2 (2008), *available at* http://www.higheredcenter.org/services/publications/stategic-planning-prevention-professionals-campus.

Graham Larkin, *What's Not to Like About the Academic Bill of Rights?* (Sept. 22, 2004), *available at* http://www.aaup-ca.org/Larkin_abor.html.

Michael O. Leavitt, Margaret Spellings & Alberto R. Gonzalez, *Report to the President on Issues Raised by the Virginia Tech Tragedy* (June 13, 2007), *available at* http://www.hhs.gov.vtreport.html.

Sara Lipka, *Discipline Goes on Trial at Colleges,* Chronicle of Higher Education (March 27, 2009), *available at* http://chronicle.com/article/Discipline-Goes-on-Trial-at/30030/.

Sara Lipka *Ties Between Colleges and Students Increasingly Look Like Contracts,* Chronicle of Higher Education (June 29, 2010), *available at* http://www.chronicle.com/article/Ties-Between-CollegesS/66088/.

Sara Lipka, *U. of Virginia Abandons Proposed Student Background Checks in Favor of Stricter Self-Disclosure,* Chronicle of Higher Education (Aug. 10, 2010), *available at* http://chronicle.com/article/U-of-Virginia-Abandons-Pro/123870/.

Sara Lipka *U. of Virginia President Meets With Governor to Push for Access to Law-Enforcement Records,* Chronicle of Higher Education (May 12, 2010), *available at* http://chronicle.com/article/A-Call-for-Access-To-Studen/65482.

Sara Lipka, *Watchdog Group Proposes Stricter Disclosure Requirement for Sexual-Assault Cases,* Chronicle of Higher Education (April 15, 2010), *available at*

Bibliography

http://chroncile.com/article/Watchdog-Group-Proposes-Str/65143.

David Lisak, Ph.D., *Understanding the Predatory Nature of Sexual Violence*, Univ. of Mass. Boston, *available at* http://www2.ucsc.edu/rape-prevention/pdfs/PredatoryNature.pdf.

Lord of the Rings (New Line Cinema 2002) (motion picture).

Mad Men (AMC 2007).

Jonnelle Marte, *New Rules for Loans*, Wall Street J. (July 18, 2010), *available at* http://online.wsj.com/article/SB127940788035718231.html.

The Matrix (Warner Bros. 1999) (motion picture).

Steve McDonald, *The Fundamentals of Fundamental FERPA,* (Feb. 21, 2010) *available at* http://www.law.stetson.edu/tmpl/academics/helps/conf/conf-sub.aspx?id=10813.

Beth McMurtrie, *College Settles Suit by 3 Students over '98 Attack in Guatemala*, Chronicle of Higher Education (July 5, 2002), *available at* http://chronicle.com/daily/2002/07/2002070502n.htm.

Beth McMurtrie, *Southern Accrediting Group Penalizes 21 Colleges*, Chronicle of Higher Education (Jan. 11, 2002), *available at* http://chronicle.com/article/Souther-Accrediting-Group-/12176.

Michigan Judicial Institute, *Your Guide to the Michigan Courts: A Quick Reference Guide to the Court System*, http://courts.michigan.gov/plc/AccessMichCourts.pdf (last visited Aug. 10, 2010).

Peter Monaghan, *Dealing With Bullies*, Chronicle of Higher Education (Sept. 12, 2006), *available at* http://chronicle.com/article/Dealing-wth-bullies/117964.

Mothers Against Drunk Driving, http://www.madd.org/Drunk-Driving/Drunk-Driving/Laws.aspx (last visited Aug. 5, 2010).

Tessa Muggeride, *ASU Settlement Ends in $850,000 Payoff,* State Press (Feb. 3 2009), http://www.statepress.com/archive/node/4020.

National Association of College and University Attorneys, *History and General Information* (2010) *available at* http://www.nacua.org/aboutnacua/index.asp.

National Association of College and University Business Officers and the Association of Governing Boards of Universities and Colleges, *Meeting the Challenges of Enterprise Risk Management in Higher Education* (2007), *available at* http://www.uncop.edu/riskmgt/erm/documents/agb_nacubo_hied.pdf.

National Association of Student Personnel Administrators, http://www.naspa.org/ (last visited Aug. 30, 2010).

National Center on Addiction and Substance Abuse at Columbia University (CASA), *Wasting the Best and the Brightest: Substance Abuse at America's Colleges and Universities* (Mar. 2007), *available at* http://www.casacolumbia.org/absolutenm/articlefiles/380-WastingtheBestandtheBrightest.pdf.

National Institute on Alcohol Abuse and Alcoholism (NIAAA), *A Call to Action: Changing the Culture of Drinking at U.S. Colleges* (2002), *available at* http://www.collegedrinkingprevention.gov/NIAAACollegeMaterial/TaskForce/TaskForce_Toc.aspx.

New York State Unified Court System, *Court Structure: Civil Court Structure*, http://www.courts.state.ny.us/courts/structure.shtml (last visited Aug. 9, 2004).

Office of Civil Rights, *Dear Colleague Letter* (April 4, 2011), *available at* http://www2.ed.gov/about/offices/list/ocr/letters/colleague-201104.pdf.

Robert M. O'Neil, *Colleges Face Ominous New Pressures on Academic Freedom*, Chronicle of Higher Education (Feb. 8, 2008), *available at* http://chronicle.com/article/Colleges-Face-Ominous-New-P/14752/#top.

Governor Deval Patrick, *Governor Patrick Signs Landmark Anti-Bullying Legislation* (May 3, 2010) http://www.mass.gov/?pageID=gov3pressrelease&L=1&10=Home&sid=Agov3&b=pressrelease&f=050310_anti_bullying&csid=Agov3.

Mary Pilon, *Student-Loan Debt Surpasses Credit Cards*, Wall Street J. (Aug. 9, 2010), *available at* http://blogs.wsj.com/economics/2010/08/09/student-loan-debt-surpasses-credit-cards/.

Bibliography

Julia Preston, *Lawyers Back Creating New Immigration Courts,* N.Y. Times (Feb. 8, 2010), *available at* http://www.nytimes.com/2010/02/09/us/09immig.html.

Pretty in Pink (Paramount Pictures 1986) (motion picture).

Real World (MTV 1992-2010).

Salvador Dali Museum, Inc., *The Dali Museum* (2010), http://www.salvadordali-museum.org/collection/collection_highlights.html.

Peter Schmidt, *AAUP Votes to Sanction Antioch U. and Censure Two Other Institutions,* Chronicle of Higher Education (June 13, 2010), *available at* http://chronicle.com/article/AAUP-Votes-to-Sanction-Antioch/65930/.

Security On Campus, Inc., http://www.securityoncampus.org (last visited August 18, 2010).

Security on Campus, Inc., *Campus Sexual Assault Free Environment (SAFE) Blueprint – 2010: Proposed Enhancements to the Federal Jeanne Clery Act and Title IX, available at* http://www.securityoncampus.org/index.pfp?option=com_content&view=article&id=2048:campus-sexual-assault-free-environment-safe-blueprint-2010&catid=58:federallegislation (last visited Aug. 21, 2010).

Lauren Sieben, *Education Dept. Issues New Guidance for Sexual-Assault Investigations*, Chronicle of Higher Education (April 4, 2011), *available at* http://chronicle.com/article/Education-Dept-Issues-New/127004/?sid=at&utm_source=at&utm_medium=en#.

Stetson Univ. Coll of Law, *Three Educators Receive Stetson Law's Facilitator Award* (March 2, 2009), http://www.law.stetson.edu/tmpl/news/article/aspx?id=5954.

Gene Stout, *Gallagher Tosses Out Observations While Throwing Food* (Aug. 21, 1987), http://www.seatlepi.com/archives/1987/8701220487.asp.

Students for Academic Freedom, *The Academic Bill of Rights* (2007), *available at* http://www.studentsforacademicfreedom.org.

Supreme Court Committee on Standard Jury Instructions, *Florida Standard Jury Instructions in Civil Cases* § 4.1 (2001), http://www.flcourts18.org/PDF/civil.pdf.

Texas A&M Univ., Dept. of Student Activities, *Letter from the Director* (Aug. 30, 2010), *available at* http://studentactivities.tamu.edu/orgmanual/stuact.

Nancy Tribbensee, *Faculty Adviser, Beware: You May Be Liable,* Chronicle of Higher Education (June 25, 2004), *available at* http://chronicle.com/article/Faculty-Advisor-Beware-Yo/29646.

Nancy E. Tribbensee & Steven J. McDonald, *FERPA and Campus Safety*, 5 NACUA Notes 4 (Aug. 6, 2007), *available a*t http://www.nacua.org/documents/ferpa1.pdf.

Don Troop, *Will a New Federal Rule Do the Trick?,* Chronicle of Higher Education (June 6, 2010), *available at* http://chronicle.com/article/New-Rule-to-Curb-Textbook-C/65788/.

Jonathan Turley, *Torti Tort: California Supreme Court Rules Against Good Samaritan* (Dec. 19, 2008), *available at* http://jonathanturley.org/2008/12/19/torti-tort-california-supreme-court-rules-against-good-samaritan.

United Educators Insurance, https://www.ue.org/home/aspx (last visited Aug. 2010).

United States Courts, *Bankruptcy Courts,* http://www.uscourts.gov/FederalCourts/UnderstandingtheFederalCourts/BankruptcyCourts.aspx (last visited Aug. 10, 2010).

United States Courts, *Jurisdiction of the Federal Courts,* http://www.uscourts.gov/FederalCourts/UnderstandingtheFederalCourts/Jurisdiction.aspx (last visited Aug. 10, 2010).

U.S. Dep't of Health and Human Services, *Office for Civil Rights*, http://www.hhs.gov/ocr/ (last visited Aug. 10, 2010).

U.S. Dep't of Educ., *Database of Accredited Postsecondary Institutions and Programs*, http://www.ope.ed.gov/accreditation (last visited Aug. 8, 2010).

U.S. Dep't of Educ., Office for Civil Rights, *The Civil Rights of Students with Hidden Disabilities Under Section 504 of the Rehabilitation Act of 1973* (Jan. 1, 1995), *available at* http://www2.ed.gov/about/offices/list/ocr/docs/hq5269.html.

Bibliography

U.S. Dep't of Educ., Office for Civil Rights (OCR), *Letter to Bluffton University in California* (Dec. 22, 2004), *available at* http://www.bazelon.org/Link-Click.aspx?fileticket=LWFnT1VirFU%3D&tabid=313.

U.S. Dep't of Educ., Office for Civil Rights (OCR), *Letter to Woodbury University in California* (June, 29, 2001), *available at* http://ahead-lists.org/down-loads/training/lissner_handouts/J-psych)%20Woodbury%20University.rtf.

U.S. Dep't of Educ., Office of Special Education and Rehabilitative Services, *Questions and Answers on Individualized Education Programs (IEPs), Evaluation, and Reevaluations* (June 2010), *available at* http://www2.ed.gov/policy/speced/guid/idea/iep--qa-2010.pdf.

U.S. Dep't of Health and Human Services, Administration for Children and Families, *Mandatory Reporters of Child Abuse and Neglect: Summary of State Laws* (2008), *available at* http://www.childwelfare.gove/systemwide/laws_poli-cies/statutes/manda.cfm.

Urban Dictionary, www.urbandictionary.com (1999–2010).

Virginia Tech Review Panel, *Mass Shootings at Virginia Tech, April 16, 2007: Report of the Review Panel Presented to Governor Kaine*, Commonwealth of Virginia (2007), *available at* http://www.vtreviewpanel.org/report/index.html.

Washington Courts, *Municipal Courts*, http://www.courts.wa.gov/appellate_tri-al_courts/?fa=atc.crtPage&crtType=Muni (last visited Aug. 10, 2010).

Paula Wasley, *Judge Dismisses Hazing Charges Against 2 Rider U. Officials,* Chronicle of Higher Education (Aug. 28, 2007), *available at* http://chronicle.com/articl/Judge-Dismisses-Hazing-Char/39465/.

Paula Wasley, *Rider U. Official Indicted in Student's Death,* Chronicle of Higher Education (Aug. 17, 2007), *available at* http://chronicle.com/article/Rider-U-Officials-Indicted/25138/.

The Who, *We Won't Get Fooled Again* (Arista Records 1970).

Wikipedia, *Boston Garden,* http://wn.wikipedia.org/wiki/Boston_Garden (last visited Aug. 27, 2010).

Wikipedia, *Celtics-Lakers Rivalry,* http://en.wikipedia.org/wiki/Celtics-Lakers_rivalry (last visited Aug. 27, 2010).

Wikipedia, *Calvin and Hobbes: Calvinball,* http://en.wikipedia.org/wiki/Calvin_and_Hobbes#cite_ref-45 (last visited Aug. 8, 2010).

Wikipedia, *Cluedo,* http://en.wikipedia.org/wiki/Cluedo (last visited Aug. 9, 2010).

Wikipedia, *Drunk Driving in the United States: History of Drunk Driving Laws,* http://en.wikipedia.org/wiki/Drunk_driving_in_the_United_States#History_of_drunk_driving_laws (last visited Aug. 5, 2010).

THE STATE OF GEORGIA

RESOLUTION WHICH ADOPTED

THE ACADEMIC BILL OF RIGHTS

A RESOLUTION

Recommending the observance of the Academic Bill of Rights at public universities in Georgia; and for other purposes.

WHEREAS, the principles enumerated in this resolution fully apply only to public universities that present themselves as bound by the canons of academic freedom contained within. Nothing in this resolution shall be construed as interfering with the right of a private institution to restrict academic freedom on the basis of creed or belief; and

WHEREAS, the central purposes of a university are the pursuit of truth, the discovery of new knowledge through scholarship and research, the study and reasoned criticism of intellectual and cultural traditions, the teaching and general development of students to help them become creative individuals and productive citizens of a pluralistic democracy, and the transmission of knowledge and learning to a society at large; and

WHEREAS, free inquiry and free speech within the academic community are indispensable to the achievement of these goals, the freedoms to teach and to learn depend upon the creation of appropriate conditions and opportunities on the campus as a whole as well as in the classrooms and lecture halls, and these purposes reflect the values – pluralism, diversity, opportunity, critical intelligence, openness, and fairness – that are the cornerstones of American society; and

WHEREAS, academic freedom is indispensable to the American university. From its first formulation in the General Report of the Committee on Academic Freedom and Tenure of the American Association of University Professors, the concept of academic freedom has been premised on the idea that human knowledge is the pursuit of the truth, that there is no humanly accessible truth that is not in principle open to challenge; and

WHEREAS, academic freedom is most likely to thrive in an environment that protects and fosters independence of thought and speech. In the words of the General Report, it is vital to protect "as the first condition of progress [a] complete and unlimited freedom to pursue inquiry and publish its results"; and

WHEREAS, because free inquiry and its fruits are crucial to the democratic enterprise itself, academic freedom is a national value as well. In a historic 1967 decision, the Supreme Court of the United States overturned a New York State loyalty provision for teachers with these words: "Our Nation is deeply committed to safeguarding academic freedom, [a] transcendentvalue to all of us and not merely to the teachers concerned." (Keyishian v. Board of Regents of the Univ. of the State of New York). In Sweezy v. New Hampshire, (1957), the Court observed that the "essentiality of freedom in the community of American universities [was] almost self-evident"; and

WHEREAS, academic freedom consists in protecting the intellectual independence of professors, researchers, and students in the pursuit of knowledge and the expression of ideas from interference by legislators or authorities within the institution itself, meaning that no political or ideological orthodoxy should be imposed on professors and researchers through the hiring, tenure, or termination process, nor through any other administrative means by the academic institution, nor should the legislature impose any such orthodoxy through the control of the university budget; and

WHEREAS, from the first statement on academic freedom, it has been recognized that intellectual independence means the protection of students as well as faculty from the imposition of any orthodoxy of a political or ideological nature. The 1910 General Report admonished faculty to avoid "taking unfair advantage of the student's immaturity by indoctrinating him with the teacher's own opinions before the student has had an opportunity fairly to examine other opinions upon the matters in question, and before he has sufficient knowledge and ripeness of judgment to be entitled to form any definitive opinion of his own." In 1967, the American Association of University Professors' Joint Statement on Rights and Freedoms of Students reinforced and amplified this injunction by affirming the inseparability of "the freedom to teach and freedom to learn." In the words of the report, "Students should be free to take reasoned exception to the data or views offered in any course of study and to reserve judgment about matters of opinion;" and

WHEREAS, the academic criteria of the scholarly profession should include reasonable scholarly options within the areas of discipline; and

WHEREAS, the value of the life of the mind was articulated by Thomas Jefferson when he stated, "We are not afraid to follow truth wherever it may lead, nor to tolerate any error so long as reason is left free to combat it;" and

WHEREAS, the education of the next generation of leaders should contain rigorous and balanced exposure to significant theories and thoughtful viewpoints, and students should be given the knowledge and background that empowers them to think for themselves.

NOW, THEREFORE, BE IT RESOLVED BY THE SENATE that to secure the intellectual independence of faculty and students and to protect the principles of academic freedom, this body strongly recommends that the following principles and procedures be observed at all public colleges and universities within the State of Georgia:

1. All faculty members shall be hired, fired, promoted, or granted tenure on the basis of their competence and appropriate knowledge in the field of their expertise. No faculty member shall be hired, fired, or denied promotion or tenure solely on the basis of his or her political or ideological beliefs;

2. No faculty member shall be excluded from a tenure search or hiring committee on the basis of his or her political or ideological beliefs;

3. Students shall not be graded on the basis of their political or ideological beliefs. Each college and university should have well known and publicly accessible policies and procedures available to students who believe they have been penalized for their social, political, or ideological beliefs;

4. While teachers are and should be free to pursue their own findings and perspectives in presenting their viewpoints, they should consider and make their students aware of other viewpoints. Academic disciplines should welcome exploration of unsettled questions;

5. Faculty members should not use their courses for the purpose of political or ideological indoctrination;

6. An environment conducive to the civil exchange of ideas being an essential component of a free university, the obstruction of invited campus speakers, destruction of campus literature, or other efforts to obstruct this exchange shall not be tolerated; and

7. Knowledge advances when individual scholars are left free to reach their own conclusions about which methods, facts, and theories have been validated by research. Academic institutions formed to advance knowledge within an area of research, maintain the integrity of the research process, and organize the professional lives of related researchers serve as indispensable venues within which scholars circulate research findings and debate their interpretations.

BE IT FURTHER RESOLVED that the Secretary of the Senate is authorized and directed to transmit appropriate copies of this resolution to the Board of Regents of the University System of Georgia and to the president of every college and university in this state.

TABLE OF CASES

A

Adarand Constructors, Inc. v. Peña, 515 U.S. 200 (1995) ... 235

Albertini; United States v., 472 U.S. 675 (1985) ... 204

Allen v. Cox, 942 A.2d 296 (2008) ... 30

Anjou v. Boston Elevated Ry. Co., 94 N.E. 386 (Mass. 1911) ... 134

Anthony v. Syracuse Univ., 224 A.D. 487 (N.Y. App. Div. 4th Dep't 1928) ... 63, 86, 187, 216

Arkansas v. Forbes, 523 U.S. 666 (1998) ... 209, 217

Arkansas Gazette Co. v. Pickens, 258 Ark. 69 (Ark. 1975) ... 254

Atria v. Vanderbilt Univ., 142 Fed. Appx. 246 (6th Cir. 2005) ... 53, 54, 85

A.W. v. Lancaster County. Sch. Dist. 0001, 601 N.W.2d 757 (Neb. 2010) ... 105, 138

B

Baldwin v. Zoradi, 123 Cal. App. 3d 275 (Cal. Ct. App. 1981) ... 57, 119

Balk v. Austin Ford Logan, Inc., 221 A.D.2d 795 (N.Y. App. Div. 1995) ... 62

Bash v. Clark Univ., 22 Mass. L. Rep. 84 (Mass. Super. 2006) ... 105, 109, 115, 172

Bash v. Clark Univ., 2007 WL 1418528 (Mass. Super. 2007) ... 167

Beach v. University of Utah, 726 P.2d 413 (Utah 1986) ... 55, 57, 59, 60, 61, 137

Beagle v. Vasold, 417 P.2d 673 (Cal. 1966) ... 144

Bearman v. Univ. of Notre Dame, 453 N.E.2d 1196 (Ind. App. 3d Dist. 1983) ... 168

Benner v. Oswald, 592 F.2d 174 (3d Cir. 1974) ... 67

Beth Rochel Seminary v. Bennett, 825 F.2d 478 (D.C. Cir. 1987) ... 82

BG&E v. Flippo, 684 A.2d 456 (Md. Ct. Spec. App. 1996) ... 131

Biakanja v. Irving, 49 Cal. 2d 647 (1958) ... 100

Blackburn v. Dorta, 348 So.2d 287 (Fla. 1977) ... 116

Bloss v. University of Minn., 590 N.W.2d 661 (Minn. Ct. App.1999) ... 172

Board of Curators of the Univ. of Mo. v. Horowitz, 435 U.S. 78 (1978) ... 40, 53, 55, 183, 184

Board of Educ. v. Grumet, 512 U.S. 687 (1994) ... 225

Board of Educ. of Hendrick Hudson Cent. Sch. Dist., Westchester Cnty. v. Rowley, 458 U.S. 176 (1982) ... 202, 223

Board of Educ. of Westside Cmty. Schs. (Dist. 66) v. Mergens, 496 U.S. 226 (1990) ... 223

Board of Regents of State Colls. v. Roth, 408 U.S. 564 (1972) ... 186

Board of Regents of Univ. of Wis. Sys. v. Southworth, 529 U.S. 217 (2000) ... 64, 79, 182, 203, 225

Boccone v. Eichen Levinson LLP, 301 Fed. Appx. 162 (3d Cir. 2008) ... 13

Booker v. GTE.net LLC, 350 F.3d 515 (Ky. 2003) . . . 156

Boos v. Barry, 485 U.S. 312 (1988) . . . 210

Borer v. American Airlines, Inc., 563 P.2d 858 (Cal. 1977) . . . 145

Boston v. Webb, 783 F.2d 1163 (4th Cir. 1986) . . . 182

Bowen v. Comstock, 2008 WL 2209722 (Tex. App. Waco Dist. 2008) . . . 43, 71

Boy Scouts v. Dale, 530 U.S. 640 (2000) . . . 203

Bradshaw v. Rawlings, 612 F.2d 135 (3d Cir. 1979) . . . 48, 57, 59, 60, 61, 137, 224

Bragdon v. Abbott, 524 U.S. 624 (1998) . . . 243

Brandenburg v. Ohio, 395 U.S. 444 (1969) . . . 198, 220

Brennan v. Board of Trs. for Univ. of La. Sys., 691 So.2d 324 (La. App. 1st Cir. 1997) . . . 168

Brooks v. Parshall, 806 N.Y.S.2d 796 (N.Y. App. Div. 3d Dep't 2006) . . . 124

Brophy v. Columbia County Agric. Soc'y, 498 N.Y.S. 193 (N.Y. App. Div. 3d Dep't 1986) . . . 124

Brown v. Board of Educ., 347 U.S. 483 (1954) . . . 52, 231, 233, 250

Burton v. Wilmington Parking Auth., 365 U.S. 715 (1961) . . . 67

Byers v. Gunn, 81 So.2d 723 (Fla. 1955) . . . 116

C

Cain v. Cleveland Parachute, 457 N.E.2d 1185 (Ohio 1983) . . . 150

Calabro v. Bennett, 737 N.Y.S. 2d 406 (N.Y. App. Div. 3d Dep't 2002) . . . 124

Caldwell v. A.R.B., Inc., 176 Cal. App. 3d 1028 (Cal. App. 1986) . . . 159

Carroll Towing; United States v., 159 F.2d 169 (2d Cir. 1947) . . . 126

Carson v. Springfield Coll., 2006 WL 2242732 (Del. Super. 2006) . . . 66

Chalk v. Orange Cnty. Superintendent of Schs., 840 F.2d 701 (9th Cir. 1988) . . . 243

Chaplinsky v. New Hampshire, 315 U.S. 568 (1992) . . . 198

Chatham v. Larkins, 216 S.E.2d 677 (Ga. Ct. App. 1975) . . . 133

Chicago Police Dep't v. Mosley, 408 U.S. 92 (1972) . . . 210

Christian Legal Soc'y at Hastings Coll. of the Law v. Martinez, 130 S. Ct. 2971 (2010) . . . 64, 79, 80, 123, 180, 182, 184, 198, 201, 202, 204, 211–213, 216, 217, 221–224, 258, 259

Citizens United v. Federal Election Comm'n, 130 S. Ct. 876 (2010) . . . 202

Clarke v. Community for Creative Non-Violence, 468 U.S. 288 (1984) . . . 204

Clay v. Texas Women's Univ., 728 F.2d 714 (5th Cir. 1984) . . . 141

Coalition of Clergy, Lawyers, and Professors v. Bush, 310 F.3d 1153 (9th Cir. 2002) . . . 182

Coghlan v. Beta Theta Pi Fraternity, 987 P.2d 300 (Idaho 1999) . . . 117

Cole v. Richardson, 405 U.S. 676 (1972) . . . 216

Coleman v. United States, 91 F.3d 820 (6th Cir. 1996) . . . 156

Collier v. Zambito, 807 N.E.2d 254 (N.Y. 2004) . . . 124

Colorado Nat'l Bank of Denver v. Friedman, 846 P.2d 159 (Colo. 1993) . . . 33

Commodari v. Long Island Univ., 62 Fed. Appx. 28 (2d Cir. 2003) . . . 65

Commodari v. Long Island Univ., 89 F. Supp.2d 353 (E.D.N.Y. 2000) . . . 66, 67

Concerned Citizens of Lake Milton, Inc. v. Mahoning County, 1995 WL 574217 (Ohio App. 7th Cir. 1995) . . . 184

Connell v. Higgenbotham, 403 U.S. 207 (1971) . . . 216

Connick v. Myers, 461 U.S. 138 (1983) . . . 202, 207, 222

Cordas v. Peerless Transp. Co., 27 N.Y.S. 2d 198 (N.Y. Ct. Cl. 1941) . . . 128

Cornelius v. NAACP Legal Def. and Educ. Fund, 473 U.S. 788 (1985) . . . 209

Craig v. Driscoll, 781 A.2d 440 (Conn. App. 2001) . . . 116

Crosby v. Florida State Bd., 506 So.2d 490 (1987) . . . 81

D

Daniel v. American Bd. of Emergency Med., 988 F. Supp. 127 (W.D.N.Y. 1997) . . . 69

Davidson v. University of N.C. Chapel Hill, 543 S.E.2d 920 (N.C. Ct. App. 2001) . . . 113, 115, 150, 171

Davidson v. Westminster, 649 P.2d 894 (Cal. 1982) . . . 120

Davies v. Barnes, 503 A.2d 93 (Pa. Commw. 1986) . . . 173

Davies v. Mann, 152 Eng. Rep. 588 (1842) . . . 147

Davis v. Monroe County Bd. of Educ., 526 U.S. 629 (1999) . . . 193, 240

Davis v. Southerland, 2004 WL 1230278 (S.D. Tex. 2004) . . . 43, 71

Davis; United States v., 442 U.S. 397 (1979) . . . 245

Davis v. Westwood Group, 652 N.E.2d 567 (Mass. 1995) . . . 131

Delaney v. University of Houston, 835 S.W.2d 56 (Tex. 1992) . . . 173

DeMarco v. University of Health Scis., 352 N.E.2d 356 (Ill. App. 1st Dist. 1976) . . . 188

De Stefano v. Wilson, 233 A.2d 682 (N.J. Super. L. Div. 1967) . . . 79

Dillon v. Legg, 441 P.2d 912 (Cal. 1968) . . . 100, 145

Dixon v. Alabama State Bd. of Educ., 294 F.2d 150 (5th Cir. 1961) . . . 52, 53, 55, 183, 190, 193, 217

E

Edgewater Motel, Inc. v. Gatzke, 277 N.W.2d 11 (Minn. 1979) . . . 159

Eisel v. Board of Educ. of Montgomery County, 597 A.2d 447 (Md. 1991) . . . 112

Elgin v. District of Columbia, 337 F.2d 152 (D.C. App. 1964) . . . 70

Eli v. New York, 901 N.Y. S. 2d 899 (N.Y. App. Div. Kings Cnty. 2009) . . . 149

Ellis; State v., 2006 WL 827376 (Ohio App. 2006) . . . 227

Englert, Inc. v. LeafGuard USA, Inc., 659 S.E.2d 496 (S.C. 2008) . . . 30

Erie R.R. Co. v. Tompkins, 304 U.S. 64 (1938) . . . 38

Estate of. See name of party

Esteban v. Central Mo. State Coll., 277 F. Supp. 649 (W.D. Mo. 1967) . . . 183

Ewing v. California, 538 U.S. 11 (2003) . . . 53, 183, 184

F

Farwell v. Keaton, 240 N.W.2d 217 (Mich. 1976) . . . 112, 117

Feldman v. Ho, 171 F.3d 494 (7th Cir. 1999) . . . 79

First Nat'l Bank of Boston v. Bellotti, 435 U.S. 765 (1978) . . . 202

Fitzpatrick v. Universal Tech. Inst., Inc., 2009 WL 2476639 (E.D. Pa. 2009) . . . 117

Flaim v. Medical Coll. of Ohio, 418 F.3d 629 (6th Cir. 2005) . . . 53, 182, 184

Fleckner v. Dionne, 210 P.2d 530 (Cal. 1949) . . . 137

Florence v. Goldberg, 375 N.E.2d 763 (N.Y. 1978) . . . 121

Fordice; United States v., 505 U.S. 717 (1992) . . . 52

Forsythe Cnty., Ga. v. Nationalist Movement, 505 U.S. 123 (1992) . . . 210

Foster v. Preston Mill Co., 268 P.2d 645 (Wash. 1954) . . . 139

Franklin v. Gwinnett Cnty. Pub. Schs., 503 U.S. 60 (1992) . . . 240

Fraser v. United States, 674 A.2d 811 (Conn. 1996) . . . 111

Frye v. United States, 421 U.S. 542 (1978) . . . 68

Fuentes v. Shevin, 407 U.S. 67 (1972) . . . 181

Fullilove v. Klutznick, 448 U.S. 448 (1980) . . . 235

Furek v. University of Delaware, 594 A.2d 506 (Del. 1991) . . . 106, 117

G

Garcetti v. Ceballos, 547 U.S. 410 (2006) . . . 202, 207, 208, 222

Garofalo v. Lambda Chi Alpha Fraternity, 616 N.W.2d 647 (Iowa 2000) . . . 130, 191

Gebser v. Lago Vista Indep. Sch. Dist., 524 U.S. 274 (1998) . . . 193, 240

Gideon v. Wainwright, 372 U.S. 335 (1963) . . . 181

Gift v. Palmer, 141 A.2d 408 (Pa. 1958) . . . 107, 123

Goddard v. Boston & Maine R.R. Co., 60 N.E. 486 (Mass. 1901) . . . 134

Goldbarth v. Kansas State Bd. of Regents, 9 P.3d 1251 (Kan. 2000) . . . 71

Gomes v. University of Maine Sys., 365 F. Supp. 2d 6 (D. Me. 2005) . . . 186, 188

Gonzaga Univ. v. Doe, 536 U.S. 273 (2002) . . . 44, 129, 177, 230

Gonzalez v. University Sys. of N.H., 2005 WL 530806 (Conn. Super. 2005) . . . 150

Gordon v. Bridgeport Housing Auth., 544 A.2d 1185 (Conn. 1988) . . . 70

Gorman v. University of R.I., 837 F.2d 7 (1st Cir. 1988) . . . 53, 75, 184, 188

Goss v. Lopez, 419 U.S. 565 (1975) . . . 53, 181, 183, 184, 249

Gott v. Berea Coll., 161 S.W. 204 (Ky. 1913) . . . 108

Gragg v. Wichita State, 934 P.2d 121 (Kan. 1997) . . . 173

Gratz v. Bollinger, 539 U.S. 244 (2003) . . . 79, 234, 235, 236

Greene v. Texeira, 505 P.2d 1160 (Haw. 1973) . . . 146

Greenman v. Yuba Power Prods., Inc., 59 Cal. 2d 57 (Cal. 1963) . . . 100

Greenya v. GWU, 512 F.2d 556 (D.C. Cir. 1975) . . . 67

Griswold v. Connecticut, 381 U.S. 479 (1965) . . . 198

Gross v. Family Servs. Agency and Nova Se. Univ., Inc., 716 So.2d 337 (Fla. App. 1998) . . . 61

Gross v. Sweet, 400 N.E.2d 306 (N.Y. 1979) . . . 149, 175

Grutter v. Bollinger, 539 U.S. 306 (2003) . . . 79, 234, 235, 236

Guardians Ass'n v. Civil Serv. Comm'n, 463 U.S. 582 (U.S. 1983) . . . 233

Guest v. Hansen, 2007 WL 4561104 (N.D.N.Y. 2007) . . . 110

H

Hack v. President and Fellows of Yale Coll., 237 F.3d 81 (2d Cir. 2000), *cert. denied*, 534 U.S. 888 (2001) . . . 65

Hacker v. Hacker, 522 N.Y.S.2d 768 (1987) . . . 80

Hall v. Hawaii, 791 F.2d 759 (9th Cir. 1986) . . . 69

Hall v. Medical Coll. of Ohio, 742 F.2d 299 (6th Cir. 1984) . . . 69

Hamilton v. Regents of the Univ. of Cal., 293 U.S. 245 (1934) . . . 49, 69

Handley, Name Change of, 736 N.E.2d 125 (Ohio Prob. 2000) . . . 82

Hanna v. Plumer, 380 U.S. 460 (1965) . . . 38

Harlow v. Fitzgerald, 457 U.S. 800 (1982) . . . 71

Harris v. Showcase Chevrolet, 231 S.W.3d 559 (Tex. App. Dallas 2007) . . . 30

Havlik v. Johnson & Wales Univ., 509 F.3d 25 (1st Cir. 2007) . . . 85, 176, 177, 179, 180, 181, 185

Hawkins v. Sarasota County Sch. Bd., 322 F.3d 1279 (11th Cir. 2003) . . . 193

Hayden v. University of Notre Dame, 716 N.E.2d 603 (Ind. App. 1999) . . . 151

Healy v. James, 408 U.S. 169 (1972)...52, 79, 198, 200, 212, 219, 220–223, 225
Heigl v. Board of Educ., 587 A.2d 423 (Conn. 1991)...70
Heinz v. Mayer, 425 U.S. 610 (1976)...206
Hess v. Indiana, 414 U.S. 105 (1973)...198
Ho v. University of Tex. at Arlington, 984 S.W.2d 672 (Tex. App. Amarillo 1998)...69
Hooper v. North Carolina, 379 F. Supp. 2d 804 (M.D.N.C. 2005)...141
Hu v. American Bar Ass'n, 568 F. Supp. 2d 959 (N.D. Ill. 2008)...67
Humphrey v. Memorial Hosp., 239 F.3d 1128 (9th Cir. 2001)...247

I

Ingram v. Pettit, 340 So.2d 922 (Fla. 1976)...155
International Soc'y for Krishna v. Lee, 505 U.S. 672 (1992)...208
Island City Flying Serv. v. General Elec. Credit Corp., 585 So.2d 274 (Fla. 1991)...156

J

Jackson v. Metropolitan Edison Co., 419 U.S. 345 (1974)...67
Jain v. Iowa, 617 NW.2d 293 (Iowa 2000)...138
Janzen v. Atiyeh, 743 P.2d 765 (1987)...82
Jasko v. F.W. Woolworth Co., 494 P.2d 839 (Colo. 1972)...134
Johnson v. Lincoln Christian Coll., 501 N.E.2d 1380 (Ill. App. 4th Dist. 1987)...85
Johnson v. State, 894 P.2d 1366 (Wash. Ct. App. 1995)...174
Johnston v. Joyce, 596 N.Y.S.2d 625 (N.Y.A.D. 4th Dep't 1993)...143
Jones v. Dressel, 623 P.2d 370 (Colo. 1981)...151
Jordan v. Jordan, 257 S.E.2d 761 (1979)...96, 135

Joseph v. Board of Regents of the Univ. of Wis. Sys., 432 F.3d 746 (7th Cir. 2005)...69
Joy v. Great Atl. and Pac. Tea Co., 405 F.2d 464 (4th Cir. 1968)...134

K

Kashmiri v. Regents of the Univ. of Cal., 156 Cal. App. 4th 809 (Cal. App. 1st Dist. 2007)...75, 87
Katzenbach v. Morgan, 384 U.S. 641 (1966)...68
Kelly; People v., 195 Cal. App. 2d 669 (1961)...227
Kemezy v. Peters, 622 N.E.2d 1296 (Ind. 1993)...156
Keyishian v. Board of Regents of Univ. of N.Y., 385 U.S. 589 (1967)...78, 216, 221, 238
Kimps v. Hill, 546 N.W.2d 151 (1996)...70
Kline v. 1500 Mass. Ave. Apt. Corp., 439 F.2d 477 (D.C. Cir. 1970)...109
Knoll v. Board of Regents of Univ. of Neb., 601 N.W.2d 757 (Neb. 1999)...105, 109, 110, 172, 173
Kobe v. Industrial Acc. Comm'n, 35 Cal. 2d 33 (Cal. 1950)...158
Kolaniak v. Board of Educ., 610 A.2d 193 (Conn. App. 1993)...70
Korematsu v. United States, 323 U.S. 214 (1944)...200, 237
Kovacs v. Cooper, 336 U.S. 77 (1949)...211
Krishna v. Lee, 505 U.S. 672 (1992)...217

L

Lakewood, City of v. Plain Dealer Publ'g Co., 486 U.S. 750 (1988)...210
Lamb's Chapel v. Central Moriches Union Free Sch. Dist., 508 U.S. 384 (1993)...201, 209, 212
Lara v. Saint John's Univ., 735 N.Y.S.2d 578 (N.Y. App. Div. 2d Dep't 2001)...168

Lemon v. Kurtzman, 403 U.S. 602 (1971) ...224, 225

Lewis v. Wilson, 253 F.3d 1077 (8th Cir. 2001) ...201

Lloyd v. Alpha Phi Alpha Fraternity, 1999 WL 47153 (N.D.N.Y. 1999) ...131, 140, 149, 191

Lovell v. Griffin, 303 U.S. 444 (1938) ...210

Lunar v. Ohio Dep't of Transp., 572 N.E.2d 208 (Ohio App. 10th Dist. 1989) ...131

M

Madison Joint Sch. Dist. v. Wisconsin Employment Relations Comm'n, 429 U.S. 167 (1976) ...201

Madon v. Long Island Univ., 518 F. Supp. 246 (E.D.N.Y. 1981) ...66

Maine Caterers, Inc.; NLRB v., 654 F.2d 131 (1st Cir. 1981) ...159

Marbury v. Madison, 5 U.S. 137 (1803) ...37

Marcus v. St. Paul Fire and Marine Ins. Co., 651 F.2d 379 (5th Cir. 1981) ...30

Marrapese v. Rhode Island, 500 F. Supp. 1207 (D.R.I. 1980) ...141

Marter v. Scott, 514 So.2d 1240 (Miss. 1987) ...157

Martin v. Board of Instruction of Higher Learning, 933 So.2d 833 (Miss. App. 2008) ...32

Martin v. Herzog, 126 N.E. 814 (N.Y. 1920) ...129

McCain v. Florida Power Corp., 593 So.2d 500 (Fla. 1992) ...99, 136

McClure v. Fairfield Univ., 2003 WL 21524786 (Conn. Super. 2003) ...163

Midwest Knitting Mills, Inc. v. United States, 950 F.2d 1295 (7th Cir. 1991) ...156

Miguel v. Guess, 51 P.3d 89 (Wash. Ct. App. 2002) ...232

Mississippi Univ. for Women v. Hogan, 458 U.S. 718 (1982) ...239

Molitor v. Kaneland Cmty. Unit Dist., 163 N.E.2d 89 (Ill. 1959) ...69

Monell v. New York City Dep't of Soc. Servs., 436 U.S. 658 (1978) ...69

Moody v. Pepsi-Cola Metro. Bottling Co., 915 F.2d 201 (6th Cir. 1990) ...32

Moran v. Kingdom of Saudi Arabia, 27 F.3d 169 (5th Cir. 1994) ...157

Moransais v. Heathman, 744 So.2d 973 (Fla. 1999) ...16

Morgan, Estates of v. Fairfield Family Counseling Ctr., 77 Ohio St. 3d 284 (1997) ...112

Morgan v. State, 685 N.E.2d 202 (N.Y. 1997) ...150

Moseley v. Lamirato, 370 P.2d 450 (Colo. 1962) ...33

Moses v. Diocese of Colo., 863 P.2d 310 (Colo. 1993) ...156

Mullins v. Pine Manor Coll., 449 N.E.2d 331 (Mass. 1983) ...17, 51, 61, 108, 109, 175

Murphy v. Steeplechase Amusement Co., 166 N.E. 173 (N.Y. 1929) ...148

N

Nally v. Grace Church, 763 P.2d 948 (Cal. 1988) ...112

Nelson v. Piggly Wiggly Ctr., Inc., 390 S.C. 382 (S.C. App. 2010) ...30, 32

Nero v. Kansas State Univ., 861 P.2d 768 (Kan. 1993) ...61, 106, 138

New York Ass'n of Career Sch. v. State Educ. Dep't N.Y., 749 F. Supp 1264 (S.D.N.Y. 1990) ...253

New York Times Co. v. Sullivan, 376 U.S. 254 (1954) ...207, 226, 262

Nichols v. Northeast La. Univ., 729 So.2d 733 (La. App. 2d Cir. 1999) ...135

Nixon v. Mr. Prop. Mgmt. Co., 690 S.W.2d 546 (Tex. 1985) ...61

NLRB v. See name of opposing party

Nott v. George Washington Univ., No. 05-8503 (D.C. Super. Ct. Oct. 2005) ...246

Nova Se. Univ. v. Gross, 758 So.2d 86 (Fla. 2000) . . . 82, 92, 113, 115, 172

O

O'Brien v. Cunard S.S. Co., 28 N.E. 266 (Mass. 1891) . . . 149
Oregon v. Mitchell, 400 U.S. 112 (1970) . . . 68

P

Pacht v. Morris, 489 P.2d 29 (1971) . . . 121
Pacific Gas and Elec. Co. v. Public Utils. Comm'n of Cal., 475 U.S. 1 (1986) . . . 202
Pakett v. Phillies, L.P., 871 A.2d 304 (Pa. Commw. 2005) . . . 149
Paladino v. Adelphi, 89 A.D.2d (N.Y. App. Div. 1982) . . . 187
Palmore v. Sidoti, 466 U.S. 429 (1984) . . . 237
Palsgraf v. Long Island R.R. Co., 162 N.E. 992d (N.Y. 1928) . . . 99
Papish v. Board of Curators of the Univ. of Mo., 410 U.S. 667 (1973) . . . 225, 227
Parker v. Board of Sup'rs Univ. of Louisiana-Lafayette, 296 Fed. Appx. 414 (5th Cir. 2008) . . . 38
Parsons v. Jow, 480 P.2d 396 (Wyo. 1971) . . . 137
Pawlowski v. Delta Sigma Phi, 2007 WL 2363146 (Conn. Super. 2007) . . . 110, 111, 116, 117, 119, 259
People v. See name of opposing party
Perry v. Sinderman, 408 U.S. 593 (1972) . . . 53, 181, 186
Peterson v. Ohio Cas. Group, 724 N.W.2d 765 (Neb. 2006) . . . 14
Peterson v. San Francisco Cmty. Coll., 685 P.2d 1193 (Cal. 1984) . . . 173
P.G.A. v. Martin, 532 U.S. 661 (2001) . . . 247
Philip Crosby Ass'n, Inc. v. State Bd. of Indep. Coll., 506 So.2d 490 (Fla. App. 5th Dist. 1987) . . . 80

Piazzola v. Watkins, 442 F.2d 284 (5th Cir. 1971) . . . 227
Pickering v. Board of Ed. of Twp. High Sch. Dist. 205 Will County, 391 U.S. 563 (1968) . . . 202, 207
Pitre v. Employers Liab. Assurance Corp., 234 So.2d 847 (La. App. 1st Cir. 1970) . . . 99
Pitre v. Louisiana Tech Univ., 655 So.2d 659 (La. Ct. App. 1995), *rev'd*, 673 So.2d 585 (La. 1996) . . . 148
Plano v. Fountain Gate Ministries, 654 S.W.2d 841 (1983) . . . 81, 82
Porubiansky v. Emory Univ., 275 S.E.2d 163 (Ga. App. 1980) . . . 150
Poulos v. New Hampshire, 345 U.S. 395 (1953) . . . 185, 211
Powe v. Miles, 407 F.2d 73 (2d Cir. 1962) . . . 66, 67
Prairie View A&M Univ. of Tex. v. Mitchell, 27 S.W.3d 323 (Tex. App. 1st Dist. 2000) . . . 69
Price; United States v., 383 U.S. 787 (1966) . . . 66
Princeton Univ. v. Schmid, 455 U.S. 100 (1982) . . . 65
Prostrollo v. University of S.D., 507 F.2d 775 (8th Cir. 1974) . . . 227
Pruneyard Shopping Ctr. v. Robins, 447 U.S. 74 (1980) . . . 65, 68, 218
Purisch v. Tennessee Tech. Univ., 76 F.3d 1414 (6th Cir. 1996) . . . 71

R

Ralphs Grocer Co. v. Workers' Comp. Appeals Bd. 58 Cal. App. 4th 647 (Cal. App. 4th Dist. 1997) . . . 158
R.A.V. v. St. Paul, 505 U.S. 377 (1992) . . . 199, 212, 226
Regents of the Univ. of Cal. v. Bakke, 438 U.S. 265 (1978) . . . 232, 235, 236, 238
Regents of the Univ. of Mich. v. Ewing, 474 U.S. 214 (1985) . . . 40, 53, 55, 183, 247

Rendell-Baker v. Kohn, 457 U.S. 830 (1982) ...65, 66

Rhodes v. Illinois Cent. Gulf R.R., 665 N.E.2d 1260 (Ill. 1996) ...110

Riviello v. Waldron, 391 N.E.2d 1278 (N.Y. 1979) ...158, 159

Roberts v. Indiana Gas and Water Co., 218 N.E.2d 556 (Ind. App. 1966) ...131

Robertson v. State ex rel. Dep't of Planning and Control, 747 So.2d 1276 (La. Ct. App. 1999) ...115, 133, 153, 173

Rodebush By and Through Rodebush v. Oklahoma Nursing Homes, Ltd., 867 P.2d 1241 (Okla. 1993) ...157

Rodgers v. Kemper Constr. Co., 50 Cal. App. 3d 608 (Cal. App. 4th Dist. 1975) ...156

Rodrigues v. Bethlehem Steel Corp., 525 P.2d 669 (Cal. 1974) ...145

Rosenberger v. Rector and Visitors of the Univ. of Va., 515 U.S. 819 (1995) ...52, 64, 79, 209, 211–213, 222, 224

Ross v. Creighton Univ., 957 F.2d 410 (7th Cir. 1992) ...41, 88, 187, 188, 250

Roth v. U.S., 354 U.S. 476 (1957) ...53, 198

Rowland v. Christian, 443 P.2d 561 (Cal. 1968) ...100

Russel v. Salve Regina Coll., 890 F.2d 484 (1st Cir. 1989) ...53

S

Saelzler v. Advanced Group 400, 25 Cal.4th 763 (Cal. 2001) ...135

Saia v. New York, 334 U.S. 558 (1948) ...211

San Antonio Ind. Sch. Dist. v. Rodriguez, 411 U.S. 1, 28 (1973) ...247, 248

Sandoval v. Board of Regents of N.M. State Univ., 403 P.2d 699 (N.M. 1965) ...109

Santana v. Rainbow Cleaners, 969 A.2d 653 (R.I. 2009) ...111

Schaer v. Brandeis Univ., 735 N.E.2d 373 (Mass. 2000) ...75, 86, 180, 186, 187, 189

Schmid; State v., 423 A.2d 615 (N.J. 1980) ...68, 197, 218

School Bd. of Nassau Cty. v. Arline, 480 U.S. 273 (1987) ...243

Shamloo v. Mississippi State, 620 F.2d 516 (5th Cir. 1980) ...200

Sharkey v. Board of Regents of Univ. of Neb., 615 N.W.2d 889 (Neb. 2000) ...138, 167, 172

Shelton v. Tucker, 364 U.S. 479, 487 (1960) ...220

Shin v. Massachusetts Inst. of Tech., 19 Mass. L. Rep. 570 (Mass. Super. 2005) ...72, 138

Shore v. Town of Stonington, 444 A.2d 1379 (Conn. 1982) ...156

Shuttleworth v. Birmingham, 394 U.S. 147 (1969) ...185, 210

Skokie v. National Socialist Party, 373 N.E.2d 21 (Ill. 1978) ...199, 201

Slaughter v. Brigham Young Univ., 514 F.2d 622 (10th Cir. 1975) ...187

Smith v. California, 361 U.S. 147 (1959) ...206

Southeastern Cmty. Coll. v. Davis, 442 U.S. 397 (1979) ...245

Southwestern Pub. Servs. Co. v. Artesia Alfalfa Growers' Ass'n, 353 P.2d 62 (N.M. 1960) ...150

Southwest Fla. Water Mgmt. Dist. v. Save the Manatee Club, Inc., 773 So.2d 594 (Fla. 1st DCA 2000) ...185

State v. See name of opposing party

Sterner v. Wesley Coll., Inc., 747 F. Supp. 263 (D. Del. 1990) ...145

Stetson Univ. v. Hunt, 102 So. 637 (Fla. 1925) ...225

Stevens; United States v., 130 S. Ct. 1577 (2010) ...199

Stropes v. Heritage Childrens Ctr., 547 N.E.2d 244 (Ind. 1989) ...156

Superior Court; People v., 49 Cal. Rptr. 3d
831 (Cal. App. 6th Dist. 2006)
. . . 227
Sweatt v. Painter, 339 U.S. 629 (1950)
. . . 233
Sweezy v. New Hampshire, 354 U.S. 234
(1957) . . . 78, 79, 234

T

Tanja H. v. Regents of Univ. of Cal., 228 Cal.
App. 3d 434 (Cal. App. 1st Dist.
1991) . . . 149
*Tarasoff v. Board of Regents of the Univ. of
Cal.*, 551 P.2d 334 (Cal. 1976)
. . . 61, 100, 106, 111, 112, 167,
229, 230
Texas v. Johnson, 491 U.S. 392 (1989)
. . . 199
Texas A&M Univ. v. Bading, 236 S.W.3d
801 (Tex. App. Waco Dist. 2007)
. . . 43, 71
Than v. University of Tex. Med. Sch., 188
F. 3d 633 (5th Cir. 1999) . . . 75,
87, 189
Thing v. La Chusa, 771 P.2d 814 (Cal.
1989) . . . 145
Thompson v. Skate Am., Inc., 940 S.E.2d
123 (Va. 2001) . . . 109
Thorne v. Deas, 4 Johns. 84 (N.Y. Supp.
1809) . . . 121
*Tinker v. Des Moines Indep. Cmty. Sch.
Dist.*, 393 U.S. 503 (1969) . . . 52,
198–200, 219, 220
The T. J. Hooper v. Northern Barge Corp., 60
F.2d 737 (2d Cir. 1932) . . . 17
Tunkle v. Regents, 383 P.2d 441 (Cal. 1963)
. . . 150
Turner v. Staggs, 510 P.2d 879 (Nev. 1973)
. . . 22

U

Union Pac. R.R. Co. v. Cappier, 72 P. 281
(Kansas 1903) . . . 103
United States v. See name of opposing party

University of Denver v. Whitlock, 744 P.2d
54 (Colo. 1987) . . . 171
*University of Tex. Med. Sch. at Houston v.
Than*, 901 S.W.2d 926 (Tex. 1995)
. . . 184, 186

V

Vangsguard v. Progressive N. Ins. Co., 525
N.W.2d 146 (Wis. App. 1994)
. . . 30
Virginia v. Black, 538 U.S. 343 (2003)
. . . 199
Virginia v. Hicks, 539 U.S. 113 (2003)
. . . 210
Virginia; United States v., 518 U.S. 515
(1996) . . . 231, 239, 240
Voorhees v. Preferred Mut. Ins. Co., 607 A.
2d 1255 (N.J. 1992) . . . 13
Vulcan Eng'g Co. v. XL Ins. Am., Inc., 201
Fed. Appx. 678 (11th Cir. 2006)
. . . 14

W

Wagner v. International Ry., 133 N.E. 437
(N.Y. 1921) . . . 139
Wallace v. Broyles, 961 S.W.2d 712 (Ark.
1998) . . . 168
Ward v. K-Mart Corp., 554 N.E.2d 223 (Ill.
1990) . . . 133, 134
Ward v. Rock Against Racism, 491 U.S. 781
(1989) . . . 204, 210, 211, 212
*Wartski v. C.W. Post Campus of Long Island
Univ.*, 882 N.Y.S.2d 192 (N.Y.
App. Div. 2d Dep't 2009) . . . 168
Washington v. Chapman, 455 U.S. 1 (1982)
. . . 227
Watson v. Duerr, 379 So.2d 1243 (Ala.
1980) . . . 138
Watts v. Wayne Co. Bd. of Educ., 412 S.E.2d
541 (Ga. App. 1991) . . . 71
Webb v. Board of Trs. of Ball State Univ., 167
F.3d 1146 (7th Cir. 1999) . . . 79
Webb v. University of Utah, 125 P.3d 906
(Utah 2005) . . . 57

Wells v. St. Petersburg, 958 So.2d 1076 (Fla. 2d Dist. Ct. App. 2007) . . . 153

White v. Burns, 567 A.2d 1195 (Conn. 1990) . . . 140

White v. Davis, 533 P.2d 222 (Cal. 1975) . . . 206

Widmar v. Vincent, 454 U.S. 263 (1981) . . . 52, 198, 202, 209, 212, 214, 223–225

Wieder v. Schwartz, 829 N.Y.S.2d 125 (N.Y. App. Div. 2006) . . . 36

Wieman v. Updegraff, 344 U.S. 183 (1952) . . . 221

Williams v. Board of Regents of the Univ. Sys. of Ga., 477 F.3d 1282 (11th Ct. App. 2007) . . . 192, 193

Williams v. Wendler, 530 F.3d 584 (7th Cir. 2008) . . . 75, 87, 182

Wisconsin v. Mitchell, 508 U.S. 476 (1993) . . . 199, 213

Wong v. Regents of Univ. of Cal., 192 F.3d 807 (9th Cir. 1999) . . . 247

Wood v. Strickland, 420 U.S. 308 (1975) . . . 71

Wooley v. Maynard, 319 U.S. 624 (1943) . . . 203

Wygant v. Jackson Bd. of Educ., 476 U.S. 267 (1986) . . . 235

Wynne v. Tufts Univ. Sch. of Med., 932 F.2d 19 (1st Cir. 1991) . . . 247

Y

Yania v. Bigan, 155 A.2d 343 (Pa. 1959) . . . 103

Yohn v. Coleman, 639 F. Supp. 2d 776 (E.D. Mich. 2009) . . . 71

Younger v. Harris, 401 U.S. 36 (1971) . . . 37

Z

Zumbrun v. University of S. Cal., 25 Cal. App.3d 1 (Cal. Ct. App. 1972) . . . 75, 187, 188

TABLE OF LAWS

CONSTITUTION, U.S.

art. I, § 8 ... 68
amend. I ... 11, 52, 64, 78, 81, 197–227, 238, 249
amend. IV ... 198, 227
amend. V ... 232
amend. VII ... 31
amend. XI ... 69
amend. XIV ... 198, 227, 232, 233, 237
amend. XIV, § 5 ... 68
amend. XXI ... 60

FEDERAL LAWS, REGULATIONS, AND COURT RULES

Administrative Procedure Act of 1946 (APA), 5 U.S.C. §§ 551 et seq. ... 39
Americans with Disabilities Act of 1990 (ADA), 42 U.S.C. §§ 12131-12134, 12181-12189 ... 232
Americans with Disabilities Act Amendments Act of 2008, 42 U.S.C. §§ 12101–12189 ... 232
Civil Rights Act of 1964, Title VI, 42 U.S.C. 2000(d)–2000(d)(1) ... 231–234, 239
Education Amendments of 1972, Title IX, 20 U.S.C. § 1681 ... 185, 189, 192
Family Educational Rights and Privacy Act of 1974 (FERPA), 20 U.S.C. § 1232(g) ... 4–5, 12, 44, 52, 166, 185, 227–230

Health Care and Education Reconciliation Act, Pub. L. No. 111-152, §§ 2201–2213, 124 Stat. 1029 ... 66, 73, 74
Health Insurance Portability and Accountability Act of 1996 (HIPAA), 42 U.S.C.A. § 201 et seq. ... 231
Jeanne Clery Disclosure of Campus Security Policy and Campus Crime Statistics Act (Clery Act)
20 U.S.C. § 1092(f) ... 64, 115, 124, 169, 170, 185, 192, 224, 230
20 U.S.C. § 1092(f)(1)–(18) ... 176
20 U.S.C. § 1092(f)(1)(F)(i)(IX) ... 177
20 U.S.C. § 1092(f)(1)(J)(i)–(iii) ... 169
No Child Left Behind Act, Title IV, Part A, 20 U.S.C § 6319 ... 185, 189
Rehabilitation Act of 1973 § 504 ... 232, 242, 245, 246
Safe and Drug Free School and Communities Act, 20 U.S.C. §§ 7101–04 ... 164, 185
Sarbanes-Oxley Corporate Accountability Act ... 254
Sherman Antitrust Act, 15 U.S.C. § 1 ... 65
Volunteer Protection Act of 1997. 42 U.S.C.A. § 14501 ... 154
United States Code
9 U.S.C. § 9 ... 36
20 U.S.C. § 1092(f) ... 64, 173
20 U.S.C. § 1232g(b)(1)(I) ... 4
20 U.S.C. § 1681 ... 231
20 U.S.C. § 1681(a)(1) ... 240
20 U.S.C. § 1681(a)(3) ... 240
20 U.S.C. §1681(a)(4) ... 231

20 U.S.C. § 1681(a)(5) ... 231
20 U.S.C. § 1681(a)(6)(A) ... 231
20 U.S.C. § 1681(a)(8) ... 231
28 U.S.C. § 1331 ... 37
28 U.S.C. § 1332 ... 37
28 U.S.C. § 1367 ... 37
28 U.S.C. § 1441 ... 37, 38
28 U.S.C. § 1446 ... 37
29 U.S.C. § 791 ... 232
29 U.S.C. § 794(a) ... 244
42 U.S.C. § 1213.1(2) ... 244
42 U.S.C. § 1981 ... 234
42 U.S.C. § 1983 ... 69
42 U.S.C. § 2000d-1 ... 233
42 U.S.C. §§ 12101-12189 ... 232
42 U.S.C. §§ 12131–12134 ... 232
42 U.S.C. § 12132 ... 244
42 U.S.C. §§ 12181–12189 ... 232
42 U.S.C. § 14505 ... 154
Code of Federal Regulations
28 C.F.R. § 35 ... 232
28 C.F.R. § 35.104 ... 244
28 C.F.R. §§ 36.301–36.310 ... 246
28 C.F.R. §§ 36.401–36.406 ... 246
34 C.F.R. § 75.740 ... 228
34 C.F.R. §§ 100–106 ... 233
34 C.F.R. § 104.3(k)(3) ... 244
34 C.F.R. § 104.3(*l*)(3) ... 244
34 C.F.R. § 104.3(*l*)(4) ... 244
34 C.F.R. §§ 104–10 ... 232
34 C.F.R. §§ 104.42(a)–104.42(b) ... 242
34 C.F.R. §§ 104.42(b)(4)–104.42(c) ... 242
34 C.F.R. § 104.43 ... 233
34 C.F.R. § 104.3(j) ... 245
34 C.F.R. § 106.15(d) ... 240
34 C.F.R. § 668 ... 81
34 C.F.R. § 668.46 ... 170, 176, 177
Federal Rules of Appellate Procedure
Fed. R. App. Prac. 4(a) ... 97
Federal Rules of Civil Procedure
Fed. R. Civ. P. 3 ... 23
Fed. R. Civ. P. 7(a)(1) ... 23
Fed. R. Civ. P. 8 ... 142
Fed. R. Civ. P. 8(a)(1)–(3) ... 23
Fed. R. Civ. P. 8(b)(1) ... 24
Fed. R. Civ. P. 8(c)(1) ... 24

Fed. R. Civ. P. 12(b)(6) ... 25
Fed. R. Civ. P. 38(a) ... 31
Fed. R. Civ. P. 38(d) ... 31
Fed. R. Civ. P. 50(a)(1)(A)–(B) ... 31
Fed. R. Civ. P. 50(a)(2) ... 31
Fed. R. Civ. P. 50(b)(1)–(3) ... 31
Fed. R. Civ. P. 56 ... 29
Fed. R. Civ. P. 58 ... 32
Fed. R. Civ. P. 58(b)(1)(A) ... 143
Fed. R. Civ. P. 59 ... 32
Supreme Court Rules
S.Ct. R. 10–16 ... 42
Circuit Court Rules
United States Court of Appeals, 1st Cir. R.
36(b)(2) ... 43

STATE LAWS, REGULATIONS, AND COURT RULES

Colorado
Colo. Rev. Stat. §§ 201–207 ... 36
Florida
Baker Act, Fla. Stat. § 394.451–394.478 ... 230
Baker Act, Fla. Stat. § 394.463 ... 230
F.S.A. § 120.52(8) ... 185
F.S.A. § 429.297 ... 141
F.S.A. §§ 440.01–440.60 ... 154
F.S.A. § 627.736(10)(a) ... 22
F.S.A. § 768.13 ... 139
F.S.A. § 768.36 ... 152
F.S.A. § 768.81 ... 152
Fla. Arbitration Code §§ 682.01–682.22 ... 36
Fla. R. Civ. P. 1.710 ... 35
Hawaii
Haw. Rev. Stat. § 662-15 ... 70
Idaho
Idaho Code Ann. § 6-904 ... 70
Illinois
Ill. Admin. Code tit. 29 §§ 305.10–305.110 ... 170
Maryland
Md. Code Ann., State Gov't §§ 12-104–12-110 ... 142
Massachusetts

Mass. Gen. Laws ch. 15A, § 22 ... 257
Mass. Gen. Laws ch. 251, §§ 1–19 ... 36
Mass. Gen. Laws ch. 258, § 10 ... 70
Minnesota
Minn. Stat. § 3.736 ... 70
Minn. Stat. § 604.01 ... 152
Montana
Mont. Code Ann. § 27-1-1102 ... 111
New York
N.Y. C.P.L.R. 1411 ... 29
Ohio
Ohio Rev. Code Ann. § 2305.51 ... 112
Texas
Tex. Civ. Prac. & Rem. Code § 84.006 ... 142

Tex. Civ. Prac. & Rem. Code § 102.003
	... 70
Vermont
Vt. Stat. Ann. tit. 12 § 519 ... 118
Virginia
Va. Code Ann. § 8.01-195.3 ... 70
Va. Code Ann. § 23-9.2:8 ... 246, 257
Va. Code Ann. § 23-9.2:10 ... 170

UNIFORM COMMERCIAL CODE

U.C.C. §§ 2-102–725 ... 85

SUBJECT INDEX

Notes are indicated by n following page numbers.

A

AAUP. *See* American Association of University Professors
Academic Bill of Rights, 79*n,* 80*n,* 303–306
Academic/conduct distinctions, 54–56
Academic freedom, 76–80, 264
 of faculty, 76–79
 safety responsibility laws and, 92
 of students, 79–80
Academic mission, 175–195
Accidents. *See also* Rescue law
 negligence causing. *See* Negligence
 second injury rule, 140
Accommodation law, 241–242, 245
Accountability
 academic core mission accountability, 250
 affirmative defenses and, 147
 affirmative duty law and, 107
 civil rights era and, 217
 in facilitator era, 62
 immunity and, 72, 154
 personal accountability of individuals, 60, 92, 93
 private institutions and, 256
 real-time decision making and, 128
 registrars and consumer accountability, 228
 student affairs administrators and, 1, 25, 65, 259, 262
 student safety and. *See* Safety law

without liability, 116, 119, 168
Accreditation
 AAUP and, 258
 processes, 50, 82–83
 student lending and, 73, 73*n*
Actual authority of student affairs administrators, 259
"Actual malice" standard, 226
"Ad damnum" clauses, 24, 142, 142*n*
Admissions
 disability discrimination and, 242
 gender discrimination and, 64, 185, 231, 239–241
ADR (alternate dispute resolution), 23, 35–36
Advisory opinions, 39
Affirmative defenses, 24, 24–25*n,* 96, 147–155. *See also* Assumption of risk; Contributory negligence
Affirmative duty law
 compliance with, 105, 107–108
 exceptions, 108
 knowledge and foreseeability, 107
 rescue law and, 102, 104*n*
 special relationships and, 108–112
Agency, law of, 87, 168
Age of consent, 151
Alcohol use
 age at which students start drinking, 58
 brain development and high-risk alcohol use, 58
 campus police/security mission and, 175
 capacity to consent, effect on, 151
 evolution of law relating to, 60–62
 Greek letter organizations vs. institutions of higher learning and, 224*n*

high-risk alcohol use, 92
no legal duty to protect college
    students, 57
personal accountability of drinker, 60
proximate cause of harm, 50–51, 50*n*
recreational sports and, 171
risk management approaches, 58, 163–
    164, 164*n*
state laws on liability, 57–58
voluntary drinkers causing injury, 137
All-comers policy of student organizations,
    222–223
Alternate dispute resolution (ADR), 23,
    35–36
Amendment of complaint, 24
American Association of University
    Professors (AAUP), 77, 256, 258
American Bar Association Model Rules of
    Professional Conduct, 27*n*
American College Personnel Association,
    18–19, 18*n*, 258
American Psychiatric Association, 12–13*n*
Americans with Disabilities Act of 1990
    (ADA), 232
Answer to complaint, 24–25, 24–25*n*
Anti-discrimination rules, 7*n*
Apparent authority of student affairs
    administrators, 259
Appeals, 32, 33–34, 42
Arbitration, 35–36
Architecture and premises maintenance
    negligence and, 135
    violence risk and, 173–174, 175
Areen, Judith, 176, 190*n*
Association for Student Conduct
    Administrators (ASCA), 56*n*, 194
Association rights, 218–224
Assumed duty, 112–121
Assumption of risk, 147–151
    abrogation trend, 116–117*n*
    express, 149, 151
    implied, 148–149
    signed forms, 149–150, 152, 171

B

Baby boomers, 47*n*
Background checks, 176
Baker Act (Florida), 230*n*
Bankruptcy court, 41
Bedside manner, effect on lawsuits and
    damages, 146
Beh, Hazel, 85
Bench trials, 31, 31*n*
Best practices, 17, 131–132
Bickel, Robert, xi, 56*n*, 104*n*
Boards of trustees, 254–260
Bodily injury damages, 141, 143–144
Bohlen, Francis H., 102
Bonfire collapse cases (Texas), 43*n*, 71*n*, 160
Brain development, 58
Breach of contract, 19, 86–87, 187
Breach of duty
    mandates/compliance, 122–123
    reasonable care. *See* Reasonable care
    reasonable person standard, 123–126
Brown University's Program in Liberal
    Medication Education, 243*n*, 244,
    244–245*n*
Bullying, 191
Bunker mentality, 21
Business invitees, 2*n*, 108
"But for" test, 135
Bystander era, 56–62, 224*n*

C

California
    duty determination in negligence cases,
        99–100, 100*n*
    public institutions of higher education
        and budget crisis, 255
Campus crime reporting, 64
Campus security, 160–171
    campus police/security missions, 51,
        174–178
    care team to assess campus safety, 170*n*
    foreseeability of criminal violence,
        109, 175
    geographic boundaries and "straddling

situations," 110
nonstudents and, 132–135
Cardozo, Benjamin, 129
Care team to assess campus safety, 170*n*
Case management orders (CMOs), 26
Case preparation with counsel, 28
Causation, 135–140. *See also* Proximate
    cause
    alcohol and, 137
    foreseeability. *See* Foreseeability
    intentional wrongs of others and, 138
    intervening or supervening causes, 137
    suicide and, 137–138
    weird or unusually extensive injuries,
        138–140
Censorship, 225–227
Charitable immunity, 154
Chartering of private institutions, 253
Cheating, 191
Chilling effect, 206–207, 210*n*, 257
Circuit courts, federal, 42
Civil actions. *See also* Litigation process
    criminal actions vs., 15
Civil rights actions, 19, 38
Civil Rights Act of 1964, 231, 233
    Title VI. *See* Race discrimination
Civil rights era, 52–56, 263
Clear and convincing evidence for punitive
    damages, 141
Clery Act of 2006, 64, 115, 124*n*, 169,
        169*n*, 176–178, 185, 192, 224
CMOs (case management orders), 26
Codes of conduct. *See* Student codes
Commerce Clause, 68
Common law, 39, 39*n*
Common meaning of language, 2
Common practices, 39
Communication, 3, 10, 21
Commuting to job, 158–159
Comparative fault rules, 142, 143, 151–153
    modified comparative fault, 152
    pure comparative fault, 152
Comparative negligence, 117*n*, 134*n*, 140
Competencies
    for student affairs administrators,
        18–19, 18*n*

for students, 243
Complaint, 23–26
Conceptualization, 3
Conduct causing harm, 120
Conduct regulation. *See* Student codes
Confidentiality. *See* Privacy
Conflicts of interest, 6
Consent
    age of, 151
    as defense to intentional torts, 149*n*
    FERPA, sharing information without
        student's consent, 228–229,
        228*n*
    medical information release, 230
    voluntary consent to risk, 151
Constitutional rights. *See also* First
        Amendment rights
    academic freedom, 79–80
    history of, 49, 52
    public law application, 64
    selective incorporation, 198
Constructive notice rules, 134
Consumer protection, 54, 85
Contingency fees, 142–143, 143*n*
Contract law, 49, 57, 74–76, 83–88,
        186–189
    actual authority of student affairs
        administrators, 259–260
    apparent authority of student affairs
        administrators, 259
    auxiliary services, specific contracts for,
        86
    contract formalities, 83–84
    contractual status of student, 53–54, 63,
        87–88, 187–188
    relational aspects, 85
    reliance, 120–121
Contributory negligence, 50, 50*n*, 96,
        116*n*, 140, 147
Controlling vs. persuasive opinions, 43–44
Controversy requirement for justiciability, 39
Corporations
    First Amendment rights of, 202,
        202*n*, 203
    private institutions with corporate
        power, 253

Counsel for institution of higher education, 4–9, 255
Counterclaims, 25
Course of dealing, 86
Court of Appeals, U.S. (USCA), 42
Courts of Appeals, state, 43, 43*n*
Court system, 36, 41–43. *See also* Federal courts; Jurisdiction; State courts
Crime reporting on campus, 64
Criminal procedure, applicability of, 188–189
Criminal vs. civil actions, liability for, 15
Custodial care relationships, 111
Custom and best practices, 131–132

D

Damages
    bodily injury, 141, 143–144
    caps, 142
    emotional distress, 145–146
    foreseeable damages, 146
    impaired future earnings, 144
    large, 142, 142*n*
    lost wages, 144
    medical damages, 143–144
    mitigation of, 140
    negligence cases, 96
    pain and suffering damages, 144–145
    property, 141
    realities of, 146
    reduction of, 32, 143
    sought by plaintiffs, 24, 140–146
Danger. *See also* Self-harm; Threat assessment
    open and obvious dangers, 133
    to others, 51, 230, 230*n*, 243, 243*n*
    reasonable care and, 172
    rescuing. *See* Rescue law
Decision making by student affairs administrators, 6–7
    process involved in, 9, 127
    real-time decision making, 128
"Deep pockets," 15
Defamation, 226
"Defending" higher education, 9–11

Defenses. *See* Affirmative defenses
Deference to educational institutions, 17, 179–180, 187, 188, 201, 223
Definitions, 3
DeJong, William, 164
De jure segregation, 233, 233*n*
Delegation of authority, 257
Demand letters, 22–23
Department of Education, U.S., regulations. *See also* Family Education Rights and Privacy Act of 1974 (FERPA); Office for Civil Rights (OCR)
    equal protection rights, 233, 240
Depositions, 26–27
Desegregation, 52
Disability law, 10, 232, 241–247
    accommodation law, 241–242
    definition of disabilities, 245
    individual basis for determinations, 246
    pretexts for discrimination, 243*n*, 247*n*
    reasonable accommodation, 245
Disciplinary procedures. *See* Student codes; Student discipline
Discovery, 26–28
Discretionary vs. ministerial functions for immunity, 70
Discrimination, 51, 64. *See also* Disability law; Gender discrimination; Race discrimination
District courts, U.S., 41
Diversity jurisdiction, 37
Dram shop liability, 51, 51*n*, 62, 62*n*
Drug use
    campus police/security mission and, 175
    capacity to consent, effect on, 151
    recreational sports and, 171
    risk management approaches, 163–164, 164*n*
Dual representation, 6
Duces tecum, 27, 27*n*
Due process, 181–186
    contract law and, 75
    limited rights of students, 53, 188, 232
    protected interests and, 182
    substantive vs. procedural, 184*n*

DUI laws, 62
Duty. *See also* "No-duty" arguments
assuming duties, 112–121
fiduciary duty, 260
to mitigate injury or damage, 140
negligence, duty owed, 96, 98–106
nondelegable duty, 159, 174
to protect college students from
alcohol-related harm, 57,
59–60

E

Economic status/class discrimination, 232,
247–250
Education Amendments of 1972, Title IX.
See Gender discrimination
"Eggshell-thin skull" rule, 139
Electronic media, content censorship of, 226
Eleventh Amendment, 69*n*. *See also*
Sovereign immunity
Emergency notification of danger, 175
Emotional distress damages, 145–146
Employment discrimination, 240
Employment relationships, xi–xii, 111. *See
also* Vicarious liability
Empowerment through knowledge, xiv
Enforcement of judgment, 32
English common law on rescue, 104
Enterprise risk management (ERM), 135
Equal protection and civil rights, 231–247
Erie and jurisdiction, 38
Establishment/impairment of religion,
224–225
Exculpatory language, 150
Experts, 28
Externships, 172

F

Facts in complaint, 24
Faculty
academic freedom of, 76–80
student harassment by, 193*n*, 240*n*
Failure to state a claim upon which relief
can be granted, 25, 25*n*

Family Education Rights and Privacy Act of
1974 (FERPA), 4–5*n*, 12, 12*n*
fines for violations, 230*n*
passage of, 52
privacy and, 227–229
private lawsuits not allowed under,
44, 230
procedures for implementing statutory
provisions, 185
professional registrars and, 52*n*, 228
proposed amendments to FERPA
regulations, 166
sharing health and safety information,
228–229
sharing information for "legitimate
educational interest," 228
sharing information without student's
consent, 228–229, 228*n*
Fear and the law, 2
Federal courts, 37–38, 41–42
Federalism, 42, 43
Federalist Papers, 11*n*
Federal lending regulation, 54, 66–67,
73–74
for-profit colleges and, 74*n*
indirect vs. direct lending, 73–74
Federal question jurisdiction, 37
Federal regulation, 50, 64. *See also specific acts*
FERPA. *See* Family Education Rights and
Privacy Act of 1974
Fiduciary duty, 260
Fighting words, 198, 199, 226*n*
Fines for violations
FERPA, 230*n*
Title IX, 240
First Amendment rights, 197–231
academic freedom and, 78
association rights, 218–224
chill, 206–207, 210*n*
content and viewpoint discrimination,
209*n*, 211–212
corporations and, 202, 202*n*, 203
establishment/impairment of religion,
224–225
forum analysis, 207–218
freedom of speech, 198–204

institutions of higher education and, 11, 52, 202–204
limited public forum, 211–217, 222, 226
narrowly tailored regulation, 209–210
nonforum, 218
nonpublic forum, 217, 226
overbreadth, 206–207, 210n
press, 225–227
privacy, 227–231
putative "speech," 201
Roberts Court and, 64, 211n
text of First Amendment, 197n
time, place, and manner restrictions, 201–202, 204–206, 225, 226
traditional public forum, 208–210
vagueness, 206–207, 206n, 210n
Florida
contributory negligence, 116n
professional standard of care, 16, 16n
Foreseeability
negligence and, 107, 109, 136–137, 136n
violence and, 172, 175
Foreseeable damages, 146
Formal demand letters, 22–23
Forms. *See* Assumption of risk
For-profit institutions. *See* Proprietary institutions, regulation of
Forum analysis, 207–218
limited public forum, 211–217, 222, 226
narrowly tailored regulation, 209–210
nonforum, 218
nonpublic forum, 217, 226
time, place, and manner restrictions, 201–202, 204–206, 225, 226
traditional public forum, 208–210
Forum shopping, 38
Fourteenth Amendment
Commerce Clause in, 68
equal protection clause, 232
selective incorporation and, 198
Fourth Amendment, 227, 227–228n
Fraternities. *See* Hazing; Student organizations
Free speech. *See* First Amendment rights
Frolic and detour by employee, 159

G

Gay students, 232, 232n
Gehring, Donald, 56n
Gehring Institute, 194
Gender discrimination, 64, 185, 231, 239–241. *See also* Sexual harassment
Georgia resolution adopting Academic Bill of Rights, 79n, 303–306
Going-and-coming rule, 158–159
Good and customary practices, 17, 17n
Good samaritans and rescue law, 103–104, 117–118, 139
Governing boards. *See* Trustees
Greek letter groups. *See* Student organizations

H

Hand, Learned, 123, 123n
Hastings Law School, 7n, 11n, 212–213n, 212–216
Hate speech, 199, 226n
Hazing, 131, 149n, 190–191, 190n
Health care providers' liability, 111–112
Health Insurance Portability and Accountability Act of 1996 (HIPAA), 231n
History of higher education law, 47–89
academic freedom, 76–80
bystander era, 56–62
civil rights era, 52–56
facilitator era, 62–64
legal insularity era, 48–52
public/private distinctions, 64–76
Hornbooks, 10
Horowitz, David, 80n
Human resource management, 155n

I

Ignorance of the law, 129
Immunity
charitable, 154
limited, 153–155
qualified immunity, 71–72, 71n

state government/state officers immunity, 69–73. *See also* Sovereign immunity
Incitement, 198, 199, 201
Indemnification, 13–16
Independent contractors, 159
Individualized Education Program (IEP), 242
Informal demands, 23
Information. *See* Siloing information
In loco parentis, 48–49, 48–49*n,* 60, 89*n,* 153–154
Insurance law
  compared to negligence, 58–59
  punitive damages, 141
Insurance policies, 13–16, 13*n,* 15*n,* 22, 146
Intangible property damage, 141
Intentional torts, 138
  consent as defense to, 149*n*
Intercollegiate athletics, 170*n*
Interdisciplinary training, 3–4, 6
Intermediate scrutiny and gender discrimination, 239
Internet policies, 226
Interrogatories and requests for admission, 28
Intervening causes, 137

J

Japanese-American internment during World War II, 200, 200*n*
Jeanne Cleary Disclosure of Campus Security Policy and Campus Crime Statistics Act. *See* Clery Act of 2006
JED Foundation, 165, 165*n,* 167
Judgment, exercise of, 9, 131–132
Judgment notwithstanding the verdict (JNOV), 32, 32*n*
Judgments, 32, 143
Jurisdiction, 23–24*n,* 36–41
  compared to justiciability, 39
  defined, 37
  forum shopping, 38
Jury trials, 31, 31*n*
  calculations of fault. *See* Comparative fault rules

Justiciability, 39–41

K

Kaplin, William, 205–206
Kennedy, Anthony, 214–216, 221
Kennedy, Edward, 263
Kent State shootings, 128*n,* 154, 190*n,* 220–221*n,* 252
King, Martin Luther, Jr., 201*n*
Knowledge and affirmative duty, 107

L

Landowner duties, 110, 110–111*n*
Last clear change doctrine, 147*n*
Law-English, 2–3
The Law of Higher Education, 88
Learned profession, 17, 17*n,* 132
Learning theory, 56
Lee, Barbara, 205–206
Legal authority to exist or operate as institution of higher education, 252–254
Legal compliance, 9–11, 129
Legal discourse, 2, 229*n*
Legal insularity, era of, 48–52
Legalisms and limits of the law, 11–13
Lemon test and establishment clause, 224–225
Lending regulation. *See* Federal lending regulation
LGBT (lesbian, gay, bisexual, and transgender) students, 232, 232*n*
Liability, 15, 262
  formula for determining in negligence cases, 96–97
  immunity. *See* Immunity; Sovereign immunity
  strict liability, 124*n*
  vicarious. *See* Vicarious liability
Liability insurance and indemnification, 13–16, 13*n,* 15*n,* 22
Liberty interests, 182
Licensees, 2*n,* 133*n*
Litigation process, 19–36

alternate dispute resolution (ADR),
35–36
appeals, 32, 33–34
complaint and answer, 23–26
costs of, 21, 33
discovery, 26–28
formal or informal demand, 22–23
post-litigation management, 34
preventative steps, 20–21
steps of, 20
summary judgment, 26, 29–31
trial, 31–32
triggering event, 21–22
Loss of consortium, 145, 145*n*
Lost wages, 144

M

Magistrates, 41
Malpractice, educational, 41, 49, 141, 250
Malpractice, medical, 140, 230
McCarthy era, 78, 78*n*
Mediation, 35
Medical damages, 143–144
Medical negligence, 139–140
Medical privacy laws, 230–231
Mental health issues
risk management approaches, 165–168
therapeutic liability, 51
Michigan courts, 43*n*
Military academies and sex discrimination,
231, 240*n*
Misfeasance, 102–105, 113, 115, 120*n*
Misrepresentation of information, 131
Mistrust, 2
Mitigation of injuries or damage, 140
Model Rules of Professional Conduct
(ABA), 27*n*
Mootness, 40
Motions for failure to state a claim upon
which relief can be granted, 25, 25*n*

N

National Association of College and
University Attorneys (NACUA),
xi, 10, 10*n*, 12*n*
National Association of College and
University Business Officers
(NACUBO), 161
National Association of Student Personnel
Administrators (NASPA)
advocacy for employment rights, 258
Certificate Program in Student Affairs
Law and Policy, 194
competencies developed by, 18–19, 18*n*
Negligence
affirmative defenses. *See* Affirmative
defenses
affirmative duty law, 107–108. *See also*
Affirmative duty law
area of litigation, 19
breach of duty, 121–135. *See also*
Breach of duty
"but for" test, 135
case formula, 95*f,* 96
causation, 135–140
comparative negligence. *See*
Comparative negligence
contributory negligence. *See*
Contributory negligence
damages. *See* Damages
duty owed, 96, 98–106
foreseeability, 107, 109, 136–137, 136*n*
indemnification for, 15
insurance law compared to, 58–59
intervening or supervening causes, 137
liability formula, 96–97
mitigation of injuries or damage, 140
prima facie case, 96
professional negligence, 16*n*
reasonable care to protect students. *See*
Reasonable care
reasonable person standard, 123–126
settlement formula, 97–98
state government/state officers
immunity, 69–73
tort reform and, 50, 63
vicarious liability. *See* Vicarious liability
Negligence per se, 129, 129*n,* 153
Negligent admission, 49
Negligent entrustment, 120*n*

Negligent hiring, 138, 159
Negligent retention, 49, 138, 159
Negotiations, use of precedent, 44
New trial, order for, 32
New York
    Board of Regents, 253, 255
    state court system, 43*n*
New York Times standard of "actual
    malice," 226
Nexus between state and private actors, 67
"No-duty" arguments, 25, 30, 57, 106,
    108, 115
Nonfeasance, 102–105, 113
Nonstudents on campus, 132–135
Notice of intent to sue, 23

O

Obscenity, 198
"Off-campus behavior," 111*n,* 115–116,
    172
Office for Civil Rights (OCR), 38, 197,
    233–234, 244, 246–247, 247*n*
Open and obvious dangers, 133
Organization chart, 257
Overbreadth, 206–207, 210*n*

P

Pain and suffering damages, 144–145
Parietal rules, 227
Pecuniary loss, 145–146
Peer-on-peer harassment, 192–193, 193*n,*
    240*n*
Personal accountability, 93
Personal jurisdiction, 23–24*n*
Persuasive vs. controlling opinions, 43–44
Plagiarism, 191–192
Pleadings, 23*n*
Post-litigation management, 34
Precedent, 43–45
Premises safety, 51, 134
Presidents, 256
Press, freedom of, 225–227
Prior restraint on freedom of association, 219
Privacy, 4–5*n*, 227–231, 260

FERPA. *See* Family Education Rights
    and Privacy Act of 1974
Health Insurance Portability and
    Accountability Act of 1996
    (HIPAA), 231*n*
Private actions, 66*n,* 177, 240, 241*n*
Professionalism, 16–19, 132
Promises and reliance, 120–121
Property damages, 141
Property interests, 182
Proprietary institutions, regulation of,
    74*n,* 253
Protective orders, 28
Proximate cause, 50*n,* 51, 96, 136–137
Public duty doctrine, 120*n*
Public law principles, 54, 56, 60, 64, 75
Public policy violations, 150
Public/private distinctions, 64–76
    contract law and, 74–76
    state action, 65–67
    state government/state officers
        immunity, 69–73
    state law and, 68–69
Punitive damages, 141
Putative "speech," 201

Q

Qualified immunity, 71–72, 71*n*

R

Race discrimination, 231, 232–239
Rawls, John, 261
Real-time decision making, 128
Reasonable care
    as affirmative duty, 109
    in bystander era, 61
    as defense, 114–115
    failure to use, 121
    mandates/compliance, 122–123
    nonstudents and, 133
    process of, 126–127
    statutes and regulations, 129
    violence and, 172–173, 176
Reasonable person standard, 122, 123–126

custom and best practices, 131–132
  information not available, 130–131
  record keeping procedures, 128
Record keeping procedures, 128
Recreational sports
  risk management approaches, 170–171
  safety of, 150
Reductionism, 9
Registered student organizations (RSOs).
    See Student organizations
Rehabilitation Act, Section 504, 232, 247*n*
Reliance, 120–121
Relief sought by plaintiffs, 24
Religion. *See* First Amendment rights
Religious student organizations, 212
Remittitur, 143
Reported appellate decisions, 33
Requests for admission, 28
Rescue law, 103–104, 117–118, 139
Respondeat superior, 156–157*n*
Restatement (Second) of Agency, 157
Restatement (Third) of Torts, 100, 101*n,*
    105–106*n,* 152
Right to jury trial, 31, 31*n*
Ripeness, 40
Risk aversion, 122, 124–125
Risk management. *See also* Campus security
  alcohol and drug use, 58, 163–164, 164*n*
  balancing with risk avoidance, 114
  campus safety and wellness, 160–171
  culture in student affairs, 160, 162–163
  custodial care relationships, 111
  defined, 161–163
  employment relationships, 111
  recreational sports, 170–171
  therapeutic/medical relationships,
    111–112
  threat assessment, 170, 170*n*
Roberts Court and First Amendment
  jurisprudence, 64, 211*n*

S

Safe and Drug Free School and
    Communities Act, 185
Safety law, 21, 57, 63, 93–106

Safety systems, 173
Safety training, 173
Sarbanes-Oxley Corporate Accountability
    Act, 254*n*
SDS (Students for a Democratic Society),
    219, 219*n*
Search and seizure, 227–228, 227–228*n*
Second injury rule, 140
Section 1981 actions, 234
Section 1983 immunity, 71
Security. *See* Campus security
Self-disclosure of disability, 242
Self-harm, 51, 167, 230, 230*n,* 243,
    243*n,* 247*n*
Sells, Benjamin, 12*n*
Settlement, 30, 31, 32
  formula in negligence cases, 97–98
Sex discrimination. *See* Gender
    discrimination
Sexual assault, 192, 240, 240*n*
Sexual harassment, 192–193, 193*n,*
    240–241*n*
Sexual orientation discrimination,
    232, 232*n*
Siloing information, 130–131, 170
Social guests on campus, 133
Social host liability, 60, 61, 61*n*
Socratic method, 7
Sororities. *See* Hazing; Student
    organizations
The Soul of the Law (Sells), 12*n*
Sovereign immunity, 69–73, 141, 154
Speech zones, 204–205
Standard of care. *See* Negligence
Standard of review
  intermediate scrutiny and gender
      discrimination, 239
  rational basis, 248
  strict scrutiny. *See* Strict scrutiny
      standard
Stare decisis, 44, 44*n*
State action, 65–67, 65*n,* 240
State attorneys general, 38, 256
State courts, 38, 42–43
State government/state officers immunity,
    69–73

State regulation. *See also specific states*
  of higher education, 50, 253
  of privacy rights, 229, 230
  public/private distinctions and, 68–69
Statute of limitations, 23*n*
Stevens, John Paul, 180, 201, 213–214
Stone, Bradford, 88
Strict liability, 124*n*
Strict scrutiny standard, 225*n*, 235,
    237–238
Strict vicarious liability, 156–159
Student affairs administrators
  advice for, 261–264
  authority questions for, 259–260
  in civil rights era, 56, 263
  competencies for, 18–19, 18*n*
  dealing with students on individual
      basis, 262
  decision making by, 6–7
  defensive practice by, 9–11
  governance rights of, 258
  law and, xiv–xv, 1–2, 259, 262
  legalisms and limits of the law, 11–13, 264
  legal rights arguments with students
      and parents, 229*n*
  liability insurance and indemnification
      of, 13–16, 13*n*, 15*n*, 22
  "lifestyle job" of, 9
  litigation process and, 19–36
  professionalism and the law, 16–19
  relationship with higher education
      lawyers, 5–8, 255
  relationship with trustees, 256–258
Student codes, 189–195
  as campus management centerpiece, 179
  discipline codes, 188, 189–190, 257
  First Amendment and, 199
  jurisdiction of, 39
  procedures, 193
  rules, 190–193
  sanctions, 193
  trends in, 194–195
Student discipline, 56, 75, 75*n*, 86–87. *See
    also* Student codes
  due process and, 183*n*
  as pretext for discrimination, 243*n*

Student handbooks, 75, 75*n*, 85, 179
Student lending. *See* Federal lending
    regulation
Student life issues. *See* Alcohol use; Drug use
Student newspapers, 225–227
Student organizations, 115–116
  alcohol use, Greek letter organizations
      vs. institutions of higher
      learning, 224*n*
  association rights, 218–224
  limited public forum and, 211
  religious student organizations and
      viewpoint discrimination, 212
  sex discrimination exceptions for Greek
      letter organizations, 231
Students for a Democratic Society (SDS),
    219, 219*n*
Study abroad, 172
Subject matter jurisdiction, 23–24*n*
Substantial factor analysis, 135
Substantial performance, 86
Suicide
  duty to prevent, 51
  proximate causation, 137–138
  risk management approaches, 165–168
Summary judgment, 26, 29–31
Supervening causes, 137
Supreme Court, U.S., 33, 42. *See also* First
    Amendment rights
Suspension and expulsion, 193

T

Tarasoff duties, 111–112
Therapeutic/medical relationships,
    111–112
Threat assessment, 170, 170*n*, 244
Threats ("true threats") and free speech,
    198, 199, 226, 226*n*
Time, place, and manner restrictions, 201–
    202, 204–206, 225, 226
Title VI, Civil Rights Act of 1964. *See* Race
    discrimination
Title IX, Education Amendments of 1972.
    See Gender discrimination
Tort law, 93–94. *See also* Negligence

Tort reform, 50, 63, 92
"Totality of the circumstances," 172
Travel time of employees, 159
Trespassers, 133
Trials, 31–32
Trustees, 254–260
    relationship with higher education
        lawyers, 5, 255
    relationship with student affairs
        administrators, 256–258
"12(b)(6) motions," 25

U

Underage drinking enforcement, 62
University of Michigan law school
    admissions program, 235–236
Unpublished case, 43*n*
Unusually extensive injuries, 138–140

V

Vagueness, 206–207, 206*n*, 210*n*
Verdicts, 31, 32, 143
Vicarious liability, 14, 153, 155–159
    scope of employment, 158
    strict vicarious liability, 156–159
Vicious propensities, 124*n*
Viewpoint discrimination, 209*n*, 211–212
Viewpoint-neutrality principle, 203*n*, 222, 224

Violence in learning environment, 171–178
    architecture and premises maintenance,
        173–174
    reasonable care and, 172–173, 176
Virginia Tech shooting (April 2007), 4,
    4*n*, 12, 12–13*n*, 54, 124*n*, 154,
    168–170
Volunteer Protection Act of 1997, 154*n*

W

Warnings
    disciplinary, 193
    safety, 134, 167
Washington courts, 43*n*
Weird or unusually extensive injuries,
    138–140
Wellness
    campus police/security mission and,
        175
    risk management approaches, 165–168
Women. *See* Gender discrimination
Workers' compensation laws, 111, 154–155
Writ of certiorari, 42
Wrongful death actions, 145–146

Z

Zone of risk, 99*n*